Ecological Psychology in Context:
James Gibson, Roger Barker, and the Legacy of William James's Radical Empiricism

RESOURCES FOR ECOLOGICAL PSYCHOLOGY
A Series of Volumes Edited by:
Robert E. Shaw, William M. Mace, and Michael T. Turvey

BF 353 .H36 2001
Heft, Harry.
Ecological psychology in
   context

Ecological Psychology in Context:
James Gibson, Roger Barker, and the Legacy of William James's Radical Empiricism

Harry Heft
Denison University

LAWRENCE ERLBAUM ASSOCIATES, PUBLISHERS
2001   Mahwah, New Jersey   London

RITTER LIBRARY
BALDWIN-WALLACE COLLEGE

The following institutions kindly granted permission to reprint photographs from their collections:
Archives of the History of American Psychology, The University of Akron; Clark University Archives; Division of Rare and Manuscripts Collections, Cornell University Library; Harvard University Archives; and University Archives, Kenneth Spencer Research Library, University of Kansas.

Copyright © 2001 by Lawrence Erlbaum Associates, Inc.
All rights reserved. No part of this book may be reproduced in any form, by photostat, microform, retrieval system, or any other means, without prior written permission of the publisher.

Lawrence Erlbaum Associates, Inc., Publishers
10 Industrial Avenue
Mahwah, NJ 07430

Cover design by Kathryn Houghtaling Lacey

Library of Congress Cataloging-in-Publication Data

Heft, Harry.
Ecological psychology in context : James Gibson, Roger Barker, and the legacy of William James's radical empiricism / Harry Heft.
    p. cm.
Includes bibliographical references and index.
ISBN 0-8058-2350-6 (hardcover : alk. paper)
1. Environmental psychology.   I. Title.   II. Series.
BF353 .H36   2001
155.9 —dc21   00-067683
                                                          CIP

Books published by Lawrence Erlbaum Associates are printed on acid-free paper, and their bindings are chosen for strength and durability.

Printed in the United States of America
10 9 8 7 6 5 4 3 2 1

For Cindi and Peter, and for my parents

"One should not try to dilute the meaning of relation: relation is reciprocity .... In the beginning is the relation."
—Martin Buber (1970)

Contents

Foreword
Resources for Ecological Psychology

Robert E. Shaw, William M. Mace, and Michael T. Turvey, Series Editors

This series of volumes is dedicated to furthering the development of psychology as a branch of ecological science. In its broadest sense, ecology is a multidisciplinary approach to the study of living systems, their environments, and the reciprocity that has evolved between the two. Traditionally, ecological science emphasizes the study of the biological bases of *energy* transactions between animals and their physical environments across cellular, organismic, and population scales. Ecological psychology complements this traditional focus by emphasizing the study of *information* transactions between living systems and their environments, especially as they pertain to perceiving situations of significance to planning and execution of purposes activated in an environment.

The late James J. Gibson used the term *ecological psychology* to emphasize this animal-environment mutuality for the study of problems of perception. He believed that analyzing the environment to be perceived was just as much a part of the psychologist's task as analyzing animals themselves, and hence that the "physical" concepts applied to the environment and the "biological" and "psychological" concepts applied to organisms would have to be tailored to one another in a larger system of mutual constraint. His early interest in the applied problems of landing airplanes and driving automobiles led him to pioneer the study of the perceptual guidance of action.

The work of Nicholai Bernstein in biomechanics and physiology presents a complementary approach to problems of the coordination and control of movement. His work suggests that action, too, cannot be studied without reference to the environment, and that physical and biological concepts must be developed together. The coupling of Gibson's ideas with those of Bernstein forms a natural basis for looking at the traditional psychological topics of perceiving, acting, and knowing as activities of ecosystems rather than isolated animals.

The purpose of this series is to form a useful collection, a resource, for people who wish to learn about ecological psychology and for those who wish to contribute to its development. The series will include original research, collected papers, reports of conferences and symposia, theoretical monographs, technical handbooks, and works from the many disciplines relevant to ecological psychology.

Series Dedication

To James J. Gibson, whose pioneering work in ecological psychology has opened new vistas in psychology and related sciences, we respectfully dedicate this series.

Preface

This book is intended as a contribution to the growing body of theoretical, empirical, and historical work in *ecological psychology*. Locating the present work in the domain of ecological psychology only serves to identify its focus up to a point, however. The term *ecological psychology* has been adopted by a number of experimental psychologists who, although sharing a broad viewpoint, otherwise hold somewhat different perspectives. As a result, for some readers the term 'ecological psychology' will call to mind the work of James Gibson, whereas for others it will suggest the work of Egon Brunswik, Roger Barker, or Urie Bronfenbrenner. Each of these psychologists at some time employed ecological psychology, or some variation of it, to refer exclusively to their specific framework. Likewise, the second generation of psychologists working from the standpoint of each of these frameworks often has taken ecological psychology to be synonymous solely with their particular point of view. For this reason, the obligatory thing to do when adopting ecological psychology as shorthand for a specific perspective is to be clear from the outset how the phrase is being employed.

So within the domain of ecological psychology, what are the theoretical commitments of this book? The ecological psychology at the core of this project is that developed by James J. Gibson, although its focus is not confined solely to that approach. Work has been underway for several decades now to extend Gibson's ideas by explicating some of its central concepts. This book participates in that effort in at least three ways.

First, the central theoretical and philosophical commitments of Gibson's perspective are articulated through an analysis of its immediate historical roots, and in doing so, the *metatheoretical foundations* of Gibson's ecological psychology are revealed. Primarily, this discussion entails an analysis of the neglected work of James Gibson's mentor, Edwin B. Holt, and more fundamentally, the later philosophy and psychology of William James who was Holt's esteemed teacher. William James has long been a very familiar figure in psychology, but his later position, *radical empiricism*, which he viewed as the culmination of his life's work, has been neglected in the discipline. This volume shows that radical empiricism stands at the heart of Gibson's ecological program, and it can usefully be employed as the conceptual centerpiece for ecological psychology more broadly considered.

Second, this book expands the scope of Gibson's framework by examining relations between it and Roger Barker's ecobehavioral approach. Barker's program is distinctive in psychology because of its recognition of ecological phenomena operating across collectivities of individuals. With his discovery of *behavior settings* in the 1960s, Barker laid bare the critical role played by extra-individual ecological phenomena in everyday life. A partial synthesis between Gibson's and Barker's frameworks is possible because of shared historical commonalities that are rooted primarily in Gestalt psychology, and because of the common metatheoretical assumptions that join them in adopting an ecological perspective.

Third, the capacity of Gibson's program to encompass sociocultural phenomena is examined. Gibson long objected to the distinction between a natural domain and a sociocultural domain. His attitude in this regard is compatible with recent reevaluations in psychology and anthropology of the relation between human development and sociocultural processes, both from an evolutionary and an ontogenetic perspective. After exploring some of this latter work, which is coming to be called *cultural psychology* in many quarters, connections between it and Gibson's ecological perspective are examined. In particular, this discussion focuses on ways in which some of the knowledge sustained and elaborated through sociocultural processes are embodied ecologically in artifacts, tools, and representations, as well as how cognitive functions can be socially distributed. In such public forms, these embodiments of knowing can be aptly referred to as "ecological knowledge"; and viewed as such, they fit well with Gibson's vision of the environment as being rich in meaning from a psychological standpoint.

And what about the other ecological psychologies that will be familiar to some readers? Some features of Egon Brunswik's approach are explored, but primarily to draw a contrast between his and Gibson's views. In contrast, Bronfenbrenner's influential ecological program is examined only briefly. The exclusion of Bronfenbrenner's work stems from some theoretical incompatibilities between his and Gibson's perspective. Although aspects of Gibson's framework were indeed influenced by the same set of ideas central to Bronfenbrenner's—namely, the work of Kurt Lewin—ultimately, Gibson parted theoretical company with Lewin, and by extension with programs rooted in his perspective. At the same time, whether Bronfenbrenner's concepts of "exosystems and macrosystems," which arguably depart from Lewin's phenomenological perspective, can be brought into alignment with the Gibson–Barker synthesis explored here is a possibility left unaddressed.

In short, the proposed synthesis of Gibson's and Barker's programs is motivated by the goal of seeking an ecological psychology that is broad in scope and, importantly, *theoretically coherent*. Rather than pursue an eclectic approach to theory, the position maintained here is that psychology will be best served by advancing theoretically coherent positions that can be submitted to logical scrutiny and empirical test. Admittedly, the framework proposed requires that adherents of Barker's perspective adjust a few features of their metatheoretical commitments; but these adjustments, in my view, serve Barker's goals quite well. Otherwise, this book attempts to remain true to both Gibson's and Barker's intentions, as I understand them.

Having indicated the book's focus, let me situate this project within a broader set of underlying concerns. Looking back over the previous century of psychology, it appears that we have made advances in the scientific study of some aspects of the human condition, while neglecting others. Specifically, although gains have been made in shedding light on those attributes we share with other animals, in the process much that is essentially human has been too often set aside. As a result, matters that should be at least the partial responsibility of psychology, such as meaning, values, and aesthetics, have too often been abandoned on the doorstep of the humanities. Experimental psychology is sorely in need of a framework that at once satisfies the theoretical rigor and empirical standards of natural science, while at the same time provides grounds congenial for inclusion of those qualities that seem to be distinctively human.

Perhaps the selective development of a problem domain is the inevitable result of adopting an analytical stance. As we focus on a particular feature in our field of experience, other features become relegated to the background—and, in some cases, even slip out of focus. But surely, a scientific psychology must be both scientific and psychological. We must make good on both counts. For reasons to be explored, I believe that ecological psychology provides some of the necessary groundwork for a psychology that is both scientifically rigorous and adequate to its subject matter.

ACKNOWLEDGMENTS

I am deeply indebted to many teachers, colleagues, and friends who have helped me to steer a course among a number of broad and sometimes seemingly conflicting concerns. I am very grateful to Joachim Wohlwill, my mentor in the interdisciplinary program in environment–behavior studies at Pennsylvania State University, who offered me critical and supportive guidance throughout my graduate studies and who continued to foster my development for many years afterward. Jack Wohlwill, who was Brunswik's last student, was a model of dedicated scholarship and synthetic thinking for all who knew him.

Walter Weimer, of the Department of Psychology at Penn State, provided a stimulating and often provocative counterpoint to work in my home department, and in so doing enormously broadened my horizons about the nature of scientific inquiry. Now, over two decades later, I continue to feel the impact of Walt's intellectual provocations.

Following graduate school I had the extraordinary good fortune to spend a year at Cornell University studying with James Gibson. He graciously allowed me to shadow him and tolerated my naïve and half-formulated questions during what was, for me, a remarkable postdoctoral year. As becomes evident in the following chapters, my contact with James and Eleanor Gibson, initially through their writings and later in conversation, transformed my thinking.

Over the ensuing decades, ongoing exchanges with many others have directly shaped my views. Among those colleagues and friends who were most influential early in my academic career were Bob Daubert, Philip Glotzbach, and Anthony Lisska. Over the past two decades, my thinking has been influenced through interactions with many generous colleagues, especially Ed Reed, Herb Pick, Alan Costall, Kent Maynard, Steve Vogel, Rita Snyder, Mark Moller, and Bahram Tavakolian.

A number of years ago, I was struck by the aptness of a book dedication to "my teacher, under whom I have never studied" (R. I. Watson, 1978). This dedication conveys a sentiment that most academics feel: namely, a profound intellectual indebtedness to the community of scholars, past and present, from whose writings we have learned so much. My teachers from these ranks, most of whom I have never met, are far too numerous to list here, but their contributions to my thinking are apparent in the following pages.

The present work has benefitted immeasurably by the critical and supportive comments of many individuals. I am most grateful to Alan Costall, Jack Sanders, and Bill Mace, who read an earlier version of this book in its entirety. Their generosity in taking on this considerable task is greatly appreciated. Also, I am indebted to Phil Schoggen for his detailed critique of an earlier draft of chapters 7 and 8. His penetrating assessment greatly improved my examination of Barker's program. In addition, I would like to thank the following individuals who graciously offered very helpful comments on one or more chapters of the book: Kerry Marsh, Paul Gump, Julie Mulroy, Anne Pick, Kent Maynard, Bahram Tavakolian, Rita Snyder, Tim Ingold, Mary Clark, Pat Zukow-Goldring, Steve Vogel, Mark Moller, Dikkie Schoggen, Jonathan Barker, Herb Pick, Endre Kadar, Dankert Vedeler, Ed Reed, Eleanor Gibson, Jon Krosnick, Tony Lisska, Bill Nichols, Philip Glotzbach, William Epstein, and Sharon Hutchins. Needless to say, the faults that remain in the book do so in spite of the best efforts of these generous colleagues. I would also like to express my gratitude to Marianna Vertullo of LEA for her expert editorial contributions and cheerful support during the final phases of this project. Finally, I thank Louise Barker for sharing with me the splendid photographs of her husband, Roger Barker.

Work on this project, and indeed on most of my scholarly endeavors over the past 24 years, has been supported by my home institution, Denison University. My semester's leave of absence from teaching responsibilities at the beginning of this project (spring 1995), and again near its end (fall 1999), both times supported by Robert C. Good Faculty Fellowships, made this project possible. Professional development support over several summers from Denison is also gratefully acknowledged. Liberal arts colleges, like Denison, with a primary commitment to undergraduate education, and that also support faculty research and scholarship, are truly treasures in the academic community.

I am also very grateful for the support and friendship of my colleagues in the Department of Psychology and across campus over the years.

Finally, there is no doubt that the long period of time during which this book has been in preparation must have seemed especially protracted to my family. I am inexpressibly grateful for their love, forebearance, support, and sacrifices. I thank Cynthia Kreger for her boundless encouragement, patience, and good cheer, and Peter Heft for tolerating my periods of solitude and preoccupation. His anticipated arrival during the project's early stages helped to inspire the endeavor, and my joy in his presence kept me energized throughout its preparation.

I consider myself remarkably fortunate for all of these experiences and for the support of so many. I look back with wonder at the role chance events and chance encounters seemed to have played in my development, and with awe and humility at the many kindnesses extended to me.

Columbus, Ohio
August 2000

Introduction

Has there been a moment since its formal founding in the late 19th century when experimental psychology was not in a state of theoretical conflict? Select any historical point during its first 120 years, and you will find psychologists embroiled in some theoretical squabble. It is true that psychology is by no means alone among the sciences in having ongoing theoretical tensions. And yet there is an important difference here. In most other sciences, especially those that share psychology's roots in natural science, these disagreements typically occur around the edges of a core set of shared theoretical presuppositions. But, in psychology, it is these very *core presuppositions* that are often being contested. Since its inception the discipline has been rife with claims from various quarters that particular theoretical approaches and conceptual tools, levels of analysis, and methods are canonical, with other contenders for that status lacking legitimacy. Psychologists continue to struggle among themselves concerning the best way to think about the subject matter of psychology, and to some extent even about identifying the proper subject matter of psychology.

What is the reason for this ongoing conflict and instability? In the aftermath of Kuhnian analyses of science, in which work in mature sciences is portrayed as being structured by an underlying common paradigm, the view of some psychologists seems to be that this turmoil reflects the ongoing preparadigmatic state that befits any immature science such as psychology. This explanation, however, lets psychologists too easily off the hook, and in so doing, covers up the source of the problem. One underlying purpose of this book is to offer a different explanation. Much of this theoretical instability can be explained by the fact that our systematic attempts to understand ourselves have been typically built on a conceptual foundation ill suited for this task. If examined closely, it becomes evident that it is a foundation made up to a significant degree of long-standing concepts from the sciences of nonliving things, that is, the sciences of the inanimate.

With a few notable exceptions, the field of psychology has been an attempt to develop a science of animate beings on the back of concepts borrowed from traditional approaches to the study of the inanimate. This juxtaposition of the animate and the inanimate at the heart of psychologists' thinking has engendered irresolvable conceptual conflicts. Moreover, after stepping back and viewing it from a distance, the picture of psychological functioning that emerges from this science sometimes seems to bear little relation to our everyday experience—and worse, it sometimes seems to violate our notion of who we are.

By sciences of the inanimate, I am referring of course, to the physical sciences–the oldest and most advanced of the modern sciences–and to particular physical science approaches at that. The collective progress made toward developing ever-sophisticated and predictive explanations of the character of the physical world is without a doubt among the most impressive intellectual achievements of the last millennium. From the analysis of matter at atomic and subatomic levels to the composition of the universe at a cosmological scale, the record of the physical sciences is imposing and admirable. It is not surprising then that in attempting to establish the groundwork for a scientific psychology, the first generations of experimental psychologists tried to emulate these endeavors by drawing on the conceptualizations of nature and the scientific methods that have proven so successful in the physical sciences.

Surely, modeling psychology after these highly advanced sciences is all to the good. Or is it? A premise of this book is that uncritical utilization of concepts and methods from the physical sciences has impeded progress in psychology precisely because some of these borrowed concepts fail to capture those qualities most characteristic of animate things. The position being advocated here instead is that psychology stands the best chance of progressing as a discipline when more than lip service is given to the fact that, first and foremost, psychology is the study of animate phenomena. Psychology needs to be built on a conceptual foundation compatible with the life sciences, and especially with the study of animals as organized, dynamic, adaptive beings, rather than on the mechanistic foundations of physical science.

This sweeping indictment needs to be qualified, however, in two respects. First, when I speak here of the physical sciences, I am referring to what is commonly called the Newtonian framework of physics and, more generally, the Cartesian metaphysics on which it is based (to be described later). Although this framework forms but a piece of contemporary theory in physics, it is the perspective that has had the greatest impact on psychology. Consequently, reference here to the influences of physics and physical concepts is not intended to describe physics as contemporary physicists view it. Rather, it refers to physics as it has historically shaped psychological thinking; that is, physics as psychologists typically view it. Alternatives to the Newtonian approach in physics, such as field theory and more recently, the analysis of dynamic complex systems, will figure positively in later discussions in this book.

Second, the varieties of theories in psychology cannot be painted with a single brushstroke. Whereas some theoretical approaches are deeply influenced by the conceptual tools of the physical sciences, others, such as organismic approaches, have explicitly sought to break from that perspective. In the case of the latter, however, there is often an uncritical assimilation of some physicalistic concepts that prevents the goals of these theories to be fully realized. This shortcoming is most evident when it comes to how the environment is handled and how the relation between the person and the environment is conceptualized—but more on these matters later.

Consider some ways in which a science of the animate differs from a science of the inanimate. At the level of human experience, animate beings, unlike inanimate things, are (a) ceaselessly *active* and b) continually in the process of engaging their surroundings in a *selective* manner. Environmental conditions are in flux, and animate beings monitor these ongoing conditions, make functional adjustments with respect to them, and engage environmental features in relation to their own goals and interests. For these reasons, (c) animate beings exist *in relation* to a flow of events, and their functioning is best understood as that of dynamic, organismic processes *in context*. Animate beings selectively engage environmental features and selectively enter places in order to benefit from the functional opportunities things and places offer. And more than this, (d) animate beings participate in the *modification* of many of these very features and places. In these respects, (e) animate beings are *adaptive agents*.

Inanimate things, as described with traditional physical science concepts, lack these dynamic, selective, relational, and constructive qualities. Inanimate things are just that, inanimate; they are inert. They are passive recipients of what environmental conditions have to offer rather than being purposive agents in the environment.[1] As such, they are not sentient. Because the properties of inanimate things are not functional properties, an appreciation of context is not necessary for the analysis of

---

[1]Categorical boundaries are rarely sharp. Where do plants fit into this conceptual division? Admittedly, they do not fit neatly into either category, but because they lack agency, for the purposes of an ecological psychology they fit into the inanimate category (J. J. Gibson, 1979). Not all animals have agency, however, as in the case of sessile animals such as sponges, so strictly speaking animate is not completely synonymous with animal.

most inanimate things. It is with respect to these attributes that the sciences of the inanimate and the animate are most fundamentally at odds. And it is our inattention to these differences, resulting in employing standard concepts from the physical sciences where functional concepts are required, which begins to erode the possibility of developing a psychology fully adequate to living things.

Recognition of the distinctive qualities of animate beings requires an essential conceptual step; and this step more fully distinguishes the approach explored in the following pages from other broadly similar ones. At the conceptual core of a science of the animate is an *ecological perspective*. Such a perspective takes as its central tenet, as its sine qua non, the *dynamic interrelation* between a living thing and its environment, with the environment considered in its full complexity, including at multiple levels of organization.

RETRIEVING ECOLOGICAL PSYCHOLOGY FROM THE MARGINS

Making a commitment to a psychology built on an ecological perspective unfortunately creates at least as many difficulties as it resolves. This is the case in large measure because some of our most basic patterns of thought, both in science and in daily living, grow out of conceptions rooted in Newtonian physics and Cartesian metaphysics. Standard physical science notions permeate our language and certainly our schooling, making particular ways of thinking familiar to the point of no longer being noticeable to us as but one way of thinking. And this is the case as much for the academic as it is for the layperson.

Consider three brief examples of this influence, each of which is discussed in more detail in the following chapters. First, our automatic and exclusive identification of the term *cause* with mechanistic antecedent-consequent relations illustrates one way that thinking from the perspective of Newtonian physics and Cartesian metaphysics has become part of the fabric of everyday discourse. With this formulation, when considering the cause of an occurrence, the tendency is to look for precipitating, antecedent events. This, however, may be too limited a view of causality when attempting to address animate phenomena.

A second example of this effect is the seemingly commonsense distinction between matter and mind, which grows in part out of attempts to describe aspects of perceptual experience in classical, physical terms.[2]

---

[2]By physical I mean employing the concepts of the physical sciences, particularly as they are used to describe the environment and environment–organism relations. I distinguish *physicalistic* and *materialistic*, the latter referring to assumptions about the "stuff" of which all things in the natural world are made (Turvey, 1992). Opposing the use of standard physicalist concepts for psychology does not entail opposing materialism. As a science, psychology must be materialistic.

Armed with this distinction between matter and mind, psychologists tend to reject one side of this distinction, traditionally the mind, or if not, then to treat mind with circumspection—in either case, to the detriment of constructing an adequate psychology. Certainly, part of the problem here is how mind has been traditionally conceptualized, and in the following, we will take a non-conventional approach to this issue.

Third, but related to the preceding example, is the apparent dichotomy between the organism and its environment. From a psychological perspective, frequently reference is made to a domain "in" the organism as against a domain "outside" the organism, as if there is a clear and obvious boundary between the two. But, the question of where to locate this boundary is not clear-cut and, as a consequence, it is far more interesting than it appears at first glance.

When venturing into the territory of ecological thinking as it applies to psychological phenomena, it is necessary to jettison such ways of thinking in order to proceed in a coherent manner adequate to the subject matter. In the absence of familiar conceptual guideposts, finding our way is fraught with uncertainty. Ecological thinking requires a shift in point of view. For this reason, it can initially feel unfamiliar and confusing, which leads to the primary purpose of this book.

The overall aim of this book is to articulate an emerging conceptual foundation for an ecological approach in psychology. Having announced such a grandiose intention, it is necessary to qualify what I am doing in this book. Fortunately, this project does not need to be cut from whole cloth—I am not so presumptuous as to attempt such a daunting task. The groundwork for an ecological psychology already exists among diverse sources in the psychological literature. To date, however, some of these ecologically-related writings have been marginalized in experimental psychology, remaining outside of the mainstream of disciplinary thought. My intention is to retrieve some of these initiatives, and by synthesizing them, give these individual efforts added strength and persuasiveness through their mutual relations. This synthesis is based partially on identifying shared *historical roots*, and partially on elucidating *theoretical complementarities*. Rather than proposing a novel perspective, the goal here is to examine in considerable detail a few existing bodies of work, which when joined together provide the needed conceptual foundation for an ecological psychology. Primarily, the focus is on the ecological psychology of James J. Gibson[3] and the eco-behavioral science of Roger

---

[3] In truth, it is inaccurate to attribute sole authorship of this ecological approach to James Gibson. As he stated repeatedly, his equal partner in this endeavor was Eleanor J. Gibson, whose efforts were and continue to be directed primarily at developmental issues from an ecological perspective. The focus here on James Gibson's work, and its historical origins, is in no way intended to diminish the contributions of Eleanor Gibson, *continued on next page*

G. Barker.[4] And of these two positions, Gibson's constitutes the core of the ecological framework advanced herein.

THREE GOALS OF THE PROJECT

With these broad intentions in mind, let me indicate three more specific goals of this book. First of all, Gibson's approach is currently the most well known of the ecological psychologies in the field of experimental psychology. At the same time, it appears to be an approach that is not easily grasped in its entirety. It has been frequently misunderstood by its critics, and even underappreciated by more sympathetic readers. *One of the goals of this book is to cultivate a deeper appreciation for Gibson's approach by articulating its theoretical commitments, in part through philosophical and historical analysis.*

The primary focus of this analysis is the later philosophy of William James and the psychological and philosophical contributions of E. B. Holt, two of Gibson's intellectual antecedents. This historical and philosophical ground has received only brief consideration in other scholarly studies of Gibson's work (Lombardo, 1985; Reed, 1988). Gibson's program is quite different from familiar formulations of psychological processes, and by extension, from the historical origins on which these mainstream ideas rest. It is partially for this reason that his ecological approach has been marginalized in the discipline. In the absence of a fuller exposition of its roots, Gibson's ecological program will continue to be vulnerable to dismissal as a maverick, quirky point of view. This book shows that, to the contrary, this approach has deep connections to critical developments in early 20th-century American philosophy and psychology, which themselves have a time-honored pedigree.

A second reason why ecological psychology can be easily pushed to the margins of the field is because, in fact, it is not one program but many different ones bearing uncertain connections. Gibson's is but one ecological psychology among several others; and the appellation "ecological psychology" points to several different, loosely joined positions rather than

---

[3]*continued from previous page*   who by any measure is surely among the outstanding experimental psychologists and scientists of the 20th century. At the same time, in spite of their commonalities, the Gibsons were not of one mind, and there have been fine differences between the way they each approach certain issues. Consequently, it is not possible to talk about "the Gibsons' view" without occasional qualification. For this reason, although most of what follows is consistent with Eleanor Gibson's ideas, it is important to stress that it is the work of James Gibson that is traced in this book.

[4] I would be remiss if I did not mention the substantive contributions of Barker's close colleagues to this endeavor, especially Louise Barker, Herbert Wright, Paul Gump, and Phil Schoggen. Reference to "Barker's program" in the following pages acknowledges his clear leadership of this group, but it is also intended at times as a shorthand for the efforts of his research team.

any shared perspective. There is considerable justification for questioning the possibility of a coherent ecological psychology among them. What, if anything, proposals for an ecological psychology share, besides a general call for sensitivity to environmental conditions variously defined, is far from clear. Consequently, *a second goal of this book is to explicate a set of foundational ideas that can serve to draw together two of the major ecological programs in psychology, James Gibson's and Roger Barker's*. This synthesis is especially worthwhile because it enables the expansion of the scope of ecological psychology in theoretically coherent ways.

Now is a propitious time for such an undertaking. The past decade has seen an increasing number of psychologists embrace several ideas that are fundamental to an ecological approach. There has been a growing recognition of the critical role contextual factors play in psychological phenomena; and reciprocally, there has been increasing skepticism about the meaningfulness of analyses that wrest phenomena from their accompanying contexts. Further, the notion of multiple and reciprocal causation has firmly taken hold in psychology, replacing single cause, unidirectional explanations of events. These two ideas— recognition of the significance of context and a sensitivity to multiple and reciprocal causes—are, in fact, facets of the dynamic, organic perspective that is the hallmark of the life sciences.[5]

For these reasons and others that could be mentioned, experimental psychology as a discipline may be moving ineluctably toward a conceptual and a methodological stance that will transform it into an ecological psychology. As becomes evident, a significant consequence of this transformation is recognition of the central role that sociocultural processes must play in an account of psychology.

Finally, a third goal of this project is *to consider the place of ecological psychology in the discipline of psychology more generally*. Because of its metatheoretical commitments, ecological psychology is well suited to take some preliminary steps to address what is certainly one of experimental psychology's most glaring deficiencies. To state the problem briefly here, the account of psychological processes offered up by the discipline often seems to have only a minor bearing on individuals'

---

[5]Such qualities also characterize some approaches in physics that have been proposed in this century as alternatives to the Newtonian framework. Indeed, Hermann (1998) convincingly argued that concepts from analyses of biological systems in recent decades are of greater value in understanding inanimate systems than is the reverse. He wrote:

> In the past, discussions of the relevance of science for the interpretation of reality, including human existence, were based on the simplification of physics. However, the close relationship of alternative interpretations of living matter ... suggests that the understanding of living, rather than inanimate systems, would be of greater use in reconciling the simplifying and complex qualities of reality. (p. 7)

everyday lives. Our present understanding of the human condition is surely more limited than any psychologist would like.

Some critics, such as Koch (1964, 1999), have attributed this circumstance in part to an impoverished conceptual language that arises from unwarranted strictures on what can be properly admitted into the discipline. A historical analysis suggests that this tendency can be traced back several centuries to the early development of the natural science attitude itself (Toulmin, 1990). A number of less than desirable consequences follow from this state of affairs. Only two are named here. First, there is the ever-widening gulf between the content of psychology and other domains of inquiry concerned with the human condition, namely, the humanities and the arts. Arguably, the problem Koch so vigorously criticized has lessened somewhat in recent years. But, it is sad to say that a great deal of psychology still falls short when it comes to offering an account of the human condition that psychologists and nonpsychologists alike recognize as adequate to their own everyday experience.

This point leads to a second consequence of an inadequate conceptual language. Because of the authoritative status of the sciences in Western culture, the "image of human nature" that psychology offers up has the power to transform how we think about ourselves. For this reason, an impoverished or an inaccurate account of human experience can reflexively and gradually become accurate or self-fulfilling in time through the imprimatur of science, even if this is an unintended outcome. For this reason, the work of psychologists, both in a research context and in the classroom, carries with it a greater measure of moral responsibility than is often recognized.

One essential quality of human experience that has received scant attention in experimental psychology is its *meaningfulness*. Unlike the world described by the physical sciences, the world-as-lived is meaningful; and clearly, much of human action is characterized by "efforts toward meaning." Individuals strive to make sense, in both mundane and elevated ways, of the constant and changing character of their lives. That continuing efforts of this nature are basic to human beings can be evidenced on those rare occasions when we experience disorientation and distress in situations lacking in meaning for us. These efforts are more commonly evidenced by the extensive and elaborate individual and sociocultural actions plainly visible around us that function to maintain meaningful structures in our lives. The discipline is in need of systematic and rigorous ways to address this central dimension of human experience. At its most basic level, meaning is a relational or contextual property of human experience, and ecological psychology can play a central role in articulating this dimension of immediate experience.[6]

In short, what is being offered here is a study of ecological psychology in context in several different, although interrelated, respects: in historical context; in relation to the other sciences, and the life sciences in particular; as a concern for phenomena occurring at multiple levels of organization; in the context of the role of sociocultural processes in psychological phenomena; and in recognition that meaning, which arises out of contextual considerations, is an inescapable quality of human experience.

OVERVIEW AND PLAN OF THE BOOK

With those introductory remarks, let us turn to an overview of the argument, along with a description of the structure of the presentation.

Part I begins with a brief discussion of psychology's perennial theoretical dilemma. From the outset, experimental psychology has been caught between, on the one hand, following successful paths established in the physical sciences and, on the other, recognizing the necessity of grounding its concepts in evolutionary theory. A dilemma arises from psychology's being thusly positioned because of some conceptual differences between the Newtonian worldview that underlies classical physical science approaches and the functional perspective of an evolutionary account of living processes. Newtonian physics is an attempt to describe a timeless world that is already in place. An evolutionary approach assumes a dynamic world continually coming into existence in often unforeseeable ways. The standard metatheoretical foundation of much 20th-century psychology, based as it is on a Newtonian–Cartesian philosophical heritage, leaves the discipline awash in tensions arising from these radically different stances. As a result, critical tensions lurk at the heart of the discipline.

An alternative metatheoretical approach more suitable for an ecological psychology had been developed and was available early in this century, although—then as now—it has attracted little attention in most psychological circles. This alternative, discussed in detail in chapter 1, is William James's philosophy of radical empiricism. It is highly ironic that in spite of James's eminence among psychologists, his philosophy of radical empiricism—which in many ways was the culmination of his life's

---

[6] Ecological psychology is not alone in identifying meaning as a central and yet neglected issue in the discipline. A major effort has been underway for a decade or more in the psychology of language to give meaning or semantics the attention it has long been overdue (e.g., Lakoff, 1986).

work—is relatively unknown to psychologists.[7] This paradoxical situation needs to be examined. James formulated radical empiricism as a means of circumventing the insurmountable problems presented to psychologies built on the Cartesian tradition. Unlike these latter positions on which evolutionary considerations can only be awkwardly imposed post hoc and that retain the exclusive mechanistic focus of Newtonian science, radical empiricism grows directly out of a functionalist, evolutionary account of psychological processes and fully embraces the reciprocity between animal and environment that such a view entails. This book shows how the perspective of radical empiricism, which fits compatibly with evolutionary theory, leads to a psychology that more fully captures the nature of human experience than does its rivals.

Radical empiricism may be relatively unknown to contemporary psychologists, but the most significant psychological product of this philosophical system has become quite visible in recent decades: I refer here to James J. Gibson's ecological psychology. Although growing in influence recently, Gibson's theory remains on the periphery of psychology for several reasons, foremost of which is its conspicuous departure from standard formulations of psychological processes. Psychologists initially confronting Gibson's ecological approach, and even those having some familiarity with it, typically have difficulty anchoring it to any existing intellectual traditions. It seems highly idiosyncratic, appearing virtually "out

---

[7] In the weeks preceding the completion of this book, I came across two very recent and problematic uses of the term *radical empiricism*, one somewhat misleading and the other inaccurate. As to the former, in an extended and detailed call for interactionism in analyses of developmental processes, Elman et al., (1999) used the term to refer to an extreme environmentalist position. Although that may be a literal rendering of the phrase, it is not at all what James's had in mind when he employed radical empiricism to refer to his philosophical position. Used in this way, radical empiricism becomes closely aligned with radical behaviorism. If radical empiricism takes on this connotation in the coming years, it would be regrettable, because in the process a distinctive viewpoint that James and others sought to develop would be lost.

More problematic is the use of the term by Capaldi and Proctor (1999), who accurately connected the term to James's philosophy, but who are quite wrong in describing James as a relativist who foreshadowed the epistemological relativism seen in much post-modernist philosophy. Only a cursory reading of James's position could lead to such a conclusion. I am sympathetic with many of the concerns that motivate Capaldi and Proctor's discussion, but I worry that their misreading of James could foreshadow a similar misreading of the present work.

As I will show, there has been a long-standing tendency to employ certain dichotomies in analyses of psychology that are rather dubious, one of which is objective/subjective vis-à-vis knowledge claims. James's radical empiricism is a rejection of this dichotomy. Therefore, while James finds the notion of "objective" knowledge (in the sense of knowledge that corresponds with external reality) problematic, that does not mean he considered knowledge to be something that minds impose on the world. To draw that conclusion is to remain within the objective/subjective dichotomy. This claim is not only inaccurate with reference to James, but also with reference to some (but not all) versions of pragmatism generated by his or John Dewey's writings.

of the blue." This circumstance has impeded ready comprehension of its essential claims, which in turn has adversely affected its wider acceptance. Reading Gibson's work does little to remedy this situation. Although he clearly indicated which theoretical traditions he distanced himself from, it is far from obvious how to ground his ecological theory in a positive manner. The presentation of radical empiricism here partially fills in this gap.

But James's radical empiricism alone does not lay the foundation for Gibson's ecological program. Although this ecological approach is an off-spring of James's philosophy of radical empiricism, Gibson's exposure to radical empiricism was apparently indirect, through his primary graduate school mentor, Edwin B. Holt, a student of James, who devoted most of his intellectual life to working out some psychological implications of James's radical empiricism. Holt's position has sometimes been called *philosophical behaviorism*. A largely forgotten figure today, Holt was very prominent in both psychological and philosophical circles during the first three decades of the 20th century. His work provides the linkage between James's radical empiricism and Gibson's ecological psychology, and it is the focus of chapter 2.

Holt's writings receive the extensive treatment that they do here precisely because his work has been forgotten by contemporary psychologists. But it is deserving of far more attention than it has received in recent decades. Not only does it provide an important extension of radical empiricism into psychological theory, and in so doing connect Gibson's ecological approach to Jamesian psychology and philosophy, but it is insightful and notable in its own right in spite of some limitations from a contemporary vantage point. By presenting as detailed examination of Holt's work as I do, I run the risk of detracting from the main purpose of developing a broad-based account of an ecological perspective. If other sources existed that reviewed Holt's ideas and demonstrated their contribution to Gibson's thought, far less space would be devoted here to this body of work. Unfortunately, this is not the case. Hopefully, my examination of Holt's contributions will help to rehabilitate the work of this important 20th-century thinker. Some of the reasons for his fall from prominence in psychology reflect the prevailing social climate in academia for much of this century and are themselves instructive to consider, if only briefly.

Having examined in detail some of the writings of James and Holt, Part II turns to Gibson's ecological theory, specifically to articulate the interconnections among the three. Although Gibson's ideas are presented here at a level accessible for the newcomer to this work, because my primary goal is to demonstrate the linkages between Gibson, James, and Holt, Gibson's ideas are not systematically reviewed. Some overviews for various audiences have been offered elsewhere (Heft, 1981, 1988b, 1997);

moreover, numerous, detailed expositions of his ideas are readily available (e.g., Michaels & Carrello, 1981; Reed, 1988), not to mention Gibson's own highly accessible books and papers. Prior general familiarity with Gibson's work is not necessary for reading these chapters in Part II; the chapters can stand on their own. But they are not intended as a substitute for a full exposition of Gibson's ecological framework.

Chapters 3, 4, and 5 that comprise Part II, examine the interconnections among the works of these individuals—and I stress their *inter*connections—because not only do major features of Gibson's ecological theory reflect the influences of James and Holt, with many of Gibson's proposals growing out of themes central to radical empiricist philosophy and philosophical behaviorism, but also aspects of Gibson's theory can reflexively address several critical and unresolved problems that arose for James in the formulation of radical empiricism. This discussion contributes to the ongoing philosophical examination of James's later work, which is experiencing somewhat of a renaissance in recent decades (e.g., Lamberth, 1999; Myers, 1986; H. Putnam, 1990, 1995; R. Putnam, 1997; Reed, 1997; Seigfried, 1978, 1990; Simon, 1998; Suckiel, 1982; Taylor & Wozniak, 1996). Hopefully, interweaving central features of Gibson's, James's, and Holt's ideas in these chapters will help the relative newcomer to Gibson's work gain a firm foothold; will give those readers with a background in this perspective new and deeper insight; and will enrich the philosophical development of radical empiricism and its allied program, pragmatism.

These chapters that comprise Parts I and II of this volume have as their collective intention to explicate and thereby *deepen* the theoretical base of an ecological psychology. This deeper conceptual base, however, remains somewhat narrow, focusing as it does primarily on matters concerning the psychology of perception and cognition. *Broadening* the conceptual base of ecological psychology is the overall intent of Part III.

The first three chapters in Part III attempt to merge Gibson's ecological psychology with the somewhat lesser known eco-behavioral program of Roger Barker. Through painstaking observational research, Barker and his colleagues made important discoveries about the structure and dynamics of the social settings within which individuals conduct their daily lives. They found that higher order ecological structures emerge from the dynamic interrelations established among individuals and environmental features, and in turn these extra-individual structures are the basis for some of the order seen at the level of individual action. I show that Gibson's and Barker's programs are complementary, with each working at different levels of ecopsychological analysis.

To date, these two ecological programs have been dealt with quite separately in the literature, but they are historically and metatheoretically compatible. Both approaches have been deeply influenced by the field-theoretic Gestalt tradition. Further, and most significantly, the theoretical linchpin between Gibson's and Barker's systems is the seminal work of Fritz Heider during the first half of the 20th century. Chapter 6 examines these Gestalt influences, as well as the related and very important perceptual work of Heider. Although Heider is well known for his contributions to social psychology (e.g., attribution theory, one of the more influential theories of the 1980s, is traceable to him), his earlier perceptual writings are less well known to psychologists.

Chapter 7 focuses specifically on Barker's ecological psychology, including a critical examination of a recent attempt to expand this program. In place of the latter, an alternative proposal is offered that draws on writings concerning dynamic complex systems. Chapter 8 considers the interrelationships between Gibson's and Barker's programs. Overall, by juxtaposing Barker's framework with that of Gibson's, it becomes possible to elucidate a theoretically coherent ecological theory of psychology that operates at multiple levels of analysis.

Ecological psychology's conceptual base is expanded further in chapter 9 where *sociocultural* processes become the focus. The framework of ecological psychology is seen as being compatible with the viewpoint in contemporary cultural anthropology that culture provides a necessary background for understanding developing psychological processes, both from a phylogenetic and an ontogenetic perspective. The quality of psychological experience that becomes most central from such a viewpoint is *meaning*, which is the very quality that is most problematic for a psychology built on the standard physicalistic concepts. The entities of physical science—or rather, natural entities considered at the level of analysis of physical science—are without meaning and value-free. It is primarily for this reason that a psychology with its roots in the physical sciences, as is the case with most contemporary experimental psychology, has precious little to say about meaning. This lacuna in contemporary experimental psychology is glaring considering that meaning and value are ubiquitous, inescapable, and arguably the quintessential features of human experience. In an ecological-functional account, where psychological processes are viewed as part of a sociocultural network of mutually supporting, adaptive relations, and where the individual as a participant in culture is recognized as sustaining, and indeed creating, cultural structures through everyday actions, meaning takes center stage—as well it must if psychology is to have much to say about the human condition. Significantly, ecological psychology suggests an approach to meaning from a third-person perspective, thereby offering a way of making this issue amenable to experimental study.

These considerations add further weight to the fundamental Jamesian insight that psychology must adopt a relational focus. Knowing will be seen as being best understood as a functional relation between the knower and the known. Rather than viewing knowing as an intra-individual process, as something primarily occurring "in" the private theaters of individuals' consciousness, it will be seen, most basically, as action-in-context. By adopting this perspective, psychological processes cannot be justifiably seen as events occurring within the boundaries of the body in any simple sense. Instead, the realm of the psychological encompasses the environment (defined relationally) to include, among other things, tools, artifacts, and representations.[8] Opportunistic discovery of tools and the intentional design of artifacts and representations demonstrate that knowing can extend into the environment itself, encompassing both the individual and the environment considered jointly. What this discussion highlights, in particular, is the *public nature of knowing*, which is embodied not only in social action but also in artifacts and other human constructions. The public availability of knowledge is seen as fundamental to sociocultural processes, and in turn, is essential for understanding many of the advanced forms of knowing that distinguish humans from other animals.

As an extension of this claim, chapter 9 proposes that knowing can be distributed among groups of individuals. It is quite commonplace that each of us participates in collective activities that no one of us could accomplish alone. This phenomenon is more than a mere division of labor where members of a group divide up a set of tasks that any one of them could, in principle, carry out. In many cases, an individual only knows one part of the collective activity. Thus, what is commonly found in the everyday world, once we begin to look for it, are instances of knowing that exist only in a distributed form across a group of individuals and across the tools, artifacts, and representations they employ. In such cases, the needed knowledge for carrying out many activities resides with no one person, but only exists en masse.

This discussion of extended and distributed cognition, compatible with the relational foundations laid by James, Holt, and Gibson (not to mention Dewey and Heidegger), helps to liberate psychology from its traditional "derma-bounded" focus—a focus that locates psychological phenomena solely within the boundaries of skin. In turn, this discussion leads to the recognition of the important place that work such as Barker's on extra-

---

[8]As should be apparent from the context, and as becomes very clear in the following chapters, the term *representation* is not used in the standard way to refer to something existing in an individual's head, in the sense of a "mental representation." Following Gibson, I am using representation to refer to environmental features such as drawings, photographs, and writing.

individual phenomena has in psychology. Knowing, or mind, if you will, extends into the functional and symbolic possibilities of an individual's sociocultural world. Recognizing this is truly an important step toward a more fully realized ecological psychology.

Finally, chapter 10 returns the discussion to its point of origin. The radical empiricist roots of ecological psychology are reexamined in light of the overall presentation. An ecological psychology built on radical empiricist assumptions, and integrated with recent ideas in anthropology, the study of technology and tools, the analysis of situated and socially distributed cognition, and dynamic complex systems will enable psychology to break free from those physical science conceptions that have constrained its growth to date. With this ecological framework at its core, the prospects for a scientific psychology that highlights rather than obscures unique qualities of the human condition become more imaginable.

I

Ecological Theory and Philosophical Realism

Prologue: Intimations of an Ecological Psychology

> And just as an individual, to be free, must verbalize the past that has resulted in his present, so an entire science must remain in dialogue with its past and analyze its hidden biases and omissions if it is not to wither away into dried-up specialties and unfulfilling evasions. (Jaynes, 1973a, p. x)

The modern conception of psychology is rooted firmly in the Cartesian perspective. The expression "the Cartesian perspective" refers to the worldview accompanying the rise of the New Science, starting roughly in the early 17th century and represented in the work of such scientists as Galileo and Kepler. It received its clearest and most systematic articulation in the writings of Descartes, and later reached formal scientific expression in Newton's imposing cosmology and physics. Thus, the phrase "the Cartesian perspective" does not refer solely to the philosophical and scientific writings of Descartes. Instead, it is intended as a label for the convergence of thought among many empirically minded Renaissance and Enlightenment thinkers who self-consciously, through logical reasoning and mathematical analysis, sought to liberate individual inquiry from centuries of institutional constraints. Its goal was, and is, to articulate the abstract, universal principles on which the natural order rests (Berlin, 1980).[1]

The Cartesian approach as applied specifically to psychological concerns recognizes two distinct domains: the *environment* and the *person*. It offers up a picture of the world consisting of matter in motion and, in contrast, a separate dynamic realm of mental phenomena where such materialistic accounts do not apply. Although phenomena of psychological interest—such as perceptual experience, thoughts, and emotions—are to be located within this domain of the person, their causes are typically sought in the material domain. What this conceptualization requires, then,

---

[1] With its emphasis on discovering decontextualized universals, the Cartesian perspective that came to be synonymous with the natural science approach differed from an alternative, but equally "progressive" approach to understanding represented by the humanists of the late 16th century (Toulmin, 1990).

is that psychological analyses come to grips with processes of both the person and the environment—and it is here where the going gets rough. For if occurrences in the environment follow physical laws that are best understood as mechanical events, and if phenomena of the mental realm follow dynamic, nonphysicalist principles, then psychological phenomena in this dualistic framework cannot be related in any straightforward way with conditions of the environment.

How then can events in the physical world and phenomena of the psychological domain be coordinated? How can lawful relations be identified between environmental conditions and persons? Because the features of the environment and the operations of the body are both describable in the common currency of physical properties and mechanical events—that is, because the mechanical operations of the physical body are co-extensive with the mechanics of the physical environment—the body can be viewed as functioning as an intermediary between the environment and the mental realm.

This dualistic Cartesian perspective, which requires the coordination of a physical mechanistic domain (environment and body) and a dynamic mental domain, is contemporary psychology's legacy from its intellectual past. In the wake of this history, psychological theories have either followed this formulation generally and uncritically, or have adopted analyses that in the manner of their rejection of dualism retain some of its most problematic features.

CONCEPTUALIZING THE ENVIRONMENT AND THE PERSON

Let us look more systematically at the way the environment and the person are conceptualized in the Cartesian perspective. The picture of the environment offered by this perspective is that of a world of inert matter in mechanical interaction. Matter and the objects composed from it are located in a container of space, their location specifiable with reference to three Cartesian coordinates, and also along a dimension of abstract time (Burtt, 1954). The various properties of objects in the world are describable in forms of physical energy, and through these energies, object properties are conveyed to the knower: Visually perceivable properties of objects are conveyed by light energy giving rise to visual experience. Tangible properties, such as solidity and texture, and sounds emitted from inanimate and animate objects are conveyed via mechanical energy and realized psychologically as tactual and auditory experience, respectively. The chemical composition of environmental features is conveyed by chemical energy and realized as taste and smell. This kind of account of the *physical* properties of the material world forms the basis of most contemporary treatments of the environment in experimental psychology.

And how have processes of the person been conceptualized? Such conceptualizations have changed in scientific circles over the past several centuries from an unholy Cartesian dualistic alliance of mechanical bodily processes and those of an unextended soul, either in interaction or in a parallel relation, to a more exclusive concern with material processes of the body. Analyses of bodily processes have themselves progressed from accounts described in purely mechanical terms, modeled after inanimate phenomena [e.g., the hydraulics of a closed system of fluids (Descartes) or the vibrations of taut strings (Newton and Hartley)], to analyses using biochemical concepts more suited to the nature of organic processes.

Taking a long view, then, this developing understanding of environmental properties and of person processes has followed different trajectories. Whereas the conceptualization of person processes has radically changed over the past three to four centuries, the concepts that psychologists employ today to describe the environment are substantially the same as those that scientists used in the days of Galileo, Descartes, and especially Newton. Looking at these different trajectories, would advances in the biological sciences have enabled a more primitive understanding of living processes to catch up with a more sophisticated understanding of the environment? Or, alternatively, in some sense, has the conceptualization of the environment in psychology failed to keep pace with changing views of the living organism? Although at first glance the first of these interpretations may seem more accurate, in my estimation, it is our conceptualization of the environment from a psychological perspective that is lagging behind.

The Newtonian revolution in the physical sciences during the Enlightenment has a counterpart in the Darwinian revolution in the life sciences of the 19th century. Evolutionary theory has obvious and important implications for the way in which psychologists think about living things, and consequently, this framework has dramatically transformed the conceptualization of the organism. Perhaps less obviously, but equally important, are the implications of evolutionary theory for how psychologists think about the environment. However, now, almost 150 years since the publication of *The Origin of the Species*, the treatment of the environment in psychology, for the most part, remains unchanged since the Enlightenment and is still couched in the language of the physical sciences.

Here is the origin of many of the theoretical tensions in experimental psychology. Put perhaps much too simply, the reason is this: The implications of the Darwinian revolution in the life sciences have yet to catch on fully in contemporary psychology. While psychological analyses of organismic processes have been transformed by evolutionary thinking, psychological analyses of the environment relevant to organismic functioning have not. In the absence of a conceptualization of the environment more in keeping with evolutionary thinking, the current analyses of psychological issues are infused with a mixture of concepts from the physical sciences and the biological sciences, not to mention verbal descriptions of first-person mental experience of psychological processes.[2]

Conceptual confusion results when psychological phenomena are described simultaneously in these various ways. And yet this is what is often done in contemporary psychology. Take the standard formulation of perception. It entails a physical description of environmental conditions and some combination of biological and experiential description applied to the individual, and oftentimes hypothetical intrapsychic processes are included as well. For example, the conventional textbook account of visual perception is a description of physical energies of light, which initiate biochemical processes in the retina and subsequent neural activity in the optic pathways and cortex, resulting in a mental representation of the environment with correlates in conscious experience.

But the conceptual frameworks provided by the physical sciences and the life sciences, as well as phenomenological analysis, are alternative descriptive systems, and each descriptive system may be more appropriately suited to one kind of phenomenon than another. What often seems to be absent in much of contemporary psychology is explicit recognition that many of its commonly used concepts stem from alternative explanatory systems. One way to conceptualize the differences between the concepts of these alternative explanatory systems is with reference to the notion of differing levels of organization.

---

[2]This complaint that evolutionary theory has yet to have a full impact on psychology might strike some readers as wildly inaccurate for at least two reasons. First, the historical record plainly shows that some psychologists embraced Darwinian theory from the founding years of the discipline, even though for many of the first generation of psychologists, such functional concerns were of minor importance because they were inconsistent with the primary goals of the discipline (e.g., the description of the contents of consciousness and their relations). Let me reiterate, however, that my claim is that evolutionary theory has had minimal impact on how psychologists conceptualize the *environment*, and in turn how that conceptualization affects one's view of the organism. A second reason that this comment might seem inaccurate is because of the development in recent decades of so-called evolutionary psychology (e.g., Barkow, Cosmides, & Toobey, 1992.) The goals of that approach, to explain present-day psychological attributes in terms of their prior evolutionary value, differ greatly from the goals of ecological psychology. Ecological psychology is an analytical framework that seeks to reveal lawful, functional relations in the ongoing reciprocal interaction of the individual and the environment. In other words, each approach asks quite different questions. That being said, there remains several substantive differences between the concepts employed by evolutionary psychologists and ecological psychologists—most notably, the way culture is conceptualized, and in turn, the place of sociocultural processes in human development (see chap. 9).

As is discussed later (chap. 8), natural phenomena can be viewed as being organized at different levels of organization, and particular conceptual resources are better suited for capturing the distinctive processes operating at one level of organization as opposed to another. For example, when a problem is identified at a biochemical level, such as how photochemicals in the retina are altered by light and then reconstituted, an analysis at the level of physical and biochemical processes is clearly most desirable. However, when psychological processes are the concern (e.g., perceiving the layout of environmental features), what is needed is an account of the functional relation between the properties of environment and an individual's actions.

A functional analysis centers on the individual's ongoing transactions with meaningful features of the environment. Accordingly, it involves a conceptualization of environmental conditions at a molar (rather than molecular) level of organization commensurate with an individual's molar, purposive actions (i.e., the self-directed actions of the whole organism). In other words, a functional analysis emphasizes the intentionality of individuals' actions, and concurrently adopts a molar analysis of the environment in relation to which these actions transpire. With this focus, psychologists are in a position to work within a framework where both facets of the environment–person relation are conceptually commensurate. And, maintaining commensurate analytical levels is crucial because in this way the ongoing, reciprocal interrelations between the environment and the person become conceivable in a coherent manner. At this level of analysis, individuals engage the environment in order to learn more about its properties and, in many instances, individually and collectively contribute to the environment's changing functional character. This kind of analytical stance, emphasizing the *reciprocity* of the environment and the person, is a central feature of an *ecological approach.*

Because it has these attributes, the ecological approach to be explored in subsequent chapters avoids many of the seemingly intractable problems and theoretical tensions associated with the standard Cartesian formulation, with its conjoining of physical variables, biological processes, and conscious experience. Perhaps more significantly, the ecological framework will create opportunities for breaking new conceptual ground in psychology.

Where does one begin to develop an ecological analysis of the environment and the individual? Many of the concepts needed for such a project, as well as the metatheoretical foundations required for its further development, have been available in the psychological literature for some time. The next section begins to draw some of these ideas together.

COLLECTING THE THREADS OF ECOLOGICAL PSYCHOLOGY

Looking for the precise historical beginning of an idea is usually an empty exercise. Intellectual progress is a cumulative and collective enterprise among a community of inquirers extended over historical time and distributed across geographical places. At some point, however, anticipatory ripples from diverse sources converge into the beginnings of a ground swell, at which time a certain idea may come to be expressed explicitly for the first time. Accordingly, in this study of ecological psychology, no single event marks its initial development; but some significant historical threads that appeared earlier in this century can be picked up.

A good place to start is Heider's (1926/1959) classic essay "Thing and Medium," and Tolman and Brunswik's (1935/1966) joint paper "The Organism and the Causal Texture of the Environment." Both papers point to a problem that has been insufficiently addressed in psychology, a problem most explicitly formulated by Heider.

Generalizing from first-person experience, it would seem that all individuals perceive a world populated with innumerable objects and features (e.g., trees, houses, tools, other individuals etc.). And yet perception as it has typically been studied in psychology begins with a consideration of the impact of physical stimulation from the world on specialized sensory receptors of the body. If contact with the world consists of physical stimulation of these receptor interfaces located on the body, how is it that individuals experience a world of features "out there" that extends away from them and among which they negotiate? How is it possible to bridge the gap, conceptually speaking, between the perceiver and the environment?

In the case of vision, by beginning an analysis of perception with retinal stimulation, the next step is to discover how the character of the experienced world can be derived from these scintillations of receptor firings. However, a prior question has been overlooked: What is the relation between the environment and visual stimulation? Or, stated more generally, what is the relation between the structure of the environment and stimulation at receptor surfaces? This is the important question raised by Heider.

The only framework for the analysis of perception available to most psychologists is one that takes physical stimulation as the appropriate conceptualization of the "stimulus." Beginning with a conceptualization of the stimulus as physical stimulation at the receptor level creates enormous, and perhaps insurmountable, theoretical and philosophical problems for any account of perception because from the outset the structural properties of the environment are absent. With such a formulation, perception of environmental features becomes, if not magical, then pure guesswork.

Alternatives to this approach are lacking because, quite simply, the structure of the environment from a psychological perspective, as contrasted with a physical perspective, has rarely been considered. Heider (1930/1959) described the situation this way:

> Everybody will concede that the perceptual apparatus belongs to an organism which is adapted to the environment; nevertheless, in discussion of perception the structure of the environment is often completely neglected, and only the proximal stimuli (for instance, the wave length of the stimuli impinging on the organs) are taken account of. (p. 35)

Heider's essay and the Tolman and Brunswik paper offered different approaches to this problem. Heider considered how structure can be conveyed via a medium, such as the air, to a perceiver. Tolman and Brunswik (1935/1966) offered a broader analysis of what they called the environment's "causal texture," wherein the probabilistic dependencies existing among environmental events can be the basis for an organism developing expectations of environmental structure (see chap. 6).

At first glance, consideration of the problem of environmental structure may seem to be only a narrow concern for the analysis of perception. But there is hardly a topic in psychology for which considerations of the nature of the environment and an individual's relation to it do not play an essential role. As Tolman and Brunswik (1935/1966) pointed out:

> All the problems of psychology—not only those of visual perception and learning—but the more general problems of instinct, insight, learning, intelligence, motivation, personality, and emotion all center around this one general feature of the given organism's abilities and tendencies for adjusting to these *actual causal textures [of the environment]*. (p. 483, emphasis added)

If this claim is warranted, analysis of the structure of the environment would seem to be a task that is crucial for understanding all manner of psychological phenomena. For this reason, analysis of the structure of the environment is among the more central tasks for psychology as a whole.[3] Notably, it is also one of the most neglected tasks in the discipline.

"Ever since Darwin" (to borrow Stephen Jay Gould's phrase), adaptive functioning has been seen as the hallmark of any viable living organism, and this requires that animals have the means to detect environmental

---

[3] More generally, there is a long tradition in philosophy, and by extension, psychology that considers perceptual experience as fundamental to all other forms of knowing. This viewpoint is explicit in phenomenological approaches, which adopt the perspective that "we *never* completely escape from the realm of perceptual reality, and even seemingly independent structures of categorical thought (of 'rationality') are ultimately founded in perception" (Edie, 1964, p. xvii).

conditions at some distance from them. And yet with few exceptions, psychologists have been employing theoretical approaches to perceiving that are tacitly, if not explicitly, structured by pre-Darwinian (i.e., by Cartesian thinking; see chap. 1). The necessary attempts to accommodate evolutionary considerations into psychological theory have typically involved little more than grafting some sort of functional analysis onto this pre-Darwinian perspective. Such a move results in attention being directed either to the peripheral sensitivities of animals and their associated proximal stimuli, or to intra-organismic processes, or to both. In all of these cases, the sole focus of the analysis is on processes of the organism. But as Heider (1926/1959) and Tolman and Brunswik (1935/1966) pointed out, such a restricted focus is incomplete. Because organisms function adaptively in an environment filled with meaningful features located at various distances from them, the earlier question remains unanswered: How can the gap be bridged between environmental conditions and psychological processes?

If the gap is conceptualized as one separating physical stimulation and psychological experience, then it is, in fact, unbridgeable. This is because to state the problem as one of discovering the relation between physical properties and psychological experience is to attempt to link conceptual resources operating at incommensurate levels of analysis. Is this then an irresolvable issue, or is there some alternative way of framing the problem? Clearly, a variant of the dualistic, Cartesian metaphysical framework will not do.

In his later writings, William James labored to formulate an alternative way of conceptualizing the relation between the environment and the person. The result was his philosophy of radical empiricism, and through this alternative, James did not so much bridge the gap as attempt to eliminate it entirely. Radical empiricism provides the philosophical and historical foundations for ecological psychology.

William James
(Archives of the History of American Psychology,
The University of Akron)

1

William James's Radical Empiricism: A Foundation for Ecological Psychology

> But through this complexity, which is due to the complexity of reality itself, we believe that the reader will find his way if he keeps a fast hold on the two principles which we have used as a clue throughout our own researches. The first is that in psychological analysis we must never forget the utilitarian character of our mental functions, which are essentially turned toward action. The second is that the habits formed in action find their way up to the sphere of speculation, where they create fictitious problems, and that metaphysics must begin by dispersing this artificial obscurity. (Bergson, 1910/1988, p. 16)

The intellectual revolution engendered by evolutionary theory was the culmination of a progression of ideas that transformed the way the life sciences look at the natural world. Displaced was the long-held schema of nature as a static chain of being (*Scala Naturae*) comprised of a succession of material entities and culminating in spiritual entities, with an admixture of matter and spirit characterizing the intermediate place of humans in that chain (Eiseley, 1958). In its place there is a dynamic realm of thoroughly natural, co-evolved entities functioning in a web of environmental interdependencies. The structural and functional properties of natural entities, and the interdependencies they share, reflect their ongoing mutual history. This view underlies an *ecological perspective* and is at the heart of the modern life sciences.

Psychology as a whole has yet to feel the *full* impact of this revolution in thinking. To adopt a Piagetian stance for the moment, it could be said that whereas psychology has assimilated an ecological perspective, it has yet to accommodate to it. That is to say, even though experimental psychology—and particularly American experimental psychology—early on recognized and attempted to incorporate a view of the essentially functional character of psychological phenomena, all the while an irresolvable tension has existed at the theoretical center of the discipline, making it difficult to achieve a coherent functional account. This tension stems from the dissonance existing between characteristics of the traditional framework on which psychology has been erected, on the one hand, and an ecological perspective, on the other. What happened historically, in brief, was that the viewpoint offered by evolutionary theory was added onto a long-standing, and in many ways theoretically incompatible, conceptualization of psychological processes. What was needed instead of an up-dating of old models, however, was a radical transformation of the kind seen in the other sciences concerned with the animate world.

The long-standing conceptualization in psychology that an ecological perspective has yet to displace is the Cartesian framework, which was described in the preceding prologue. Dewey (1896) pointed out in the early years of the discipline that the new functional perspective being offered by the field of scientific psychology was in fact the same old wine in new bottles. With his usual prescience, he argued that until vestiges of the Cartesian framework are fully dislodged from psychological theorizing, accounts of psychological processes will continue to harbor intractable problems, such as the relationship between mind-body. These problems will remain in spite of intentions to the contrary, and even in spite of efforts to brush these merely philosophical problems aside as irrelevant to a science of psychology.

Specifically, Dewey argued that the newly emerging distinction between *stimulus* and *response*, which in succeeding decades was to become the primary conceptual unit for 20th century psychology, was a restatement of the Cartesian distinction between environmental properties and organismic properties. Instead of embracing the *unitary, coordinative relation* that reflects an animal's ongoing, adaptive functioning in an environment, this distinction maintained the Cartesian disjointedness between the environment and the organism. A Cartesian soul no longer may have been explicitly present in the stimulus–response formulation; but, the Cartesian gap between the environment and the individual remained. The problem of bringing stimulus and response into alignment is the same species of problem as that of bringing into alignment the physical world and mental experience. If the response side of the dichotomy is defined in nonphysical terms, then the difficulty is explaining the interrelations between physical processes of the world and the mental processes of the organism. If the response is defined solely in physical terms, then it can be proposed that the relations between environment and organism are fully mechanistic in nature. But by taking this step, we may have traded one set of problems for another. The environment–organism connection is explained mechanistically at the considerable cost of omitting many essential qualities of human processes, such as purpose and meaning. Thus, the gap between the physical environment and human experience looms as large as ever. Worse, a limited or—if the limitations go unrecognized—a distorted conceptualization of human experience takes up residence in our account. In order to move beyond Cartesian dualism, something more radical is needed than the substitution of stimulus–response terminology for the categories of environment/body-mind.

What is lacking is an adequate functional account of living processes that have co-evolved with respect to a set of environmental conditions and maintain a dynamic and reciprocal relation with those conditions. The functional view of psychological processes provided by evolutionary theory cannot merely be added to a Cartesian framework; but this is precisely what has happened in much of psychology's recent past.

A PSYCHOLOGY OF ADAPTATION

William James (1842–1910) did more than anyone else among the first generation of psychologists to introduce an evolutionary perspective into psychological theorizing. Without question, in this regard, psychology was profoundly affected by his efforts. In the wake of James's psychological writings in the late 19th century (as well as the influential, earlier work of Herbert Spencer and others), American psychology took on a decidedly functional outlook. The immediate and long-term effects of James's efforts showed in that most psychologists began to couch traditional concepts in a functional framework.

But James's intentions were much more ambitious than a terminological shift. It is clear, particularly in his later writings, that James attempted to incorporate a naturalistic perspective into psychology in such way as to avoid problems arising from the unavoidable clash he saw between a functional approach and a traditional Cartesian view.

If the manner in which James attempted to resolve the tension between these perspectives is to be recognized, and the possibilities of a more coherent functional theory is to emerge, greater attention must be paid to the full body of work James produced, and not just to the writings he explicitly titled "psychology." The culmination of James's work in psychology, broadly considered, is his philosophy of *radical empiricism*, which appeared in explicit form during the first decade of the 20th century.[1] This project provides much of the needed conceptual groundwork for an ecological psychology. Indeed, the conceptual underpinnings of James Gibson's ecological approach are traceable to James's later philosophical position.[2] Moreover, radical empiricism can be employed as a philosophical foundation for an ecological psychology that extends beyond the purview of Gibson's work. The primary purpose of this chapter is to provide the basis for these claims. Accordingly, the radical empiricist framework that James developed is described through a selective examination of his writings.

A Reluctant Dualist of the 1890s

James's attempts to resolve the tension between a functional and a Cartesian perspective occupied much of his career. The position offered in his radical empiricist writings is partially the result of these efforts, creating the possibility for a new approach to many of psychology's central issues. In this regard, Whitehead (1925) claimed that Descartes and James shared a common role in the history of philosophy and psychology:

> Neither philosopher finished an epoch by a final solution of a problem. Their great merit is of the opposite sort. They each of them open an epoch by their clear formulation of terms in which thought could profitably express itself at particular stages of knowledge, one for the seventeenth century, the other for the twentieth century. (p. 147)

---

[1]*Essays in Radical Empiricism* (1912/1976) was published posthumously, although James initially assembled its contents for his students' use during the 1906–1907 academic year. *A Pluralistic Universe* (1909/1996) and *Some Problems of Philosophy* (1911/1996), also published posthumously, followed. James's later philosophy and psychology referred to generally as radical empiricism is presented primarily among the essays in these books. *Pragmatism* (1907/1978) and its sequel *The Meaning of Truth* (1909/1978) also comprise essential pieces of this effort (see later).

When possible, I have used throughout the pagination of the Harvard editions of James's published work. The first date indicates the original date of publication, and the second date refers to the Harvard edition publication date. The exceptions are *A Pluralistic Universe* and *Some Problems of Philosophy*, where I used the University of Nebraska Press editions, and *Psychology: A Briefer Course*, where I used the Notre Dame University Press edition.

[2]In addition to radical empiricism, James's later philosophical writings included a metaphysical proposal for a pluralistic universe. The relation between these two aspects of his later work are discussed briefly in chapter 4.

The epoch that James opened did not become explicitly articulated until his later philosophical writings, although its seeds can be found in the work of his early and middle career (D. A. Crosby & Viney, 1992; Reed, 1997; E. I. Taylor, 1992).

The highlight of the middle portion of his career, and perhaps his masterwork, is *The Principles of Psychology* (1890/1981). What was distinctive about the vision of experimental psychology proposed in this seminal work was its commitment to a biological and evolutionary perspective. It was unlike the experimental psychology burgeoning on the Continent, mostly in Germany and being spread by students of its laboratories to England and North America. The latter psychology was characterized by analyses of the contents of mind and the manner of their relations, by the study of psychophysical correspondences, and by the amassing of chronometric data concerning a wide variety of psychological and psychomotor functions. The psychology James proposed sought to connect analyses of mental functioning with biological processes, and with brain processes in particular. Importantly, underlying this project was the functionalist assumption that biological processes, and correlatively, psychological phenomena, reflect an organism's coming to terms with the character of its environment. This was the Spencerian gospel that James tried to spread.

James staked out his position at the very beginning of *The Principles*. He asserted that "few recent formulas have done more real service" than Spencer's claim that "the essence of mental life and bodily life are one, namely, 'the adjustment of inner to outer relations'" (p. 19).[3] James subsequently had some critical things to say about leaving Spencer's "formula" simply at that. Yet, because it acknowledged that "minds inhabit environments which act on them and on which they in turn react," and in turn because it required investigators to take "mind in the midst of all of its concrete relations" (p. 6), this formula resting as it did on an evolutionary perspective was more likely to help form an understanding of psychological phenomena than was the kind of experimental psychology being promoted in places like Leipzig and Würzburg. This latter psychology bore the stamp of Cartesian metaphysics, which as James put it, "treated the soul as a detached existent, sufficient unto itself" (p. 6).

Indeed, like Descartes's model of a thinker engaging in the *cogito*, the introspective psychology practiced by Wundtians, and to a lesser degree by their rivals of the Act Psychology school, explicitly examined psychological states apart from the concrete, everyday world. Moreover,

---

[3]It is the emphasis on "adjustment" that distinguishes this perspective from psychophysics.

the institutionalization of experimental procedures and of a formal context for studying mental contents, which was instantiated in the distinction between a subject and the experimental conditions, further served to sever the relation between psychological processes and the world (Danziger, 1990).

Although James's biological approach to psychology, with its emphasis on the evolutionary history of the organism, was widely embraced at the time of the publication of *The Principles* as an important new beginning for experimental psychology, the discipline as a whole did not take his recommended further step: to study the "mind in the midst of its concrete relations." Instead, experimental psychologists, although generally adopting James's functionalist perspective, continued to follow the lead of what he sarcastically called "the brass-instrument psychologies" of the European laboratories and to model its experimental methodology on the approach of the physical sciences. Nor does the kind of approach that James proposed characterize much of the experimental psychology of more recent decades, even though *The Principles* continues to be venerated as one of psychology's greatest works. Ironically, although this veneration is well deserved, it often seems to be for reasons not entirely in keeping with James's intentions. James's promotion of the Darwinian perspective in *The Principles* did not substantively alter psychology's adherence to a Cartesian framework: The knower studied by experimental psychologists remained detached from the concrete particulars of daily life.

How can this incongruity between James's intentions and how James has been read be reconciled? If attention is limited to *The Principles*, it is not very difficult to understand. Its basis is reflected in the ambivalence that James himself expressed in this work concerning the place of concerns about the relation between mind and environment in the study of psychology—an ambivalence that he resolved shortly after its publication and that partially accounts for divergent readings of this work.[4]

---

[4]For an interesting case study of conflicting ways in which James can be read, compare the chapters by Rock (1990) and by Reed (1990) in Johnson and Henley's (1990) centennial reexamination of James's *The Principles*. Both authors compared James's approach to perception to other theoretical approaches, and their accounts are contradictory. Rock argued that James is working in the tradition of Helmholtz and more recent theorists who proposed that perception involves making an inference about the character of reality based on perceptual cues: "James explicitly endorses what nowadays has come to be called the likelihood principle, which Helmholtz [promoted]" (p. 198). Reed, in contrast, stated outright that James "disagrees with Helmholtz that the explanation of [spatial perception] is due to some (unconscious) different *mental* interpretation" (p. 233). Part of the reason why theorists with different theoretical commitments can all find their roots in James's *The Principles* is due to the ambivalence conveyed by that book. But a more critical, if understandable, determinant is a selective reading of the corpus of James's work.

James reluctantly accepted a Cartesian dualistic perspective in *The Principles*. He was certainly aware of the numerous problems associated with dualism; indeed, the seeds of the alternative he was developing appeared in essays prior to the publication of *The Principles* (e.g., "The Function of Cognition," 1885, later published in *The Meaning of Truth*, 1909/1975). But he attempted in this book to keep his philosophical concerns and his psychology separate and to write a psychology book free of "metaphysical" issues. Accordingly, he differentiated between a physical world and a mental realm primarily because it is with this distinction that psychologists seemed to naturally work. He tried to hold the line in *The Principles* that a philosophical critique of dualism was beyond the bounds of a psychological analysis of the sort offered in that project.

However, his student and first biographer R. B. Perry (1935) pointed out that James soon had second thoughts about this provisional adoption of dualism:

> The whole trend of his philosophical thought before and after the publication of the *Psychology* [i.e., *Psychology: The Briefer Course* (1892)] had been *against* that provisional makeshift. He now saw with increasing clearness that he could not hold one view as a psychologist and another as a philosopher; and as his rejection of dualism became a more and more dominant motive in his thought, he saw that he would have to correct his psychology. (p. 273)

Support for Perry's claim can be found in James's *Psychology: The Briefer Course* (1892/1985), *The Principles* more compact sibling, wherein he concluded:

> When, then, we talk of 'psychology as a natural science,' we must not assume that that means a psychology that stands at last on solid ground. It means just the reverse; it means a psychology particularly fragile, and into which the waters of metaphysical criticism leak at every joint. (p. 334)

His reconsideration of the provisional dualism adopted in *The Principles* is stated even more explicitly in the 1895 essay "The Knowing of Things Together," where he wrote, "I have become convinced since publishing that book that no conventional restrictions *can* keep metaphysical and so-called epistemological inquiries out of the psychology books" (James, 1895/1920b, p. 399).

It is clear, then, that by 1895 James had given up the view expressed in *The Principles* that psychology and philosophy could be kept separate even on a provisional basis. He recognized that the philosophical problems plaguing a psychology embracing mind–body dualism could not be eliminated simply by ruling it out of bounds. As a result, in his subsequent writings, James proposed to work toward the articulation of, what he called in a letter, "a non-dualistic formulation of the canvas of experience" (cited in Perry, 1935, I, p. 649).

The apparent disjunction between James's psychological writings appearing in the 1890s and his explicitly philosophical writings published in large measure during the first decade of the 20th century has led some commentators to conclude that James divided his career into a psychological phase and a philosophical phase (e.g., Hergenhahn, 1992; Leahey, 1994).[5] The psychological phase is presumably reflected in *The Principles of Psychology* (1890/1981), *Psychology: Briefer Course* (1892/1985), and *Talks to Teachers on Psychology* (1899/1958), although he had been at work and publishing parts of *The Principles* from the late 1870s on. The philosophical phase is presumably reflected in the books *Pragmatism* (1907/1975), *The Meaning of Truth* (1909/1975), *A Pluralistic Universe* (1909/1996), *Some Problems of Philosophy* (1911/1996), and *Essays in Radical Empiricism* (1912/1976). However, dividing James's thought and career into a psychological period followed by a philosophical period is an inaccurate characterization of his work. Apart from the fact that such a division omits other topics about which James wrote extensively—such as will, belief, and religious experience—it suggests a cleaving of his intellectual journey that is far too pat. *The Principles*, besides being a thorough review of the experimental literature of his day and James's own proposals for the development of psychology, was also deeply and, in many places, explicitly philosophical (e.g., see chap. 5, The Automaton Theory). In fact, aspects of what would later be his radical empiricist philosophy can be found in *The Principles*. It can be seen, then, that his short-lived intentions to keep psychology and philosophy separate were not even realized in this work. Reciprocally, James's later philosophical writings reexamine many of the same issues explored, perhaps in a theoretically preliminary fashion in his "psychology" (E. I. Taylor, 1992). D. A. Crosby and Viney (1992) estimated that of the 25 topic areas they identified in *The Principles*, 15 are reassessed in *Essays in Radical Empiricism* alone.

Before examining James's attempts to address the dualism lying at the heart of traditional psychological theory, and consequently, his broader effort to develop a metaphysics that accords with his psychology of adaptation, a few brief comments on post-Jamesian psychology are

---

[5]Herganhan wrote that in 1892 James "decided that he had said everything he could say about psychology, especially experimental psychology [and] he decided to devote his full attention to philosophical matters" (p. 311). Leahey (1992) stated, "After writing *The Principles*, James abandoned psychology for philosophy and developed his own brand of pragmatism" (p. 262).

needed. After all, the behaviorist psychology that began to appear during the last years of James's life and that came to dominate psychology for the next half century (and more) was a framework that explicitly rejected considerations of mind. Thus, is it not accurate to state that the Cartesianism that troubled James, with its assumption of the dual realms of matter and spirit, dropped out of psychology early in this century with the emergence of behaviorism? If so, many of the philosophical problems with which James was concerned no longer applied to psychological theory after J. Watson's (1913) behaviorist manifesto took hold. However, this is an unwarranted claim.

Behaviorism and Dualism

Among the numerous influences that gave rise to the behaviorist program were James's pragmatism (or at least a narrow application of it)[6] in combination with the positivist writings of individuals like Comte and Mach. In its classic form, as it is presented persuasively and colorfully by Watson, behaviorism rejected the existence of any unobservable, mental entities. From this classical behaviorist perspective, all that exists are physical entities, and physical entities are in principle observable. Therefore, all that is relevant to a science of psychology is behavior and measurable (i.e., observable) happenings in the body, both which can be directly linked mechanistically to the material properties of the physical environment. This latter dictum was subsequently relaxed slightly by Hull, Tolman, and others, who allowed for the inclusion of unseen "intervening variables" as long as they could be ultimately tied to observables. James's pragmatist approach to meaning, transformed by Bridgman's operationism, also had a belated hand in loosening these strictures, but only a little. Collectively, these developments had the effect of excluding, in any meaningful way, so-called mental processes from mainstream psychological inquiry for at least 50 years.

This outcome was certainly not what James had intended with his pragmatism and with his critical stance toward dualism.[7] James would have disapproved of the narrowed focus of classical behaviorist psychology, with its transformation, if not outright exclusion, of some of the most distinctive qualities of human experience. James also sought to

---

[6]Among other things, pragmatism is an attempt to deal with the problem of meaning, such as the meaning of concepts. Prompted by proposals of his colleague C. S. Peirce, James argued that the meaning of a concept rests in the practical and ideational consequences that result from utilizing it (see later). A simple application of James's pragmatism is operationism, which had a significant influence on behaviorism as it developed. Here the meaning of a concept devolves entirely on how it is measured or otherwise assessed. But this is an exceedingly narrow use of James's pragmatist proposal.

[7]In turn, Watson clearly distanced himself from James's views (see J. Watson, 1930/1970, chap. 1).

include all psychological phenomena that were observable. But, for James, observable meant "that which can be experienced." This is a decidedly broader standard than Watson applied, which only permitted physical entities for inclusion.

By deciding a priori that "the observable" and "the physical" are synonymous, Watson applied a nonempirical criterion, indeed a metaphysical criterion, to determine what counted as empirical. What is empirical for him are only certain kinds of occurrences, namely, physical occurrences. This approach undermines the very bedrock of what constitutes the empirical, namely, *phenomena*, which refers to anything experienced from a human point of view. How could a psychology adequate to humans admit only certain phenomena while excluding others?

Apart from this problem, there is a further reason why these behavioristic developments in psychology would not have pleased James. Although because of Watson's influence behaviorists subsequently became more careful in their use of mentalistic terms—and this was indeed an important step forward—they never truly closed the door on a dualistic framework. Unwittingly, they kept dualism alive, as it were, off stage. And James felt that psychology must move fully beyond dualism in order to progress.

But surely the preceding assertion that behaviorists contributed to keeping dualism alive must be wrong! After all, the elimination of dualism was the raison d'etre of most post-Watsonian behaviorists. As it was carried out, however, Watson's formulation of behaviorism maintained a place for a Cartesian mind. As Heidbreder argued in her seminal work *Seven Psychologies* (1933), the way the classical behaviorist program was set up *required* the very thing that it denied—namely, a nonnatural view of mind. His psychology was defined in large measure in terms of what it was not. In his efforts to eliminate the non-natural from psychology, Watson—and others following in his thinking—conflated the mental with the spiritual or nonnatural: What is mental is by definition nonnatural. Having done that, he then proceeds to excise the mental as a legitimate concern in a scientific psychology. Because psychology is a natural science, and because the mental refers to nonnatural processes, the mental must be excluded from psychology. Thus, he allowed the physical world and bodily processes as the only proper subject matter for a psychology that aspires to be a science.

At the same time, it is obvious when examining Watson's writings that he recognized as legitimate many of the phenomena that the term *mind* generally refers to because he offered explanations for several of them, as in his accounts of remembering and language. But, because Watson found it necessary to equate the natural only with physical and bodily processes narrowly construed, his treatment of these phenomena in his psychology distorted these processes to such a degree that they were almost unrecognizable to anyone outside of an exceedingly narrow physicalistic perspective. They certainly did not constitute a rich account of such phenomena. Why did he not simply state that remembering and language do not go on, that they are akin to sprites and goblins, and be done with it? Watson could not do this because in order to offer an adequately encompassing psychological system, these are among the numerous phenomena of "mental life" that he must address. So these "mentalistic" phenomena remain.

But Watson's claim that mental phenomena are non-natural is a "straw-person" argument when it is critically directed, as he did so, at James, Dewey, and even Titchener. They did not equate mental phenomena with the spiritual or nonnatural, nor is it necessary to do so. Mental processes, like other psychological phenomena, should and can be treated as natural phenomena, that is, as natural events associated with complex biological organisms. Why assume, as Watson did, that what might be called mind is supernatural? Heidbreder (1933) explained:

> But only because the mind-body distinction is used in a prescientific sense do such connotations arise. … If something like a dread of the supernatural did not lurk in the background, there would be no reason why such events as sensations, emotions, and thoughts, in the form in which they immediately present themselves to the person who has them, should not be *conceived simply as natural events in the natural world*. (Heidbreder, 1933, p. 283, emphasis added)

Why not then, as James did, simply recognize perceiving, thinking, imagining, and remembering to be natural processes? That is, why not include in psychology all that can be experienced, and assume all that can be experienced is perforce natural? Apart from Heidbreder's claim that Watson's thinking harbored "a dread of the supernatural" (she added, "Only those who believe in ghosts are afraid of them," p. 23), there were a variety of influences that led Watson to adopt this physicalistic viewpoint. One influence that has the greatest bearing on the focus of the present discussion was the teachings of a mentor, the biologist Jacques Loeb, who is best known for his work on *tropisms*.

Beginning in the mid-1800s, scientists such as Helmholtz sought to link the processes of living systems with the current ideas in physics. Among other things, the deepening understanding of the physiological and biochemical processes underlying living systems "strengthened the view that biological activities could be subsumed under the same concepts that also define inanimate systems" (Herrmann, 1998, p. 117). Loeb was one of the most influential biologists in the late 19th century promoting this view. A result of these efforts was the description of biological systems in terms of molecular, lower level processes. This approach is continuous with the goals of the Cartesian perspective to articulate underlying, unifying principles at work in nature; and it has consequences:

> Inherent in the scientific thought of the past centuries has been the resolve to create a representation of reality that is free of complexity. Examination of complexity as a noteworthy concept in its own right was to be avoided. Phenomena that could not be reduced to the simplicity of ideal systems [i.e., closed systems] were to be disregarded. ... This tendency became particularly frequent in dealing with biological systems. (Herrmann, 1998, p. 125)

Certain phenomena are disregarded because the simplicity sought requires minimizing variables in what are otherwise complex systems. The alternative approach, as indicated in this quotation, is to take *complexity* itself as a problem to tackle. But the argument for recognizing complex systems as such was not effectively made in biology until later in the 20th century. So, under the influence of this way of thinking, Watson sought to subsume psychology under physics and in so doing disregarded or greatly simplified phenomena that did not seem to fit with the prevailing view of reductive, inanimate processes.

As already noted, almost 20 years prior to publication of Watson's (1913) behaviorist manifesto, Dewey (1896) argued in his now classic critique of the reflex arc concept that the nascent stimulus–response psychology left a place for Cartesian thinking. That is, Dewey's objection to the stimulus–response formulation was not in its supposed break with the dualistic tradition—which is the way Watson must have taken it given his criticisms of the functionalists—but rather in its failure truly to make this break and offer a fresh approach. Subsequent developments in psychology bear out this judgment. Precisely because this break was not fully made, when references to mental processes reappeared in psychological discourse in the 1950s and 1960s, the neobehaviorist framework could be stretched without too much theoretical effort to assimilate their return. There had remained a place for the treatment of cognitive processes in the behaviorist metatheory, even though Watson sought to exorcize these concepts. The dualistic roots of this form of behaviorism were always lurking in the background despite efforts to repress them.

Thus, the rise of behaviorism did not render James's concerns about dualism obsolete. The tensions that concerned James early in this century between the Cartesian framework and a functional perspective remained; and, if anything, the Cartesianism became more hidden and harder to recognize. But this perspective can still be found in the information-processing models of the 1970s and 1980s, as well as in much contemporary cognitive science (H. Putnam, 1990, p. 251).

And there is another reason why the neobehaviorist renewal of interest in perception, language, memory, and other cognitive processes would not have pleased James. As pointed out earlier with Watson, mentalistic phenomena could only be assimilated into the behaviorist framework at a cost. In the highly restrictive language of most behaviorist frameworks, mental phenomena become unrecognizable to anyone but experimental psychologists who operate from this perspective. George Miller, one of the leading voices of the cognitive revolution of the 1960s, pointed out in retrospect this inadequacy of the field:

> What seems to have happened is that many experimental psychologists who were studying human learning, perception, or thinking began to call themselves cognitive psychologists without changing in any obvious way what they had always been thinking and doing—as if they suddenly discovered they had been speaking cognitive psychology all their lives. ... In my opinion, however, the use of these mentalistic terms is still constrained by a positivistic philosophy of science, so that *now* we have in effect an oxymoron: non-mentalistic cognitive psychology. (G. Miller, cited in Bruner, 1983, p. 126, emphasis added)

As psychologists have returned to the study of cognitive phenomena, two familiar options for addressing psychological processes appear open: First, they can talk uncritically about mental functions in a manner that keeps them distinct from, and hence detached (in a Cartesian sense) from environmental conditions. This tack creates a tension between a mentalistic perspective focusing as it does on intra-organismic processes, and a functionalist-evolutionary perspective that stresses the reciprocal relations between animal and environment. Second, they can try to reduce mental functions completely to material processes and, in the process, brush aside their distinctive psychological qualities.

Is there some way of bypassing these seemingly never ending problems about matter and mind, which are never far from the surface in psychology? What is required is a radically different approach to the apparently dual character of psychological phenomena. William James's radical empiricism is such an attempt. By providing an analysis of psychological experience that is grounded in the concreteness of everyday life, James's radical empiricism seeks to offer a descriptively rich account of psychological phenomena from a thoroughly naturalistic vantage point. And in so doing, it establishes the foundations for an ecological psychology.

A WORLD OF EXPERIENCE

Among James's significant intellectual efforts is an attempt to formulate a philosophical system that avoids some of the seemingly insolvable problems stemming from Cartesian (metaphysical) dualism. This dualistic approach makes the claim that there are two fundamentally different "entities" that need to be considered in any psychological analysis: matter and mind. A wide variety of accounts of knowing embrace metaphysical dualism either explicitly or more often tacitly. In his landmark essay, "Does Consciousness Exist?" (1912/1976),[8] James explicitly rejected metaphysical dualism and all schools of thought that are related to it, and importantly, he began to provide an alternative way of conceptualizing mind.

The primary focus of this essay was a critical assessment of the notion of mind as a nonmaterial entity. He saw this approach to conceptualizing the mind as a vestige of otherwise discarded ways of thinking: It is "a mere echo, the faint rumor left behind by the disappearing 'soul' upon the air of philosophy" (p. 4). But James did not want to be understood as rejecting mental phenomena outright, as some later behaviorists did "for undeniably 'thoughts' exist" (p. 4). He intended to deny that mind refers to an entity: "There is, I mean, no aboriginal stuff or quality of being contrasted with that of which material objects are made, out of which our thoughts of them are made" (p. 4).

James proposed that instead of beginning with a metaphysical dualism, which gives rise to numerous vexing problems, suppose instead that "there is only one primal stuff or material in the world, a stuff of which everything is composed" (p. 4). He called this "primal stuff" *pure experience*. From this starting point, a conceptualization of mind is developed that offers a real alternative to those based on dualistic approaches.

Pure experience is that undifferentiated experience that is immediately and prereflectively encountered. It refers to "the immediate flux of life," or that which is most directly and naively experienced. It can be thought of as proto-phenomenological (Suckiel, 1982). James was making an empirical claim about what is most fundamental in our experience; he identified pure experience as the ground of all knowing while trying to avoid suppositions that go beyond direct observation. This is an empirical claim because when looking to that which is most fundamentally experienced, "we never come across anything else except pure experience, and therefore there is no point in postulating anything more. ... The burden of proof is on those who claim there is something more" (Sprigge, 1993, p. 114). What James was willing to admit into his philosophy at the outset was only that which can be

---

[8]In the case of many of James's essays, such as "Does Consciousness Exist?," initial publication was as a journal article appearing prior to its inclusion in the cited collection. In the present case, this essay appeared initially in 1904 and was reprinted in 1912. For a chronology of James's writings, see McDermott (1977, pp. 811–858).

experienced, and "pure experience" is the most basic of that which can be experienced.[9]

What then is the nature of pure experience? This proves to be a tricky question to answer. Pure experience is most elusive because knowing from the outset is a *selective function*, and pure experience provides the "material" for this selection. In other words, pure experience as such may be best viewed as an idealized starting point for James's analysis—akin to a mathematical limit (Seigfried, 1978). According to James (1912/1976), "Only new-born babes, or men in semi-coma from sleep, drugs, illnesses, or blows may be assumed to have an experience pure in the literal sense, of a *that* which is not yet any definite *what*, though ready to be all sorts of whats" (p. 46). Significantly, in its indefinite state, pure experience is "ready" to become something definite: Pure experience embedded as it is in a person–environment relation is poised to be dynamically differentiated.

Having said that, James still tried to identify qualities of this aboriginal ground of knowing. He did so by describing pure experience as a multiplicity of "sensible natures" (James, 1912/1976, p. 15): "It is made of *that*, of just what it appears, of space, of intensity, of flatness, brownness, heaviness, or what not" (pp. 14–15).[10] Sprigge (1993) aptly described pure experience as being comprised of "definite somethings occurring as distinguishable items in streams of personal and, by hypothesis, of impersonal, experience" (p. 117).[11] Collectively, this ongoing stream of experience is a manifold of possibilities for knowing, or what James called sometimes a "quasi-chaos."

As already noted, the reason why pure experience is itself rarely encountered and why it may be best thought of as a limit concept is

[9]There is considerable debate among James scholars concerning how best to characterize his metaphysics. Some philosophers, perhaps most prominently the New Realists (see chap. 2), viewed James's position as a neutral monism (Sprigge, 1993). To the extent that James was adopting a neutral monism in his radical empiricism essays, it does appear that he had difficulty maintaining this perspective in subsequent work, most especially in *A Pluralistic Universe*. Some would even argue that a pluralistic viewpoint is evident in his radical empiricism essays (see footnote 11).

Much of the confusion about neutral monism appears to turn on whether James's notion of pure experience is a metaphysical or epistemological claim (Flanagan, 1997; Gale, 1997). I do not intend to explore this matter at this point, however. How best to characterize James's metaphysics is one of many debates among James scholars that will come up in the following pages. Although I acknowledge these points of disagreement and offer a few suggestions, an examination of the lengthy and complex debates about James's work that fill volumes of scholarly analysis would detract from the main purpose of this book.

[10]James was apparently quoting Shadsworth Hodgson here (see McDermott 1977, p. 179, footnote 47).

[11]The difference between this definition of pure experience as a multiplicity and the one given earlier referring to pure experience as consisting of "one stuff," as well as other facets of James's analysis, has generated considerable discussion among philosophers as to whether his metaphysics was a monism or a pluralism. It would appear that most Jamesian scholars today see him as developing a pluralistic (*continued on next page*)

because, in actuality, selective functions are "always already" at work—to employ a Heideggerian locution. These selective functions comprise *knowing*, which is "a particular relation towards one another which portions of pure experience may enter" (James, 1912/1976, p. 4). Thus, the defining characteristic of knowing—and this point cannot be overemphasized (and is drawn on throughout this book)—is *selectivity*; and through this function, some of the myriad possibilities of structure in the quasi-chaos that is pure experience are realized. Immediate experience consists of things and their relations. Knowing is an activity that traces out lines of potential structure in immediate experience; structure is not imposed on experience. From this viewpoint, James submitted that consciousness is a function in experience, rather than an entity. (For the contemporary reader, perhaps the term *awareness*, rather than *consciousness,* is less burdened with distracting connotations and conveys more of the functional character James intended.)

In James's metaphysics, the aboriginal world of experience is *not*, then, composed of two entities, matter and mind; rather, it is an undifferentiated, latent multiplicity of "stuff." What is initially differentiated or selected is a dimension of experience, a relation with its termini being the *knower* and the *object known.* Hence, the knower is not introduced into his framework as an isolated Cartesian observer standing apart from the object thought about. Rather, in James's psychology, the knower appears from the outset in relation to the thing known because of the essential selective character of knowing.

Moreover, the knower and object known each become realized as different constellations of relations themselves coexisting ultimately in a ground of pure experience. The claim that these are coexisting domains differentiated within experience has important implications for James's analysis. Consider this idea through the following example. James (1912/1976) asked the reader to begin with a perceptual experience, "the room he sits in, with the book he is reading at its centre" (p. 7). The traditional, dualistic approach would suggest that there is, on the one hand, the room and the book "out there," and on the other hand, one's experience of them, a representation of them "in" the mind. However, such "'representative' theories of perception ... violate the reader's sense of life, which knows no intervening mental image but seems to see the

---

[1]*continued from previous page* metaphysics [e.g., H. Putnam's, (1990) Jamesian "pluriverse"; Sprigge, 1993).] The analysis offered in chapter 4 raises the possibility that he might have been able to maintain some sort of metaphysical monism if he saw how to do that, and there suggestions are offered as to how he might have done so. Even so, James was consistently an "epistemological pluralist" in the sense of recognizing that because any individual viewpoint is limited, all viewpoints need to be given thorough consideration.

room and the book immediately just as they physically exist" (p. 8). Instead, James asked us to consider our experience of the room as simultaneously being a part of two different sets of relations within experience. One constellation of relations, traceable to the reader's history, provides one context for the experience: The room as it is a part of the reader's own history is a part of a series of relations that led up to being in the room. At the same time, a different set of relations, traceable to the room's history, provides a second context: "The very same *that* [i.e., the room] is the *terminus ad quem* of a lot of previous operations, carpentering, papering, furnishing, warming, etc." (p. 9).

There is a degree of independence between these two constellations of relations. The room is a particular place that has a separate past and future relative to the perceiver. Likewise, the perceiver's history, although intersecting the room at times runs separate from the room and will continue to do so. However, in spite of this independence, when the room is experienced by the perceiver, it is one thing considered from two points of view. That is, even though the room is locatable in two distinct constellations of experience, the physical and the mental, it does not have two existences (i.e., as a physical object in the material world and a mental representation of that object). It is a single experience that functions simultaneously in two different contexts.

How can two domains, such as matter and mind, be talked about in the same breath without invoking a dualistic ontology? Here James (1912/1976) offered a simple yet persuasively transforming analogy that enables the reader to overcome old habits of thinking:

> The puzzle of how one identical [experience] can be in two places is at bottom just the puzzle of how one identical point can be on two lines. It can, if it be situated at their intersection. ... It could be counted twice over, as belonging to either group, and spoken of loosely as existing in two places, although it would remain all the time a numerically single thing. (p. 8)

Experience is unitary, but at the same time, it can simultaneously be part of two constellations of relations, that is, a part of two distinguishable contexts. In the present example, a constellation of relations that is the room and a constellation of relations that is the perceiver are the two different contexts in question. The same "given undivided portion of experience [e.g., the room] ... in one group figures as a thought, in another group as a thing" (p. 7).

To summarize the discussion so far, there is a multiplicity of potential structures that can be realized in pure experience through the selectivity that characterizes knowing. The object known and the knower are each embedded in contexts of relations that have their own distinguishable structures. The knower and the object known are coexisting domains of relations, and any particular experience can be located simultaneously in both domains:[12]

> The experience is a member of diverse processes that can be followed away from it along entirely *different* lines. The one self-identical thing has so many relations to the rest of experience that you can take it in disparate systems of association, and treat it as belonging to opposite contexts. (p. 8, emphasis added)

This analysis of the multiplicity of potential structure in pure experience, and of the selective function of knowing as the process by which some of these structures are realized, establishes the basis for James's philosophy of radical empiricism as an alternative to metaphysical dualism.

One further, and very significant, point needs to be added to this introduction to James's radical empiricism. Selection of structure in experience involves following a set of relations in experience, and this is possible only because the relations between experiences are themselves experiencible. Relations in experience are "transitional experiences *which the world supplies*" (James, 1912/1976, p. 14, emphasis added). That is, the lines of structure selected out by the knowing function are not imposed on the thing known, but are identified or discovered *in it*. (This point is discussed more fully in chap. 4). As already emphasized, pure experience has an intrinsic, latent structure. The next section looks at why the claim that relations are discoverable in experience is of paramount importance for James in the development of an alternative metaphysics.

At this point, three basic claims can be identified that characterize James's philosophy and justify his calling it a philosophy of radical empiricism. The following summation is derived from his introduction to *The Meaning of Truth* (1909/1978):

- The first claim is the insistence that only those things that can be identified or discovered in experience are to be included in one's philosophical system. That is, James is offering an *empiricist* philosophy.
- The second claim concerns *what* can be found in experience: "the relations between things, conjunctive, as well as disjunctive, are just as much matters of direct particular experience, neither more so or less so, than the things themselves" (James, 1909/1978, p. 173). This "statement of fact" is what makes James' empiricism *radical* be-

---

[12]This statement needs to be amended after the distinction between percepts and concepts is introduced later.

cause, as is shown later, experiencible *relations* are precisely what have been neglected in empiricist and in rationalist philosophies.

- The third claim follows directly from the preceding one, and it asserts James's belief that the world itself possesses an inherent, discoverable structure:

the parts of experience hold together from next to next by relations that are themselves parts of experience. The *directly apprehended* universe needs, in short, no extraneous trans-empirical connective support, but *possesses in its own right* a concatenated or continuous structure. (p. 173, emphases added)

Instead of developing James's radical empiricist program further at this point, it is useful to consider some historical issues. In order to appreciate fully the philosophical significance of this position, and what was at stake for James in formulating radical empiricism, it is necessary to place his position in its historical context.

THE HISTORICAL CONTEXT FOR RADICAL EMPIRICISM

The dominant philosophical positions of the late 19th century can be seen in part as variations of two types of responses to an epistemological problem. The epistemological problem is how to account for the apparent order or structure in experience. After all, our experience of the world is not chaotic but ordered. What is the basis for this order? The two types of responses to this question were *empiricism* and *idealism*.

But why does order need to be accounted for in the first place? This question comes up because of the metaphysical assumption that the universe is fundamentally composed of *elements*. In other words, what is found most basically in the world are distinct elements, or "things," with various properties. This assumption is closely tied to a particular kind of materialistic view of the physical world. Anticipated in the writings of Democritus in the 3rd century B.C., the view that the material world is most fundamentally made up of elementary "atoms" came to be the dominant post-Renaissance conceptualization of the physics traceable from Galileo through Newton to contemporary physics (with some notable exceptions; see Introduction). The epistemological claim that experience is at its foundation a collection of elementary sensations obviously parallels this fertile idea in physical science.

The late 19th-century discovery that the retina is a mosaic of receptors gave added epistemological weight to the view that knowledge is built up from elementary sensations. If sensory input, and primarily visual input, is the primary source of knowledge, then it would appear that experience gets chopped up into bits straight away, independent of what reality is truly like.

But our immediate experience of the world is not merely of separate elements such as sensations, it also consists of relations among things, including causal relations that, not incidentally, are a cornerstone of mechanistic science. There appears to be considerable orderliness in our experience of the world. Consequently, given the assumption that experience is composed of elements, a central problem to be explained is the basis for the order that is found among these entities. James vividly put the problem this way in *The Principles:*

> This multitude of ideas, existing absolutely, yet clinging together, and weaving an endless carpet of themselves, like dominoes in ceaseless change, or bits of glass in a kaleidoscope,—whence do they get their fantastic laws of clinging, and why do they cling in just the shapes they do? (James, 1890/1981, p. 17)

The *empiricist* response to this problem—or specifically, the British Empiricist response—is that order in immediate experience is based on the synchronous and successive relations that have previously obtained among the elementary sensations of experience.[13] For example, two elements of immediate experience, such as the visual appearance of a fire and the heat from it, co-occur regularly; hence, we come to understand that, in some way, these sensations are related. Eventually, we come to believe that they are both properties of a common object. To take a second example, whenever a particular moving object makes contact with a stationary object, the latter is propelled in a particular direction. From experiences such as these we discover *causal relation:* Given conditions x and y, *ceteris paribus*, outcome z will result. It is through repeated sensory exposure to these kinds of associations of a synchronous and successive nature among sensations that we come to know the lawfulness of the world.

However, this associationist account of the lawfulness in our world brings with it an epistemologically significant, and to many including Kant and James, a distressing implication. As Hume brilliantly analyzed, there is an inherent and unavoidable arbitrariness to this explanation. If our knowledge of the order among elements and events—and hence the lawfulness of the world—is solely based on previous experiences of successive and synchronous co-occurrences, then it follows that given a

---

[13]The fact that the word "experience" has multiple meanings in English can be a source of confusion. Experience (and, by extension, empirical) can mean immediate experience as "the act or process of directly experiencing events or reality"; and it can also mean *prior experience* as "the fact or state of having been affected by or gained knowledge through direct observation or interpretation" (*Webster's Ninth New Collegiate Dictionary*, 1990). In the following pages, which of these two meanings is intended should be clear by the context.

different set of previous experiences, one would be led to knowledge of a world with a completely different structure. In other words, if the known relations among elements are explainable solely in terms of their co-occurrence in prior experience, then in principle any set of known relations in nature is possible in light of the possible orders prior experience can take (Robinson, 1981). Such a capricious view of knowledge obviously does violence to the possibility of coming to understand a stable and lawfully independent universe of the sort Newton proposed, much of natural science envisions, and psychology assumes.

But why does knowledge depend on prior experience to discover the relations in the world? Why can't the individual simply see the world and its relations as they are? The empiricist does not have this option open because it is assumed that the world that is immediately perceived is composed of elements. Hence, relations only arise out of past acquaintance with "what goes with what" synchronically or successively. The world as an ordered, structured universe is derived from prior experiences; it is not immediately perceived. Thus, rather than relations in experience being based on the discovery of the existing structure in the world, they are based on conclusions or inferences that individuals separately draw based on what has come before in their own experiences. The particular knowledge we each hold about the world reflects habitual ways of thinking. We come to believe that the world is thus and such; its order or lawfulness is not something we directly or immediately experience. And because of the inductive nature of these inferences, our knowledge is inherently uncertain and always potentially in error. We never know whether the very next instance of a phenomenon will conform to the pattern suggested by prior occurrences or whether it will deviate from this pattern. As a result, an associationistic view of relations in experience—that relations arise solely out of synchronous and successive occurrences in experience—necessarily leads to Humean skepticism concerning stability and order in the world and certain predictability of occurrences in that world.

The *idealist* response to this problem—as formulated by James's contemporaries and intellectual rivals, Royce and Bradley—follows broadly the kind of approach Kant offered in reply to Hume's skepticism. For Kant, it was unacceptable that knowledge could be so arbitrary. A philosophy for the Age of Enlightenment must offer more of a solid epistemological foundation than that. And yet Hume's analysis was a logical consequence of the view that knowledge is based solely on elementary sensations. Accordingly, Kant proposed that the order in experience originates elsewhere. If it is not derived from prior experience, then it must have its origin in the structured process that is knowing itself. That is, the order is based on a priori structuring processes, rather than a posteriori conclusions. In a similar vein, the idealists of James's day claimed that the relations or order in experience has its origins in ideas (i.e., in the contents of individuals' minds) and individuals' ideas are themselves partial reflections of an a priori Transcendent source, the Absolute. Royce, for example, whose work was deeply influenced by Berkeley's idealism as well as by Kant, claimed that what is experienced is not the physical world, but an idea presently in consciousness. For Royce, the basis for knowledge of the world is explainable by the fact that an idea is part of the Absolute, and as such, points beyond itself to a wider realm. So my knowledge of the causal relations between two ideas presupposes an understanding of causation that goes beyond the present experience. This understanding is indicative of my ideas' involvement or connection to a wider realm of Absolute Truth.

This sort of idealist philosophy played a central role in philosophical debates early in this century. Because James formulated radical empiricism mostly as a response to idealism, it is necessary to have some minimal familiarity with this position in order to appreciate James's philosophical writings (Conant, 1997; Moller, 1997; Sprigge, 1993). Although idealism is no longer fashionable, the kind of approach it represents is still very much alive in appeals to unknowable, inherited structures that are found in contemporary rationalist explanations in psychology and philosophy.

James was dissatisfied with the idealist position for several related reasons, including the following: First, by adopting this type of view, absolute idealists were assuming a metaphysic that runs counter to the naturalism that is central to James's thought and to all 19th century scientific thought. Second, James found this kind of approach unsatisfactory because like mechanistic accounts, but for entirely different reasons, the idealistic universe (what James called a "block universe") was somewhat static and its relations determined. Such a view did not leave room for the novelty and change that were in evidence in the evolutionary record as well as in daily life. Similarly, it did not leave room for the place of individual choice that was so vital to James's moral stance (Kuklick, 1977, p. 177; H. Putnam, 1990). James (1912/1976) wrote "The 'through-and-through' universe seems to suffocate me with its infallible impeccable all-pervasiveness. Its necessity, with no possibilities; its relations, with no subjects, make me feel as if I had entered into a contract with no reserved rights" (p. 142).

Moreover, the connection of individual minds in a common Absolute did not recognize the pluralism of consciousness among individuals. Finally, absolute idealism separates the activity of understanding from everyday experience and locates it in interaction with a transcendent realm, whereas James sought an understanding of experience in its everyday concreteness as is reflected in his pragmatist writings, as well as in so many of his essays.[14]

James criticized the positions of both the British Empiricists and the Absolute Idealists because of a common assumption they shared that he felt was deeply flawed. Both assume at the outset a world of immediate experience that is essentially disjointed, composed fundamentally as it is of elements:

> The result is that from difficulty to difficulty, *the plain conjunctive experience* has been discredited by both schools, the empiricists leaving things permanently disjoined, and the rationalist remedying the looseness by their Absolutes or Substances, or whatever fictitious agencies of union they may have employed. (James, 1912/1976, p. 26, emphasis added)

But James did not see the need to accept this assumption of the disjointedness of experience. He had been deeply influenced by his senior Harvard colleague Chauncey Wright's claim that:

> the order we observed in things wanted explaining only if we supposed a preliminary or potential disorder, but this was a gratuitous notion since things were orderly; if there was no antecedent chaos, there was no reason for a cosmic "glue" to prevent things falling asunder (Kuklick, 1977, p. 176).

Empiricism and idealism fail to recognize the orderliness of experience because they both fail to take relations in experience as real aspects of immediate experience itself. James's alternative to these views, radical empiricism, asserts that the relations providing the structure in our experience of the world are intrinsic to the experience: These relations are "as 'real' as anything else in the system" (James, 1912/1976, p. 22). In other words, James claimed that the empiricists were not empirical enough, and "he looked to empiricism itself as a means of escape" (Perry, 1935, p. 557).

Recognizing that relations are part of immediate experience allows one to approach a number of long-standing theoretical difficulties in new ways. First, the resolution to the problem of accounting for the order in experience does not need to be sought in a mechanistic associationism that the empiricists embrace and that Hume demonstrated, if one is intellectually consistent, leads to skepticism. Nor need it be sought in some intrinsic, but unobservable, structuring process of the act of knowing (or in the Absolute), which the rationalist propose and that leads

---

[14]These comments are reflective of some of James's general views about idealism. He carried on a detailed and lively debate with Royce and with Bradley for many years. The specifics of these exchanges go beyond the scope of this chapter. The interested reader should see the studies by Kuklick (1977) and Sprigge (1993).

analysis to posit some empirically inaccessible, and historically at least, an unnatural realm. Relations are to be found in immediate experience itself. Order is an intrinsic quality of encountering the world.

Second, the vexing problem of the relation between the knower and the object known can be viewed in a new light. Limiting the focus here to perception, if the perceiver and the object were "absolutely discontinuous entities" as philosophers from Descartes to Royce supposed, then "the 'apprehension' by the former of the latter, has assumed a paradoxical character which all sorts of theories had to be invented to overcome" (James, 1912/1976, p. 27). If the object known and the knower are "discontinuous," how can this gap be overcome? (Recall that this was the question which concluded the Prologue.) The British Empiricist approach embraced a representational viewpoint, which "put a mental 'representation,' 'image,' or 'content,' into the gap, as a sort of intermediary" (James, 1912/1976, p. 27) between the knower and the world. However, introducing a mental representation into the account only introduces a new gap—this time between the world and the representation. If what is directly experienced is a mental representation of the world, what can be said about the relation between this mental representation and the world? As Berkeley showed incisively in his analysis of the primary–secondary quality distinction, if a mental representation of the world is what is directly experienced, then what has yet to be explained is how the world independent of the perceiver can be known.[15]

But the gap between the knower and the known is introduced because relations in immediate experience are assumed to be imposed. James argued that both approaches overlooked a crucial fact: "All the while, in the very bosom of the finite experience, every conjunction required to make the relation intelligible is given in full" (James 1912/1976, p. 27). Like the empiricists, he adopted the perspective that knowledge is derived from sensory experience; but he went further than traditional empiricists by adopting a radical stance toward this assumption. The origins of all knowledge—entities and their relations—are to be found in immediate experience. James did not begin with perceiver and object as discontinuous entities, but with undifferentiated experience; and relations, including the relation between knower and known, are part of immediate experience. This is his philosophy of radical empiricism.

Radical empiricism offers a fresh approach to knowing, even on the contemporary scene. It proposes that the potentially known is latent in the world and knowing is manifested as differentiation of structure in "pure

---

[15]In making this argument, Berkeley was offering support for the view that ultimately what is real is the stuff of ideas, that is, Spirit, rather than matter.

experience" through the continuing transaction of knower and known. As a result, this approach calls for a detailed analysis of potential knowledge in the ongoing knower–object known relation. It claims that our initial knowledge of objects and their relations is immediate, and in so doing, it eliminates the seemingly unbridgeable gap between knower and world. Rejecting elementary sensations as the grounds for knowing, radical empiricism obviates the need for either a posteriori or a priori processes to provide the missing structure. Beginning with the notion of pure experience, even as a limiting concept, the knower and world have a direct, unmediated relation.

COGNITION FROM A RADICAL EMPIRICIST PERSPECTIVE

To back up for a moment, in radical empiricism, knowing refers most fundamentally to a functional relation in experience between a knower and an object known. The defining characteristic of knowing is *selectivity*. Through knowing processes, structure is selected out of, or differentiated from, immediate experience. It is now time to consider the *products* of selective processes. To use James's terminology, two products of the selectivity of knowing processes are *percepts* and *concepts*.

James's treatment of these notions differs in important ways from their treatment in traditional Cartesian-grounded theories. Most standard formulations view perception as "precognitive"; that is, they view perception as being subordinate to cognition and not as a mode of knowing in its own right. For James, percepts and concepts are both products of knowing. Or, to make the distinction in terms of processes, perceiving and thinking are both *cognitive processes*; they are both distinctive modes of knowing. The terms *cognition* and *cognitive* are used here, and throughout this book, to refer to the various processes of *knowing*, including perceiving and thinking, and this usage is consistent with Gibson's perspective (Reed, 1991).

Although Gibson's ecological approach specifically and most fully addresses the nature of perceiving, it is clear that he felt this approach could be extended to other aspects of cognition as well (see J. J. Gibson, 1979, chap. 14). Reed (1991, 1993) made useful contributions in this direction. What might seem problematic, of course, is how to address thinking, imagining, and so on without slipping into a representationalist viewpoint. That is, how can these psychological processes be addressed while maintaining the claim that experience of the environment is direct? Embedding an account of cognition in James's philosophy of radical empiricism will point the way, assisting in explicating the line of thought Gibson seemed to be following in this regard.[16]

Percepts and Concepts

From the perspective of radical empiricism, the ground of knowing (i.e., the field of pure experience) is a quasi-chaos of latent structure. The selectivity that characterizes the knowing function differentiates this field of experience initially along lines of order intrinsic to the field. This initial differentiation of experience is the *perceiving* process, and it has the quality of immediacy. Through it, "the mind enjoys direct 'acquaintance' with a present object" (James, 1911/1996, p. 28). There are no intermediaries between the perceiver and the thing perceived. Perceiving is direct.

This claim clearly sets radical empiricism apart from varieties of the dualistic theories. As noted earlier, in the latter cases, perception is not direct; there is the thing perceived, and there is one's mental representation of it, along with the attendant, uncertain relation between the two. It is the representation that is immediately experienced, and as a result, the representation stands between the object and the perceiver. Thus, in any dualistic approach, objects have a duplicity; they exist "in fact" as a feature of the physical world, and they exist "mentally" as a representation of the physical object.[17]

To reiterate for emphasis, in radical empiricism the thing perceived is "all the time a numerically single thing" (James, 1912/1976, p. 8). It is not a replica of something else more real. For example,

[a sheet of] paper seen, and the seeing of it are only two names for one indivisible fact which, properly named, is *the datum, the phenomenon, or the experience*. The paper is in the mind and the mind is around the paper are only two names that are given later to one experience. ... *To know immediately ... is for mental content and object to be identical.* (James, 1895/1920b, pp. 378–379)

---

[16]Although James's analysis of perception and cognition recur throughout his writings, he gave the most sustained attention to these matters in *The Principles of Psychology* (1890/1976) and *Some Problems of Philosophy* (1911/1996).
[17]In consideration of mental representations, one could distinguish between metaphysical and epistemological dualism, where with the latter, unlike the former, one asserts that mental representations are immediately experienced and objects are experienced indirectly, while remaining agnostic about the metaphysical status of both. In the case of either dualism, one is faced with explaining the relation between objects and mental representations. Consequently, Humean-type problems associated with mental representations (see earlier) remain.

It is only when reflecting on experience after the fact that two names are applied—the object and the experience of the object—to this immediate, single experience.

In addition to being direct, perceiving is ongoing. It is continuous, unbroken, ceaseless; and it is also multimodal. As is seen more fully later, perceiving is ongoing because it is an activity of an individual. Perceiving transpires as an individual engages the world, as the body moves with respect to the world's features, and largely for this reason, experience is in flux. The continuity of the perceptual flux is punctuated by boundaries that gradually flow one into the next. In fact, "boundaries" is probably misleading, suggesting an edge that is rigid and impermeable. Better put, there are transitions in perceptual experience "which are overflowed by what they separate," and whose parts "compenetrate and diffuse into its neighbors." Consequently, it is a "big, blooming, buzzing confusion, as free from contradiction in its 'much-at-oneness' as it is all alive and evidently there" (James, 1911/1979, p. 32, emphasis added).

"Blooming, buzzing confusion" is one of the most frequently quoted phrases from James, and it is commonly misinterpreted. To see this description as attributing chaos to immediate experience, such that mind subsequently must impose order on it (a common "presentist" take on this phrase) distorts what James had in mind. James described immediate experience as having a potential order that is "free from contradiction." It is not a chaos, but a "quasi-chaos" (James, 1912/1976, p. 32). As such, order is not imposed on experience, but rather order is discovered within experience itself—within the relation between the knower and the thing known.

Perceiving, then, is a direct, unmediated, selective discovery of structure in immediate experience. And it is a selective process that transpires continuously over time: Percepts "are singulars that change incessantly and never return exactly as they were before" (p. 253).

It is obvious, however, that our immediate experience is not limited to percepts. For if it were, experiences would merely be fleeting, and it would be impossible to "step out of" the continuing flow of events in order to take a somewhat detached stance. As James (1911/1979) vividly put it, "We should live simply 'getting' each successive moment of experience, as the sessile sea-anemone on its rock receives whatever nourishment the wash of waves may bring" (p. 39).

It is against the backdrop of this flow of percepts that the character of concepts is to be understood. Thinking, like perceiving (indeed, like all knowing), is a process of selectivity. Perceiving is an action that entails selection of a flow of immediate experience out of the potential ground that is pure experience. Thinking or conceiving entails, in turn, selecting and fixing particular parts of this perceptual flow. Through this process, concepts are carved out of immediate perceptual experience at a remove from action and are abstracted from it. Abstracting from the immediate flow of experience makes it possible for the knower to isolate, and then to classify or otherwise manipulate, these extracted "moments." This cognitive capability enlarges the knower's epistemic potential in incalculable ways. As James (1911/1979) put it:

> The substitution of concepts and their connections ... for the immediate perceptual flow, thus widens enormously our mental panorama. ... With concepts we can go in quest of the absent, meet the remote, actively turn this way or that, bend our experience, and make it tell us whither it is bound. We change its order, run it backwards, bring far bits together and separate near bits, jump about over its surface instead of plowing through its continuity, string its items on as many ideal diagrams as our mind can frame. (p. 39)

The system of concepts selected out of the perceptual flow may help the knower to better discern the structure latent in that flow by drawing connections and identifying structure that may be discernible only at a remove from it. Thus, concepts play an important epistemic role, enabling the individual to better comprehend the structure of the environment (although their role is not limited to this). And, in doing so, concepts have important potential value for our daily actions: Concepts extracted from the perceptual flow, "verbally fixed and coupled together, [let us] know what is in the wind for us and get ready to react in time" (James, 1912/1976, p. 47).

But James was emphatic that the truth value of concepts is incomplete if this abstracted and collated order is left free standing without continual, renewed contact with perceptual experience. Allowed to function independently of the structure available through perceiving processes, the relations among concepts can take on a character that is disconnected from experience of the world. This creates possibilities for imagining novel circumstances and arrangements, which is a rich and valued part of everyone's experience. But because concepts are interwoven into our immediate experience of the world (i.e., they become part of what we immediately experience) when conceptual structures are not recognized as derived structures, and instead are taken to be identical with the world that is the ground of experience, concepts have the potential to mislead. So, although the conceptual order may allow the perceiver to adapt to a wider environment, this outcome is not guaranteed. And an autistic conceptual system, a system characterized by false beliefs and unfounded prejudices that does not reconnect harmoniously with the world, leaves us functionally adrift, or worse:

> Whenever we intellectualize a relatively pure experience, we ought to do so for the sake of redescending to the purer experience. ... If the intellect stays aloft among its abstract terms and generalized relations and does not reinsert itself with its conclusions into some particular point of the immediate stream of life, it fails to finish out its function and leaves its normal race unrun. (James, 1911/1979, p. 47)

For this reason, James repeatedly cautioned the reader about the hazards of intellectualizations ("vicious intellectualism") that are not ultimately and continually grounded in perceiving. Individuals often fail to recognize, he stated, that what they might take to be qualities of immediate experience are instead abstracted products derived from immediate experience. This kind of error James referred to as "the psychologist's fallacy" (see later), and it is a hazard to be avoided particularly in psychological theorizing, which is especially susceptible to it.

With his concern for the consequences of concepts breaking loose from their perceptual moorings, James followed a very different line of thinking than that of rationalist theorists. For, unlike the latter, James was not privileging the conceptual order—quite the contrary. Knowledge resides ultimately in the direct relation between a knower and the immediate perceptual flux. To make this claim is not to deprecate the value of concepts. Concepts, "monstrous abridgements though they be" (James, 1911/1979, p. 53), are necessary because of the sheer plenitude of immediate experience and the limitations of percepts. However, one must always bear in mind that concepts are derivative and are in need of continual reevaluation and revision against immediate experience. "Use concepts when they help, and drop them when they hinder understanding; and take reality bodily and integrally up into philosophy *in exactly the perceptual shape in which it comes*" (James, 1911/1979, p. 53).

Concepts should serve the functional needs of individuals (although not these needs alone), enabling individuals to better understand the structure of the environment and themselves in it. But this intellectualized, abstract structure is always hypothetical. The "truth" status of any portion of the conceptual order is ultimately determined by its relation to percepts; Consequently, the conceptual order must be continuously assessed "pragmatically" by examining concepts in relation to subsequent immediate experience. Here are the beginnings of the program of *pragmatism*, the other half, and the better known half, of James's later philosophy.

Pragmatism and Knowing

H. Putnam (1990, 1995) claimed that the unifying concern in all of James's work is ethical and moral. From a biographical standpoint, this assertion can be situated in the circumstances of James's life and times. He lived in the midst of the transition between, on the one hand, a 19th-century frame of mind grounded in ways of thinking that assumed some foundational bedrock and, on the other, the coming anti-foundationalism of the 20th century (Diggins, 1994). The tension between these two epochs was brought to the forefront of his awareness being raised by a father who was at once a philosopher/theologian and a radical thinker (Feinstein, 1984; Lewis, 1991). From an early age, James was confronted with a clash of seemingly different worlds: a world of knowledge based on certain religious truths versus a world of uncertainty; and a world of determinant mechanisms versus a world of volition and choice. Through the development of *pragmatism*, James tried to come to grips with some of the problems the coming modern world posed, such as finding a conceptually coherent way of discussing what it means to say that something is true and of evaluating what is a correct and appropriate action. A brief consideration of pragmatism is useful here because it further clarifies the significance of radical empiricism—both for psychological theory and for the practice of science generally. Also, some aspects of these matters are useful in later discussions of the ecological program.

Although pragmatism is relatively well known in psychological circles, it is usually viewed apart from its connection to radical empiricism. Indeed, James (1909/1978) indicated that they can be viewed as logically independent (p. 6). But this is not to say they are unrelated. James saw pragmatism as a vital part of his radical empiricist metaphysics. To the extent that pragmatism is a useful way of talking about the discovery of truth and its verification in experience, it provides support for radical empiricism: "It seems to me that the establishment of the pragmatist theory of truth is a step of first-rate importance in making radical empiricism prevail" (James, 1909/1978, p. 172). Reciprocally, pragmatism provides a way of thinking about verification that accords with radical empiricism (Suckiel, 1982).

James's intention in formulating a pragmatist approach to verification and meaning was to provide an alternative to traditional "correspondence" approaches. From the standpoint of the Cartesian dualistic perspective, determination of the validity of a specific knowledge claim is based on how well a particular idea in the mind ("in here") maps onto conditions in the world ("out there"). A true belief in an individual's conceptual scheme is one that corresponds to conditions in the world. Likewise, *meaning* entails a referential relation between an idea held by an individual and an object in the external world. Thus, a correspondence theory of truth and meaning rests on a distinction between a mental realm and an external world.

Clearly, such an approach to assessing knowledge claims and meaning would not be congenial to James. The possibility of this kind of a correspondence runs counter to James's metaphysics, which explicitly rejects the two worlds distinction between the mental and the physical and instead seeks to build a view that is consistent with Darwinian thinking. As Rorty recently (1999) explained:

> Pragmatists hope to break with the picture which, in Wittgenstein's words, "holds us captive"—the Cartesian–Lockean picture of a mind seeking to get in touch with a reality outside itself. So they start with a Darwinian account of human beings as animals doing their best to cope with the environment—doing their best to develop tools which will enable them to enjoy more pleasure and less pain. (pp. xxii–xxiii)

For James, validity and meaning are assessed entirely within experience. And how might this be accomplished? James proposed that the validity of an idea and its meaningfulness can only be assessed in terms of the effect holding it has in relation to other parts of experience. If ideas are viewed as functioning in a tool-like fashion to allow individuals to better realize relations in experience, then an idea can be assessed as being true or false—workable or unworkable—in a practical or pragmatic sense. If, for example, a particular concept enables an individual to anticipate occurrences in immediate experience (i.e., among the stream of percepts), or it enables the individual to apprehend new and coherent relations with other concepts, then this concept has truth value, and its meaning is established within the context of these relations. To the extent that an idea plays these kinds of functions, it is true pragmatically. According to James (1909/1978), "Any idea that will carry us prosperously from any one part of experience to any other part, linking things satisfactorily, working securely, simplifying, saving labor; is true for just so much, true in so far forth, true *instrumentally*" (p. 34). Ideas and beliefs viewed as "tools" serve as intermediaries between parts of experiences. A tool is an extension, and in some cases an amplification, of the body's capacity to act on the world (see chap. 9). And, as such, rather than operating in a realm apart from the world,

> there is no way in which tools can take one out of touch with reality. No matter whether the tool is a hammer or ... a belief or a statement, tool-using is part of the interaction of the organism with its environment (p. xxiii). ... [The] distinction between inside and outside ... is one which cannot be made once we adopt a biologistic view. (Rorty, 1999, p. xxvii)

The following example adapted from James illustrates the pragmatic viewpoint with regard to the relation between ideas or concepts, on the one hand, and percepts, on the other. How do I assess the validity of my idea of how to get from my home to my office at the college? If my idea of the way from one place to another corresponds with what I perceive as I travel, and if following this sequence of ideas literally leads me to my office, then the route as conceived by me was valid. This particular idea, or set of ideas, functions as a tool in immediate experience to guide my behavior; and it allows me to look ahead. Why isn't this account a correspondence analysis? It is not because the process unfolds entirely within experience; it is not a mapping between two parallel domains of mental experience and the physical world. What is being described is a relation or series of relations in experience, with one constellation of this relation being the knower and the other the object known. "Knowledge of sensible realities thus comes to life inside the tissue of experience" (James, 1912/1976, p. 29). These concepts may or may not be corroborated by our ongoing immediate experience, but in any case, this process of corroboration itself needs to occur within experience.

When a concept is assessed and verified in relation to other experiences, it may substitute for another experience, such as another concept. Returning to the previous example, if I believe that following an alternative path will lead me to my office more quickly than the path I already follow, I can test this possibility within experience; and if verified (it gets me there), it can replace the previous belief as a better choice. The practical effects of holding a concept do not reside in a relation between a concept "in mind" and an effect perceived "in the world," but instead in a relation between different aspects of experience. Concepts and percepts are both happenings in experience; and "the only function that one experience can perform is to lead into another experience; and the only fulfillment we can speak of is the reaching of a certain experienced end" (James, 1912/1976, p. 32).

Clearly, this approach to verification clashes with the seemingly commonsense view of truth as correspondence to reality, the view that the discovery of that which is true is a process of revealing the absolute reality behind appearances. But from a pragmatist perspective, attaining truth in the preceding sense is not the aim of knowing. As Rorty (1999) expressed concerning the claim that "truth is the aim of inquiry":

> But I think we pragmatists must grasp the nettle and say that this claim is either empty or false. Inquiry and justification have lots of mutual aims, but they do not have the overarching aim called truth. Inquiry and justification are activities we language-users cannot help engaging in; we do not need a

goal called "truth" to help us do so, any more than our digestive organs need a goal called health to set them to work. (pp. 37–38)

Forming concepts and beliefs is something complex biological creatures such as ourselves do in order to be better in touch with the flow of experience, rather than uncovering fixed and transcendent universal truths. It is a natural process of complex animals attempting to function adaptively in relation to changing environment–person relations, rather than a rarified occurrence in a detached mental realm.

An objection to this viewpoint is that it appears to justify an extreme relativism of meanings and values, where anything goes. But this is *not* at all the case *from an ecological perspective*, at least. To extend the metaphor of concepts and beliefs as tools that connect different parts of experience, remember that not any tool works for every task. The situation at hand permits some tools to function effectively, and some more effectively than others, and it also rules out the adequacy of many others. As James argued in his original formulation of the position, the validity of a concept or belief is to be evaluated with respect to its "practical effects," that is, in terms of where it leads. Thus, ideas can be more or less useful, and sometimes of no use at all. But, isn't "usefulness" an arbitrary criterion? Rorty (1999) attempted to clarify:

> When the question "useful for what" is pressed, [pragmatists] have nothing to say except "useful to create a better future." When they are asked, "Better by what criterion?", they have no detailed answer, any more than the first mammals could specify in what respects they were better than the dying dinosaurs. ... When asked, "And what exactly do you consider good?", pragmatists can only say ... with Dewey, "growth." "Growth," Dewey said, "is the only moral end." (pp. 27–28)

In contrast, if verification or truth value is viewed against an absolute reality "out there" beyond appearances, and knowing is a process of establishing correspondences with that preestablished reality, then growth is limited to conformance to some plan. Such a view is *ahistorical* because the ground of knowing is fixed. As such, it runs counter to an evolutionary perspective in which change is a constant condition of circumstances, and animals continuously make efforts to learn more about rich and changing organism–environment conditions (chap. 9).

One may choose to speak casually as if there is an experience, idea, or concept "in mind" and a world "out there"; but it should not be forgotten that in doing so, one is all the time dealing with either intellectualized, abstract experiences (concepts) or concrete, direct experiences (percepts). In each case, they are occurrences in immediate experience.

The systems of conceptual orders allow the knower to contemplate possibilities yet explored through perceiving, and even possibilities not directly explorable. James (1912/1976) wrote:

> The paths that run through conceptual experiences ... are highly advantageous to follow. ... [They] sweep us on towards our ultimate termini in a far more labor-saving way than the following of trains of sensible perception ever could. Wonderful are the new cuts and short-cuts which the thought paths make. (p. 32)

But—to reiterate—ultimately, the paths through the conceptual orders must terminate in percepts if these concepts are to be more than fictions. Fictions are fine, in fact often delightful, when understood to be fictions; but otherwise, they are hazardous. Percepts both verify and ground concepts. Independent of their relation to percepts, concepts may be mere fancies and unreal imaginings. They constitute knowledge about the world and ourselves in the world only insofar as they eventually are coherent with direct perceptual experience.

The Material World as a Conceptual Order

Systems of concepts substitute an intellectualized or abstracted order in experience for the immediate perceptual flow. Among these conceptual systems, "all abstracted and generalized from long forgotten perceptual instances" (James, 1912/1976, p. 34), James included the "worlds" of commonsense discourse, of scientific concepts, of mathematics, of ethical propositions, of logic, and of music. "*The intellectual life of man consists almost wholly in his substitution of a conceptual order for the perceptual order in which his experience originally comes*" (James, 1912/1976, p. 33).

With this notion of conceptual systems in hand, it becomes evident that in his rejection of mind–matter dualism, and by replacing it with "pure experience" as a metaphysical starting point, James was not denying the existence of the material world. To do this would have been as unreasonable as it would have been to deny the existence of mind. What he was doing in the case of the material world, as he did in the case of mind, was to reformulate what the matter at hand is. Instead of taking the material world as the starting point of an epistemological analysis (i.e., instead of claiming that material properties of an external world are there or are present from the outset), he proposed that what we take as the material world is a conceptual realm abstracted from direct perceptual experience. It is a world that we posit to stand apart from an individual's perceptual experience, and we shape it to varying degrees. It is a conceptual order that serves as a description of the world we assume to be common to all perceivers.

There are alternative descriptions of the material world, from those of naive discourse to those offered by the physical sciences. In all cases, a conceptual order is posited which, to varying degrees of precision and consistency, rests fundamentally on the ongoing perceptual stream of immediate experience. The various conceptual orders serve different functions. The world of naive experience serves as the context within which we negotiate with others in our culture at large; whereas the world of the physical sciences is a rarefied realm for more technical, specialized, and more precise (but in many ways, more limited) exchanges.

We may be inclined to believe that ultimately the physical science realm is more real than the commonsense realm (e.g., that molecules and atoms are more real than tables and chairs). But, in fact, they are merely alternative intellectualized descriptions of the immediate flux of perceptual experience (Stebbing, 1960). Moreover, in comparison to immediate perceptual experience, conceptual realms are quite malleable. Alternative physical descriptions of the world of experience have been proffered over time and across cultures, as have commonsense descriptions of the world. But it is important to recognize that in the end if these descriptions are going to have verisimilitude, this will be a malleability within constraints, namely, the constraints of immediate perceptual experience. The synthetic conceptual orders must be corroborated against the structure of perceiving.[18] And even in the absence of corroborative evidence, a conceptual order may be held onto until the anomalies between percepts and concepts overwhelm the conceptual order.

On what grounds can one justifiably assert that the conceptual world offered by physical science may be both more precise and more limited than the conceptual world of everyday discourse? Stebbing's (1960) insightful analysis of physical as compared to naïve descriptions of reality help form an understanding of why this is the case.[19] Drawing on Berkeley's critique of the materialists' treatment of visual experience, Stebbing revealed: "It seemed to Berkeley that the metaphysics of Descartes and Newton resulted in the description of a 'real world' that had all the properties of the sensible world *except the vital property of being*

---

[18]Here a distinction should be drawn between analytic conceptual orders, such as mathematics, logic, and music, and synthetic conceptual orders. Whereas the latter can be corroborated with respect to perceived structure of immediate experience, the former are corroborated, more or less, with respect to their internal consistency.

[19]I was led to Stebbing's work by following J. J. Gibson's (1966) reference to it. The kind of argument Stebbing offered clearly reinforced Gibson's thinking about the primacy of the ecological level of analysis.

seeable" (p. 78, emphasis added). For example, the property of color cannot appear in a materialist account of the "real world" because color as such is not to be found in light conceptualized as waves in a Newtonian physical world. Color vision in terms of the conceptual domain of physics is not the same as immediate visual experience itself. These are separable domains, and a physical account of the basis for color experience is not an account of color experience itself. To return to Stebbing's (1960) discussion: "It is Berkeley's merit to have realized that the Cartesian–Newtonian philosophers, seeking to account for a *seeable* world, succeeded only in substituting a world that could in no sense be *seen*. He realized that they had substituted a theory of optics for a theory of visual perception" (Stebbing, 1960, p. 78).

It will be helpful to explore this example a little further because it will assist in the developing notion of alternative levels of analysis (which has come up at various points thus far), and in turn, illustrate the irreducibility of a given analytical level. The description of perceived color using the conceptual tool of spectral wavelengths provides a very real gain in precision for distinguishing among different color experiences. With this tool, exceedingly fine distinctions can be made among colored objects by referring to their relative differences in selective spectral reflectance. But it is important to recognize that this is also a limited description of color perception. For one thing, perceived colors are not simply reducible to the dimension of spectral frequencies. Rather, the phenomenology of color experience is multidimensional. There are "modes of color appearance," such as surface colors, volume colors, film colors, and luminous colors (D. Katz, 1911/1935). To illustrate, a red object and a red liquid may convey the same measurable wavelengths of light (i.e., spectrometric readings are identical); but comparatively, the colors in each case appear to be qualitatively different such that it is difficult to make accurate comparisons between the redness of a red cloth and a red liquid (Beck, 1972). As this example demonstrates, a scientific conceptual order can bring with it considerably more precision than description based on the conceptual world of everyday discourse that is closer to immediate experience. But, at the same time, scientific discourse is typically more limited than everyday discourse and cannot simply substitute for it.

Another conceptual order of great importance to psychology in addition to the material order is the biological order. In *The Principles*, James argued persuasively that an adequate psychology could only be one that included an analysis of the biological conditions that underlie psychological processes. It should be clear now that it is possible to make this argument—and in contemporary psychology it is indisputable—and at the same time reject a reductive materialism. To utilize a particular conceptual language to describe the underlying

WILLIAM JAMES'S RADICAL EMPIRICISM

biological correlates of some psychological experience is not to offer an account that is identical with the experience itself, only more precise. The biological description (the conceptual system) cannot wholly substitute for the experience as perceived; it is abstracted from experience. Thus, rather than take neurophysiological description as a neutral foundation onto which all psychological phenomena can, in principle, be reduced, contemporary neuroscience can be seen as a highly sophisticated *conceptual* system. Its validity can be instrumentally (or pragmatically) demonstrated in terms of how well it helps with an understanding of phenomena of immediate experience or in understanding other concepts—that is, how well it allows us "to get into satisfactory relation with other parts of our experience."

Moreover, from this viewpoint, it becomes apparent why a science properly called "psychology" can never be eliminated by a sufficiently complete neurophysiological analysis. The psychologically relevant questions and puzzles that more reductive, neurophysiological analysis can help to explain are identified as phenomena of immediate experience. That is, psychological considerations set the problems for a psychologically relevant neuroscience to address.

The Coalescence of Percepts and Concepts

What is the relation between percepts and concepts? For the most part, conceptual orders do not replace or override the intrinsic structure of perceptual experience. Instead, percepts and concepts imperceptibly merge together. The experience of our mental life is largely an interweaving of the immediate structure of perceiving and the abstracted systems of concepts. The failure to recognize that, for James, the perceived structure runs through "instrumentally true" concepts can lead one to mistakenly view him as a constructivist—as holding the view that concepts fashion percepts. But to do so is to misread James. When functioning jointly, percepts and concepts coalesce. The concepts:

> return and merge themselves again in the particulars of our present and future perception. By those *whats* we apperceive all our *thises*. Percepts and concepts interpenetrate and melt together, impregnate and fertilize each other (James, 1911/1979, p. 34).

It is the case, as already mentioned, that some concepts may not adequately coalesce with percepts, but instead be left "flocking with their abstract and motionless companions." But those kinds of concepts are apt to have little instrumental value for the individual. By contrast, concepts with "cash value" bring "the mind back into the perceptual world with a better command of the situation there" (James, 1911/1979, p. 36).

Because concepts and percepts typically are highly interwoven, a challenge for psychology is to be able to separate the two adequately for analytical purposes. Under certain circumstances, failure to do so can lead to considerable confusion about the nature of knowing. A case in point here is revealed in James's criticism in *The Principles* of the notion of "sensation."

Traditional approaches to knowing, especially those following along the lines set out by the British Empiricists, assume that the initial psychological datum, the building block for all empirical knowledge, is a sensation. Among early experimental psychologists, an example of a visual sensation would be a sensory patch of color, and among analytical philosophers, it would be a "sense datum." In more contemporary analyses of visual perception, the essential element might be an edge or any other simple or complex element (see van Leeuwen, 1998). However, James argued that empirically (i.e., from the point of view of immediate experience) a simple element, however it is construed, is never a characteristic of perceiving. In fact, he turned this taken-for-granted claim on its head. He proposed that what is taken to be a sensation is an intellectualization of immediate perceptual experience. In the opening paragraph of the chapter "The Stream of Thought" in *The Principles* (1890/1981), James offered:

> Most books start with sensations and proceed synthetically, constructing each higher stage from the one below it. But this is abandoning the empirical method of investigation. No one ever had a simple sensation by itself. Consciousness, from our natal day, is of a teeming multiplicity of objects and relations, and what we call simple sensations are results of discriminative attention, pushed often to a very high degree. (p. 219).

James considered this type of misattribution to be a serious error in psychological analysis. The previous quotation continues: "It is astonishing what havoc is wrought in psychology by admitting at the outset apparently innocent suppositions, that nevertheless contain a flaw. The bad consequences develop themselves later on, and are irremediable, being woven through the whole texture of the work" (p. 219). One of these seemingly innocent, but erroneous, suppositions is that "sensations, being the simplest things, are the first things to take up in psychology" (p. 219). This supposition is the foundation for the elementaristic approach discussed earlier.

An analytical error of this sort is an instance of what James described as "the *great* snare of the psychologist" (James, 1890/1981, p. 195), namely, "the psychologist's fallacy." This fallacy involves taking what is the product of a psychological process for the process itself. It is a confusion of ends and means. So whereas a sensation may be the product of a process of perceiving-followed-by-intellectualization of perceptual experience, often it is mistakenly taken to be a constituent of the process. From this viewpoint, the standard claim long presented in most psychology textbooks that perceiving begins with the detection of simple sensory data that are then elaborated or synthesized ("processed") by the perceiver has the account exactly backward. And this analytical error is far from inconsequential for psychological theory, because it gives rise perhaps to psychology's "most fictitious puzzle," namely, the choice between "presentative or representative perception" or between direct or indirect perception. It pits the naïve experience that we perceive the world directly against the view that we immediately detect elementary sensations from which a mental representation of the world must be constructed if one is to deal with perceptual phenomena. This account presents the puzzle of "whether an object is present to the thought that thinks it by a counterfeit image of itself, or directly and without any intervening image at all" (James, 1890/1983, p. 195).

But this is a "fictitious puzzle" because one of the alternatives is built on the fallacy of taking a product of intellectualizing about perceiving, such as a sensation or an edge, as a fundamental, constituent feature of perceiving. Psychologists are susceptible to this analytical error because of the coalescence of percepts and concepts. It is difficult indeed to untangle the intellectual contributions to experience based on reflection from the immediate qualities of perceiving.

Furthermore, unlike immediate experience, which is dynamic, mental representations constructed from elementary sensations (or what have you) tend to be static. Visual perception has long been conceptualized as a matter of capturing still images of the environment along the lines of a camera obscura or, more recently, a photographic camera. However, a static image, like its elementary constituents, is a product of intellectualizing about the perceiving process. As James (1890/1981) argued, "What must be admitted is that the definite images of traditional psychology form but the very smallest part of our minds *as they actually live*" (p. 246, emphasis added). He continued:

> The traditional psychology talks like one who should say a river consists of nothing but pailsful, spoonsful, quartpotsful, barrelsful, and other moulded forms of water. Even were the pails and pots all actually standing in the stream, still between them the free water would continue to flow. It is just this free water of consciousness that psychologists resolutely overlook. (p. 246)

Famously, James (1890/1981) argued that experience is like a stream, "it is nothing jointed, it flows" (p. 233). The remainder of this chapter offers some initial comments on this immediate experiential flow and its basis.

EXPERIENCE AND ACTIVITY

An essential quality of immediate psychological experience is an "apprehension of something *doing*, an experience of activity" (James, 1911/1979, p. 82). The fact of the active nature of experience has its origins in our existence as corporeal, mobile animals. Recognizing the embodied nature of experience will anchor James's analysis, and knowing itself, more concretely in everyday experience.

Duration and Context

The discussion of radical empiricism up to this point may have obscured an important dimension of experience. My primary concern so far has been to show how James attempted to offer an alternative to dualistic metaphysics by proposing undifferentiated, pure experience as the ground for all knowing. Out of this field of experience is differentiated a distinction between knower and known, as well as the domains of percepts and concepts. What was only mentioned in passing, but is a fundamental quality of pure experience, is that it is ongoing, having the quality of duration (Bergson, 1888/1960). Immediate experience is extended in time; it flows.

Unfortunately, use of the word "time" as in the phrase "extended in time" is potentially confusing. Time here does not refer to the discrete units of seconds, minutes, or hours; time as apportioned into discrete units of time is conceptual, not perceptual. Time in that sense is an abstraction or intellectualization of the immediate duration of experience. It is a scheme based on a technology that makes it possible to divide duration into measurable units. As such, it has a rich cultural history (Boorstin, 1985; Crosby, 1997; Landes, 1983). Immediate experience, unlike time, is not doled out in discrete droplets; it is a continuous passage of events or experiences that possess duration. It goes on.

However, to say that psychological experience is continuous rather than discrete does not mean that it is homogenous. James saw immediate experience as a textured flow. In an often quoted passage, he described the "stream of thought" this way: "As we take, in fact, a general view of the wonderful stream of our consciousness, what strikes us first is this different pace of its parts. Like a bird's life, it seems to be made of an alternation of flights and perchings" (James, 1890/1983, p. 236).

As a textured flow, lines of connection run through it. Hence, psychological experience is always extended, pointing ahead. With the flow of experience "goes the sense of its relations, near and remote, the dying echo of whence it came to us, the dawning sense of whither it is to lead" (James, 1890/1981, p. 246). As a result, awareness is never just of the present 'now'; it is suffused with what came before and what is ahead. As James (1890/1981) expressed it, *"The knowledge of some other part of the stream, past or future, near or remote, is always mixed in with our knowledge of the present thing"* (p. 571). That is, there is a halo, or "fringe" to any present portion of experience that points to what is coming 'next' and to other relations in ongoing thought.

This quality of parts of the stream of experience reflecting near and distant relations grows out of its structured continuity and has important implications for understanding meaning. Take the case of an utterance. A particular word spoken in a sentence is meaningful because of its position in the overall expressed idea. It is anticipated by that which precedes it, anticipates what follows, and is part of the overall idea within which it is embedded: "Annihilate a mind at any instant, cut its thought through whilst yet uncompleted, and examine the object present to the cross-section thus suddenly made; you will find, not the bald word in process of utterance, but that word suffused with the whole idea"(James, 1890/1983, p. 271). The meaning of a word resides in its relation to the context of the object of thought. In order to highlight the significance of this issue of context for James, it may be useful to review one last time the tradition he was opposing here, if only to extend this critique a bit.

James was taking a stand against the view that the contents of mental experience are an assemblage of distinct elements, such as individual sensations or ideas. He wrote bluntly, *"A permanently existing 'idea' or 'Vorstellung' which makes its appearance before the footlights of consciousness at periodic intervals, is as mythological an entity as the Jack of Spades"* (James, 1890/1981, p. 230). James opposed this view on empirical grounds, that is, based on an examination of his own experience; and he also opposed it on logical grounds in light of physiological considerations. Our nervous system is continuously being stimulated and hence continuously changing because our bodies are active. "Experience is remoulding us every moment, and our mental reaction on every given thing is really a resultant of our experience of the whole world up to that date" (p. 228). To reexperience the same identical thought one previously had would mean that it occurred "the second time in an unmodified brain" (p. 227). But the intervening of experiences have made this a "physiological impossibility." We never step twice into the same stream. This vision of dynamic, ongoing brain functioning—a view long pushed to the margins of psychophysiology in spite of the best efforts of the prominent neuroscientist Lashley (1950/1951)—is presently gaining a foothold in cognitive science through dynamic models of distributed processing (see, e.g., A. Clark, 1997; Port & van Gelder, 1995; Thelen & Smith, 1994).

The role that context plays in meaning is important in James's analysis because it is the only way by which sense can be made of his claim that we never experience exactly the same idea a second time, and yet also acknowledge that obviously, in some sense, we experience an idea as being "the same" as one previously encountered. What remains the same across encounters is not the same identical idea, but rather a common structure, an "object-in-context." This relation can be preserved over occasions, just as a melody can remain the same despite being transposed into a different key or played on different instruments.

Selectivity and the Body

Taken in isolation, James's well-known discussion of the stream of thought might lead to the conclusion that the individual passively experiences a flow of events: The stream of thought with its substantive parts and its transitive parts may seem merely to course through conscious awareness. Such a rendering would not align with James's psychology. As already seen, from the outset, the knower as agent selectively engages the ground of experience.

From the point of view of radical empiricism, a knower with selective interests and concerns is immersed in a field of experience that has a plentitude of potential structure. Knowing is characterized by selective activity within the constraints of the structure making up the immediate ground of experience. This perspective recognizes both the richness of potential experience and the selective nature of knowing processes. Both are essential ingredients in James's radical empiricist vision. The world presents the individual with potential knowledge through its inherent structure, and the perceiver realizes the object known by engaging the flow selectively.

It should now be apparent why James could only give partial support to Spencer's "formula" that "the essence of mental life and bodily life [is] the adjustment of inner to outer relations" (James, 1890/1981, p. 19). To the extent that this view is taken as describing merely a mechanical adjustment of organism to environment, it omits the selective activity of the knower in this relation. Perceiving is not merely mechanical because the purposes and interests of the knower play an essential role (James, 1878/1920a). In "Are We Automata?" (1879, and later incorporated with modification into *The Principles*), James compared the active nature of perceiving with the activity of a sculptor. Just as it could be said, erroneously, that perceiving is a passive process, so "well might one say that the sculptor is passive, because the statue stood from eternity within the stone. So it did, but with a million different ones beside it" (James, 1890/1981, p. 277). The intentions of the sculptor cannot be left out of the account. However, in recognizing James's view of perceiving as an activity, it is important not to take this view to mean that the perceiver's knowledge or intentions are merely imposed on a fully malleable world. Like an unsculpted block of marble, the world offers resistance along the lines of its inherent, and perhaps yet unrealized, structure. Many patterns are possible and others ruled out, in correspondence with the potential structures therein; what can be perceived/sculpted is constrained by the world/marble. Anything does not "go." Here, in ideas developed about 25 years prior to the formal presentation of radical empiricism, it can be seen that James viewed knowing as a selective process whereby some of the latent possibilities in the environment are made manifest.

Critically, selectivity is an action, and as such "it comes with desire and a sense of a goal; it comes complicated with resistances which it overcomes or succumbs to, and with the efforts which the feeling of resistance so often provokes" (James, 1912/1976, pp. 82–83). More broadly, this experience of effortful, goal-directed activity is "synonymous with the sense of 'life'" (p. 82).

Can more be said about the nature and origin of this experience of activity? Most fundamentally, it is anchored in the experience of our embodiment in the world. In the introspectionist climate of James's day, there was some debate among his contemporaries as to whether or not activity is a part of our mental experience, and if it is, what might be the nature of this experience. James applied the pragmatic method to this debate in his 1904 presidential address to the American Psychological Association. If activity has any meaning, it "must lie in some concrete kind of experience that can be definitely pointed out" (p. 81). James identified that concrete experience as the experience of the body:

> The world experienced (otherwise called the "field of consciousness") co-mes at all times with our body at its centre, centre of vision, centre of action, centre of interest. … The body is the storm centre, the origin of co-ordinates, the constant place of stress in all that experience-train. Everything circles round it, and is felt from its point of view. The word "I," then, is primarily a noun of position, just like "this" and "here." (James, 1912/1976, footnote, p. 86)

At the heart of selective activity is the fact of our being embodied knowers. Fundamentally and concretely, we are active beings. We move around and act on environmental features. We experience the environment through our bodies, and reciprocally, we experience our bodies through engaging the environment. Here James was laying some of the groundwork for the significant philosophical analyses of later philosophers such as Merleau-Ponty (1962), as well as those who followed in the 1980s and 1990s, on the role of the body in our experience of the world and our place in it.

This discussion of embodiment, appearing in one of James's late essays, was anticipated in his earlier, influential treatment of the self in "The Consciousness of the Self" in *The Principles*. In this rich and provocative chapter, James took on several problems, including the elusive one of specifying the nature of the self. Most notable, and at the time radical, were his efforts to anchor the self in empirical phenomena, in keeping with his later pragmatism. This led James to identify two facets of the empirical self: the "material selves" that include one's body, clothes, family, property, and the "social selves," which are established through the relations we form with others. James pragmatically justified calling these properties of the self because if they are violated or assailed in some way, this event is experienced as an assault on one's personhood. More relevant to the present discussion, however, is the "self of selves" or what he called "the spiritual self"—that seemingly unitary entity that we feel to be located centrally at the core of our being. The best James can do, however, in trying to find a central self on empirical grounds is to identify it with the movements of the body: *"Whenever my introspective glance succeeds in turning round quickly enough to catch one of these manifestations of spontaneity in the act, all it can ever feel distinctly is some bodily process, for the most part taking place within the head"* (James, 1890/1983, p. 287). Elaborating on this perhaps surprising observation, James stated: "If the dim portions which I cannot yet define should prove to be like unto these ... *it would follow that our entire feeling of spiritual activity, or what commonly passes by that name, is really a feeling of bodily activities whose exact nature most men overlooked*" (p. 288).

James's thoughts on the spiritual self extend and, more importantly, ground Hume's unsettling analysis two centuries earlier. Hume was unable to locate a self among his sensations and ideas, and as a result, he concluded that "the self" was a belief, a habit of mind to account for the apparent continuity of experience. James, however, found evidence for the self, or rather the selves, in our immediate experience of the activities of our body, including both gross movements or "executions," and subtle actions or "adjustments." He called the latter actions "primary reactions" because we may "feel them as the birthplace of conclusions and the starting point of acts" (p. 289).

Actions of the body would seem, then, to give rise to two different dynamic aspects of experience: the "intra-specific" flow of bodily events that we identify with the self, and the "extra-specific" flow of environmental features as we move through the world. These two dimensions of experience contribute to the ongoing stream of experience. It is the active character of humans as embodied agents that resides at the "storm centre" of our experience.

To conclude this overview of radical empiricism, it can be seen that, for James, selectivity in relation to a field rich in latent structure is the sine qua non of knowing, and selectivity is a directed action of "the body." Knowing refers to a wide range of directed actions from intelligent behavior to abstract thinking and reasoning. Knowing is not the operation of a disembodied soul, the "entire function of which is to think," but it is an activity of a natural being, an animal, in the natural world. Through directed actions, particular structures in the field of potential or "pure" experience become realized; some of these realized structures are tied directly to the field of experience (percepts) and others are derived from it (concepts). Moreover, what James called percepts and concepts can be applied not only to experience of objects, but also to experience of the self, where our actions are immediately experienced and from which concepts "of self" are derived in a self-reflexive manner.

Finally, James's analysis of embodiment and experience invites us to consider the ways in which knowing as an embodied action is reflected in what is known. James did not directly examine this question, but it is taken up in chapter 3 when the discussion turns to a consideration of Gibson's ecological theory. There, and among the other chapters of part II, the discussion outlines how the framework James offers in radical empiricism serves in part as the basis for central features of ecological theory.

Edwin B. Holt
(Harvard University Archives)

2

Edwin B. Holt
and Philosophical Behaviorism

Consciousness, whenever it is localized at all … in space, is not in the skull, but is "out there" precisely wherever it appears to be. (Holt, 1912 , p. 353)

The preceding overview of radical empiricism constitutes a first step toward laying out the primary philosophical groundwork for James Gibson's ecological psychology, as well as for ecological psychology more generally considered. However, based on Gibson's citations of James's work there is no evidence that he was directly familiar with many of James's writings other than *The Principles of Psychology*. Although much that was to follow in James's subsequent work is anticipated in *The Principles*, these foreshadowings are subtle and most easily seen with hindsight. So what then accounts for the striking and deep parallels between William James's radical empiricism and James Gibson's later ecological approach?

Looking for parallels in the work of two theorists separated in time, such as James and Gibson, may be merely an interesting, if somewhat facile, exercise, or it may have real historical and theoretical value. It is a mere exercise when there exists little evidence of a historical or intellectual connection between the two theorists, and similarities between separate bodies of ideas are merely traced. The analysis begins to take on value when the ideas being compared enrich each other. And it is more valuable still if it can be established that the theorists of concern are linked historically. The latter two features apply in the present case. A direct historical and intellectual linkage between James's radical empiricism and Gibson's ecological psychology can be readily identified in the person of Edwin B. Holt, James's student and then colleague at Harvard and Gibson's primary graduate school mentor at Princeton.

In the role of a graduate school mentor, Holt more than any other individual had the most direct influence on the overall development of Gibson's thinking.[1] Although this claim is justified over the course of the next several chapters, for now it can be simply noted that in his autobiographical essay, J. J. Gibson (1967a) described himself as a "Holtian philosophical behaviorist." It becomes evident in the following that Holt's primary intellectual commitment was to promote and extend William James's radical empiricism. In the absence of evidence that Gibson had any more than a selective exposure to James's writings, it is most likely that his knowledge of radical empiricism came through contact with Holt. There can be little doubt that the radical empiricist perspective permeated much of Holt's teachings. By conveying this perspective to his students, as well as through his own unique contributions, Holt directly contributed to the formulation of Gibson's ecological psychology.

If the only goal here were to trace out these connections, then the following discussion of E. B. Holt's work would be considerably briefer and even take a slightly different form. The fact is, however, that the secondary literature on Holt is scant. He is presently a forgotten figure in contemporary psychological and philosophical circles. Holt's current status contrasts sharply with the fact that during the first few decades of the 20th century, he was one of the more prominent theoretical psychologists in the United States and abroad. Holt's prominence and influence diminished, however, as he gradually disengaged from academia during the later part of his career largely for personal reasons. Today, with few exceptions, Holt is remembered by only a handful of active psychologists, most of whom were trained in the 1940s and 1950s when his writings remained in the collective memory of the discipline. It is because he is a relatively unknown figure on the contemporary scene that this chapter offers a somewhat extensive overview of his work, highlighting its influence on the development of ecological psychology to be sure, but going beyond those considerations.

Apart from serving a goal of this project to trace the theoretical and historical connections between the ideas of James and those of Gibson, Holt's work should also be of interest to contemporary experimental psychologists and cognitive scientists because his was one of the first psychological frameworks to propose a *purposive molar behaviorism*. The kind of purposive behaviorist approach that Holt offered has had a major impact on psychology, especially on cognitive psychology, through

---

[1]Chapter 6 explores other influences, and these too have Jamesian roots, albeit less direct ones.

the work of another of Holt's influential students, Edward C. Tolman. In many respects, the purposive behaviorism that Tolman developed during his career, following along the lines of Holt's thinking, helped to set the stage for the reemergence of interest in cognitive processes after midcentury. Thus, Holt's writings provide new insights into the historical roots of neobehaviorist cognitive psychology, as well as into the beginnings of ecological psychology.

Finally, and of more general significance, the body of Holt's work represents a notable attempt by one of James's students to extend radical empiricism in new directions. Accordingly, with the renewed interest over the past few decades in James's writings, and in his later philosophy in particular (see Introduction), Holt's work should be of interest to contemporary James scholars.

EDWIN B. HOLT: A BRIEF BIOGRAPHY

Holt did not publish a memoir of his life and career. Biographical information and analyses of his work are presently limited to two obituaries, one by Leonard Carmichael (1946) and the other by Herbert S. Langfeld (1946), who were colleagues and friends of Holt, and to a chapter in Kuklick's (1977) important survey of philosophy and psychology at Harvard.[2] Although Kuklick's analysis is a detailed treatment of Holt's ideas, it does not examine Holt's years at Princeton, which is the period Gibson studied with him. Holt receives only brief mention in current histories of psychology (e.g., Hergenhahn, 1992; Hilgard, 1987; Hothersall, 1995; Leahey, 1992.)

A Chronology of Life Events

Edwin Bissell Holt (1873–1946) was born on August 21 in Winchester, Massachusetts. After attending Amherst College in 1892, he enrolled at Harvard where he received a B.A. in 1896. Holt entered Harvard Graduate School of Arts and Sciences in 1897, but these studies were interrupted the next year by brief military service (1898) during the Spanish-American War. Following military service, Holt attended medical school at the University of Freiburg for a year (1899), spent another year (1900) at Columbia University where he received an A.M. degree, and then returned to graduate studies at Harvard to receive a Ph.D. in 1901.

Holt's Harvard mentors were William James, Hugo Münsterberg, and Josiah Royce. Apart from being drawn to James for intellectual reasons, Holt probably found James's informal style and iconoclastic tendencies

---

[2] The biographical material in this chapter is drawn primarily from these three sources.

appealing (see, e.g., Barzun, 1983; Simon, 1996). No doubt, Holt must have been one of the students in James's circle who was once described by an observer of the Harvard scene as being "flippant like James" (cited in Harlow, 1931). Holt and R. B. Perry, who later became James's earliest biographer, are generally considered two of James's most able students. Following his Ph.D., Holt remained at Harvard for 18 years, first as an instructor from 1901–1905, and then as an assistant professor from 1905–1919. During this later period, he spent a year during World War I working as a volunteer in a government office in Washington, DC. Holt had been an inspiring teacher at Harvard, attracting some of its brightest students.[3] He submitted his resignation from the Harvard faculty in 1919, leaving a full-time job in academia for the remainder of his life.

After his departure from Cambridge, Holt lived briefly in New England, California, and British Columbia, eventually settling on the coast of Maine. Holt's friend and former Harvard colleague, H.S. Langfeld, who had become chair of the psychology department at Princeton, lured him to teach there annually during its spring semester beginning in 1926. About his tenure at Princeton, Langfeld (1946) wrote:

> He was an unusually good teacher. His voice was pleasant, his language distinguished, his exposition clear, his interest sharp, and his criticism often caustic. ... Most of his precepts were in the evening; often students would stay through two precepts and on into the night, and accompany him home about one o'clock in the morning. (p. 254)

James Gibson began undergraduate studies at Princeton starting in 1922, staying there to pursue graduate work, and completing his Ph.D. thesis in 1928 under Holt's direction.[4] In an autobiographical essay, J. J. Gibson (1967a) described Holt as "a great teacher [who] had a contempt for humbug and a clarity of thought that has never been matched. ... He shocked his students by violent predictions in the mildest possible manner of speaking" (p. 9). Holt continued teaching part time at Princeton until his retirement in 1936. Appreciation of Holt as a teacher is reflected in an editorial that appeared in the Princeton undergraduate newspaper at the

---

[3] Among these students was Walter Lippman, who was to become perhaps the most influential journalist in the United States during the middle decades of the 20th century (Steel, 1980). Lippman also became well acquainted with James, who at this time was retired from teaching, through regular weekly teas at the James's house.

[4] In view of Langfeld's description of Holt's evening work habits, one cannot help but wonder whether Gibson's unorthodox work schedule began at Princeton. As Gibson's students discovered, he was rarely available until the afternoon, having typically concluded his previous day's work in the early hours of the morning. In addition, Langfeld's (1946) description of Holt's writing style could also be readily applied to Gibson: "Holt wrote slowly and with great care. His style however, was easy, clear, and graceful. Words interested him. He had an unusually wide vocabulary and an uncanny ability in selecting exactly the right word or phrase to express his meaning. He disliked unusual words if a common one would do, and his expressions were direct and to the point." (p. 255)

time of his retirement (reprinted in Carmichael, 1946). There he is described as combining "an extraordinary teaching ability with world renowned scholarly research," and as being exceedingly kind and helpful to "bewildered and troubled undergraduates" (Carmichael, 1946, p. 479). For the 10 years following his retirement, Holt lived in Tenants Harbor, Maine, with his long-time male companion, George X. Bernier, until his death in 1946. He is buried in Winchester, Massachusetts.

Holt's Withdrawal from Academic Life

To backtrack somewhat, Holt's motives for resigning from Harvard, and partially withdrawing from faculty life, are noteworthy: first in terms of what they reveal about the growing professionalization of academic life at Harvard and other universities in the early decades of this century—changes that have shaped the university climate in the United States to the present day—and second, about social constraints and prejudices that existed in academia at that time, and to a lesser degree still do today.

It is clear that Holt's partial withdrawal from faculty life can be attributed in large measure to his disenchantment with academia. During his 25 years at Harvard, he had witnessed the beginnings of a change in the American university. Holt's ideal was the scholar whose sole goal was the quest for knowledge. However, Holt saw academic life transformed from solely an intellectual calling to an occupation motivated by concerns for

E. B. Holt's house in Maine
(Courtesy of George Carey)

personal advancement. This change was precipitated, in his view, by the ascendance of faculty motivated by self-interest and self-promotion. Holt's critical thoughts on these matters were no doubt shaped in part by James's 1903 critique of academia, "The PhD Octopus" (James, 1903/1911). Holt's 1919 letter of resignation to President Lowell expressed these sentiments:

> From the side of the young instructor the system operates thus;—he is eager to "get on," and so must become as soon as possible "well-known." He therefore reads immature papers at Christmas meetings of his scientific society, writes others for his professional journals, scrambles old notes and threadbare formulae together into a "textbook," palavers with everybody who has the slightest academic influence, and turns himself generally into a publicity bureau. All this he substitutes outright for anything resembling the sober and honest pursuit of truth, and for all save the most perfunctory attention to the instruction and guidance of his students. (quoted in Kuklick, 1977, p. 432)

He held this negative assessment of the motives of many academics for the reminder of his life. In one of his last published articles, Holt (1935) wrote: "And we, if we have had close contact with scientists, know that scientific ambition and prestige are commonly as grimly self-centered as the manoeuvers of any highwayman" (p. 186).

Without intending to minimize these concerns, there were also personal factors that probably also served to embitter and alienate him from academic life in Cambridge and beyond. First, Holt's active intellectual and social life at Harvard, which centered around a group of fellow philosophers and psychologists, including Yerkes, Langfeld, and Perry (cf. Hilgard, 1987, p. 829, n. 8), was dissolving prior to the time of his resignation. As described in most detail by Kuklick (1977), some members of this group left Cambridge to pursue various career opportunities, and others who had married withdrew from this circle of male companions to familial responsibilities. Kuklick (1977) commented, "Perhaps these events should have meant little, but Holt was maudlin about his male friendships. When a romance of his own ended unhappily, he felt bereft of both intellectually stimulating comrades and an emotionally supportive companion" (p. 421). Kuklick's description of Holt's "maudlin" demeanor concerning male relationships is a characterization he seems to have picked up from Holt's correspondence with Yerkes, and it is probably a pejorative allusion to Holt's homosexuality. Whether or not Holt was generally open about his sexual orientation while at Harvard is uncertain; but at Princeton, Holt apparently made little secret of it.[5] In any case, it is

---

[5] According to Ed Reed (personal communication, April 27, 1992), Gibson's biographer, Gibson was aware of the intimate relationship between Holt and Bernier. However, it seems that the nature of Holt's and Bernier's relationship was not common knowledge to residents of Tenant's Harbor, Maine, although they were still remembered in 1997 by local townsfolk.

not unreasonable to suppose that both the dissolution of his social group at Harvard, as well as the conflicts engendered by being homosexual in the academic world of Cambridge early in the century, took its toll on him personally.

Second, Holt had accepted the responsibility of caring for his aging mother who, over the very years that his social life became strained, required increasing care. This filial labor apparently isolated him further from the academic community at Harvard. It also led him to turn down a promising academic position at the University of Manchester.[6] There is some indication that Holt ultimately regretted that decision, which would have led him to become a faculty colleague of Samuel Alexander, who at the time was the most prominent of the English Realists (Langfeld, 1946). Intellectually, Alexander might have played the role of an elder colleague and mentor, filling the void after James's death in 1910. Not coincidentally, Holt resigned from Harvard immediately following his mother's death, his care for her perhaps being his last remaining tie to Cambridge.

Any further dabbling into "psychohistory" would be irrelevant to the goals of this chapter. The significance of these background matters is that they contribute to an explanation for Holt's growing alienation from academia. More generally, as abbreviated as these considerations are, they serve as an indication that life for homosexual academics for much of this century has probably been exacting, no doubt adversely affecting countless careers.[7]

The Principal Phases of Holt's Scholarship

Although there is considerable continuity in Holt's writings throughout his career, several distinguishable phases can be identified. His first experimental work was in the area of visual perception, and representative of this activity is "Eye-Movement and Central Anesthesia" (1903), which was based on his doctoral dissertation completed under Münsterberg's direction. Holt continued working actively in the Harvard laboratories, serving as acting director for a year during Münsterberg's leave of absence (1910–1911).

Around this time, Holt's published work took on a more philosophical cast as he joined with five others to develop a program they called "The

[6] Hilgard (1987) wrote in a critical tone about Holt's feelings of obligation to his mother. He described Holt, rather uncharitably, as being "tied to his mother's apron strings" (p. 272). Hilgard's brief biographical sketch of Holt contained other similarly "chatty" and unflattering comments. Hilgard's treatment of Holt seems unnecessarily harsh and petty. It leads one to wonder if this is the sort of hostility Holt frequently faced as a result of his sexual orientation.
[7] Roger Brown's (1989) candid autobiographical essay offers much insight into the difficulties faced by homosexuals in academia.

New Realism."[8] The work of this group began initially as separate efforts to respond to Josiah Royce's attack on James's realism from an idealistic perspective. Jointly, in an attempt to defend and extend radical empiricism, the group published a platform for their program in 1910 (Holt et al., 1910). In 1912, the major statements of this group were published in the multi-authored volume *The New Realism: Cooperative Studies in Philosophy* (Holt et al., 1912), to which Holt contributed a chapter on illusory experience from a realist perspective. Appearing after this volume, but in fact completed several years earlier (1908), was *The Concept of Consciousness* (1914/1973), which was Holt's first detailed statement of what might be called his philosophical behaviorism.[9] And, as becomes evident, it was in part an attempt at a rapprochement between James's and Royce's positions. Like radical empiricism, the program of the New Realists and Holt's early writings in particular are most readily understood as responses to the subjectivist character of idealism.

Holt attended the now famous meeting at Clark University in 1909 where Freud delivered his only lecture on psychoanalysis in the United States.[10] In the widely reprinted photograph taken at this meeting, Holt can be found standing several rows behind his mentor, William James. Holt was deeply impressed with Freud's theories, and he found many important connections between them and the purposive behaviorism that he was developing. Holt saw Freud's stress on motivated action directed toward some psychological end as being congenial with his own purposive emphasis, and he attempted to recast some of the motivational aspects of Freud's work into behaviorist terms in *The Freudian Wish* (1915a)—a highly influential, although somewhat controversial book. Particularly relevant to the present discussion was an essay Holt appended to this volume, "Response and Cognition," which had been separately published as a series of journal articles (Holt, 1915b, 1915c).

Throughout the 1920s Holt was engaged in writing the first volume of *Animal Drive and the Learning Process: An Essay Toward Radical Empiricism*, which appeared in 1931. This book deals with issues of learning and development primarily from a psychobiological, rather

---

[8] The New Realists consisted of Holt and Ralph Barton Perry (Harvard), W. P. Montague and Walter B. Pitkin (Columbia), E.G. Spaulding (Princeton), and Walter T. Marvin (Rutgers).

[9] In 1973, *The Concept of Consciousness* was reissued as part of a *Classics in Psychology* series published by Arno Press.

[10] Freud's presentations were reprinted as *Five Lectures on Psychoanalysis* (1909/1977).

PSYCHOLOGY CONFERENCE GROUP, CLARK UNIVERSITY, SEPTEMBER, 1909

Beginning with front row, left to right: Franz Boas, E. B. Titchener, William James, William Stern, Leo Burgerstein, G. Stanley Hall, Sigmund Freud, Carl G. Jung, Adolf Meyer, H. S. Jennings. *Second row:* C. E. Seashore, Joseph Jastrow, J. McK. Cattell, E. F. Buchner, E. Katzenellenbogen, Ernest Jones, A. A. Brill, Wm. H. Burnham, A. F. Chamberlain. *Third row:* Albert Schinz, J. A. Magni, B. T. Baldwin, F. Lyman Wells, G. M. Forbes, E. A. Kirkpatrick, Sandor Ferenczi, E. C. Sanford, J. P. Porter, Sakyo Kanda, Hikozo Kakise. *Fourth row:* G. E. Dawson, S. P. Hayes, E. B. Holt, C. S. Berry, G. M. Whipple, Frank Drew, J. W. A. Young, L. N. Wilson, K. J. Karlson, H. H. Goddard, H. I. Klopp, S. C. Fuller

Clark University Conference, 1909:

William James is third from the left in front row; E. B. Holt is third from the left in the back row.
(Clark University Archives)

than a philosophical, perspective. Holt returned to some of his philosophical concerns in essays published in the mid-1930s. He also maintained an ongoing interest in social psychology, regularly teaching a course on this topic at Princeton and publishing one chapter expressing his views in this area. During the last decade of his life, he apparently worked on the second volume of *Animal Drive and the Learning Process;* this volume never reached published form.

A UNIVERSE OF NEUTRAL BEING

Apart from his experimental research on vision, Holt's earliest work was an attempt to contribute to the nondualistic metaphysics that James had begun in his radical empiricist essays. Holt's *The Concept of Consciousness* (1914/1973) had an unmistakable Jamesian stamp (although James had reservations about the book), and it offered several novel ideas to this philosophical approach. But, in its efforts to accommodate aspects of Royce's idealism, it is flawed in ways that even Holt recognized in retrospect. Still, some of Holt's most significant contributions are introduced in this book, and there is much to be learned even in its shortcomings.

A Hierarchy of Universes of Discourse

Holt attempted to take certain aspects of Royce's metaphysics and logic and turn it to use in a realist framework. Royce's idealist philosophy (see chap. 1) attributed the coherence in immediate experience to a transcendent order to which individual minds were connected. Logic for Royce is more than a method of reasoning; it reflects various universes of order, identifying most significantly the Absolute and in turn "derived from it the more limited order systems defining the world of spatio-temporal objects" (Kuklick, 1977, p. 422). Holt followed Royce in arguing that logic reveals the structure of "what *is*"; but, whereas for Royce this order is subjective (idealistic), in Holt's adaptation it is ontologically neutral arguably in the same way as James's world of pure experience. Logic as a system provided Holt with a way of considering the structure of reality in ontologically neutral terms, and as a way of understanding how different systems of thought are related. Thus, logical terms and propositions are the basic elements of a universe of neutral being, and out of their relations are formed various "universes of discourse," such as mathematics, geometry, physics, chemistry, and psychology. In distancing himself from idealism, Holt wrote concerning these universes of discourse that "the entities (objects, facts, etc.) under study in logical, mathematics, and the physical sciences are not mental in any usual or proper meaning of the word 'mental'" (Holt et al., 1912, p. 472).

The structure of this system is that of a nested hierarchy, with each successive universe of discourse dependent on those operating at more abstract levels. Identifying each level or order of being with symbolic logic is important for Royce and for Holt because the successive universes of discourse can be generated deductively (in principle at least) from underlying, more fundamental logical propositions. According to Holt, "Any system of being ... arises from a certain Given consisting of terms and propositions, which generate of their own motion all further terms and propositions that are in the system" (p. 16). A particularly clear and succinct description of Holt's hierarchical universe was provided by Kallen (1916), another student of James's and a notable philosopher in his own right:

> Nature appears in this perspective as a self-generating hierarchy, moving from the simple to the complex; from the one or few, to the many; from the "neutral" to the psychical and material; from the indifferent to the valuable. ... [The various levels of the hierarchy] all derive from the simple entities of logic, which are the walls of the world and the foundation of reality. (p. 599)

This hierarchy consists of "entities" or "manifolds of being" that are connected by "external relations," and the differing organization at the various levels results in different properties as one moves through the hierarchy. By external relations, Holt and the New Realists meant that entities of the different systems of order are independent. However, in arguing for a metaphysics of external relations, Holt insisted that he is not proposing a dualism of substance:

> This pluralism ... has nothing to do with the dualism of mind and matter, or any other pluralism of substance. If the terms and propositions of logic must be substantialized, they are all strictly of one substance, for which perhaps the least dangerous name is neutral-stuff. (Holt, 1914, 1973, pp. 51–52)

In fact, Holt argued, concern about substance has deflected our efforts to develop a comprehensive account of the varieties of phenomena in our world, monistic accounts such as materialism or idealism typically giving short shrift to one or another category of phenomena. A neutral ontology removes these impediments, making a comprehensive account possible. Holt explained:

> Now in logic the question of substance is of the most trifling interest, if it can be said to be of interest at all; for clearly in any system the fundamental entities, or the members of the fundamental class (K), are all of one "substance" and differ only in respect of position, *et cetera*, being generated by some repetitive process. (pp. 62–63)

What Holt was doing here was bringing together aspects of the positions of two of his Harvard teachers: the subjectivist idealism of Royce and the radical empiricism of James. It becomes clear as the discussion in this volume proceeds, however, that Holt was borrowing Royce's perspective to bolster James' metaphysical claims more so than the other way around.

Importantly, and in line with the independence of external relations, the fact that this universe is of one "neutral-stuff" does not "prevent the entities of different complexity from having very different properties" (p. 63). Holt illustrated how properties can change while substance does not by stating that although water is the same substance as hydrogen and oxygen, the properties of water cannot be reduced to these constituents. It takes hydrogen and oxygen in particular amounts and in a particular arrangement to account for water: "And of course the progress of science shows countless cases in which an apparent difference in substance has resolved itself into a difference of form but an identity of substance" (pp. 63–64).

This claim that entities of a common substance can have different properties is an important feature of Holt's examination of the structure of being. Particular properties may be specific to a given level or order of complexity, although ultimately the "neutral substance" of this domain as a whole is the same as that of its constituents. Even though in his later writings Holt did not advocate a view of "neutral," fundamentally logical entities at different levels of complexity, his claim of a "continuity of substance" throughout a natural hierarchy was an enduring theme in his work.

Holt extended this argument to properties operating at the level of complexity that is mind: "It takes all the components of my experience together and just in their given order to constitute my idea, consciousness, or mind" (p. 89). Whereas mind is not substantially different from its constituents, and indeed its constituents (i.e., neurophysiological processes) can be studied from the starting point of mental phenomena, the *properties* of mind are distinct from the properties of the nervous system.

Although Holt was concerned in writing this book with idealism's monistic solution to the mind–body problem—namely, that all things are ultimately connected to a transcendent realm—contemporary discussions of mind, however, are often confronted with a monism of a different type, namely, that of a physicalistic kind. Such approaches typically adopt a reductionistic stance toward perceptual experience, as well as consciousness or awareness generally. However, if all mental experience is reducible to physical entities, how is it possible to account for qualities characteristic of mentation short of either denying their existence, or alternatively, creating a separate mental realm that has secondary status relative to the physical world?

For Holt, if the view is adopted that mental properties are *irreducible*, although not without identifiable constituents, then perceptual experience of an object is neither reducible to physical properties, nor divisible into objective, physical properties (primary qualities), on the one hand, and subjective, mental properties (secondary qualities), on the other. Objects of experience simply are. In adopting this view, Holt agreed with Berkeley's stance that, "those immediate objects of perception which according to you are only appearances of things, I take to be the real things themselves ... you will have them to be empty appearances I real beings" (quoted in Holt, 1914, p. 123). However, he disagreed with Berkeley about what those "real beings" are. Unlike Berkeley, Holt was "not for changing things into ideas, but rather ideas into things" (p. 123). Here, without explicitly stating so, Holt was adopting James's perspective of pure experience where objects of experience are ontologically neutral. And, in so doing, he amended Berkeley's dictum "to be is to be perceived" (*esse ist percipi)*: "It may be true that to be X is to be perceived, but only on the condition that X is" (p. 95).

But in agreement with Berkeley, Holt rejected matter as primary. What is primary are the things of experience: "But it is to be remembered that the real objects about us, which can never be explained away, are not 'Matter'; they are just objects, while 'Matter' is the stuff that philosophy has declared these objects are made of" (p. 122).

Surprisingly little direct mention is made of James's philosophy in this book, but the imprint is unmistakable. By claiming that what is primary are objects, neutrally considered, and that ways of experiencing those objects can be identified with different universes of discourse, including that of physics, Holt echoed James's notion of pure experience and his analysis of concepts, respectively.

The Failings of Holt's Early Framework

The system that has been sketched here, however, is not fully compatible with James's perspective, and Holt came to realize that for this reason it did not ultimately suit his purposes. The property differences among levels of being, derived as they are from logic, are essentially *static*. Although logic seemed an appropriate choice as the underlying framework for his system because it carried with it little ontological baggage, it is unsuitable for conveying the *functional* and *dynamic* qualities of James's perspective.[11]

---

[11] It is likely that James was not favorably disposed toward Holt's logical analysis. In a note to an editor (June 27, 1904) concerning the publication of his essay "Does Consciousness Exist," James wrote: "Young Holt, assistant in Münsterberg's laboratory, was here while I was writing my article, & we talked it over very much. He also disbelieves in Consciousness absolutely, and has an extremely vigorous and original, but to me in many points very obscure system on the literary stocks" (quoted in editors' appendices (continued on next page)

This criticism was offered in Kallen's (1916) insightful review of the book. Kallen argued that logic offers a "formal staticism which has a denatured activity," and accordingly, it excludes essential attributes of "being," such as duration, change, possibility, and potentiality. Kallen claimed:

> A proposition and its implicates are simultaneous and instantaneous. One implies and posits all; all imply and posit one. The mere being of "simples" is thus necessarily coincident with their combination into all sorts of complexes. There can be no possibilities, no potentialities in Mr. Holt's world. ... Activity, change, time, in the usual signification of these terms are purely illusions, being definable by means of instantaneous and simultaneous relations of *before* and *after*. (pp. 600–601)

Kallen criticized Holt for offering a view that emphasizes "being" rather than "becoming" or "doing," and therefore for proposing a view that is not in keeping with James's dynamic approach. Kallen's criticisms ring true. (They also point to one essential facet of James's ideas that have been neglected in psychology the 20th century; see chap. 5). In the view presented in Holt's book, "All being reduces to coordinations of immutable, self-repeated simples. ... The world is petrified, and plurality, motion, change, and life have still to be accounted for" (Kallen, 1916, p. 603).

This is a criticism that Holt (1920, p. 377) later acknowledges to be justified. Accordingly, he did not employ this Roycean inspired framework in any of his subsequent work, where his writings henceforth take on a more dynamic character. Still, the system he offers in *The Concept of Consciousness* has heuristic merit in that it offered a novel approach to thinking about psychological phenomena. It is a perspective that contrasts sharply with theoretical variations of Cartesian dualism, that promulgates James's later writings on consciousness as a relation (see next section), and perhaps most important, that subsequently allowed Holt to think about mental phenomena in nondualistic ways. The *strengths* of the framework Holt developed in this book are most evident in his treatment

---

[11]*continued from previous page)*   to the Harvard edition of James's *Essays in Radical Empiricism*, p. 211). James was certainly referring here to Holt's *The Concept of Consciousness*, which was completed in 1908 and published in 1914. James was not positively inclined toward highly formalized psychological systems such as this one. Kallen (1937) wrote that James had reservations about

> "a certain technique of handling some form of language where interest in the symbols and formulae and their manipulation displaces concern about the realities they stand for. James, being the great master of language, found that form of manipulating it a device either for concealing intellectual poverty or for obscuring reality" (p. 76).

One wonders whether James's dissatisfaction with aspects of this work in part accounts for Holt's delay in publishing it until after James's death and also for the scant reference to James in this book.

of perception. When Holt applied the framework developed in *The Concept of Consciousness* to the domain of perception, some of his most important contributions to the collective project of the New Realists are expressed. Thus, before going on to examine some other issues from *The Concept of Consciousness*, the next section discusses the platform of the New Realists.

THE PROGRAM OF THE NEW REALISTS

The collective effort of the six philosophers who identified themselves as the New Realists can be seen mostly as an attempt to defend and expand James's radical empiricism and explore some of its implications. Differences among the six existed and remained unresolved throughout their somewhat brief association. What united them was a critical stance toward subjectivist accounts of knowing and a resolute defense of realism.

As already noted, this group initially produced a brief platform (Holt et al., 1910) consisting of separate statements by each participant that were claimed to "represent the same doctrine." By drafting different statements, the participants obviously wanted the differences existing among them, as well as the commonalities, to be preserved and duly noted. These statements were followed by *The New Realism: Cooperative Studies in Philosophy* (1912). In addition to a joint introductory chapter by the six, each philosopher contributed an extended essay to this volume. Finally, two commentaries—Montague on Holt's chapter and Holt's reply—were appended to the book. Clearly, the six were unable to get beyond some of their differences, and as a result, this book stands as a less than unified contribution of the group as a whole.

The New Realists were as one, however, in their objection to philosophies that take as their starting point a knower's awareness of his or her own mental states—that is, philosophies that take ideas to be *the* fundamental property of reality. This means that not only did they reject Roycean idealism, but also (and most pertinent to contemporary issues) they objected to any account of knowing that claims that what individuals know immediately are only their own personal knowledge states (e.g., mental representations). Such views take subjective experience or ideas to be primary. Instead, like James and Dewey, they embraced a thorough-going *naturalism*. From this standpoint, as Montague (in Holt et al., 1912) put it, "Cognition belongs to the same world as that of its objects. It has its place in the order of nature. There is nothing transcendental or supernatural about it" (p. 475).

Although knowing and the object known both belong to the natural order, they are independent; there is an "independence of things known and the knowing of them" (Holt et al., 1912, p. 34). There is a relation of externality, as already mentioned, between a knower and an object.

Objects that are known exist independently of a knower and are not altered by their being known. In Montague's words,

Realism holds that things known may continue to exist unaltered when they are not known, or that things may pass in and out of the cognitive relation without prejudice to their reality, or that the existence of a thing is not correlated with or dependent upon the fact that anybody experiences it, perceives it, conceives it, or is in any way aware of it. (In Holt et al., 1912, p. 474)

According to this claim, there is a reality of things and events that exists independently of its being known. In contrast, the assumption that knowing processes and objects known have a "relation of internality" means that objects are altered through the process of knowing them (consider this claim either from the point of view of Humean associationism or Kantian transcendentalism). Starting from this assumption, individuals can never know the world independently of their own experience. And one important consequence, if this is so, is that individuals cannot jointly experience in any fundamental way a *common world* (see chap. 4). Instead, individuals only have immediate awareness of their own private, intrasubjective experiences. This latter claim is a tenet of the Cartesian metatheory discussed previously, and it has led historically to the view that the world considered independently of a knower cannot be directly experienced.

In modern psychology, this is the position reflected by most theories of cognition, although sometimes only tacitly. There are two versions of this viewpoint, as pointed out previously, both of which claim to embrace realism (for how could a modern scientific theory not do so?), but in the process leave the claim for realism in a precarious position. The first version stems from the British Empiricist tradition and assumes that individuals construct mental representations of the environment, and it is the mental representations that are immediately experienced. The second version stems from varieties of Kantian-inspired views claiming that what is detected by the senses is transformed through the act of knowing, and hence what is directly known is a synthesis of input and a priori structuring processes. In both views, an independent world is inaccessible to direct experience, and the psychologically meaningful world—the world that is phenomenologically primary—is experienced privately by each individual. Knowing is something that happens solely in a knower. Further, depending on which specific version of either type of theory is adopted, the world independent of an individual's experience is either that world described by physics, or it is unknowable in principle.

Instead of viewing knowing as largely a process occurring in a knower, the New Realists following James claimed that knowing or cognition is a relation between a knower and an object known. Importantly, the object is not altered as a part of this relation, but instead, by establishing a cognitive relation with an object, a knower comes to know that object as an independent entity with preexisting properties. Holt et al. (1912) explained:

> The realist believes that he thus discovers that the interrelation in question is not responsible for the characters of the thing known. In the first place being known is something that *happens* to a preexisting thing. The characters of that preexisting thing determine what happens when it is known. Then, in the second place, when the knowing takes place, these characters are at least for the most part undisturbed. (p. 34)

Thus, in their view, the world exists independently of the knower, and the knower can know that world. It follows from this that different knowers can know the same world: There are empirical grounds for shared understanding.

How can the process of knowing be conceptualized as a direct relation between functionally independent domains? The way in which James approached this problem has already by covered. In *The Concept of Consciousness*, Holt offered a useful discussion of this process of direct knowing, and he reiterated this account in a more abbreviated and slightly revised form as part of his contribution to *The New Realism* volume.

Perceiving and Remembering from a New Realist Perspective

In Holt's formulation, perceptual experience can be thought of as an external relation between two orders of being where the manifold that is the psychological order transects a portion of the manifold that is the domain of physical objects. The critical concept here is that of a "cross-section," which Holt defined as any portion of one manifold that is defined or articulated by principles specific to a different manifold. The roots of this idea in James's radical empiricism should be apparent (see chap. 1). An analogy that is modified slightly from Holt helps to clarify the notion of a cross-section. Consider a boat with a searchlight moving along a shoreline and illuminating successive features of the landscape. The shoreline features considered independently of the boat comprise one "manifold"; but the particular features that are successively illuminated are not determined by principles of the shoreline manifold. The determining principles are connected to a second manifold, comprised of the combined movement of the boat and the intensity and breadth of the light. This second set of factors, attributes of the second manifold, define the cross-section of landscape that is illuminated over some passage of time. Significantly, the cross-section is neither the shoreline, nor the boat, nor the searchlight each considered separately. Rather, it is that portion of the shoreline illuminated by the moving boat. That is, the cross-section is defined by a *transaction* between two distinguishable systems.

With this example, Holt shows why he would object to a representationalist claim that perceived objects are "in" the mind or constructed by the mind. Such a claim makes no more sense than the claim that the shoreline features are "in" the searchlight. Likewise, the objects of experience are not dependent on psychological processes for their existence. The landscape, of the previous example, can itself be described independently of the boat and light. Their relation is one of externality.

Working from this analogy, an individual selectively engages some features of the environment and not others, and the features constituting the cross-section are determined by the individual's "specific response" (to use Holt's and Perry's terminology) to the environment at a particular time. That is, the environment for an individual at a particular time—that which is manifested from the range of possibilities comprising the environmental manifold—is delimited in terms of what that individual responds to. Hence, the effective environment is established relationally, and yet the environment and the individual are independent. (This point is discussed in the context of Gibson's approach in chap. 3.) Holt proposed, "In order to ascertain what entities belong to the cross-section of any given animal, one only has to discover what entities the animal responds to with a specific reaction" (p. 180). Defining the effective environment for an individual in this relational manner as a "cross-section" lays some of the conceptual groundwork for Gibson's concept of affordances (chap. 3).

Further, it can be seen how this approach provides philosophical grounds for a realist epistemology. By defining experience as a cross-section, Holt was stating that "all the objects that one perceives, including the so-called 'secondary qualities,' are 'out there' just where and as they seem to be" (Holt, 1914/1973, p. 353). Perception is not mediated by mental representations. Perception is direct.

Unlike the largely static nature of the logical universe of Holt's first book, he did admit into this New Realist account of perceiving the Jamesian notion of change over time. Rather than conceptualizing perception "causally" as the "entry, maintenance, and exit of sensations and perceptions," he views perception as a cross-section of a manifold that moves in space and also in time: "The temporal succession of possibilities from moment to moment is a manifold that is both extended in time and progressive with time. The entities contained in any one span, are together in consciousness but not simultaneous" (p. 212). In other words, the cross-section is more than a slice in time; "the knowledge-mass is a temporal sequence, like a rhythm or a melody" (p. 244). The theoretical significance of this claim becomes apparent shortly.

Furthermore, Holt already recognized in the earlier book that consciousness as a cross-section of the material world is selective and partial, and more can be discovered with further transactions between the two manifolds or domains. Therefore, there is an ongoing possibility for knowing more about the structure of the environment manifold. Herein resides one aspect of the pluralism of Holt's position: The possibility always remains open for the discovery of new knowledge and multiple perspectives. This point of view will prove central to Gibson. In his otherwise somewhat critical review of *The Concept of Consciousness*, Kallen (1916) noted approvingly that Holt's recognition of these dynamic attributes of perceiving "does greater credit to his common sense than his [theoretical] consistency" (p. 601), and it points to places in his analysis where "the passion for logic becomes checked and overlaid by an equally strong passion for fact" (p. 607).

Holt's analysis of memory from the point of view of his framework has some heuristic value. The main theoretical problem that Holt faces here is how "past events can be in present knowledge" (p. 223). At issue is how to account for memories without positing a mental representation that is a residue of previous experience. To do so would be to posit a mental entity that could also be invoked in an account of perception, and this move would lead Holt back to the kind of mentalistic position he wanted to avoid. This question is a challenge for any direct realist account, and Holt seemed to meet it with only partial success. All the same, it is an interesting attempt.

Remembering is not literally recall of the past. Adopting the Jamesian assumption that thought is an ongoing, ever-changing stream, it is not possible to go backward in time to relive a previous occurrence. Instead, in the case of a remembered experience, one is aware that a presently experienced "now" occurred sometime in the past. Stated in terms of Holt's framework, remembering occurs when ongoing experience is transected by a temporal knowledge system. This temporal manifold consists of knowledge as to when events occurred relative to others. Thus, in the case of a particular remembered experience (Y), as opposed to perceptual experience (Z), one is aware that an event has occurred sometime in the past, as opposed to "now," because the event has a prior position in the time manifold. For instance, it is known to have occurred serially after X but before Z. A perceptual experience per se has temporal duration, but when it occurred is marked by its position in the temporal manifold.

Taking this analysis one step farther, mental experience in James's and Holt's ontologically neutral sense arises from the intersection of two systems, and the object of experience is located at this intersection. In the case of perceiving, the intersection in question is one of the knower and the environment manifold. In the case of remembering, it is an intersection of two sets of relations in the domain (i.e., among the constellation of relations) of the knower: the cognitive order and knowledge of a temporal order of events. In such a view, both perceiving and remembering occur "now." They are both immediate and unmediated experience. However, they differ functionally in the following way. Perceiving can lead to more knowledge being discovered about another order, namely, the environment manifold. In contrast, "memory surveys that which is not further accessible to our volition" (Münsterberg, quoted by Holt, p. 253).

Apart from this specific formulation, this kind of distinction between perceiving and memory will prove to be of some help to Gibson, and it is an important one for any ecological theory of knowing. If perceiving is viewed as a process by which animals remain functionally adapted to the environment, and significantly, as a process that enables them to broaden their adaptive functioning to an ever-widening range of environmental properties, then it is essential that perceiving be viewed as making possible the discovery of new things in the environmental manifold. But if the representational line of thinking is followed, there are problems here. A representational theory of perception is essentially a memory-based account—that is, there is a claim that perceiving is driven by the activation of previously generated mental representations. If this is so, then there is the problem of reconciling the conservative nature of mental representations with the requirement that they also need to be modifiable. This problem is not theoretically insurmountable, as is evidenced by Piaget's impressive efforts in this regard. But this solution brings with it all of the difficulties attendant to a representationalist account of perceiving. Moreover, if experience is most immediately of a mental representation, is it possible to distinguish between past and present experiences (see Reed, 1988, pp. 302-303)? Indeed, what does present experience even mean in this context? The approach Holt is advocating proposes that perceiving and remembering are qualitatively different experiences.

Illusory Experience from a Realist Perspective

One other topic that Holt devoted considerable attention to in *The Concept of Consciousness* is errors in experience. This is an issue that he returned to address even more fully in his contribution to *The New Realism: Cooperative Studies in Philosophy* (1912). The latter chapter, entitled "The Place of Illusory Experience in a Realistic World," is a clearer exposition of these issues, and it is this presentation that is considered here.

The problem that Holt tackled in his contribution to this multi-authored volume is one for which it would seem a realist is most vulnerable. How can nonveridical experiences, such as illusions, be accounted for in the context of a realist theory? It would seem that phenomena such as illusions and perceptual errors contradict any position such as neorealism that claims perception is direct and unmediated. Gibson's ecological theory of perception has been repeatedly attacked on these same grounds, and his response to these criticisms followed Holt's lead.

The nature of Holt's response is to start with an examination of the premises of the problem as it is typically formulated. This kind of strategy, one encountered frequently in James's writings, is a good one to adopt because it might head off considerable effort directed at difficulties that in fact are solely created by the way an issue is framed. Holt pointed out that framing the question, as is usually done, as essentially a problem of *correspondence* (i.e., one of entailing a comparison between a percept residing "in" the mental realm and the environment "outside") prejudges the matter. Viewing illusions as errors of correspondence presumes the comparison of the illusory experience in consciousness to the true state of things in the world, and that the latter is an unproblematic, objective realm. According to Holt (1914/1973):

> Of course, the fact that opinions differed and that some must be wrong, would not have led to the supposition that opinions belong to a subjective realm, had it not at the same time been tacitly or openly held that the objective world could contain no errors, contradictions, or untruths. (p. 189)

In other words, the question presupposes the kind of physical world envisioned by Galileo and Newton—a world of perfect predictability and lawfulness, a world wholly devoid of chance or unexpected occurrences. In this universe, physical properties such as shape and size remain constant unless they are undergoing systematic, predictable change. Whereas knowledge of this world may be probable and approximate, events of the physical world have definite, lawful properties. With this view of the world, perceptual errors and illusions must be "in the mind" not in the world.

The New Realists, following James, rejected the correspondence analysis that underlies this way of putting the issue. Such a view requires a distinction between an outer domain that is the world and an inner domain of consciousness, and considers how well the latter may or may not map onto the former. Consciousness is not a property of an intra-subjective domain. Instead, " … consciousness, whenever it is localized at all (as it by no means always is) in space, is not in the skull, but is 'out there' precisely wherever it appears to be. This is for me at least, one of the cardinal principles of realism" (Holt, 1912 , p. 353). What might it even mean to say that consciousness is "in" your skull? Even though it can be said that the brain is in the body, does it follow that consciousness is "in" anything? Holt argued that although there are numerous relations between the nervous system and consciousness, one of these need not be that of "spatial inclusion."

Only if the relation of knower and known is accepted as one of "inside and outside" does it make sense to treat error and illusion as correspondence problems. It is precisely this sort of distinction that James's radical empiricism, and Holt's elaboration of it, does not accept. Consciousness is not a mental state as such; it is a *relation*, an "awareness of" an object of experience. The notion of correspondence does not fit with this type of framework. Two distinct domains are not being mapped accurately or imperfectly onto one another; rather, awareness is relational.

Given this viewpoint, what then is the status of illusions and their like? If they are not "in the skull," and they are not errors of correspondence, where and what are they? Holt addressed this question by invoking an analogy of a "mirror space." A layout of objects that is perceived in a mirror is different in certain respects from the layout of the objects independent of that mirror. For example, object relations are reversed in mirror space relative to those in the world. In addition, we cannot move about in the mirror space as we can in the perceived layout. In short, there is an absence of correspondence in some respects between the reflected object layout and the layout as such. However, is mirror space an illusion or an error? Is the mirror space unreal, subjective, illusory, or erroneous? On the contrary, mirror space meets all of the standard criteria of objectivity. Different observers will report the same reflected layout; observations by a single observer are replicable; it is possible to take measurements of the reflected layout; and reliable and precise predictions can be made. With regard to the latter point, once the way in which reflected light from objects interacts with a mirrored surface is understood, mirror space is thoroughly predictable. Using Holt's terminology, mirror space is a cross-section of the layout of objects and the reflective properties of the mirror.

Working from the analogy of mirror space, one can begin to see how to understand illusions from a realist perspective. Given the realist description of perception as a cross-section of the perceiving function and the environment, perceptual errors and illusions would not be viewed as occurring "in" the perceiver, but rather in the interaction of the perceiver and the world. It is from this perspective that Holt addressed the status of illusions. Perceptual errors and illusions are real parts of experience. Illusions arise under particular specifiable, objective conditions. The problem is not one of correspondence, or a lack thereof, but one in which circumstances lead to a lack of coherence or consistency within perceptual experience.

Holt cited the visual phenomenon of the bent stick in water. Is this commonplace visual illusion subjective or unreal? This phenomenon is only "unreal" if the reality of any aspect of this situation is denied: namely, that the stick is partially immersed in water and water has refractive properties that differ from those of the air. A stick in water is truly bent in visual experience. There is nothing illusory or unreal about it. If the situation is modified such that the stick is viewed out of water, then it now appears straight. In the process of removing the stick, did subjective experience change while the stick remained the same? Putting the question this way reintroduces the objective–subjective distinction. Instead, it is more accurate to say that the viewing conditions have changed. One is no longer dealing with the same situation, that is, the same object-in-context. The difference in appearance of the stick under the two conditions then is not a lack of correspondence between experience versus reality. It is a lack of consistency between how an object looks under one set of "real" conditions versus how it looks under different set of "real" conditions. There is a lack of coherence within experience.

Rather than confirming the subjectivity of all perception, as illusions such as this are typically taken to do, this example demonstrates that "illusory phenomena" are explainable, in principle, with reference to the conditions under which they are experienced. In other words, illusions are quite real. The "illusion" of some illusions is a result of isolating parts of a more complex stimulus array for consideration, as is the case with the stick in water. Other illusions and errors can be approached in the same way, such as the Muller-Lyer and the Ponzo. In these cases, there is typically an inconsistency between some portion of the stimulus configuration when viewed in isolation versus when it is viewed as a part of the configuration (see J. J. Gibson, 1966, pp. 312–313). Efforts to understand why the appearance of an entity changes under varying conditions are valuable—Holt's analysis hardly puts the question of the nature of various illusions to rest. But it clearly points out that there has been much confusion about what illusions and the like indicate about the nature of perception and reality.

Apart from addressing the matter of illusions, this analysis should assist in clarifying Holt's realist position in general. The realist position is "as things are perceived *so they are*"—which is to be distinguished from the claim "as things are perceived *so they really are*." The latter claim does not leave open the possibility that under different circumstances things might indeed look different, or the possibility that things without a counterpart in the material world, such as dreams and hallucinations, are truly experienced. Holt et al. (1912) argued, "But while all perceived things are things, *not* all perceived things are *real* things. ... For the gist of realism is not to insist that everything is real, far from it, but to insist that everything that is, is and is as it is" (pp. 358–359).

Finally, Holt used the example of mirror space to elaborate his critical stance toward mental representation. Mirrors reproduce objects through reflection, but do they in any meaningful sense represent those objects? If representation is used in the manner that it is in most discussions of epistemology, this claim would have to mean that mirrored images "derive their nature from the mirror itself, and [are] intrinsically subjective mirror-stuff" (p. 369). But of course no one would subscribe to such a view because it would lead to "no end of silly talk," such as the need to invoke some "mirroring spirit." Obviously, mirror space "is a reproduction of identicals without change of their 'nature.' ... [This view] affords no footing for speculations as to a subjective reality of representations" (p. 369). Aren't considerations of perception of the world in terms of mental representations equally problematic? The direct realist believes that they are.[12]

COGNITION AND THE ENVIRONMENT

Holt's writings took a decidedly more psychological turn in *The Freudian Wish* (1915a) and in his monographs, "Response and Cognition (1915b, 1915c)," reprinted as a supplement to that book and arguably his most important essays. In previous publications, Holt was writing for the most part as a philosopher with psychological interests. These two offerings are the reflections of a philosophically sophisticated psychologist. Further, it is in these two publications, and particularly the monograph, that we can illustrate the most explicit links between Holt's position and the later perspective developed by Gibson. One of these linkages, and indeed, a central theme of the monograph, is the idea of "the recession of the stimulus."

---

[12] The historically minded reader may want to know what became of the New Realist program. It was soon overshadowed by the so-called Critical Realists who adopted the view that realist epistemology must be based on the immediate experience of objects in consciousness. In effect, they returned to the kind of dualistic epistemology of the British Empiricists, while rejecting metaphysical dualism (Sellars, 1920/1960). But this was not the only factor contributing to the relatively short life of New Realism. The lack of cohesion among the group certainly contributed as well. Montague (1937/1960), for one, felt that in its attempt to address the criticisms of direct realism from the standpoint of illusions that the position "degraded the pure members of [the physical world] to an unseemly parity with objects of error and fantasy" (p. 488): he argued for a sort of Platonist realism ("subsistential realism") in which universals exist independent of minds. Further, he objected to the move toward behaviorism by Holt and others as degrading "the mind to a mass of 'specific responses'" (p. 488). A third factor is that the New Realism, Critical Realism, and concurrent trends in thought more compatible with scientific developments contributed to dislodging Idealism from its position as major philosophical perspective. Recall that the New Realism arose in large measure as a reaction to Idealism. With its principal adversary removed from the field, the basis for the cohesion among this group of otherwise differing realists gave way. Looking back, Holt wrote (1931) with tongue in cheek and with a parting shot at the Critical Realists:

> In the minds of all serious thinkers at the present time, the traditional alignment, in which clodhopping materialists stoned with their rude slings the true children of light, the idealists, who replied with deadly lightning from on high, is a long since forgotten episode. The enemies have become friends and have intermarried. ... [However], the children of the children of light ... incapable in fact of thinking dynamically at all, are still conceiving their world in terms of substance. (pp. vi–vii)

This idea enabled Gibson to take the first critical steps in the development of ecological psychology.

Molar Behaviorism and the Integrated Act

Holt's initial concern in "Response and Cognition" was how psychology can best progress as a science, and here his sympathies were explicitly with the newly emerging behaviorist program. Holt was in step with the positivist character of the functionalist-behaviorist position that was very much on the rise during the first two decades of the century. J. Watson's (1913) manifesto, "Psychology as the Behaviorist Views It," appeared just two years before Holt's "Response and Cognition."

Holt's ideas soon diverged in significant ways from this newly emerging, behaviorist starting point, however. He saw limitations in the focus adopted in most behaviorist accounts, with these limitations inhibiting theoretical and empirical progress. Holt noted two facets to this problem of restricted focus. First, he objected to the reductionistic strategy adopted by many behaviorists. He argued that behavior is a "coordinated totality" of the whole organism, which is not reducible to its components. Although behavior is unquestionably a product of a functioning nervous system, it is most appropriately studied holistically (i.e., at a molar rather than molecular level of analysis) because unique functional properties, not present at lower levels of functioning, only make their appearance at molar levels. This claim, which has Jamesian roots, alone distinguishes him from classical behaviorists of a Watsonian orientation. The conceptual grounds for this emergentist view were developed in *The Concept of Consciousness*, which was examined previously; and the promotion of a holistic orientation is clearly a point of commonality between the monograph and this earlier work.

Significantly, as already noted, this molar perspective was promoted most vigorously and effectively throughout the middle decades of the 20th century by one of Holt's students, Edward C. Tolman (1932). As evidence of Tolman's success in this regard, he is justifiably cited by commentators on the "cognitive revolution of the 1960's and 70's" as leading the way to an emphasis on the molar and purposive analysis that was to characterize much of the later cognitive approach. Indirectly, then, Holt too became an important influence in this vein, although he surely would not have felt comfortable with many of the ways in which this cognitive approach was ultimately expressed in theory and research.

Much of the difficulty Holt would have had with post-1960s cognitive psychology grows out of a second limitation that it shares with its behaviorist predecessors—and this criticism reveals the most original part of Holt's functional focus. The second limitation of most behaviorist accounts, as well as more contemporary cognitive approaches, is that they seek explanations of behavior in "immediate stimulus conditions." Or, stated inversely, they do not seek explanation of behavior beyond proximal stimulus conditions. Holt rejected the idea that behavior, by which he always meant complex integrated actions of an organism, is a function of stimulation on the periphery of the body, such as at the level of sensory receptors. He argued that when considering *integrated behavior*, "any correlation between it and the stimuli which are immediately affecting the organism becomes increasingly remote" (Holt, 1915a, p. 164). Behavior considered as a "coordinated totality" needs to be viewed as functionally related to some distant object or situation. This is his claim of "the recession of the stimulus," and it is examined in more detail in the next section. Before taking that up, a few metatheoretical comments are necessary.

With this molar and distal focus, Holt argued that explanation in psychology can take the same general form that it does in other natural sciences: namely, identifying lawful functional relations in the natural world. At the most basic level, psychological inquiry should begin with the question, "What is an organism doing?" From a functional perspective "a fairly *accurate description* of this activity will invariably reveal a law (or laws) whereby this activity is shown to be a constant function of some aspect of the objective world" (Holt, 1915a, p. 166). However, if one selects too molecular an analysis of behavior or too limited a focus of the relation between behavior and some feature of the environment or both, then a lawfully predictable, functional relation between the behavior and the environment will not be discernable.

Failing to adopt the appropriate level and breadth of analysis has significant theoretical consequences for psychological explanation. Characteristics of immediate, peripheral stimulation alone are not adequate in accounting for behavior above the level of organization of reflexes and molecular, physiological activity. Given this state of affairs, and in the absence of functional explanations linking behavior to distant environmental features, psychologists have often been led to account for complex behavior by positing unobservable mental phenomena that, at a minimum, mediate between environmental stimulation and behavior. Holt (1915a) concluded, "Is it any wonder that having ignored the *objective functional reference of behavior*, we are led into the superstition of 'ideas' in the 'sensorium' which have an 'objective reference' to the environment?" (p. 171) Theorists do not typically seek to discover the distal environmental referents of behavior "and to assuage this ignorance … fabricate a myth" (1915a, p. 93).

This argument is a further point of commonality between the monograph and Holt's earlier more philosophical writings. The philosophical *bete noir* for the New Realists was the representational theory of knowledge. Here Holt was indicating a *methodological reason* for the resilience of this problematic view. It arises from failing to look for lawful relations between molar behavior and distal, objective features of the environment. This argument had a profound impact on Gibson's theoretical writings and is one of the basic claims that drove his experimental work.

A second consequence of failing to adopt the appropriate level and breadth of analysis of behavior is an error of a different nature than that of positing unseen mental processes. In the absence of identified lawful relations between a distal, environmental referent and behavior, the goal-directed nature of integrated action can go unrecognized. In such cases, the precipitating cause of a response is seen to be some proximal event, such as peripheral stimulation or some preceding response, as in hypothesized response chains. Holt (1915a) referred to such accounts as "bead theories," comparing causal linkages to adjacent beads on a string. The result of this limited focus then is just the sort of *mechanistic* approach to psychological functioning that dominated psychology throughout the 20th century.

Holt (1915a) claimed that proximate explanations are sought because

> the often too materialistically-minded biologist is so fearful of meeting a certain bogy, the "psychic," that he hastens to analyze every case of behavior into its component reflexes without venturing first to observe it as a whole. In this way he fails to note the recession of the stimulus and the infallibly objective reference of behavior. (p. 78)

The approach Holt advocated restores the validity behind teleologically tinged accounts of behavior without including the echoes of vitalism that often accompany them, and which in turn would vitiate a naturalistic approach: "The whole truth of teleology is taken up, and rectified, in that objective reference which behavior as *function of an object* provides for" (Holt, 1915a, p. 203). Identifying this "infallibly objective reference to behavior" requires turning away from a search for proximate "causes," as the stimulus recedes into the complex network of preexisting structures that is the environment.

The Recession of the Stimulus

The call for a distal rather than proximal focus in an analysis of the environment and the individual needs to be examined in more detail. Consider an example Holt (1915a) offered:

> The man is walking past my window; no I am wrong, it is not past my window that he is walking; it is *to* the theater; or am I wrong again? Perhaps the man is

a journalist, and not the theater, nor yet the play, but the "society write-up" it is to which the creature's movements are adjusted. (p. 162)[13]

When asking the question, "What is the individual doing?," the answer will vary as a function of what we choose as the particular focus of the person's action; and clearly some choices provide more adequate answers than others. If the response is that the man is walking past the window, does this choice provide an explanation for these actions? Because it is unlikely that merely walking past the window is the goal of the action, with this limited view the focus of the action is not apparent. Alternatively, perhaps then the only way to specify the goal is to assume it is unobservable, that is, it is a goal state in the person's mind inaccessible to an observer. These two possibilities are the standard options seen to be available, and they both leave much to be desired for different, and obvious reasons.

However, if this unit of behavior is instead seen as part of a more comprehensive or integrated action, then the man can be viewed as walking past the window for some identifiable purpose. Accordingly, the action stands in a functional relation with a goal that can be objectively specified. In this example, the goal, in fact, is part of a configuration of social motives. The man is not just walking to the theater, or even going to watch a performance, but more comprehensively, he is in the process of preparing a "society write-up" for the newspaper. The reason for (or cause of) his actions is best understood if the appropriate grain of analysis is adopted. Moreover, note that the reason for his actions is best understood as a social psychological motive, indicating the need in some instances for an analysis of the environment from a sociocultural perspective (see chap. 9).

How can the appropriate focus or level of analysis be identified in any given instance? What complicates the answer to this question is that the level is not fixed, but shifts with changes in attention or awareness and with increasing integration of behavior and the corresponding environmental referent of that action. With increasingly integrated action, and concomitantly more comprehensive goals, the "stimulus" (i.e., that toward which action is directed) recedes. It becomes locatable at more distal and molar levels of the environment. Recognizing that the appropriate level of analysis shifts with attention and with the level of integration of action, in principle the relevant environmental referent, and thus the appropriate environment–individual functional relation, can be specified by identifying what the individual is doing in that instance of action. The appropriate level of analysis of the environment in any particular case will be the level that is functionally commensurate with the integrated behavior in question. Consider the following example from Holt (1915a):

---

[13] Holt, like his student Gibson, had an interest in the theater (Langfeld, 1946).

> When one first learned to walk, the process involved lively consciousness of pressure on the soles, and at different intensities of the two feet; of visible objects which one carefully watched in order to steady oneself, etc. etc. One now walks with head in the air and in almost total oblivion of the steadying visual objects ... now one *walks*, or perhaps not consciously even this; for one may consciously not be walking or running, but catching a train, thinking over a lecture, bracing oneself to do a sharp stroke of business. (pp. 186–187)

As responses become more complex with development and learning, instead of viewing this change as an elaboration of a sequence or chain of responses, Holt saw it as a process whereby earlier response patterns become integrated into successively more complex forms of behavior. Accompanying this integration of action is "a recession of the stimulus" toward which action is directed and to which it is lawfully and functionally related.

Molar Behaviorism and Selectivity

With his recognition of the changing functional relation between individual and environment as a shifting focus of attention or awareness, Holt was clearly adopting the Jamesian view that selectivity is the sine qua non of cognition. Bearing this in mind enriches the claim that cognition (and consciousness) is a functional relation between knower and object known. More precisely, it is a relation of an agent to an object. The terms *consciousness*, *attention*, and *awareness* do not refer to inner mental states; they all refer to the referential character of all psychological functions. Holt (1915a) proposed:

> In the view now before us, consciousness and "the subjective as such" are done away with. Consciousness is not a substance but a relation—the relation between the living organism and the environment to which it specifically responds; of which its behavior is found to be this or that constant function; or, in other words, to which its purposes refer. (p. 96)

In retaining consciousness or awareness in his account, Holt differed sharply from other behaviorists. Although Holt was very sympathetic to most of the aims of behaviorism, including making objectivity the criterion for determining what are to count as data in a science of psychology, he felt that the behaviorist program is "in danger of making the materialist's error, of denying *facts*, as well as the theory of consciousness" (p. 207). For Holt, as for James, consciousness, in the sense of awareness, was an undeniable fact of the knowing functions. In accusing behaviorists of making a "materialist's error," Holt was drawing a distinction between an objective and a reductionistic analysis—a distinction typically not made by some of his behaviorist contemporaries or by many later behaviorists. By the materialist's error, he meant the reduction of functional processes to component material states. With the reduction of complex, integrated actions to its components, functional properties of the organism–environment relation, such as agency and awareness, drop out of the analysis.

Consciousness has reappeared in the later decades of 20th-century contemporary psychological theory, but in ways that are rarely built on the sort of relational viewpoint that Holt and James proposed. Viewing consciousness as, for example, an emergent property of a complex brain is not enough, because it treats consciousness as a mental property as such, distinct from perceiving and thinking. Viewed in this way, its function is seen as highlighting certain contents of mind, thereby isolating them in the "footlights of consciousness." In this attempt at restoring an unavoidable quality of experience that had been excised by behaviorists who commit the error of materialism, consciousness or awareness becomes detached from cognitive functions, to be treated as a separate faculty apart from perceiving and thinking. With such usage, awareness becomes awareness per se, and as such it conjures up the "spirit" behaviorists rightly sought to exorcize.

Consciousness is better viewed in the first instance as a natural phenomenon that emerges with the complex environment–behavior relations accompanying the development of cognition. As such, awareness is not distinct from perceiving and thinking. It is the essential quality of these cognitive functions (Reed, 1996a). Perceiving and thinking are processes of selection. For Holt, in particular, perceiving is a process of selecting environmental referents for action; accordingly, what is perceived are those objects toward which action is directed, and "not some pale 're'presentations' thereof" (Holt, 1915a, p. 97). He continued, "That about which a man thinks is clearly ... numerically identical with that upon which his *actions turn*, and with that which, when he comes near enough, he *sees and handles*" (p. 97, emphases added). The perceiver is aware of the object directly, awareness is not some searchlight to be directed at one or another content of mind.

Reconsider a question raised earlier: Taking awareness as an intrinsic feature of the functional relationship between the environment and the behaving organism, how is it possible to determine what an individual is aware of? As a first pass at this question, the focus of awareness can be specified by determining what environmental referent the action is directed toward. "The attentive level at any particular moment is the most comprehensive field to which the organism is at that moment specifically responding (of which its behavior is a function)" (p. 188). Attention is reflected in the bracketing established in the functional relation between the environment and action.

Importantly, for Holt, attention is rooted in actions of the body. He wrote: "The most highly integrated behavior system that is in action determines the personal level of attention" (p. 188); as a result, shifts in attention are "nothing but this selected procession of environmental aspects to which the body's ever-varying motor adjustments are directed" (p. 189). Although this account of attention needs further elaboration, treating attention in this way helps to demystify it. By rooting attention in integrated action and anchoring it in an environmental object, Holt (unlike many of his fellow behaviorists) did not have "ontological" difficulties with notions such as consciousness, awareness, and attention. These terms refer to selective functions of a *knower in context*; and like James, the "knower" from a psychological perspective is identifiable with bodily processes. Holt pointed out, "Clearly this knower can be nothing but the body itself; for in [my version of] behaviorism, the body is aware, the body acts" (p. 174). This emphasis on the central role of the experience of the body in transaction between the knower and the object known plays an important role in the ecological account of perception developed by Gibson, although Gibson's approach differs markedly from Holt's in several respects.

One difference to be mentioned briefly here is that Holt was essentially offering a motor theory of consciousness; that is, attributing awareness to the functioning of behavior (e.g., muscle) systems. This idea was very much in the air early in the century, and it reflects some of Münsterberg's influence on Holt. Motor theorists attempted to offer a functional and materialist-linked explanation of consciousness without resorting to the kind of sensation-based view promoted by Wundt and Titchener.[14] Gibson (1967a) later commented on the elegance and sophistication of Holt's approach (p. 9), and even adopted it for a time, but ultimately abandoned it for an alternative based on exploration and adjustment (see chap. 3).

Finally, and more generally, Holt claimed that the approach he proposed can be eventually applied to all cognitive functions, not just perceiving. By beginning the analysis with the assumption that "a total situation comprising *both organism and environment* is always involved," an account of cognition results that will avoid some of the problems typically accompanying mentalistic explanations. He proposed, "I venture to predict that behaviorism will be able to give *a complete account of cognition* without invoking the services of the metaphysical subject nor any one of its swarming progeny of Ego's" (p. 177). Holt's prediction has yet to be realized. Although the language of psychology may have changed, the conceptual, if

---

[14] Münsterberg's position on consciousness clashed with that of his mentor Wundt, and instead, was more compatible with James's overall approach—a fact that contributed to his selection by James's to take over directorship of the Harvard laboratory (see Kuklick, 1977, pp. 187–189).

tacit, reliance on "inner mental states" continues. Perhaps with assimilation of ecological psychology into the mainstream, a relational theory of cognition will become a reality some day.

HOLT'S PSYCHOLOGY OF LEARNING AND DEVELOPMENT

Following his departure from Harvard in 1919, Holt published only a few reviews and commentaries. He was apparently occupied for the next decade with the preparation of the first volume in a planned two-volume work called *Animal Drive and the Learning Process: An Essay Toward Radical Empiricism*. This first volume appeared in 1931, and it was the only part of the larger project that was to be published. However, based on comments Holt made in the first volume about his plans, the general thrust of the second volume can be anticipated.

James Gibson was a student of Holt's during the later stages of the preparation of the first volume. Thus, the themes of this work were likely to have permeated Holt's teachings at this time and accordingly have been very familiar to Gibson. Indeed, much can be learned about the underpinnings of Gibson's later ecological theory from an examination of this now relatively obscure book.

In this work, Holt was as forcefully opposed to dualism as he was in his early writings, but he was no longer "neutral" concerning the "stuff" of the universe. What was only intimated in the "Response and Cognition" monograph was now very clearly expressed. Holt explicitly adopted here the "physicalistic" stance of a behaviorist, although in doing so he distinguished between physicalism and materialism, as becomes evident shortly.

A psychology based on a physicalistic orientation is largely physiological, and indeed, most of this volume is a physiological analysis of behavioral development and learning. This characteristic of the book makes it a significant departure from the earlier writings. It appears that Holt set out to write a book decidedly unlike anything else he had written, perhaps to defy a view that he was only familiar with the theoretical and philosophical, perhaps to distance himself from philosophical squabbles with other New Realists and with their successors the Critical Realists.[15] In this vein, what is surprising at first glance about this book, given the nature of his earlier work, is the apparent absence of philosophical considerations. Apart from an essay by the philosopher H.C. Brown (1931) on materialism, which is appended to the body of the book, Holt engaged in little philosophical analysis.

---

[15] For a discussion of some of these differences, see Harlow (1931), Kuklick (1977), Lovejoy (1930), Montague (1937/1960), and pertinent readings in Chisholm (1960).

However, *Animal Drive and the Learning Process* is not as much of a departure from earlier themes as it first appears. In a sense, Holt was making good on a long-standing promissory note. What he tried to accomplish with this book was the provision of the biological, developmental, and functional foundations for the molar behaviorism that he had been advocating since the appearance of "Response and Cognition." As such, he viewed this work as an extension of James's project of radical empiricism. In the preface, he was very clear about his intentions for this work:

> William James did not live to apply his doctrine of Radical Empiricism in a detailed way to the problems of psychology. We shall never know just what picture he would have given us. We do, however, know that the ghost-soul of metaphysical dualism would have been completely eliminated. The following essay on Animal Drive is an effort to carry on in the spirit, at least, of Radical Empiricism. (p. vi)

In this vein, Holt asserted that James would have agreed with the claim that "conscious phenomena are to be explained entirely, without reserve or residue, in *physical* terms, and specially of course in terms of physiology" (p. v). These comments indicate that although the book is, in part, a physiological treatise, it has broader philosophical goals. Holt promised in this preface to address philosophical issues explicitly in the second volume of this book. But, the second volume never appeared.

The Reflex-Circle and the Adient Response

From the prefatory comments to this first volume alone, it is clear that Holt's physicalism is not straightforward, because there he distinguished between a physicalistic account and a materialistic account: "As at the outset we are brought face to face with the question, whether a 'radically' empirical and physiological theory is necessarily 'materialistic.'" These considerations will lead "at a later point" (i.e., vol. 2) to an examination of "the very categories, 'mind,' 'matter,' and 'reality,' as psychological phenomena" (p. vii).

The physiological approach he adopted broadly follows along the lines of the more well-known work of Sherrington (1906) and later of Goldstein (1934/1995), which emphasize organized and integrated actions of biologically complex systems. From this holistic perspective, primary interest is in functional properties unique to complex living systems—properties that are absent when the focus is directed solely toward lower level material processes. That is to say, Holt's goal was not to transmute the properties of complex living systems into a set of simpler, fundamental processes, but instead he sought to understand their complexity as such.

The theme of irreducible properties at higher orders of complexity can be traced throughout Holt's writings to his first book, *The Concept of Consciousness*. Twenty years later, he was attempting to offer a physiological account of psychological functioning at a degree of complexity that preserves the functional properties of living systems. On these grounds, Holt claimed that his system, although physicalistic, was not materialistic.[16]

Holt was seeking a physiologically grounded and, at the same time, a psychologically adequate account of behavior. In proceeding toward this goal, he wanted to avoid the "verbal magic" of mentalists, where unreal mental states are suggested by terms that in fact have no tangible referents. In addition, he wanted to avoid the "exorcism by verbal denial" of psychological phenomena that is engaged in by many behaviorists. His goal was "to present the outline of a nonfaculty psychology in terms wholly of physical and physiological [i.e., natural] processes" that can account for psychological phenomena. He continued: "For I am convinced that these are the only terms in which we can find the solution of any of our psychological problems" (p. 7).

Holt's analysis began with a discussion of organismic development, reflective of his behavioristic inclinations. As for his developmental perspective, he was critical of any account examining development solely as a maturational process—that is, as a process of unfolding from some intrinsic potential. Such a view struck him as "finalistic" or teleological, pointing to some unseen cause. Instead, he argued that developing organismic processes require the *co-presence* of supportive external conditions. The pattern of development manifested is an expression of organismic processes in conjunction with particular external influences. In other words, development at every point is an interactive process, and its lawful nature can be described as a functional relation between behavior and environment. This claim, of course, applied to behavior generally, is the central theme of "Response and Cognition."

---

[16] At first glance, Holt's advocacy of physicalism, but not materialism, seems to run counter to my support of materialism, but not physicalism (see Introduction). The differences, however, are solely terminological, not substantive; but these terminological differences are a possible source of confusion. By physicalism, I (but not Holt) mean reductive tendencies and, especially, the application of *physical concepts* in attempts to understand psychological processes. By materialism, I mean the common "stuff" of which all natural entities are composed, and as advances have been made in physics research, the notion of matter today surely offers a greater range of possible conceptualizations than in Holt's day. His embrace of physicalism is support for a naturalistic attitude toward all psychological phenomena, whereas his negative stance toward materialism most certainly is based on wanting to avoid suggesting a matter–mind distinction and his opposition to reductionism. I suppose I could minimize the possible confusion here by adopting Holt's usage, but the connotation of physical as in traditional concepts employed by the physical sciences (versus the life sciences), justifies the change.

The contribution on the side of the organism to development and learning is *activity*, and what the environment contributes, put in the simplest of terms, is *resistance*. An active organism encounters obstacles, for example, barriers to movement, and these encounters are felt; they are stimuli. That is, the organism encounters stimuli through action; stimuli are not imposed on a passive organism.

A primary motive of the organism is "to get more of the eliciting stimulus" (p. 40)—assuming for the moment that the obstacle is neither too intense nor otherwise noxious. These behaviors are characterized by a tendency to "go out to meet the stimulus, get more of it, repeat or reproduce the stimulation" (p. 41). As a result, the initial movement is perpetuated ("a circular reflex"), moving against the stimulating effects of an environmental resistance. Importantly, for a behavior to move against a particular source of stimulation adequately that action must take into account properties of the particular source. Consequently, this pattern of behavior, what Holt called "the reflex-circle," eventuates in behavior that is both purposive and structured in relation to the object: "The 'reflex-circle' always starts with an aimless, chance innervation of muscle, but ends with a reflex established which is always *a response that intelligibly refers to the stimulus*, and one that is often distinctly 'purposive'" (p. 40, emphasis added).

Here Holt wanted to be understood as describing the essential psychological attribute of complex living organisms throughout their life span: "For it is observable that the fundamental character of the normal organism, both in infancy and in adult life, is an out-reaching, outgoing, inquiring, examining, and grasping one" (p. 41). The imprint of this behavioral approach, which at its core recognizes the active, *exploring* organism, can be seen in Gibson's later conceptualization of perceptual systems.

The term that Holt used to describe this fundamental behavioral attribute of out-reaching is "adience." An adient response is one "which gives the organism *more* of the stimulus" (p. 41, footnote). In understanding Holt's conception of adience, it is important to note that for him responses are *patterns* of action. That is, he was emphasizing the integrated nature of responses. In most instances, a single reflex-arc that results in micro-movement is artifactual.[17]

Consider an example of a primitive adient response: postural tonus with respect to gravitation. The downward pull of gravitation is an unremitting force in the environment. Organisms actively respond

---

[17] Merleau-Ponty (1942/1963) made the same claim about reflexes in his book *The Structure of Behavior*. There are striking parallels between Merleau-Ponty's work, especially in perception (Merleau-Ponty, 1962), and Gibson's later theory (see Glotzbach & Heft, 1982).

against this resistance and in so doing maintain continual stimulation from this pervasive source. Thus, with experience, organisms develop complex, coordinated movements that maintain an upright posture by, in effect, moving toward or against this source of stimulation. This basic, but hardly simple case, shows how an integrated response of an organism refers to the stimulus. Indeed, here as in other cases, the development of integrated action requires an environmental referent. Behavior– environment relations are synergic. According to Holt (1931), "It is not to be wondered at that integration cannot be found by looking merely within the organism, for it is always *a progressive negotiation between the organism and its environment*" (p. 217, emphasis added).

This universal tendency toward adience is the basis for a lifelong process of "education of sensory surfaces" of the entire organism—from the proprioceptive receptors in the muscles and joints to the "teleceptors, reacting to distance stimuli, such as the eye, the ear, and the nose" (p. 62). Over time through the synergic relations of environment and behavior, actions are transformed from gross, unpatterned motions "into motions that more and more definitely and more and more discriminatingly respond to particular features of the world about it" (p. 73). Psychological development is a process of the narrowing down and refining of action with reference to specific environmental features.

The Locus of Freedom

The first step in the integration of an organism's behavior, then, is establishing an external referent. With ongoing interaction, more extensive functional integration in activities develop, and in turn there is a "recession" of the environmental referent—and so on in an ongoing cycle of integration of action and differentiation of environmental structures.

Two features of this ongoing integrative process need to be stressed. First, as already noted, the increasing integration results in a sharpening of actions. Second, this sharpening or differentiation of actions is with reference to increasingly precise or differentiated environmental features. Here is an extension of the notion of adience. By responding adiently (i.e., to seek more stimulation) with reference to increasingly specific stimuli, the range of responses becomes narrowed and fine-tuned. This relation establishes a locus of freedom for the action.

This locus, or range, of activity provides constraints, "being that which makes for the unity and integration in the behavior of the organism" (p. 217). At the same time, within this range of activities that refer to aspects of the environment, "random movement still has the freedom to play." That is, the locus of freedom allows for exploration within relationally established constraints. These constraints contribute a purposiveness in the context of exploration:

> Every response ... defines a residual locus of freedom; every additional response that is simultaneously in force makes the action more definite and precise, and by just so much narrows down the residual locus of freedom. Within this ever narrowing locus, random activity can still play. (p. 221)

And this account of "random movements with the locus set by one or more sustained adiences, gives us the very pattern (indeed the definition) of all 'exploration'" (p. 216).

The notion of freedom of action within constraints is important for understanding the functionally dynamic character of all psychological processes. At the level of the individual, it makes systematic and yet spontaneous exploration intelligible. If the discovery of structure is left to purely random activity, the prospects of uncovering structure related to what is already known becomes a hit or miss affair. However, if no room is provided for spontaneous action, then the possibility of discovery is foreclosed. The locus of freedom for complex, integrated behaviors becomes a way of reconciling these two apparently competing tendencies. Chapter 8 returns to this perspective in an attempt to understand how settings can be understood as constraining behavior within group situations, while simultaneously creating possibilities for individual growth and discovery.

The integration of actions is not to be conceived as a single unified response, but rather as an order or structure resulting from the confluence of numerous interacting responses. The action is multifaceted, and it takes the particular form it does because it is "a compromise ... between many simultaneously stimulated but more or less conflicting responses." Significantly, no factor operating solely on the side of the organism contributes to the integration of responses "to lessen in any systematic way the occurrence of tensions and conflicts." Instead, the *functional relation* established between environmental referent and action that is the locus of freedom, "which is defined [relationally] by many simultaneously sustained responses, [is] a principle which makes for integrated action" (p. 262).[18]

The concept of locus of freedom, then, is an elaboration of the framework Holt developed in "Response and Cognition." Integrated, complex actions are viewed in terms of a direct functional relation with environmental referents. Because investigators have failed in many cases to

---

[18] Holt argued that this principle sheds considerable light on the topic of personality. He noted the observations of Morton Prince (incidentally, to whom this book is dedicated) who stated: "Personality ... is many sided, one side being manifested in one situation, another in another and so on. Thus apparently, a person in actual life exhibits contradictory traits, but it is the situations that are responsible for the seeming paradox" (Holt, 1931, p. 263).

ask "what is the organism doing?", the appropriate level of complexity in action and its concomitant environmental reference are not often identified.

Holt believed that he provided the conceptual foundations for an account of how cognition derives naturally from the "physiological learning process" without introducing "any 'psychic' principle ... as a *deus ex machina* in explaining mental phenomena" (p. 256). When the relations between an organism and the environment are considered at a level of complexity that takes into consideration the whole organism, new functional properties emerge. Holt reasoned:

> If from our strictly physiological start we do come upon mental phenomena, or perchance the general mechanism of mind, it will be because we have reached a new "emergent level" ... that is, because nerves and muscles when organized in a more complex unity necessarily give rise to a new phenomenon which not at all resembles nerves and muscles. (p. 256)

Nothing new has been added ontically—this remains a thorough-going "physicalistic" or naturalistic framework. Instead, there is a transformation of the existing processes at a new level of organization—the kind of *transformation of function* that can be found throughout the natural realm. [The supplemental essay by H. C. Brown (1931) in the book provides extended support for this claim.] Moreover, it is a transformation of organismic processes in context, not just a transformation of the organism per se. Whatever physiological changes have occurred to support these advanced cognitive processes, their psychological qualities can only be manifested in relation to setting conditions.

One final feature of Holt's analysis needs to be added. Coupled to the initial question, "What is the organism doing?" is "With respect to what feature in the environment is action directed?" An answer to the latter question can sometimes be guided by phenomenological considerations. This point is most apparent when examining changes in the functional relations between environmental features and action. Consider the following example: Holt described an occasion when he found himself locked out of a friend's house where he was staying. The windows of the house initially went unnoticed; but after discovering that he was locked out, "my adience toward the interior of the house, although blocked as overt action, was still in force as tonus and posture; and ... the windows *taken as* holes, orifices of ingress, excited reflexes which ... were in motor harmony (synergy) with my adient set to the interior of the house" (p. 245). The relation between the environment and action changed, and that change is reflected in shift of awareness. The "motor set" picks out a feature toward which it can be directed, and reciprocally, a feature identified for its action potential establishes a behavioral tendency in the individual. This is a response "circle" rather than a unidirectional cause; and cognition and awareness are functional characteristics of the relation that is established between environment and action.

This passage and others in the book illustrate that Holt was inclined toward a motor theory of consciousness wherein conscious awareness is linked to actions of the body. As mentioned earlier, Gibson ultimately rejected this view, seeking instead to tie awareness to the pick up of information while retaining the reciprocal character of Holt's framework (see chap. 5). Quite apart from the matter of conceptualizing awareness, however, this example illustrates how Holt would sometimes utilize phenomenological description to reveal the nature of changing functional relations between person and environment. This is a quality that is used effectively by both James and Gibson as well (chap. 4), and points to a way phenomenological description can be employed in the service of psychological analysis.

In sum, the framework that Holt offered is physicalistic and yet holistic; nondualistic and yet psychological and phenomenological; purposive and yet nonteleological. It is a view that stresses the activity of organisms in relation to environmental opportunities and constraints. It is a dynamic framework that describes psychological functioning as a process whereby individuals stay in touch with and thereby learn more about properties of the environment.

Toward a Psychology of Cognition

From some brief comments in *Animal Drive and the Learning Process*, it seems clear that in the planned second volume Holt wanted to explore the theoretical implications of this account of "physiological learning" for a psychology of cognition. He intended to do this by elaborating many of the themes developed in "Response and Cognition." At the conclusion of Volume 1, he stated: "From the point where we now stand it is but one short step to a definition of awareness and consciousness in terms of physiological process; and it is a step which I previously outlined (1915, pp. 153–203)" (Holt, 1931, p. 263). This reference is the entire "Response and Cognition" essay. Further indication of this future direction is revealed in the following comment: "The principle of locus of freedom narrowed and made precise through the simultaneous action of so many responses throws more light on the mental life, and the so-called 'field of consciousness' than any other *single* principle that I know of" (p. 219). Holt added in a footnote that this claim corresponds to what he elsewhere "somewhat loosely called 'the recession of the stimulus.'" The footnote continued: "The reader will perhaps perceive that we have here, *in part*, the physiological basis of 'abstract' thinking" (p. 219).

The psychology of cognition that he envisioned (and hence the form volume 2 might have taken) can be dimly made out from these comments. It is likely that Holt's psychology of cognition would have been a framework built along the lines of James's distinction between percepts and concepts (chap. 1), as Holt already began to do in *The Concept of Consciousness*. At all times, cognition is to be seen as growing out of a concrete situation comprised of the relations between the knower and the object known. The varieties of cognition (e.g., perceiving, remembering, imagining) refer to functional relations that are possible in conjunction with referents laying along a dimension between the objective and subjective poles of experience. Holt's idea of the recession of the stimulus, initially presented in "Response and Cognition," may be applied here, whereby actions of the knower become increasingly fine-tuned in relation to environmental features both increasingly differentiated and increasingly "remote." Extending this idea, it might be supposed that at some point in development (and phylogeny), the organism acquires the capacity to select as a referent for action a feature already abstracted from the perceptual field on prior encounters. Action with this abstracted feature (a "concept" in James's sense) as its referent can come to manifest a "functional autonomy," and in so doing it can extend the individual's cognitive possibilities. With contextual support, the individual can reflect on present events (thinking) and past occurrences (remembering) and to project future possibilities (imagining).

It bears repeating that in all such cases, like the case of perceiving, cognition is a *functional relation* between action and referent. By employing "the principle of recession of the stimulus" in a more abstract fashion than heretofore, this relation can be seen as being "transformed" into different functional possibilities.

Finally, because experience is ongoing, it is the case that perceiving, thinking, remembering, and imagining are all happening "now," that is, they are events presently occurring. In the case of "remembering," the event experienced now is "known" to have happened at an earlier time, and in "imagining," the event experienced now has yet to happen. Borrowing the imagery of Holt's (1914/1973) first book, ongoing experience transects a temporal knowledge system in such cases.

These speculations about the direction that Volume 2 might have taken with respect to cognition are merely an extension of James's discussion of percepts and concepts from the perspective of Holt's molar behaviorism. No doubt these ideas would have been developed in much richer detail and taken in some unforeseeable directions in the second volume of *Animal Drive and the Learning Process*.

A RETURN TO A PHILOSOPHICAL PSYCHOLOGY

Holt's last published writings do not shed any further light on the direction that his thinking about cognition might have taken. The "Response and Cognition" (1915b, 1915c) essays stand as the best published indication of his thoughts in this vein. In his final essays, Holt returned to a more philosophical style of analysis, elaborating some of the themes central to his earlier work and tying up some loose ends.

In "The Argument for Sensationism as Drawn from Dr. Berkeley," Holt (1934) appeared to be targeting the Critical Realists whose writings overshadowed the work of the New Realists in the American philosophical community. This work reviewed the epistemological debate concerning the question of how one can know about the world itself if "the mind 'knows' *only* its own sensations" (p. 509). This problem was central for the New Realists 20 years earlier, and it was a source of contention between them and the Critical Realists, who regressively (from a New Realist standpoint, at least) reintroduced the claim that what is known immediately are objects in consciousness (also see fn 12). In this essay, Holt critically examined the logic of Berkeley's and Hume's discussion of representationalism and found it wanting (see Holt, 1934, pp. 514–515). More polemically, he accused philosophers who support such a position as having an "aversion to reality." As James did in his radical empiricist approach, Holt pointed out that, unlike the representationalists' analysis, his approach rests on an assumption that objects of experience "are *not* a 'mere' heap, flux, collection, congeries, or kaleidoscope." Instead, "the elements composing the [phenomenal object] ... present a stable organization in phenomenal space and phenomenal time" (p. 518). Moreover, Holt emphasized, as he did in his previous book, that in the end knowing processes are real, bodily actions of an animal. Arguing for a motor theory of consciousness, he claimed that "movements point to the objects. ... And what the organism so does is its consciousness, its mind" (Holt, 1934, p. 523).

In his final publication, "Materialism and the criterion of the psychic" (1937), Holt recapitulated his "philosophical behaviorism." His goal for psychology was to be able to explain in thoroughly physical (natural) terms the distinctive characteristics of psychological phenomena. In this vein, Holt argued that the psychic is ultimately referable to bodily processes: "If we can open our eyes to obvious facts we shall see that the only knower, the only active self that there is, is the physical body simply; that and nothing else" (p. 38). Perceiving, thinking, and knowing are bodily activities; and asserting his motor theory of awareness, he posited that neuromuscular functioning of the body "creates the mental contents and governs in every respect what they shall be and in what succession they shall flow" (p. 41).

Perceiving, thinking, and imagining are not happenings in some nonmaterial realm. Rather, these functions are just some of the things that the body of a complex biological organism does. To say "I think" refers to a complex bodily process in the same way that "when I say that 'I digest my food well,'" what is being referred to is a different, if simpler, kind of biological process of the physical body. In neither instance is it the case that "any spiritual inner being is implied" (p. 49). Also, to extend the analogy, digesting is an action of the body on some other structures. Digesting is a functional relation, and in the absence of digestibles, it is an unrealized potential function. Likewise, cognitive functions are potential activities of an animal in relation to other structures. Holt's final prescription for psychology is to study "the sensorimotor activities of a living organism in a concrete situation" (p. 50). "The knower," he continued, "is a concrete material body in a concrete material environment, and the cognitive relation exists between the two" (p. 51).

Looking back over Holt's writings, there is much continuity. His early psychological writings, excluding his initial experimental work on vision, were largely theoretical in style. As he recognized the static nature of his initial system presented in *The Concept of Consciousness*, he came to look at the organism in a more dynamic way, and this emphasis led to a molar functionalism built on a detailed empirical analysis of behavior and development. Lest this biological emphasis seem like a movement away from his initial philosophical and theoretical concerns, these final articles show a closing of the circle as he returns to the philosophical questions that he explored earlier in his career.

A FORGOTTEN PSYCHOLOGIST OF "THE OLD DAYS"

Although Holt's intellectual interests persisted throughout his career, his productivity diminished in step with his waning enthusiasm for academia. Some insight into his later attitudes toward academia and toward institutions and social structures generally can be gleaned from his late and acerbic essay, "The Whimsical Condition of Social Psychology, and of Mankind" (1935). Holt taught social psychology for many years while at Princeton, and this essay provides the only glimpse available into his social psychological orientation, although for reasons to be mentioned, his views in this essay were likely more politically conservative than those he held at Princeton in the late 1920s. Finally, this essay offered a clearer sense of his personality toward career's end than any of his later publications.

Holt was blunt in his criticism of the field of social psychology. He accused social psychologists of a "mental blindness" toward the one underlying fact of all social behavior: namely, that "man, no less than every other living creature, is always and inevitably self-interested, ego-centric" (p. 173). Holt viewed this claim as an obvious extension of his concept of adience: "Adience, in short, is the physiological term and egotism, selfishness, self-interest are the behavioristic terms for one and the same thing" (p.186).[19]

Because this is the primary social motivation of humans, Holt cautioned the reader to be wary of ideologies and the leaders who promote them. In truth, leaders are intent on pursuing self-interest, often to the detriment of the masses. He saw this problem as especially acute at the time this essay was written in the early 1930s. ("We are well within the penumbra of a new Darkness.") He specifically expressed his concern about the mounting armaments in Western countries and directed much pointed criticism toward communist Russia. He urged us to recognize our essentially self-interested motives and then work toward the development of a society in which we can "pursue a wiser, more far-sighted self-interest" (p. 202). This latter prescription is one of the few bright moments in an otherwise gloomy assessment of the human condition.

Although it is true that this analysis could be seen as one possible extension of adience, it is not logically necessary that it be the only one. Social actions motivated by self-interest are not the only possible social transformation of the adient response tendency of perceivers to "go out to meet the stimulus [and] get more of it" (Holt, 1931, p. 41). Indeed, it would appear to be an excessively narrow consideration of the range of "interests" that his mentor, William James, claimed directed selectivity in cognition and action, and a movement away from James's pluralistic outlook.

Moreover, it is not entirely consistent with the picture of Holt's social psychology presented in Gibson's notes. Reed (1988, chap. 4) pointed out that Gibson and his fellow graduate students pursued Holt's suggestion that actions of the group not only can constrain individual action, but sometimes can enhance it. This latter possibility is not reflected at all in the Hobbesian tone of Holt's late essay. It is probably the case that the cynicism projected in this essay is attributable, at least in part, to the accumulation of frustrating circumstances of Holt's life up to that time. He remained estranged from mainstream academic psychology throughout this latter portion of his career, and due in part to intolerant social attitudes, he continued to live his personal life in a relative isolation. Moreover, at the

---

[19] Following this sentence, Holt wrote: "It may seem on first thought, for instance, that scientific curiosity is a very different thing from the lust for power; but it seems not so different to the animals that are mutilated and destroyed in research laboratories. They know only too well that scientific curiosity is an instance of the lust for power" (Holt, 1935, p. 186). These comments sustain the concerns expressed in his 1919 letter of resignation from Harvard cited earlier in this chapter.

time this essay was written, the United States was in the depths of the Depression, and visible on the horizon was the sociopolitical turmoil in Europe and the military buildup worldwide that would eventuate in World War II.[20] These contextual factors, in combination with his theoretical stance, rather than the latter considered alone, may account for much of the essay's embittered tone.

Assessing the lasting impact of Holt's scholarly work, Kuklick (1977) offered a fairly negative assessment, which he attributed at least in part to Holt's critical attitude toward the academic establishment:

> When he died in 1946 the academic establishment had its revenge. Remembered as one of the most respected psychologists of "the old days," Holt received a few tributes and was forgotten—only a few students and no institution remained to keep his work alive. (p. 433)

Kuklick was correct. Holt indeed was largely forgotten. But in view of the fact that Edward C. Tolman and James J. Gibson were among these "few students" who kept his work alive through their own writings, how truly successful the "revenge" of the academic establishment was is in need of reevaluation.

---

[20] In his generally critical biographical sketch of Holt (see fn 6), Hilgard (1987) attributed his political conservatism to a fear of losing inherited finances during the Depression years.

II

The Ecological Approach
and Radical Empiricism

Prologue: Three Generations of Psychologists

Typically when confronting Gibson's ecological approach for the first time, it is difficult to place it in a familiar theoretical framework. As discussed in the Introduction, the ecological approach appears to be an outlier, being located on the fringe of the theoretical traditions most recognizable to contemporary experimental psychologists.

As a corrective to this situation, the overriding goal of Parts I and II of this book is to show the ways in which some of the core assumptions and central features of Gibson's ecological approach are embedded in an established philosophical theory—William James's radical empiricism. The problem is that this theory is relatively unknown to most contemporary psychologists despite James's prominence in the field. Part I presented the primary features of James's radical empiricism, as well as extensions and modifications of it in the philosophical behaviorism of his student and Gibson's mentor, E. B. Holt, who most certainly introduced James's ideas to Gibson. Here in Part II, the focus shifts to the ecological approach and its relation to these two theoretical antecedents. The next three chapters interweave a presentation of the primary features of Gibson's ecological approach with the work of James and Holt just examined. The main purpose in doing so is to explicate the interrelations that exist among them. For the reader somewhat new to this ecological approach, these chapters introduce the ecological approach in the context of some of its historical roots. For readers already familiar with Gibson's approach, these chapters clarify some of its primary theoretical foundations and commitments.

A second goal of the following three chapters is to show ways in which aspects of Gibson's ecological approach can further James's philosophical program. In developing radical empiricism, James ran up against several problems that seemingly forced him to alter his initial hopes for this philosophical approach. Some of the concepts that Gibson developed, which themselves are partial outgrowths of James's thinking, can be utilized to realize the initial intent of radical empiricism. Whereas the specific issues in question here may be of greatest relevance to readers interested in James's work, more generally the discussion serves as further evidence of the interconnections between radical empiricism and ecological psychology.

So much for overall goals. To be more specific, chapter 3 adopts a broader focus than the others by examining the perspective shared by James, Holt, and Gibson concerning the relation between the individual and the environment. Chapter 4 examines in detail a defining feature of both James's and Gibson's position, namely, that *relations* are an intrinsic property of psychological experience and of the stimulus information for perceiving, respectively. Chapter 5 addresses another shared feature of James's thought and Gibson's framework: the central position given to the temporal character of psychological experience. These discussions demonstrate the deep relations among these programs, and they show that a continuing dialogue between these programs will serve to enrich each of them.

Before proceeding, however, a few qualifications are in order. First, clearly James and Holt were not the only influences on Gibson's work. A more complete picture should also consider the influence of sensory psychophysics, Gestalt psychology, experimental phenomenology, and comparative analyses of sensory systems (see Reed, 1988). Some of these influences are taken up in Part III. These other influences notwithstanding, most fundamental—and indeed what prepares Gibson's receptivity to several of these other influences—is his formative exposure to the perspectives of James and Holt.

Second, it is important to recognize that the functionalist and pragmatist perspective initiated in large measure by James was very much in the air during the years that Gibson was a student (Diggins, 1994; White, 1947). To a large extent, this orientation among American psychologists and philosophers can be attributed to James's influential writings, as well as those of Dewey, Mead, and others. In any case, besides whatever direct influence James's thought might have had on Gibson, these ideas were also a significant feature of the intellectual atmosphere of the 1920s and 1930s. Gibson was certainly influenced as much by this general climate of ideas as he was by the particulars of James's position.

One indication of this more pervasive influence on Gibson's thought is revealed by the manner in which he identified himself in psychology. He described himself as "a behaviorist."[1] He was a member of a generation of psychologists who rejected mentalism of any kind and embraced the goal of establishing predictable functional relations between environmental

---

[1]Gibson indicated this to me when I first met him in fall 1975. After asking me "what kind of psychologist" I was (fortunately I cannot remember the incoherent answer I must have given at the time), he informed me to my surprise that he was a behaviorist. I subsequently came to understand what he meant.

conditions and behavior. Almost all forward thinking experimental psychologists during the first three decades of the century were behaviorists in this general sense. At the same time, there were diverging lines of thought within the behaviorist camp. Gibson's affiliations were with the molar and purposive behaviorism of Holt and Tolman, which had its roots in James's writings, rather than the reductionistic and mechanistic behaviorism of Watson, Pavlov, and Hull, which derived from trends at the time to subsume the functional properties of complex biological systems under classical physics.

James J. Gibson, 1960s
(Division of Rare and Manuscripts Collections,
Cornell University Library)

3

Perceiver–Environment Relations

It is amazing how hard it is to get back to the idea that we do, after all, normally perceive what is out there, not something "in here." (H. Putnam, 1990)

James Gibson's (1904–1979) views on perception, and knowing generally, slowly evolved over several decades, with a notable shift in his thinking occurring about midcareer following the publication of *The Perception of the Visual World* (1950a). Although the influence of William James's radical empiricism can be seen throughout Gibson's career, it was with this shift, when Gibson began to formulate his ecological approach, that his ideas and those of James most clearly converged. For this reason, the discussion begins from the perspective of Gibson's mature system, the ecological approach, with aspects of his earlier views considered in due course.

ANIMAL–ENVIRONMENT MUTUALITY AND LEVELS OF ANALYSIS

Psychological Functioning as a Relational Process

J. J. Gibson's *The Ecological Approach to Visual Perception* (1979) begins with the presentation of an ecological perspective. Essential to this perspective are two claims: that the relation between the animal and the environment is best characterized as a mutuality and a reciprocity, and ecological phenomena are to be found at an intermediate range of scale and duration.

To take each of these assumptions in turn, the recognition of *mutual relations* between the animal and environment stands in contrast to

109

standard accounts that draw a sharp distinction between the physical environment, on the one hand, and psychological processes (variously conceptualized), on the other. With such a bifurcation, the properties of the environment and the properties of the animal can be defined independently of one another, and the causal influences typically flow from the environment to the animal. The environment can be described physically as a realm of swarming molecules, intersecting rays of electromagnetic energy, a sea of diffusing chemicals, or what have you. The animal can be viewed as a complex biological mechanism through which course electrochemical events.

From the point of view of neurophysiology (i.e., from a *physical-physiological level of analysis*), some properties of an animal can readily be considered independently from the larger environment in which the organism is presently situated. For example, the operation of neurotransmitters and enzymes in the synaptic cleft can be examined regardless of whether the environment beyond the skin of the animal is its natural habitat or the controlled conditions of a scientific laboratory. However, functional properties of animals considered as integrated organisms cannot be so understood.

At a *functional level of analysis*, animal and environment "make an inseparable pair. Each implies the other" (J. J. Gibson, 1979, p. 8). Consider, for example, the acts of reaching and of grasping. Whereas it is possible to talk abstractly about reaching and grasping as pure acts, independent of an environmental referent, in fact their *psychological expression* is always based on the co-influence of bodily and environmental properties. Reaching and grasping have referents. An individual does not reach per se, but reaches toward something; and, importantly, the biomechanics of reaching vary as the relative location of the object to the body changes. In the same fashion, although it is possible to talk abstractly about the act of grasping, the expression of grasping is structured in part by the properties of the object about to be grasped. The biomechanics of grasping are co-determined by bodily processes and object properties, such as size, shape, and texture. In short, the neat separation that can be drawn between environment and animal at a physical/physiological level of analysis is not present at an ecological/psychological level of analysis. Psychological processes are relational processes (Heft, 1980, 1989). Said differently, in the domain of perceiving and acting, the psychological encompasses both organism and environment.

J. J. Gibson (1979) explained the difference between a physicalistic view and an ecological view in the following way:

> The mutuality of animal and environment is not implied by physics and the physical sciences. The basic concepts of space, time, matter, and energy do not lead naturally to the organism–environment concept or to the concept of a

species and its habitat. Instead, they seem to lead to the idea of an animal as an extremely complex object of the physical world. The animal is thought of as a highly organized part of the physical world but still a part and still an object. This way of thinking neglects the fact that the animal-object is surrounded in a special way, that an environment is ambient for a living object in a different way from the way that a set of objects is ambient for a physical object. (p. 8)

This "different way" in which the environment surrounds an animal will be exemplified in a later consideration of ecological optics (chap. 4). It becomes more clear at this point that there is a dynamic relation—a *reciprocity*—between the animal and its environment considered from an ecological/psychological perspective. This dynamic quality is revealed in different ways. For one thing, an animal seeks out or adjusts to present features of the environment; and, in many instances, the animal alters the environment to better fit with its aims. Either way, actions are structured by environmental properties, either present or anticipated; and those actions in turn often affect the character of the environment. These dynamic reciprocities are not typically considerations when the animal is viewed solely as a part of a physical world.

A further difference between physical and psychological phenomena is their *scale* (J. J. Gibson, 1979, chap. 1). A physicalistic framework operates at the extremes of size, from atomic and subatomic analysis, on the one hand, to cosmic analysis, on the other. The psychological level operates at an intermediate range of size, at a scale comparable to an organism considered holistically and purposively.[1] A description of the environment commensurate with this level of analysis is an *ecological description*. This chapter and the next look more closely at this level of analysis.

Differences in scale between the physical and the ecological/psychological domains can also be drawn concerning duration of events. Considered within a physical framework, events can transpire in microseconds, at one extreme, and a scale of billions of years at the other.[2] The ecological scale of events is commensurate with the living activities of animals considered as whole organisms. The duration of naturally occurring events (e.g., a diurnal cycle) should not be confused with time. The latter refers to artificial systems constructed by humans for parceling

---

[1] A more detailed discussion of the notion of levels of analysis is presented in chapter 7.

[2] In his novel book *Continental Drift*, Banks (1985) reflected on these different scales of duration:

> The metabolic rate of history is too fast for us to observe it. It's as if, attending to the day-long life cycle of a single mayfly, we lose sight of the species and its fate. At the same time, the metabolic rate of geology is too slow for us to perceive it, so that, from birth to death, it seems to us who are caught in the beat of our own individual human hearts that everything happening on this planet is what happens to us, personally, privately, secretly. (p. 42)

up the passage of events into units of seconds, minutes, days, weeks, and so on. Events and temporal structure are explored further in chapter 5.

The Psychological–Physical Distinction in Radical Empiricism

Holt's Metaphysical Hierarchy. Distinguishing between the physical and the psychological in terms of *levels of analysis* is a recurring theme in Holt's writings, and thus most likely one with which Gibson was familiar through him. In Holt's (1914/1973) early work, it is a conception he apparently appropriated in part from Royce (chap. 2). A theoretical consequence of this view is the irreducibility of organisms when they are taken as integrated functional systems. That is, the functional properties of organisms considered at a molar level of analysis are not reducible to more molecular levels. Recall that in making this claim, Holt was not suggesting that there are differences in substance between these levels. What changes are the properties that can be found among entities at each level of analysis. It is properties, in many cases functional properties, that change—not substance.

Furthermore, the notion of levels of analysis is implicit in Holt's concept of "the recession of the stimulus." Also recall that Holt proposed as increasingly molar levels of behavior are considered, a functional analysis requires that more molar or distal stimuli need to be identified.

Whereas the focus of Holt's (1914/1973) early analysis is metaphysical and its scope is comprehensive, Gibson's goals as a psychologist are more modest, limiting his attention to psychological events and the intermediate scale of complexity—the ecological level—where these phenomena are found. In his writings, Gibson's recognition of the need to draw distinctions among conceptual levels goes back at least as far as his seminal paper, "The Concept of the Stimulus in Psychology" (1960), wherein he explicitly referred to Holt's notion of the "recession of the stimulus." As his work became more ecological in the 1960s and 1970s, the notion of levels of conceptual analysis, which is common in theoretical biology (see chap. 7), becomes more sharply articulated. It is Gibson's intention to describe and analyze some of the distinctive psychological properties that are present at an ecological level of analysis, with the conception of animal–environment mutuality at the center of his vision.

The Physical World as a Conceptual Domain. William James also sharply differentiates between psychological and physical entities, but he went about this in a different way than drawing a "levels of analysis" distinction. Instead, in radical empiricist philosophy, he distinguished between that which is immediately experienced and that which is an abstraction from experience. It is only entities in the psychological domain that are immediately known. Entities in the physical domain are known only indirectly as abstractions from direct experience. This, of course, refers to the critical distinction James drew between *percepts* and *concepts* (see chap. 1).

Knowledge of the physical domain is always conceptual; it is a product of thinking about immediate experience, an intellectualization. It is a rarefied "universe of discourse," to borrow a phrase from Holt. In contrast, properties of the psychological domain, such as affordances of the environment, can be known directly through perceiving. This is not to say, however, that concepts do not interact with perception—a point furthered later. Gibson did not utilize James's percept–concept distinction directly. But, given the strong commonalities among other aspects of Gibson's and James's positions, this distinction can be used both in explicating Gibson's ecological framework and his treatment of cognition in particular.

In an effort to understand phenomena operating at some level of analysis, if a descriptive framework appropriate at another level is employed, then some of the essential properties of the phenomena of primary interest may be overlooked. Worse, the account of their most defining properties may be distorted. Some of the explanatory factors for a given phenomenon can indeed be found at lower and even higher levels of analysis, but a comprehensive understanding of it cannot be concentrated at any single level. Insisting on an exclusively physical-biological account of psychological properties is problematic in exactly this way. And when the primary interest is psychological phenomena, the costs of reductive explanations are considerable. Not only is it possible to lose sight of the phenomena of initial concern, but failure to recognize that something has been lost in our reduction can do violence to our sense of who we are. Instead, following along the lines of Jamesian–Holtian *epistemological pluralism*, multiple coexisting systems do exist, and they need to be addressed in conceptually distinct ways.

Having said this, the various levels and starting points of analysis are not on equal footing either methodologically or phenomenologically for James or for Gibson. The domain of percepts, in a Jamesian sense, is the ground against which all other claims must be checked. This is the central tenet of James's pragmatic theory of truth. Likewise for Gibson, there is an experiential primacy of the ecological-psychological domain. The immediate perceiver–environment relation is primary for both James and for Gibson. It is out of this primary relation, and importantly, out of the latent structure that is present in this relation, that all other domains of analysis emerge as conceptual systems. There is a primacy of perceptual experience in James's radical empiricism and Gibson's ecological psychology, and it is this primacy that gives a phenomeno-logical cast to a good deal of their writings.

PHENOMENOLOGY AND ECOLOGICAL PSYCHOLOGY

With considerable justification, some might object to including phenom-enology as one of the essential features of the ecological approach. Gib-son was, at best, ambivalent about the value of phenomenological description. But it is important to explore this issue because phenomenological description recurs in his work and is put to good use. Gibson employed phenomenological description, not as a substitute for experimental work, but as a propadeutic to it (MacLeod, 1964). Moreover, sensitivity to the character of direct experience is a point of commonality between James's and Gibson's work. For both, phenomenological de-scription is a good starting point for identifying significant psychological phenomena that warrant more detailed analysis.

Phenomenology in William James

James's writings have often been cited as paving the way for phenomenol-ogy in philosophy, having influenced phenomenology's presumptive founder, Edmund Husserl (Edie, 1987; Wild, 1969; Wilshire, 1968). Indeed, MacLeod (1969) claimed that James anticipated Husserl's contributions (and Heidegger's too) and stated them far more clearly. The term *phenom-enology* does not appear in James, but the term James uses to convey its methodological connotation is *introspection*. Introspection for James was a less controlled and less prescribed activity than the introspective proce-dures employed by many of his contemporaries, most notably Wundt. This difference reflects the fact that James's analyses were driven more by the phenomena at hand than by a particular codified method. Said differently, they were more problem driven than method driven. For this reason, the rigor to be expected from scientific analysis is not always found in James's discourse, although he drew heavily on the experimental literature of his day. At times, he traded off formalized rigor for an unparalleled verisimili-tude. His acute and profound sensitivity to immediate, everyday experi-ence, coupled with his prodigious gifts for verbal expression, lead readers to recognize in his writings familiar moments in their own lives. This recurring experience of self-recognition is one of the joys of reading James's psychol-ogy and is certainly one reason for its continuing popularity.

To cover some ground briefly examined earlier, for James, maintaining a sensitivity to immediate experience is the only way to keep psychological theorizing true to the phenomena. In *The Principles*, James discussed one of the "great snares" of psychological analysis as being "the psychologist's fallacy." This fallacy entails a *"confusion of his* [i.e., the psychologist's] *own standpoint with that of the mental fact* about which he is making his report" (James, 1890/1981, p. 195). By this James meant that there is a difference between immediate psychological experience as such and an analytical description of the experience, which is at a remove from it. Being a description at least once removed from phenomena, "the psychologist's standpoint" has a transforming effect on a description of the immediate phenomenon by virtue of what the psychologist brings to immediate experience. As a result, what may be described as a basic datum may be in actuality a highly intellectualized abstraction.

How can the qualities of immediate experience (percepts) be preserved in a psychologist's analysis? And how can abstractions (concepts) remain ultimately grounded in experience? These goals can be approached by continually checking analytical claims about immediate experience against immediate experience itself. The only way to insure that our theorizing does not become wholly fanciful and unrelated to the reality of our immediate experience is to bring our conceptual analyses back to their perceptual grounding. Failing to do this opens the investigator to the possibility of committing the psychologist's fallacy—a consequence of which is the construction of artificial accounts of psychological phenomena.

James cited *representationalism* as one example of the commission of this fallacy, and it is a claim that has taken on added importance in psychology and in the philosophy of mind over the course of the 20th century. This position asserts that in the act of perceiving, our immediate experience is of a representation of the environment "in the mind," rather than of the environment as directly perceived. But this error leads to no end of problems.

The claim that perceptual experience of the environment is mere appearance and illusory and that what individuals know immediately are their mental constructions of the world reflects the position of many contemporary perceptual theorists. From Plato's writings to contemporary representationalists, there continues to be a distrust of immediate perceptual experience in favor of a presumed fundamental and reliable reality beyond appearances (Reed, 1996b). It is true that appearances can be misleading and illusory at times; but, instead of flying from appearances, instead of elevating abstractions to the status of reality, James argued that we should continually "return to the things themselves," to borrow a phrase from Husserl.

One reason why a conceptual analysis of what is fundamentally "real" can produce an account that is very different from a description of immediate perceptual experience is that perceiving as compared to experiencing concepts have different qualities. Perceiving is dynamic, transpiring over time, with the "moments" of perceiving continuous, blending into one another. In contrast, concepts are static and discrete (James, 1912/1979; also see chap. 5). As a result, when a conceptual analysis of experience is offered in place of an immediate, perceptual description, reality will usually be seen as fundamentally static and elementaristic. This kind of view (which was the sort the British Empiricist school promoted and is incorporated into much contemporary experimental psychology) led to many of the philosophical problems that James sought to address. It also produced the kind of perceptual theory that Gibson's ecological approach was intended to displace.

Gibson and Phenomenology

Gibson's writings are filled with fruitful phenomenological observations of perceptual experience, several of which are examined shortly. A few comments are necessary initially, however, in order to head off a potential confusion. The phenomenological strain in Gibson's writings may seem difficult to reconcile with his consistent criticism of mentalistic accounts of perceiving. This apparent inconsistency derives from the fact that phenomenology, as it has been employed in psychology, has often taken the form of a subjective, mentalistic theory. In contrast, Gibson identified himself as a behaviorist, and as such he was a positivist. Isn't there an inevitable tension between phenomenology and positivism?

The answer is no, not necessarily. Both phenomenology and positivism assert that knowledge is ultimately grounded in immediate experience. One finds calls for phenomenology in the writings of early positivists, such as Ernst Mach and Moritz Schlick (Sprigge, 1993). Indeed, Husserl, the founder of phenomenology as a philosophical school, claimed that "it is we who are the genuine positivists" (quoted in Edie, 1987, p. 3). What differentiates positivism and phenomenology is the path each subsequently follows. The history of positivism leads to operationism and physicalism, later to logical positivism and neobehaviorism. The history of phenomenology runs from Husserl to Sartre and leads to existentialist and humanistic psychologies. These two end points are indeed in tension, but they stem from a common root.

However, not all phenomenological thought followed the kind of course just described. Several phenomenological philosophers, most notably, Merleau-Ponty and Heidegger, took exception to the subjectivistic slant of Husserl's initial program of phenomenology. Merleau-Ponty specifically saw that phenomenological philosophies were in a position to reject the objective–subjective dichotomy that plagues traditional philosophical thought: "Probably the chief gain from phenomenology is to have united extreme subjectivism and extreme objectivism in its notion of the world" (Merleau-Ponty, 1962, p. xix). And what is the notion of "the world" from a phenomenological standpoint? In brief, it is

> an account of space, time and the world *as we "live" them*. It tries to give a direct description of our experience as it is, without taking account of its psychological origin and the causal explanations which the scientist, the historian, or the sociologist may be able to provide. (Merleau-Ponty, 1962, p. vii, emphasis added)

Gibson's phenomenological leanings, with their roots in James's vision, are decidedly more in accord with Merleau-Ponty's phenomenology (Glotzbach & Heft, 1982), and Heidegger's as well (Kadar & Effken, 1994), rather than with the Husserlian tradition.

Where would the behaviorist Gibson have developed sympathies for phenomenological description? Early in his career, Gibson would have been exposed to this way of thinking through contact with James's student, Holt, and in turn, through James's writings. But also, Gibson would have learned about this research attitude during his students years from Langfeld, chairman of the psychology department at Princeton. Langfeld received his Ph.D. in 1903 from the University of Berlin, having studied with Carl Stumpf, one of the early advocates of a phenomenological approach to experimental psychology and himself a student of Brentano.[3] Stumpf's teachings provided some of the groundwork for the Gestalt movement of the next generation of psychologists.

In his years at Smith College, Gibson was also deeply influenced by both Kurt Koffka and Fritz Heider (see chap. 6), who helped bring the European phenomenological orientation to the United States. But perhaps as influential as any of these earlier influences was Robert MacLeod, who was largely responsible for bringing Gibson to Cornell. MacLeod's student years were spent in Europe, where he was greatly influenced by the experimental phenomenologist David Katz. MacLeod was the preeminent advocate in the United States of adopting phenomenology as a propaedeutic to an experimental psychology (MacLeod, 1964). Along these same lines, J. J. Gibson (1967a) recognized the affinities between some of his ideas and those of Albert Michotte, who along with Katz was perhaps the most preeminent experimental phenomenologist in Europe (Thines, Costall, & Butterworth, 1991).

To repeat what was stated earlier: Gibson was not a phenomenologist. His behaviorist antipathy to anything sounding mentalistic would prevent him from ever accepting that mantle. At the same time, over and over in his

---

[3] Also, recall from chapter 3 that Langfeld was instrumental in bringing Holt to Princeton. One additional historical note: James and Stumpf were close colleagues and good friends.

writings it is evident that he thought sensitivity to "naive experience" could contribute in important ways to experimental psychology. Indeed, MacLeod (1974) described Gibson as "probably the best experimental phenomenologist since David Katz. He first looks at the phenomena, all the phenomena, before he tries to explain them" (p. 12).

Admittedly, phenomenological description is a rather vague designation. What is it, and what is it not, at least to Gibson and James? Gibson's orientation can be glimpsed through his early struggles in his first book with the distinction he drew between the *visual field* and the *visual world* (J. J. Gibson, 1950a). This distinction refers to two modes of experiencing in vision. The visual field consists of

> a patchwork of colors something like a picture. ... [It] has boundaries, roughly oval in shape, and extends about 180 degrees from side to side and about 140 degrees up and down. The boundaries are not sharp, but they are easily attended to. ... The visual field is clear in the center and vague in the periphery. (J. J. Gibson, 1979, p. 206)

The visual world, on the other hand, consists of objects and layout, is un-bounded, and is everywhere clear. It surrounds the perceiver and is extended, in principle, indefinitely.

Although it might seem that the visual field is simpler and more primitive and thus is the product of adopting the phenomenological attitude, in fact, the opposite is the case. The description of the visual field offered earlier is a highly intellectualized distillation of immediate visual experience of the world. Although it might seem that descriptions based on a patchwork of sensations, sense data, or some other elementary units must be primary in experience, for James they reflected instead a detached, abstracted assessment of the experience of perceiving the environment. Recall James's critical view of sensation, discussed in chapter 1. As odd as it might seem at first, a sensation, and the visual field more generally, are concepts, not percepts, to employ Jamesian terminology. They reflect abstraction from immediate experience, and not immediate experience itself. However, the assumption that sensations (and their like) are the fundamental units of perceiving lies at the heart of many 20th-century psychological theories across diverse domains of the discipline—from perception and cognition to personality and social psychology. James predicted that theories built on this assumption would be plagued with numerous difficulties.

Gibson's attitude toward the visual field–visual world distinction changed in his later work. Whereas it was central in his first book, it is virtually absent from his later writings. When the term *visual field* appeared at all in the later work, Gibson used it primarily as a foil to clarify what he meant by the "world that is perceived." The uncritical use of this distinction in the first book reflects the fact that Gibson had yet to break away fully from traditional perceptual theory and its sensation—perception distinction, with visual field and visual world corresponding to each, respectively. Reed (1988) rightly described *The Perception of the Visual World* as "a last-ditch attempt to avoid a complete restructuring of perceptual theory" (p. 148). However, despite its many merits, this effort proved to be a failure, and such a restructuring was needed.

As Gibson later noted, the visual field and the visual world do not reflect two different modes of perceiving: Instead, what is perceived is the world. In fact, in his last book, Gibson noted parenthetically that the title of *The Perception of the Visual World* (1950a) "promoted confusion" because it suggested an unnecessary distinction, as if something other than the world could be *perceived* (p. 207). With hindsight, he remarked that he should have called his first book *The Visual Perception of the World*.

Consistent with this shift, a number of Gibson's most important discoveries that grew out of a phenomenological attitude came after the 1950 book. The next subsections consider four of them: optical flow and its counterpart egomotion, occluding edges, and affordances.

Optical Flow. Perhaps the clearest example of a phenomenologically rooted concept in Gibson's approach is *optical flow*. This term refers to the visual streaming or outflow of environmental features that one experiences when moving forward, and inversely, the convergence or inflow of environmental features in the direction from which one is traveling. These patterns of visual streaming are generated by a perceiver moving in an environment. For this reason, optical flow is an excellent example of the *relational* character of psychological phenomena (i.e., perceiver–environment mutuality) because it is only present through the joint contribution of an active perceiver and environmental properties.

In his autobiographical essay, J. J. Gibson (1967a) attributed the saliency of this phenomenon to childhood experiences as the son of a surveyor for the railroads: "I knew what the world looked like from a railroad train and how it seemed to flow inward when seen from the rear platform and expand outward when seen from the locomotive" (p. 127). It would be historically inaccurate to claim that the idea of a moving point of observation in perceiving only appears in Gibson's later ecological theory. His sensitivity to this aspect of visual experience can be found in a remarkable paper "A Theoretical-Field Analysis of Automobile-Driving" (J. J. Gibson & Crooks, 1938; see chap. 6).

These observations leading to and including the description of the optical flow field subsequently gave rise to a detailed analysis of the visual control of locomotion and object manipulation (J. J. Gibson, 1958, 1979, chap. 13). He discussed some of these actions in a preliminary fashion as a set of rules for carrying out particular goals. For example, "to approach is to magnify a patch in the [visual] array" (J. J. Gibson, 1979, p.

233). Importantly, these rules refer to visual information that is produced through movement. They are not rules of movement in the sense that they do not indicate what muscle or groups of muscles need to be moved or how they should be moved: "Any group of muscles will suffice if it brings about the relation of the animal to its environment stated in the rule" (J. J. Gibson, 1979, p. 233). They are rules of movement only in the sense of indicating what end is sought in the array of visual information, and any movement leading to this end is functionally equivalent to any other. In his ground-breaking formulation of perceptual systems, J. J. Gibson (1966) wrote: "The movement systems are characterized by 'vicarious action' of different muscles. The classification [of different systems] is not based primarily on the anatomy of body members but on purposes" (p. 57). These ideas can be traced to discussions of "integrated action" offered by Holt in *Animal Drives and the Learning Process*, (examined in the preceding chapter; see also the discussion of perceptual systems later).

The notion of optical flow has been an impetus for Gibson's recognizing the importance of perceiving from the point of view of a moving observer, and also for realizing that perceiving involves a co-awareness of the environment and the perceiver. The study of optical flow and, to a lesser degree, of egomotion (see the next section) has been an active and productive research area. For some representative research, see Cutting (1986), Lee (1974), Lee & Lishman (1977), Stoffregen (1985), R. Warren (1976), and W. Warren (1998).

Egomotion.   Accompanying the experience of optical flow, and perception of the environment generally, is the experience that it is "I" who is moving through the environment. This is not a Cartesian experience of the "I," a disembodied entity that is self-aware as it thinks. This "I" is much more concrete than that; it is the source of action and it can literally be seen by the perceiver. It is "I" as purposive agent.

Gibson pointed out that persistent features in the field of view are indications of one's own bodily presence. One's nose is visible, and frequently so are other parts of the body such as the head, fingers, and hands, as well as trunk, legs, and feet in contact with the ground. Each of these parts of the body are quite distinctive occluding edges in the field of view. For example, motions of one's body occlude features of the environment in distinctive ways, as when perceivers notice their own hand movements. Of course, the most persistent occluding edge that specifies the body is the nose, which is always in the field of view under normal viewing conditions.

The limbs are distinctive in the field of view as animate shapes that the perceiver never sees as closed forms; they are "semiobjects." The arms, hands, fingers, and legs move distinctively in the field of view, and under normal circumstances they "enter and leave the field [of view] at its lower edge, or else the field sweeps down to reveal them" (p. 120).

Movements of the head are also perceivable in visual information by a characteristic "*sweeping* of the field of view over the ambient array during head turns and the *wheeling* of the field over the array during head tilts" (J. J. Gibson, 1979, p. 118). Accompanying these motions, portions of the environment come into view while others go out of view in distinctive ways.

What these phenomenological observations indicate is that the self is perceived simultaneously with the environment. Put in another way, accompanying exteroception is always ego- or interoception: "The optical information to specify the self, including the head, body, arms, and hands, *accompanies* the optical information to specify the environment. The two sources of information co-exist" (p. 116).

This information specifies the self in the field of view. The directly perceivable self, what Neisser (1988) aptly called the "ecological self," is a persisting feature of visual experience. Previously, this idea was anticipated in James's (1890/1981) treatment of the "empirical self" (chap. 1).

To highlight the ways in which Gibson's approach differs from more standard views, it is useful to recall the efforts of earlier empiricist thinkers to discover evidence for the self in immediate experience. Perhaps most famously are Hume's efforts to find evidence of the self in sensations:

> For my part, when I enter most intimately into what I call *myself*, I always stumble on some particular perception or other, of heat or cold, light or shade, love or hatred, pain or pleasure. I can never catch *myself* at any time without a perception, and never can observe anything but the perception. (Hume, 1739, quoted in R. Watson, 1971, p. 59)

Not finding the self in sensations, Hume conjectured that the notion of a self is only "an act of imagination." Following Gibson's lead and looking for empirical evidence of the self in the dynamic flow of information, instead of in the static elements of sensation, it can be found right there under (and at the bridge of) our nose! In this case, as with other puzzles arising out of static and discrete views of stimulus information, the difficulties take on a different and more tractable form when perceiving is considered to be a dynamic process involving the detection of information over time. From this primary ground, that is, from the ground of perceiving (or percepts, to use James's terminology), more abstract notions of self (which are concepts) are derived through self-reflective processes. Such abstract notions of the self could include what Neisser (1988) called the extended self, the private self, and the conceptual self.[4]

Occluding Edges. Gibson's keen attention to immediate experience can also be found in his discovery with George Kaplan of the occluding edge (J. J. Gibson, Kaplan, Reynolds, & Wheeler, 1969; Kaplan, 1969). An *occluding edge* is a contour of a visible object where a second object or surface either becomes gradually hidden or becomes gradually revealed. This change in the field of view is created by the movement of an object as it covers a second object or it goes behind a second object, as in the case of a ball rolling in front of or behind a screen, respectively. Occluding edges also accompany movements of the perceiver in the production of motion parallax (i.e., the greater relative displacement of near versus far objects relative to the background). Thus, an occluding edge is specified by the relation between two textured surfaces. There is *deletion* of texture as an object goes out of view behind a second object, and *accretion* of texture as an object comes into view from behind a second object. Accretion of texture corresponds to the experience of seeing one object appearing from behind another, whereas deletion of texture corresponds to the experience of one object going behind another.

This seemingly simple observation has deep implications for perceptual theory. Phenomenologically, the surface that was visible and is now covered is still experienced as *persisting* even though it is "presently" out of sight. Similarly, the surface that was not previously visible, but now is as it emerges from behind an occluding edge is experienced as having existed prior to the present moment. These phenomena reveal a quality about perceptual experience that has been overlooked in more traditional theories using elementary sensations as their starting point: "It is certainly reasonable to describe perception as extending into the past and the future, but note that to do so violates the accepted doctrine that perception is confined to the present" (J. J. Gibson, 1979, p. 190). Although violating the accepted doctrine, this observation is consistent with James's view that immediate experience is "no knife edge," but rather that it has duration, being extending simultaneously forward and backward in time. This issue is considered in more detail in chapter 5. For now it is sufficient to note that the discovery of an occluding edge and its implications stem from adoption of a phenomenological attitude.

---

[4] Another facet of self proposed by Neisser (1988), but not included here, is the interpersonal self. As he defined it, the interpersonal self is not a product of reflection, but like the ecological self is co-perceiving in the course of perception-action.

Affordances.   A final example of the phenomenological tendency in Gibson's later writings is his influential and controversial idea of *affordance*. This idea is be treated in detail in the next section. Here its phenomenological roots are briefly highlighted.

An affordance is the perceived functional significance of an object, event, or place for an individual. For example, a firm, obstacle-free ground surface is perceivable as a surface on which one can walk. In contrast, a boggy surface or a surface cluttered with obstacles (e.g., a boulder field) is typically perceived as impeding walking. Or, to take a different kind of case, depending on its apparent size, an object may appear to be graspable with one hand or only with two hands. As these examples indicate, the perceived functional character of an environmental feature establishes possibilities and sets limits on actions.

Affordances point to an important but often overlooked quality of the world—that its features are meaningful for an active perceiver. An appreciation for these properties of the environment is growing both through theoretical writings in ecological psychology (e.g., Heft, 1989; Noble, 1981; Reed, 1993; Sanders, 1997, 1999) and in the body of experimental findings it has generated (e.g., Carello, Grosefsky, Reichel, Soloman, & Turvey, 1989; Cornus, Montagne, & Laurent, 1999; Heft, 1993; Heft & McFarland, 1999; Mark, 1987; Mark, Balliett, Craver, Douglas, & Fox, 1990; Rochat, 1995; Stoffregan, Gorday, Sheng, & Flynn, 1999; W. H. Warren, 1984; W. H. Warren & Whang, 1987). It should not be difficult to recognize the phenomenological character of affordances. If these roots require further substantiation, then the reader can turn to numerous parallels of this idea that appear throughout the phenomenological literature, including the works of Merleau-Ponty and Heidegger.

Affordances would seem to have a peculiar metaphysical status to those accustomed to thinking about meaning as an attribute that minds impose on the world. Gibson was claiming, instead, that affordances are perceivable properties of the world. For this reason, the idea of affordances has generated considerable theoretical debate. Consider next some of the theoretical properties of affordances and the relation of this idea to radical empiricism.

PERCEIVING AFFORDANCES

Much has been written over the past 10 years about Gibson's controversial idea of affordances. It is not my intention here to review the issues and debates surrounding this idea.[5] Instead, this section examines some of the primary characteristics of affordances and the roots of this idea.

---

[5] See, for example, Ben-Zeev (1984), Chow (1989), Costall and Still (1989), Ginsburg (1990), Heft (1980, 1989, 1990), Heil (1979, 1981), and Noble (1981).

Gibson cited as antecedents of the concept of affordances the influence of psychologists working in the Gestalt tradition, and in particular, Koffka and Lewin (J. J. Gibson, 1979, pp. 138–140). The phenomenological stance shared by these approaches has already been noted. Gibson raised these cases primarily to distance his conceptualization from theirs. (The commonalities and the differences between Gibson's work and the Gestalt program are taken up in chap. 6.) The formulation he proposed has its roots in James's radical empiricist writings, although Gibson did not explicitly draw this connection in his discussion. That relation is explored here. In the process, one of the primary conceptual challenges that this idea presents must be addressed. Affordances are claimed to possess two distinctive and seemingly contradictory characteristics: First, they are relational properties, and second, they are properties of environmental features existing independently of a perceiver. These issues are sorted out in turn.

The Relational Nature of Affordances

To restate the definition already offered, an affordance is a property of the environment that has perceived functional significance for an individual. A critical feature of this definition concerns the last phrase: Affordances are specified relative to an individual perceiver. That is, a feature of the environment may present certain affordance possibilities for one individual, but not for another, owing to some structural and/or functional attributes of that individual. For example, a surface may be perceived as being sit-on-able by an individual if it appears to be supportive of his weight and is positioned approximately knee-high. A surface that appears to deviate too much from these criteria—that is, it does not appear to able to support one's weight, and it is relatively too low or too high—will not be perceived as offering this affordance property. Clearly, whether a surface is perceived to be sit-on-able depends, among other things (such as intention), on the particular individual in question.

This variable quality of affordances is one of the features that makes it a peculiar, and hence controversial, descriptor of the environment. It is peculiar because, traditionally, properties of the environment have been taken to be constant. The centuries' old distinction between primary and secondary qualities rests on such a view. Going back at least as far as Galileo, perceived properties of the world were distinguished from the perceiver's own contributions to experience in terms of the constancy of the former. Properties such as mass, number, shape, and location in space and time are invariant across different perceivers and invariant over different encounters with them by the same perceiver. Their constancy suggests that these properties are attributes of the object itself, describable independently of any single individual's viewpoint. For this reason, these "primary qualities" of objects are often designated as *objective qualities*.

In contrast, other properties of objects are inconstant, varying across perceivers and across occasions for a particular perceiver. For example, different individuals may experience the degrees of warmth–coldness of the same object differently as a function of a prior level of adaptation to temperature. Or, the same object may seem to vary in warmth–coldness for the same perceiver at different times for the same reason. Similarly, odors, tastes, and colors are inconstant. If it is assumed, in keeping with the Cartesian–Newtonian framework, that properties of the environment are relatively constant (i.e., that the world has stability and permanence), then the perceiver must be the source of these inconstancies. Hence, these "secondary qualities" of warm–cold, odor, taste, and color are considered to be *subjective qualities*.

The concept of affordances cuts across the grain of this time-honored, but psychologically problematic, distinction. With the idea of an affordance, Gibson was proposing a class of properties that has perceiver-specific qualities and also is a property of the environment. From the point of view of the objective–subjective dichotomy, such a property is incomprehensible. A feature of the environment, by definition, preserves its properties independently of who is perceiving it. Perceiver-relative properties of the environment would seem to be a contradiction. But this is only the case if the standard metaphysical distinction between objective/physical properties and subjective/mental properties is adopted. Gibson, like James and Holt before him, rejected the appropriateness of this distinction for psychological analyses:

> An important fact about the affordances of the environment is that they are in a sense objective, real, and physical, unlike values and meanings, which are supposed to be subjective, phenomenal, and mental. But, actually, an affordance is neither an objective property nor a subjective property; or it is both if you like. An affordance cuts across the dichotomy of subjective-objective and helps us to understand its inadequacy. It is equally a fact of the environment and a fact of behavior. It is both physical and psychical, yet neither. An affordance points both ways, to the environment and to the observer. (J. J. Gibson, 1979, p. 129)

What is perhaps most intriguing about affordances (or most perplexing, depending on your point of view) is their metaphysical status. In standard psychological theories, the referents for most psychologically relevant concepts are either located in the environment (objective) or located in the mind (subjective). Affordances do not neatly fit into either one of these designations. This is a rather peculiar concept from the perspective of Cartesian dualism, to say the least!

Affordances and Radical Empiricism

The concept of affordances has its roots in James's radical empiricist philosophy and the related functionalist approach to psychology. (For an excellent overview of functionalism, see Heidbreder, 1933/1973). E. Gibson (1982) explicitly described the development of the affordance concept as reflecting "a renascence of functionalism." Along these lines, Noble (1981) persuasively demonstrated the functionalist and pragmatic qualities of this idea.

Recall that at the heart of the formulation of radical empiricism was a metaphysical concern (chap. 1). James sought a conceptual framework that would circumvent the morass of the world–mind dichotomy. If world and mind are conceived to be different in substance, as they are in metaphysically dualistic theories, then any interaction between them would necessarily be of an imposed nature. The object properties in one domain must somehow be imparted to entities in the other domain. An instance of this relation in the case of perception would be physical energy in the world stimulating a receptor surface at the world–perceiver boundary, initiating neural activity in the perceiver, and eventuating in the experience of a sensation. The model operating here is that of independent physical objects mechanically imparting effects from one to another in a "push-pull" manner. Explaining how one object might impart motion (or some form of energy) to another object, such as a physical energy initiating a neurochemical response in a receptor, is manageable when the interacting objects are conceptualized in terms of a common "substance." But explaining how influences are passed between qualitatively different entities, such as a physical energy causing an experiential quality such as a sensation, is quite a bit trickier—indeed, if an explanation in the form of any standard causal account is even possible.

James's approach to these difficulties was, in effect, to view such intractable problems as being a product of how the issue is conceptualized in the first place. Instead of assuming at the outset two substantively different domains, matter and mind, James proposed just one domain—metaphysically neutral, pure experience. Thus, there is no primordial boundary in any metaphysical sense between what is taken to be world versus mind; there is no "outside" standing over against an "inside." Instead, what is objective versus subjective is not "an intrinsic quality of an experience but the way that one classifies the experience" (Kuklick, 1977, p. 322). The distinction between world and mind refers to two "contexts of associates" differentiated from pure experience. And to experience X at a given moment is to experience an entity that resides simultaneously in more than one context within experience (see chap. 1).

The possibility that an object of experience can participate simultaneously in two (or more) contexts is described colorfully by James as being "double-barrelled." An object of experience taken in one context is an aspect of the knower and taken in a different context is an aspect of the object known:

> And since experience can figure in both groups simultaneously we have every right to speak of it as *subjective and objective both at once*. The dualism connotated by such *double-barrelled* terms as "experience," "phenomenon," "datum," and *"Vorfindung"* ... in philosophy at any rate, tend to more and more replace the single-barreled terms of "thought" and "object." (James, 1912/1976, p. 7, emphases added)

To the list of double-barrelled terms James offered here can now be added Gibson's idea of affordances, as well as the related view of the essential exteroceptive-introceptive duality of perceiving (e.g., simultaneously perceiving of optical flow and egomotion). For both James and for Gibson, experience has this dual quality. And as a consequence of the intrinsically selective character of knowing processes, the perceiver's experience of an object can momentarily be in relation to either constellation of associates—that is, at any given instant it might be experienced as "objective" or "subjective."

This treatment of the double-barrelled nature of conscious experience seems to be precisely what Gibson had in mind with the concept of affordance. Gibson made no mention in his brief history of the affordance concept of James's formulation (J. J. Gibson, 1979, pp. 138–140). However, it is not unlikely that he would have picked up this sort of conceptualization through his contact with Holt.

Moreover, what he may have learned either directly or indirectly (the latter is more likely) through Holt's teachings is the neorealist commitment to the assumption of *external relations* in experience (see chap. 2). This is the view that the things experienced have an independent existence. In other words, things have a place both in experience and in the world independent of experience (see later).

The alternative to this view is the assumption that things exist by virtue of their being experienced, that is, their existence depends on their being experienced. It would be the rare psychologist who subscribed to this latter view, but the New Realists argued that to assume "the mind can have for its direct object only its own ideas and states, and external objects, if they exist at all, can only be known indirectly by a process of inference" is tantamount to that view (Holt et al., 1912, p. 474). For if all individuals can know directly are their own mental states, then the object represented by that mental state depends on that mental state for its existence from the point of view of an individual perceiver. And at the outset, the point of view of the perceiver is all the psychologist has to work with.

Holt was emphatic that the objects of experience existed independently of the perceiver even while they were perceived through the selective ("specific") responses of the perceiver. Is this a perspective that he would have communicated to Gibson as a student? It is not unlikely.

Support for this possibility is evidenced by the fact that Holt's other prominent student, Edward Tolman, also held this view, which led to his concept of "manipulanda." Tolman (1932) defined "manipulanda" as

> the character of objects which support ... motor activity (manipulations). They derive in character from the *independent* physical character of the environmental object *and* the response-organ make-up of the given organism. They are such properties of environmental objects as lengths, widths, weights, resistances, solidities, fluidities, etc. But they are these properties *defined not as such, and in themselves*, but in terms of the range and refinements of manipulation they will support in the given organism. They are stand-on-able-nesses, pick-up-able-nesses, sit-in-able-nesses, etc. etc. (p. 448)

Tolman was clearly anticipating the idea of affordance that Gibson would explore more fully 40 years later. Tolman employed more positivistic language than Gibson did in his later discussions, and it is clear that these perceived functional qualities did not take on nearly the theoretical significance for Tolman as they did for Gibson. But, all the same, the similarity in these ideas it is striking. With the term *manipulanda*, Tolman was proposing a Jamesian double-barreled notion that referred to properties of the environment and the organism considered jointly.

It is impossible to say whether Gibson was sensitized to the Jamesian notion of the duality of experience through his contact with Holt, or by reading Tolman, or both. (In his 1941 paper on the concept of "set," Gibson cited Tolman's book *Purposive Behavior in Animals and Men*, 1932, where "manipulanda" is presented.) But there would seem little doubt that James's perspective, conveyed through Holt and/or Tolman, prepared the way for Gibson's later development of the concept of affordances. In the absence of citations to either the pertinent passages in James's or Holt's writings, or to Tolman's concept of manipulanda, it would appear that either Gibson was unaware of these theoretical antecedents of affordances, or he had forgotten about them by the 1970s. Another possibility is that in striving to clarify the concept of affordances, he only identified in his history of the concept (J. J. Gibson, 1979) the similar, although ultimately contrasting, views of the Gestalt psychologists. In any case, this way of thinking was clearly familiar to him for a long time (see J. J. Gibson, 1950a, pp. 198–199).

One last point concerning James's analysis of the double-barrelled nature of experience: For James, the kinds of experiences that most clearly reveal this double-barrelled quality are what he called "affectional experiences." Whereas in most cases through the selective process of knowing, an experience is readily classified as "objective or subjective" in terms of its relations to one or another context, this possibility is much more difficult with experiences that have a particularly strong evaluative character. James pointed out that we often talk as if affective qualities have both inner and outer manifestations, as in the expressions, "The sky is threatening" or "The situation is inviting." Indeed, such descriptions he claimed are the basis for much of the aesthetic and rhetorical force of language: "The man is really hateful; the action really mean; the situation really tragic—*all in themselves apart from our opinion* (James, 1912/1976, p. 72, emphasis added). These are features of the world from which we cannot easily separate ourselves, and especially our emotions. They get "under our skin" and possess properties with particular salience for us:

It is those very appreciative attributes of things, their dangerousness, beauty, rarity, utility, etc., that primarily appeal to our attention. In our commerce with nature these attributes are what give *emphasis* to objects; and ... produces immediate bodily effects upon us. (James, 1912/1976, p. 75)

These kinds of affectional facts of experience reflected real properties of objects for both James and Gibson. For both theorists, such experiences indicate a moral dimension to the perceived world, an "independent reality of values" (J. J. Gibson, 1971, p. 8; also see Costall, 1995; Reed, 1996b).[6] This issue is discussed further in the last chapter.

Affordances as "Percepts"

Meaning is commonly considered to be an exclusive feature of the domain of abstract thought. In this regard, as in others, perceiving and thinking are sometimes assumed to be distinct processes. The development of the concept of affordance, and similar efforts by James and by the Gestalt psychologists (chap. 6) were intended to indicate that meaning is also a feature of perceptual experience. This is not to suggest, however, that meaning in perceptual experience and meaning considered in abstract thinking are the same, but rather to indicate a way in which perceiving like thinking is an act of cognition (A. Pick, 1997).

---

[6] Reed (1988, p. 55) reported the following comment Gibson wrote to himself at the beginning of the notes for his social psychology course in 1936: "Give a lecture on *values* as the *objective* aspect of human motivation (economic, sexual, social, ethical, aesthetic values)."

In his discussion of what it means to perceive the meaning of an affordance, Gibson pointed out that "to perceive an affordance is not to classify an object" (J. J. Gibson, 1979, p. 134). Gibson was drawing here a distinction between perceptual meaning and conceptual meaning. What is the nature of this difference? How does perceived meaning of affordances differ from conceptual meaning?

James's distinction between percepts and concepts can be of some initial assistance here. Affordances are percepts rather than concepts in the Jamesian sense of these terms. Affordances are a part of the ongoing flow of immediate experience specified by perceptual information, and concepts are abstractions from that flow. In other words, affordances are directly perceived and concepts are derived. As directly perceived properties of the environment, affordances are not experienced as belonging to particular categories. "You do not have to classify and label things in order to perceive what they afford" (J. J. Gibson, 1979, p. 134). In contrast, categorization is the work of second-order processes; it is a thinking about immediate experience, a creating of what James called concepts.

Because of these different origins, some of the properties of meaning considered from a perceptual standpoint may differ from conceptual meaning. Affordances (perceptual meanings) and concepts (conceptual meanings) differ with respect to the determinateness of their meaning boundaries. Wittgenstein (1953)—following up some ideas from James no less—demonstrated convincingly that there are no necessary and sufficient conditions for determining the grounds for inclusion of a *concept* in a particular category. Categorical boundaries are indistinct and indeterminate: "Members of a category may be related to one another without all members having any properties in common that define that category" (Lakoff, 1987, p. 12). Instead, objects included in a common category share a "family resemblance" rather than a determinate list of features. The case would appear to be different for affordances. Because affordances are specified relative to some action by an individual, they do have determinate boundaries. Most fundamentally, and in the simplest cases, they are delimitable relative to the body-scaling of the individual (e.g., Mark, 1987; W. H. Warren, 1984). Although there may not be necessary and sufficient conditions to determine what counts as, for example, a stair qua concept, for a stair to function as an affordance for an individual there is such specificity. To be perceived as affording stepping-up-on, the horizontal surface of the stair must appear to be solid enough to support the perceiver's weight and to be within a certain height relative to the standing surface. A stair either does or does not afford climbing-on for an individual. Thus, although there may be interindividual variation for judging affordance boundaries, the reason for it is due to differences in body scaling and not indeterminate categorical boundaries.[7] In short, a distinction can be drawn between affordances and concepts in terms of how precisely their meaning boundaries can be specified.

A property that affordances and concepts share is that instances of either can have multiple meanings; however, there are differences in the ways each manifests this property. In the case of affordances, multiple perceptual meanings stem from the multiple functions an object can serve. For example, when looking for something to hold down papers on a windy day, a book will serve that purpose; it will also play the role of a door-stop or a window prop, or as its initial intended function as a repository of information. A book has multiple affordances, and each can be revealed as the perceiver's intentions change (Heft, 1989). The range of possible meanings of an affordance is constrained by the possible uses an object can be put to, which is in principle limited even if it is not specifiable in advance. The multiple meanings of concepts are far less limited because use does not constrain their possibilities.

Even though concepts may be ultimately derived from perception–action experience (Lakoff, 1987), as James pointed out (see chap. 1), they can become detached and autonomous from everyday realities. It is this characteristic that gives concepts their great creative power, such as can be seen in the arts. However, this same characteristic gives concepts the potential to violate the realities of the everyday in unfortunate ways, as has been shown, for example, by ideologies that allow us to dehumanize the other (J. J. Gibson, 1939; Sampson, 1993). By assessing concepts pragmatically against direct experience, their validity can be tested, it is true. But when concepts are instantiated in social structures, they acquire the power to transform the realities of everyday life and, in doing so, undercut possibilities for their empirical refutation. For this reason, conceptual systems can be pernicious, as the history of the past century amply demonstrates. This is a variation in

---

[7] Some experiments on perceiving affordances seem to contradict this claim. Several researchers have found that perceivers make consistent errors (either overestimations or underestimations as a function of conditions) when making judgments, such as whether an object is within reach or whether a surface affords stepping up on (e.g., Carello et al., 1989; Rochat, 1995). Such findings suggest that affordances are judged as approximations rather than with precision. However, there is evidence indicating that these small margins of error may be artifacts of the methodology employed (Heft, 1993; Heft & McFarland, 1999). Specifically, much affordance research has required participants to judge whether some action (e.g., reaching for an object) is possible, without having the participant engage in the action. Such a procedure transforms what is typically a perception–action task into a reflective judgment. When this feature of the procedure is controlled, and accuracy of affordance estimates is based on actions by the participant, these judgments have been found to be precise.

a social context of what Whitehead (1925) called the error of "misplaced concreteness" and what James's called the "psychologist's fallacy" where the products of our thoughts are taken to be the basis for our thoughts.

The Apparently Contradictory Character of Affordances

There appears to be a contradiction in the way Gibson characterized affordances (Costall, 1986; S. Katz, 1987; Noble, 1981). It is claimed that affordances are properties of the environment specified relative to an individual perceiver, and yet they exist independently of an individual perceiver. How is it possible to have it both ways? If a property exists relative to a perceiver, then isn't its existence dependent on the perceiver? Conversely, if a property is independent of a perceiver, then how can it be relational with respect to a perceiver?

Ben-Zeev (1984) and Heft (1989) adopted a similar (although not identical) approach to overcoming this apparent contradiction. This approach rests on the distinction between the potential functional properties of the environment considered with respect to an individual and the functional properties of the environment that are actualized, that is, selected by that individual as an intentional agent. For a particular individual in a specific locale or place, there is a range of affordances potentially available to be engaged. These affordances exist whether or not they are presently perceived because they inhere in the structure of the environment.

A toddler in a preschool playroom, for instance, has available to her a number of functional opportunities presented by the furnishings as a result of their design and structural properties, and considered in relation to that child. There are chairs to sit on, tables on which to work, playhouses to play in, objects to manipulate, and so on. These possibilities are present whether or not that child engages them—they are attributable to properties of the features themselves—and in this sense they exist independently of that child. That this range of possibilities is relationally established is evident when it is recognized that there are also environmental features that do not present functional opportunities because of their properties considered in relation to that child. For example, the door to a storage area that can be opened by the teacher will not likewise afford opening for the child if the door handle is located out of a child's reach. The door as a passage does not exist as a potential affordance for the child. But it remains an independent, functional property of the environment vis-à-vis an adult.

As further evidence of the independent character of affordances, individuals can make affordance judgments with respect to possibilities for others. Children, for example, can reliably assess the affordance possibilities of environmental features for adults (Heft & McFarland, 1999; Rochat, 1995).

Thus, in principle, it is possible to specify the affordances in a place available to an individual relative to, for example, body-scaling, motor skills, and so forth, or even available to a group of individuals who share particular functional characteristics. These affordances exist independently in that place regardless of whether or not any individual is presently experiencing them because they are properties of the environment. This distinction between potential and actualized structure is central to James's philosophy of radical empiricism, and it can be usefully applied to resolve the apparent dilemma concerning the status of affordances. (The potential–actual distinction and some of its implications for ecological psychology are explored further in chap. 5.) Moreover, the potential–actual distinction brings with it recognition of the intentional nature of perceiving, an essential characteristic of acts of knowing generally, or in Jamesian terms, the selectivity of the knowing relation.

A different objection is sometimes raised concerning the claim that affordances are both relational and independent. Most of the affordances in the everyday environment, such as those in the previous example of the preschool classroom, are human made—that is, they are the products of social activities. Doesn't the fact that humans construct a great deal of their world undercut the claim that affordances are independent properties of the environment? Whereas it might be valid to say that the affordances of "natural" features exist independently of a perceiver, surely this cannot hold in the case of "socially constructed" affordances and human perceivers.

It is critical in evaluating this objection to be clear that the term *construct* can be a bit misleading, especially given the way the term has been used in theories of cognition. Humans do not construct environments *de novo*. It is more accurate to say that humans (and other animals) alter existing properties of the environment (Reed, 1996a, p. 27). And putting the matter this way overcomes the dualism between the natural and the social that is implicit in this objection. As J. J. Gibson (1979) stated:

> This is not a *new* environment—an artificial environment distinct from the natural environment—but the same old environment modified by man. It is a mistake to separate the natural from the artificial as if there were two environments; artifacts have to be manufactured from natural substances. … There is only one world, however, diverse, and all animals live in it, although we humans have altered it to suit ourselves. (p. 130)

If it is accepted that the natural–social distinction is artificial and hence misleading, what remains of the objection that "affordances are not independent of individuals because typically they are constructed by individuals" seems to hinge on what the term *independent* means in the present context. Independent does not mean separate from organisms (human and other animals) such that their actions have no effect on the environment. Instead, the issue of the independence of affordances follows along the lines of what earlier in the century was called external relations and was a focus of much of the New Realist analysis (chap. 2). Montague (in Holt, et al., 1912) succinctly stated the position concerning the independence of relationally specified features of the environment as follows:

> Realism holds that things known may continue to exist unaltered when they are not known, or that things may pass in and out of the cognitive relation without prejudice to their reality, or that the existence of a thing is not correlated with or dependent upon the fact that anybody experiences it, perceives it, conceives it, or is in any way aware of it. (p. 474)

None of these New Realist claims about the external relations between knower and known is inconsistent with recognizing that most features of the environments in which human beings live are constructed by them. A constructed environmental feature (e.g., a building), continues to exist when it is not known by some individual; and its features, and even its existence, are not dependent on an individual experiencing them.

But a problem still remains. Costall (1999) argued that the ecological approach seems to treat environments "as existing prior to, and independently of, organisms, and adaptation ... as a 'fitting in' of organisms to those pre-existing conditions" (p. 413). However, because the human environment is a product of sociocultural activities, it cannot be said to be independent in the sense of existing prior to human activities (also see Costall, 1989, 1995). This is a valid point. But it does not undermine the ecological claim that affordances exist independently of individuals once the historical nature of sociocultural processes are added to the account. As is discussed in detail later (chap. 9), the sociocultural world, including social processes, institutions, and so on, is a product of individuals' ongoing collective transactions with the environment over historical time. Because of the dynamic and changing nature of the environment as a result of human actions (setting aside other sources of environmental change for the moment), the reciprocity, or "mutualism," of individual and environment must be given its due. But at any specific moment for an individual, the environment is "already there" as a context for that person's actions.

Adopting a sociohistorical perspective, then, (i.e., if a temporal dimension is added to the consideration of environments; Lynch, 1976), the environment can be viewed both as a product of individual actions and as existing independently of them. The affordances of the environment are there for individuals, in a sociohistorical sense, as a context for their actions.

THE EXPERIENCE OF THE BODY IN PERCEPTION

Complementing affordances, on the other side of the perceiving duality, is the perceiver. Indeed, perceiving is perhaps more accurately characterized as co-perceiving because through the pick up of information the individual concurrently perceives the environment and the self. "Exteroception" and "interoception" are inseparable (J. J. Gibson, 1979); and a consideration of their inseparability offers considerable insight into the embodied nature of perceiving.

Although both James and Holt placed much emphasis on the role of the body and movement in knowing, Gibson took this notion much farther than either of them did. His discussion of the role of the body in perceiving was developed in ways similar to Merleau-Ponty's phenomenology of perception (Glotzbach & Heft, 1982). James, Gibson, and Merleau-Ponty shared the claim that the self (the body) is a directly experienced facet of everyday activity.

In the earlier discussion of the phenomenological character of Gibson's thinking, some of the visual information for self-perception were described. Persisting parts of the field of view are the nose, and frequently the extremities and parts of the trunk. Through these sources of information, the self as an embodied perceiver is visually present at all times in the field of view. Movement of the entire body through locomotion is specified in a different way: namely, through the generation of perspective structure. As one move through the environment, there is a flow of optical structure generated by these movements. Simultaneously, invariant structures specifying features of the environmental layout are revealed (chap. 4).

Any motions in the visual field that result from self-produced actions of the head or whole body differ from all other motions in the visual field in at least one important respect: they are controlled by the perceiver/agent and hence, are usually reversible. Moving one's body to the left may result in the occlusion of an object behind a surface; the object can be revealed again by reversing the action. Visual phenomena as simple as this specify the presence of self as an agent.[8]

---

[8]For this reason, although motion presented through film is compelling, it cannot be confused with self-produced motion, because only with the latter can aspects of the field of view that have gone out of view be brought back into view by the perceiver. In fact, this difference between cinematic presentation and everyday experience is precisely what the developing technology of virtual reality can bridge.

In addition to the presence of the body in visual experience, the body plays a fundamental role in how things are perceived by serving as a frame of reference for action. Particularly compelling evidence for this claim can be found in experimental studies of affordances where dimensions of the body are modified. For example, Mark (1987) had individuals judge whether seats afforded sitting on under two different conditions: when participants were wearing blocks on their shoes that elevated their height and when they were standing on the ground as they normally do. Participants' affordance judgments varied directly with these modifications in body size, clearly indicating that functional properties of the environment are perceived dynamically in relation to the body rather in relation to some fixed metric. The notion of affordances and much of the research generated by it indicates that the body is at the center of perceptual experience. This view is very much in keeping with James's psychology and his radical empiricist philosophy.

Self-Perception and Radical Empiricism

With his introspective (i.e., phenomenological) method, James's analysis of the body is one part of his wider assessment of awareness of the self. In order to understand how the body fits into his framework, it is first necessary to consider his distinction between "the me" and "the I."" The me" refers to "sensible occurrences," instances of an individual's own presence and one's own activity, and the recollection of those occurrences. As such, "the me" is "only a loosely construed thing, an identity 'on the whole,' just like that which any outside observer might find in the same assemblage of facts" (James, 1890/1981, pp. 352). "The I" is the felt unity of these occurrences, as the present moment of experience reflexively appropriates previous moments; as such, it is "the hook from which the chain of past selves dangles" (p. 323).

What precisely is the origin of this felt unity? As discussed in chapter 1, whenever James pushed forward his analysis of the origins or foundations of "the I," all that he finds is some movement of the body—"the 'I' meaning for the Thought nothing but the bodily life which it momentarily feels" (James, 1890/1981, footnote, p. 324).

Moreover, the body serves as our frame of reference in our dealings with the world. In his late essay "The Experience of Activity," James explained that what we know of the world comes "at all times with our body at its centre" (James, 1912/1976, p. 86.) He continued:

> Where the body is is "here"; when the body acts is "now"; what the body touches is "this"; all other things are "there" and "then" and "that." These words of emphasized position imply a systematization of things with refer-

ence to a focus of action and interest *which lies in the body*; ... no developed or active experience exists for us at all except *in that ordered form*. (p. 86, emphasis added)

Commenting on James's position concerning the centrality of the body in knowing, Wild (1969) wrote: "The living body which exists as a finite thing in the world ... plays a major role in the constitution of the very same world" (p. 377).

Gibson's claim that self is present in the perceptual field, and James's parallel claim that ultimately the felt self refers to perceivable bodily activities, lead both of them to the same conclusion about the standard distinction between the objective and subjective domains: Instead of being separate metaphysical domains, the objective and subjective are different "poles of attention" (J. J. Gibson, 1979). If the environment and self are co-perceived, then whether individuals are experiencing a feature of the environment or the self at any particular moment depends on what they choose to notice. The information specifying both is simultaneously available to be perceived, and objective versus subjective experience is a matter of selection. Thus, the objective–subjective dichotomy, as traditionally construed, breaks down. Instead, "all that is experienced is, strictly considered, objective" (James, 1890/1981, p. 290). He continued that subsequently: "this Objective falls asunder into two contrasted parts, one realized as 'Self,' and the other as 'not-Self'; and that over and above these parts there *is* nothing save the fact that they are known" (p. 290).

Experience of the self is present in the case of both percepts and concepts, and indeed, in all cases of selection—that is, of knowing. James anchored experience of the self in a "feeling of bodily life," rather than the kinds of perceptual information Gibson later identified. However, it is unlikely that James would have objected to including this perceptual information as bases for experiencing of the self. Recall that James too identified empirical evidence of the self. As is shown in the next chapter, Gibson's concept of information would have been useful for James in a number of ways.

Holt's Concept of Adience and the Body

In *Animal Drive and the Learning Process* (1931), Holt tried to lay the theoretical foundation for a view that places the body at the center of all learning and knowing. Because his treatment of the body is intended to be thoroughly physicalistic, Holt's framework in this book is lacking the phenomenological character found both in James and in Gibson, and in some of Holt's other writings as well. However, the intentional character of action that can be seen in the phenomenological literature can be found in the way Holt conceptualized the body in the learning process. Although Holt did not use the term *intentionality* (it being, insufficiently physicalistic for his aims in this book), his central notion of "adience" arguably had an intentional flavor nevertheless.

Holt viewed behavior as directed toward the source of stimulation, not merely a consequence of stimulation. An adient response (chap. 2) is that action by which the organism gains "more of the stimulus," and because of this behavioral tendency, actions can be seen as patterns of "out-reaching, outgoing, inquiring, examining, and grasping" (Holt, 1934, p. 41). All behaviors of animals, except for the random movements of highly immature animals, always have an "objective reference":

> The movements that have been organized within the matrix of purely random motility, *all refer* to that factor ... *outside* the organism, which has stimulated the movement. ... And these movements cannot be described except with reference to some factor or factors outside of the organism. They are now not merely "reflexes," they are responses; they are aimed or oriented as the early random movements were not. And *external reference* is the great significant feature of this first step in integration. (p. 170)

Holt viewed behavior as one facet of a synergic relation between the environment and the behaving organism. There is an ongoing cyclical process of stimulation and responding against that same stimulus in order to gain more of it (i.e., adience). In the course of this ongoing process, action becomes more precisely directed toward increasingly specific characteristics of the stimulation. Behavior becomes more finely tuned relative to environmental features, and this greater differentiation of action is the ground for further action.

James's view of the body as the "centre of vision, centre of action, centre of interest" is clearly evident in this behavioristic account offered by Holt. Different aspects of Holt's account are articulated subsequently by his two most prominent students: Tolman further developed the referential nature of behavior in his framework of purposive behaviorism. The synergic relation between behavior and environment, with directed actions of the individual playing a central role, is developed by Gibson through his important concept of a "perceptual system."

Adience and Perceptual Systems

Holt's conceptualization of behavior as reflected in the notions of the reflex-circle and the adient response is a departure from the reflex arc model that underlies most behaviorist and behaviorist-inspired models (e.g., information-processing models). In the reflex arc model, there is a unidirectional causal chain from stimulus to response. In Holt's framework, behavior is an ongoing, cyclical process in which stimulation imposed from without initiates an adient response, which leads to further stimulation, and so forth. In contrast to the reflex arc conceptualization, it is an attempt to come to grips with the complexity of animal–environment relations. Gibson took Holt's effort several steps further with highly significant consequences for theory and research.

J. J. Gibson (1966) emphasized that stimulation (and in his later writings, stimulus information) is obtained by the organism rather than being imposed on the organism. Stimulus information is obtained as a result of self-produced actions; it is not forced on the organism. This view differs somewhat from Holt's, who posited that the reciprocal exchange between the organism and the environment is set in motion by imposed stimulation. It is with this point that claiming Holt to be fully promoting an intentional theory is questionable. In Gibson's theory, stimulus information is detected by an intrinsically active organism whose exploratory actions do not need to be triggered by the environment. Holt did leave room in his account for self-initiated actions; but these actions are unsystematic and random movements. Thus, the only intentional or objectively referenced actions are *adient responses*: "The 'reflex-circle' always starts with an *aimless, chance* innervation of a muscle, but ends with a reflex established which is always a response that intelligibly refers to the stimulus, and one that is often distinctly 'purposive'" (Holt, 1934, p. 40, emphasis added).

The reason why Holt included this initial step of stimulation is that he was attempting to develop a conception of "animal drive" that, to his mind, was thoroughly biological, and thus not attributable to unseen inner (vitalistic) states. Accordingly, he viewed behavior as fundamentally a release of stored food energy in the receptors and muscles initiated by the environment. With this conceptualization, Holt explicitly acknowledged the congruence of aspects of a Pavlovian approach with his own. Further, here it can be seen that Holt remained tied to an S-R framework, although with the concept of adience he approached breaking free of it.

In contrast, Gibson's view of an active organism, whose systematic and controlled actions do not have to be initiated by stimulation, creates theoretical possibilities for an account of perceiving that are not available in Holt's position. As is discussed in the next chapter, a perceiver who engages in exploratory actions creates opportunities to detect invariant structure in the perceptual field that otherwise are not readily detected. Holt's conception of the origins of an adient response ultimately contrasts with the ecological view because at the outset, according to his view, behavior is reactive and unsystematic rather than active and directed.

This viewpoint constrains Holt's perspective in a significant way relative to Gibson's. The notion of adience does not lead to the idea of stimulus information in Gibson's sense of the term (chap. 4). Stimulus information is revealed by exploratory movements of the perceiver. An adient response, which is initiated by imposed stimulation, would only lead to more stimulation, not more stimulus information (J. J. Gibson, 1966).

A further difference between Holt's notion of adient responses and Gibson's emphasis on exploratory actions in perceiving concerns the account of awareness to which each leads. As noted previously, Holt seemed to embrace the kind of motor theory of consciousness promoted by Münsterberg, one of his influential teachers. According to this view, perceptual awareness is produced by motor responses when engaging specific objects or by anticipated motor responses. It involves "having an experience," which is a product of the body's functioning. In Gibson's framework, the perceiver does not "have an experience"; the perceiver experiences the environment through exploratory activity. Awareness is an inherent quality of the process of picking up stimulus information. "The pickup of information specifying x necessarily involves some awareness of x" (Reed, 1996a, p. 98). Or, as J. J. Gibson (1979) put it, "Perceiving is an experiencing of things" (p. 178). Holt and Gibson, then, differed markedly in ways they approached the phenomena of perceptual awareness. However, neither offered a well-articulated analysis of perceptual awareness.

In spite of these differences, Holt's notion of a reflex-circle clearly paved the way for Gibson's notion of a perceptual system. Two characteristics of the perceptual system with roots in Holt's work are, first, the view that perceiving organisms function in an integrated fashion, rather than in terms of discrete responses, and second, the view that there is an ongoing reciprocal loop in perceiving–action functions. The integrative and coordinated nature of behavior is a central theme in Holt's *Animal Drive*. The view that environmental stimulation and behavior are reciprocal and ongoing functions was also offered by Holt, although not in as fully developed a manner as presented by Gibson with the idea of a perceptual system.[9]

Clearly, Gibson was influenced by Holt's ideas on the coordinated and directed nature of behavior, and its synergic relation to environmental stimulation. But Gibson was able to move beyond Holt's narrower

---

[9]Floyd Allport (1955), a third prominent student of Holt's, offered what he called "a dynamic structural theory of behavior," which was also built on a cyclical or systems view of perception. Allport's book clearly was influenced by Holt's writings, but its more proximate influence was the developing field of cybernetics. The latter also clearly influenced Gibson's thinking (as becomes evident later in chap. 7), and it shaped some of Roger Barker's work as well.

physicalistic approach to offer a view of a more thoroughgoing perception–action system centered in the perceived body. That is, Gibson was able to break completely from a stimulus–response psychology, which was a step Holt could not quite take. Gibson's perceiver is a thoroughly active and purposive perceiver; and with this perspective, J. J. Gibson (1966, 1979) was able to return to and expand on James's largely undeveloped idea of the role of the "body" in experience.

James J. Gibson, 1970s
(Division of Rare and Manuscripts Collections, Cornell University Library)

4

Relations and Direct Perception

> The parts of experience hold together from next to next by relations that are themselves parts of experience. The directly apprehended universe needs, in short, no extraneous trans-empirical connective support, but possesses in its own right a concatenated or continuous structure. (James, 1909/1996, p. 7)

The metatheoretical starting point for both William James's philosophy of radical empiricism and James Gibson's ecological psychology is the mutuality between the knower and the object known, which was the focus of the previous chapter. From there, they turn their attention to the nature of the *context* within which knowing processes transpire. The objects and events of the environment are embedded in a rich web of relations. Critically, these relations can be perceived by the knower; they are "in" the environment and not imposed on it.

The previous chapter considered an example of such a relation in experience: Individuals perceiving their own body and actions in relation to the environment. Accompanying any act of perceiving is information specific to oneself; hence the environment–perceiver relation is present in every act of perceiving. This ubiquitous and fundamental perceived relation is but one instance of a more extensive set of relations among objects and events available to be experienced by a perceiver. Recognizing this web of structural relations in the environment opens up new ways to conceptualize perceiving and thinking. One significant implication of the view that relations are available to be perceived is that the environmental context presents the individual with open-ended possibilities for knowing (chap. 5).

This chapter examines Gibson's approach to the environmental context for knowing using James's radical empiricism as a backdrop. In so doing, their commonalties are revealed, including some of the theoretical consequences that grow out of their shared point of view. One significant commonality to be considered is the place of relations in their theoretical positions.

RELATIONS IN PURE EXPERIENCE AND IN THE AMBIENT ARRAY

The world that we experience is not a chaotic amalgam of disconnected objects that enter and leave our field of attention willy nilly. Nor is it a neat, orderly, and fixed domain. There is diversity in the field of experience as well as change; but it is diversity and change with a discernible degree of structure, stability, and continuity. Providing the coherence among objects and events are *relations*. Certain objects occur with other objects or in certain contexts, whereas some objects never occur with certain other objects or never in certain contexts. Certain events always precede other events, and other events only follow certain events, whereas certain events preclude the occurrence of other events, and so on. In short, we experience objects and events and their relations.

A central concern for James in his philosophy of radical empiricism is the *source* of these relations (see chap. 1). James objected to the two standard explanations of the origins of relations in experience: (a) The *empiricist* view is that relations in experience are due solely to "habits" of thought and action (i.e., beliefs) based on the contingencies of past occurrences. In this case (following Hume), relations are not parts of sensory experience; nor do they rest on any substantive, extra-mental foundation. Order is apparent, not real. It is something that is imposed on sensory experience by the associative workings of mind. (b) The *intellectualist* view is that relations in the world are added to experience by either structuring intellectual processes/mind (rationalism) or by a transcendent Absolute (idealism). In these cases, the order has a real basis, but this basis lay outside of experience itself. In James's view, both of these approaches are fraught with deep problems. (Some of James's objections to these approaches were discussed in chap. 1.)

Seeking an alternative to both of these options, James proposed that the relations among entities in experience are intrinsic to experience. Relations are there to be perceived: "The relations between things, conjunctive as well as disjunctive, are just as much matters of direct particular experience, neither more nor less so, than the things themselves" (James, 1909/1978, p. 7). In order to account for relations in experience, then, it is not necessary to propose that relations reflect the beliefs separate individuals have come to hold about experience, or to turn to sources outside of immediate experience. The experienced world itself has order. Objects and their relations are there to be discovered through processes of knowing. Knowledge is possible through the discovery of structure intrinsic to the "quasi-chaos" of immediate experience. This claim lies at the heart of his radical empiricist program.

James's claim that relations are to be found in experience has at least two significant consequences. First, because relations are intrinsic to experience, direct perception of the environment—rather than perception by way of a mental intermediary—becomes feasible. Second, owing to the richness of these relations, on the one hand, and the selective agency that is the hallmark of knowing, on the other, there is an inexhaustible number of possible structures that can be differentiated from immediate experience. This is not to say that immediate experience is infinitely malleable, however. The relations that are present do place real evidentiary constraints on knowing. Indeed, what is known can and should be pragmatically tested continually to evaluate its truth value.

Similarly, Gibson's account of direct perception in his ecological theory turns on the claim that relations among perceived objects are intrinsic to experience. Gibson expressed this idea in a different way than did James, namely, in terms of ecological optics (see later). By exploring this issue, Gibson was able to take his discussion of relations in experience to a deeper level of specificity than James, although admittedly Gibson's program is comparatively more limited in its scope. But then, the psychologist Gibson was concerned with a more restricted set of issues than the philosopher James. In spite of this difference, Gibson approached the question of the basis for order or organization in perceptual experience along the very same trail blazed by James.

One way the similarity in their approaches can be seen is that Gibson identified his ecological approach as occupying the same metatheoretical niche that radical empiricism carved out in relation to other approaches to knowing. In a discussion of the basis for perceptual organization, Gibson contrasted the empiricist approach, wherein elements are connected through association, with the Gestalt approach, wherein the inherent organizing forces of the brain are posited as supplying the connections. Like James, Gibson rejected both of these options. He claimed that neither an associationist nor a rationalist account is necessary because stimulus information is "*already* organized and therefore do[es] not have to have organization imposed on [it]" (J. J. Gibson, 1966, p. 267).

Gibson supported this position through the development of the concepts of the "ambient optic array" and "stimulus information." Significantly, both of these concepts bolster the radical empiricist perspective because they instantiate the Jamesian claim that relations are intrinsic to experience.

What Is There to Be Perceived?

Both James and Gibson recognized the value of phenomenological description (chap. 3). However, as a scientist, Gibson followed Koffka's (1935) lead by going beyond the phenomenological question of "What do things look like?" to ask two further questions: a functional question followed by a more analytical one. The functional question is "What properties of its econiche does an animal perceive in carrying out its various activities?" The analytical question is "What conditions make these functionally significant properties available to be perceived?"

J. J. Gibson began his later books (1966, 1979) by asking, "What is there to be perceived?" Unlike most psychological treatments of perception, Gibson raised this question before introducing a consideration of the perceiver and the nature of perceptual processes. And from an evolutionary perspective, this approach makes good sense. After all, perceptual processes evolved against a set of background conditions, enabling animals to function successfully in their econiche. Moreover, to varying degrees, animals modify the environment to be more suitable for their purposes. A consideration of the econiche, then, reveals a great deal about the kinds of ecological problems perceptual and cognitive processes evolved to address.

Gibson's preliminary answer to these questions is that the perceptual systems of animals have evolved to support perceiving and utilizing the *affordances* of the environment. To make a start at enumerating what some of these affordances are, the functional supports that a particular animal needs in its daily commerce must be considered (Heft, 1988a). To illustrate, terrestrial animals require supportable surfaces that afford locomoting in order to reach resources such as food and shelter. They also need to be able to detect barriers or obstacles that could impede locomotion to those resources. Thus, surfaces of support and objects that may impede locomotion are some of the affordances of the environment for a terrestrial animal, as are concave surfaces that can be used as shelters, detached objects that can be used as tools, transportable materials that can be used for building, and so on (see J. J. Gibson, 1979, chap. 3).

(It is important to bear in mind that what is being proposed here in general terms is a method for describing the salient functional features of the animal's econiche. This approach should not be taken as offering an account of the history of the animal–econiche relation. Accordingly, it is not simply the case that a preexisting set of functional needs or skills determine what features of the environment the animal adapts to. Surely, the interrelations involved are more complex. Whereas functional needs or skills might drive adaptation in some cases, particular functional needs also develop because they enable the animal to exploit existing resources in the environment and thereby increase the species' viability. That is, there is a co-evolution of animal and environment.)

Identifying affordances of the econiche is preliminary to an analytical question: "What is it about the structure of the natural world that makes it possible for an animal to detect functionally significant environmental properties?" Gibson's hypothesis in the case of vision is that these properties are carried by information in reflected light. Attempting to work out this possibility led Gibson to develop a new area of inquiry he called "ecological optics."

Ecological Optics

The centuries' old field of physical optics has exhaustively examined how light interacts with translucent bodies such as lenses, and as a consequence, it has produced detailed and invaluable knowledge about these phenomena. By comparison, however, little attention has been paid to the issue of how light reflecting off of opaque surfaces is structured by those surfaces. With his ground-breaking work on texture gradients, Gibson (1950) established the importance of the surface qualities of objects for perceiving. From this starting point, he was led in later work to considerations of how reflected light in the environment can give rise to an array of potential information about the layout of surfaces.

J. J. Gibson (1966, 1979) proposed that surrounding any position or potential point of observation in the environment is an array of light reflected from the layout of surfaces present.[1] This array of reflected light—the *ambient optic array*—is variously structured by surface features such as texture, pigmentation, and angle in relation to the light source. What results (i.e., what the array is comprised of) are discontinuities in the reflected light, and these discontinuities with their sources in the surface layout can be described as a projected set of solid visual angles of reflected light.[2] The apexes of the dense and nested collection of solid visual angles of reflected light are located (i.e., they converge) at, practically speaking, an infinite number of positions in the immediate environment at which a perceiver could establish a point of observation. Because the ambient optic array is structured by the character of the surface layout, it is possible to consider if these solid visual angles of reflected light at a point of observation can serve as *information* specifying surface layout.

---

[1]Gibson's account of the structure of the ambient array was modified slightly between his 1966 and 1979 books. The description employed here mostly draws on that used in the later book and departures from it are only for the sake of clarity.

[2]Considered on a two-dimensional plane, an object can be described as projecting a visual angle of a particular extent to the eye. In the everyday (three-dimensional) environment, objects project solid visual angles to the eye of a perceiver.

This conceptualization is but a first step, however, because it has long been known that a geometric projection of the configuration of surfaces in the surround to a hypothetical point "in space" is equivocal in relation to its source (i.e., the reflecting surfaces). An identical projection of reflected light to a single point can be produced by a family of different configurations of surface layout. Suppose, for example, that there is an elliptical shape (the base of a cone of reflected light) in the field of view at a particular observation point. This shape carried in the reflected light could, in principle, be due to the reflection of light from a family of surface shapes, ranging from circular to increasingly acute elliptical shapes. In other words, there is a many-to-one mapping relation between surface layout possibilities and projected light. This is the problem of "equivalent configurations." Because projected shape is equivocal from an observation point, standard theories of perception have seen it necessary to posit something along the lines of supplemental processes that function to offer a reasoned guess as to which of the possible shapes is the most likely distal source of the projected shape.

If this kind of perceptual equivocality were commonplace—and standard accounts of perception claim that it is—animals would continually find themselves in a rather precarious position in the environment. Their well-being from moment to moment would depend on making the correct "guess" as to the present environmental circumstances. On its face, such a strategy does not seem very sound from an evolutionary perspective; but, it may be the best one can do under the circumstances.

Alternatively, perhaps the circumstances have been misconstrued. The apparent equivocality may have been created in large measure by the way the optics of the situation have been conceptualized. Gibson agreed that the potential for equivocality of reflected light to a single point of observation exists, but that situation constitutes a special case—namely, when the environment is perceived from a static or "frozen" vantage point. More commonly, and almost always available to perceivers, is the possibility of moving rather than remaining stationary. And what may be equivocal information from a stationary point, rarely is from a moving point of observation. As the perceiver moves with respect to a continuous series of observation points, (the idea of a "point" of observation now becoming an idealization), correspondingly there is generated a changing array of structured light available to be detected. What is especially interesting about this changing array of structured light is that, typically, while some portions of it change, others do not. Particular relations in the reflected light remain constant or invariant across changes. These invariants correspond to persisting properties of the surface layout.

Thus, introducing changes in the ambient optic array through exploratory movements of the perceiver, or alternatively, as a result of movements of the object, results in the potential for optically isolating those structures in reflected light that are invariant from those that are not. More simply put, exploratory movements create opportunities for the perceiver to detect invariant structures in reflected light, which in turn specify persisting features of the environment.

Invariants as Stimulus Information.   What is meant by invariant information revealed through change in the ambient array? It refers to higher order relations in the structure of reflected light that do not change in the context of an otherwise changing array. Consider the following example: A classic problem in the study of visual perception is that of shape constancy. Take a cube positioned on a tabletop and a fixed position from which to perceive it. From a stationary position, there appears a projected shape that includes perhaps two or three surfaces. If a different stationary position is adopted, a different projected shape would be visible. How does it happen that when the perceiver walks around the cube, what is experienced is an object of a constant shape even as the projected form of the cube changes with every change in the perceiver's position?

The standard empiricist approach to this problem is to suppose that cues are available to be utilized by a perceiver in constructing an hypothesis based on prior experiences as to the object's true shape. Less common in the 20th century, although experiencing a resurgence of late, is the rationalist position that perceivers automatically impose a particular order (in this case, shape) on a projected pattern of stimulation (form), with the basis for this pattern attributable to the way the mind naturally (i.e., has evolved to) structures certain types of input. In both cases, cognitive processes are applied to a present pattern of stimulation, and the outcome of these processes is the experience of the three-dimensional shape presumably underlying and accounting for appearances—that is, the reality that lies behind appearances is "inferred." In both cases, perceivers do not experience the environment as such; instead, what is experienced is a mental construction, namely, the environment elaborated by mental processes.

Is it possible, however, that the structure present in the ambient array is such that the three-dimensional shape can be directly perceived? Gibson took this tack. In the case of the present problem, it is hypothesized that what specifies object shape is that structure in the reflected light that remains constant across transformations generated from a moving point of observation. Because this structure remains invariant, and because it is specific to a particular object shape (i.e., there is a one-to-one mapping relation between the two), it could be said with justification that this invariant structure in reflected light can serve as information for the presence of this object (rather than some other object) in the immediate environment.

But this statement does not go far enough. The next step must be taken and this invariant must be identified, which is a difficult task. It is toward this effort that much basic work in an ecological approach to vision has been directed, and a great deal of this work remains to be done.[3] Through some of the initial work, a clearer sense of what invariants are has emerged. This conceptualization can best be illustrated by way of a relatively simple example. Consider the case of a line of fixed length as it undergoes a 45-degree rotation around a vertical axis. Possibly, an individual observing this rotation might be uncertain as to whether the line is remaining constant in length but turning around an axis (rotation), or if it is changing in length rather than rotating (foreshortening). It can be demonstrated, however, that particular relations are preserved as the line undergoes rotation. Taking any four distinct points (A, B, C, D) along the line, it can be shown that as the line rotates, the ratio of the ratios (AC/BC) and (AD/BD) remain constant from position to position. This ratio of ratios is a *cross-ratio*. So, for example, the cross-ratio (AC/BC):(AD/BD) at the initial position is equal to the cross ratio (A'C'/B'C'):(A'D'/B'D') at a second position (Meserve, 1955). The equivalent cross-ratios indicate that a set of invariant relations is preserved across the transformation.

The invariance of cross-ratios illustrates the presence of a geometric relation in the changing visual array that can specify a line of fixed length undergoing rotation. More generally, it illustrates that there are invariant properties of the optic array considered dynamically that can serve as information for perceiving constant object properties (Cutting, 1986; Johansson, von Hofsten, & Jansson, 1980).

Whether a perceiver on any given occasion detects an invariant is another matter. The claim being made here is that invariant relations are present as *potential information* for a perceiver. The array of perceptual information is considered independently of a perceiver. If perceivers detect this information, then perforce they will perceive (be aware of) a line of a fixed length undergoing rotation. To return to the example of the line undergoing rotation, it is quite possible (although considerably more difficult) to look at this kind of display as if it were a foreshortening rather than a rotation. In doing so, the perceiver selects information in the array of available information that is specific to foreshortening (i.e., an elastic transformation) instead of information specifying a rotating line of fixed length (i.e., a rigid transformation), although this is difficult to maintain for very long. (It is difficult to maintain, because if indeed the event is a rigid object undergoing rotation, information for an elastic event is not fully

---

[3]Indeed, as Neisser (1978) pointed out some time ago, the identification of stimulus invariants is "the largest outstanding promissory note in ecological optics" (p. 24). This statement remains only slightly less true today.

specified, and hence such an experience is unstable.) Perceiving is a process of selection, as James emphasized.

Presumably, the previous problem of perceiving the constant cube shape of the object while moving around it can be solved in this same way, although here we would be dealing with a more complex set of invariant cross-ratios (J. J. Gibson, 1979). Research is ongoing to explore the most appropriate way of understanding the invariants that are the basis for complex perceptual phenomena such as shape constancy (e.g., Pizlo, 1994; Pizlo & Stevenson, 1999). The set of invariants would uniquely specify a particular shape. But this is not to say that mistakes will not be made. On some occasions, object shape will be misperceived; indeed, it should be possible to predict which shapes will be confused because of similar cross-ratios. What is being claimed is that the information specifying a particular object shape is available to the perceiver, and the object is perceived through the pick up of that invariant information. As a result, perceiving object shape accurately is not a result of mentally constructing the object, but rather is a result of detecting a specific invariant structure. In other words, it is an instance of *direct perception*.

Often invariant information specifying features of the environment is revealed through perceiver–environment interaction, as in the case of a perceiver moving around an object. It is also the case that when objects, and especially animate objects, move in relation to a stationary perceiver, invariants are revealed. Thus, exploratory actions of the individual are not essential in all cases; but some source of change in the ambient array, whether induced by the perceiver or the object, greatly facilitates isolation of invariants.[4]

Finally, the account of shape perception offered by the ecological approach appears to overcome a logical inadequacy inherent in the approach of standard accounts of perception that posit supplemental, cognitive processes. It assumed in these approaches that an object's "true" three-dimensional shape is underdetermined by the projected two-dimensional form. For this reason, it is only by going beyond this projected form to take into account cues about surface slant that it is possible to infer (or, as Helmholtz said, "imagine") what the three-dimensional shape is. There is a fundamental problem with this formulation, however. To briefly take up a Jamesian objection (discussed further later), how can stimulation lacking in some property—in the present case, depth—give rise to this same property? That is, how can essentially

---

[4]Gibson claimed that sometimes, as in the case of picture perception, invariants can be perceived in a frozen array of stimulus information. Such cases are much more complex and at the present time not well understood. Gibson's approach offers very different grounds for approaching picture perception than do representational theories (J. J. Gibson, 1971, 1979, chap. 15). Costall's (1993) essay on this approach is recommended.

"depthless" views (sensations) of a cube give rise to the experience of a three-dimensional object (perception)? It could be argued, in reply, that three-dimensionality is a contribution solely of perceiver processes along the lines of Kantian a priori categories. But this kind of move puts the world as a common ground for experience out of reach, and as such it teeters on the brink of solipsism.

These difficulties can be side-stepped if instead of conceptualizing the problem as one of restoring three-dimensional structure to a two-dimensional projection that underdetermines perceptual experience, it can be claimed that the information available to be perceived specifies what is presently experienced. Although information to a fixed point of observation may underdetermine perceptual experience, information to a moving point of observation usually does not. The claim that invariant information specific to an object can be detected along a path of movement extends this possibility that "depth" can be directly perceived.

Importantly, this brief discussion of invariants leads back to the fundamental claim of radical empiricism. Relations do not need to be imposed on entities in perceptual experience if they are present there to begin with. In ecological terms, these relations include higher order invariants that are available to be detected from a moving point of observation in the ambient array. Structure and order are discovered in the dynamic of knower–object known reciprocity.

James on the Perception of Size Constancy.   The conceptual tools Gibson utilized to develop ecological optics, such as the notion of mathematical invariance, were relatively new in James's day (Cutting, 1986), and there is no apparent evidence that James was familiar with these ideas. However, James anticipated the kind of relational analysis of perceiving and an emphasis on invariants that Gibson later developed. James's analysis of the problem of size constancy foreshadows Gibson's account, and a brief examination of his proposal provides a further indication of the theoretical linkages between James and Gibson.

In *The Principles*, James examined this problem through the case of perceiving a stick being rotated. He proposed that the perceiver becomes exposed to the true length of the stick when it is in the frontal-parallel plane. As the stick is rotated, its apparent length is gradually foreshortened until its far end is occluded by its near end. At that point, when

the far end is ready to be eclipsed, the difference of its distance from the near end's distance must be judged equal to the stick's whole length; but that length has already been judged equal to a certain optical sensation of breadth. *Thus we find that given amounts of visual depth-feeling become signs of fixed amounts of visual breadth-feeling.* (James, 1890/1981, p. 849)

That is, constant length, and hence breadth, is perceived as a fixed extent that varies lawfully across the rotation of the object. With sufficient exposure, the perceiver comes to experience a certain "space-feeling" that is the object's length irrespective of its relative orientation:

> The *measuring* of our space-feelings against each other mainly comes about through successive arousal of different ones by the same *thing*, by our selection of certain ones as feelings of its *real* size and shape, and by the degradation of others to the status of being merely *signs* of these. (p. 899)

It is true that James's analysis here, with its references to judging, signs, and selection/degradation of space-feelings, could be read as consistent in many ways with contemporary constructivist views; or it could be read as a process of extracting invariant relations. In either case, James was groping toward the kind of analysis of stimulus information that Gibson later developed. Three characteristics of James' account are most notable in this regard: First, he was engaging in an analysis of relations in visual experience. Second, the informative relations specifying object size grow out of experience with an object under transformation. Third, the constant size of the object is detected in visual information alone; that is, supplementation of visual information with other modes of information (e.g., motor) is not necessary. In these respects, there can be seen a foreshadowing of Gibson's later ecological analysis.

Ecological Optics and the Recession of the Stimulus

There can be little doubt that Gibson's approach to perceiving generally, and ecological optics in particular, are rooted in large part in Holt's teachings. Holt took perceiving to be a functional adjustment of a whole organism to a distal feature of the environment. In doing so, Holt was proposing a distinctive kind of behaviorist approach—namely, one that contrasted sharply with the molecular view of behavior, the peripheralist orientation to sensory stimulation, and the proximal stimulus focus offered by other behaviorists. Holt's behaviorism sought lawful relations between purposive behavior and distal environment features.

The most original feature of Holt's account of perceiving is his notion of "the recession of the stimulus" (see chap. 2). He argued that as increasingly complex actions (i.e., activities at higher levels of organization and integration) are considered, the effective source of stimulation for that behavior "recedes" from the periphery of the body to more distant features of the environment. Holt urged psychologists to attempt to identify the distal features toward which any particular goal-directed actions are directed, and in so doing to uncover lawful relations between the environment and action.

The impact of Holt's "recession of the stimulus" on ecological theory can be seen in the development of Gibson's ideas. In his early "pre-ecological" writings, J. J. Gibson (1950a) attempted to understand how distal environmental features are perceived, and he proposed to do so by examining the higher order patterns of (proximal) retinal stimulation, which is a more molar level of analysis of the stimulus than was (or is, even today) customary. (The proposal that higher order patterns of stimulation be examined reflects the influence of Gestalt thinking on his work; see chap. 6). Gibson demonstrated that the perception of properties of the visual world such as surface slant or relative distance—properties of a greater complexity than those considered in most psychophysical research—could be potentially accounted for with reference to higher order patterns of retinal stimulation. But by retaining the proximal–distal distinction and focusing on the higher order pattern of retinal stimulation, Gibson had not yet completely embraced Holt's notion of the recession of the stimulus.

Gibson recognized in the decade following the publication of *The Perception of the Visual World* that a more adequate and coherent account of perceiving is provided by a detailed analysis of environmental layout as specified in the ambient optic array rather than by patterns of stimulation on the retinal surface. In effect, Gibson eventually abandoned the proximal-distal stimulus distinction in the analysis of perceiving. And in so doing, his later ecological theory becomes a realization of Holt's argument for recession of the stimulus object. By focusing on the affordances of the environment as the source of information, and the ambient optic array as the medium for information, the effective stimulus for perceiving resides in the environment, not on receptor surfaces.

The claim that Holt's influence is stronger in Gibson's later work can be supported by concrete evidence as well as the preceding theoretical change in his Gibson's approach. Gibson cited Holt as an influence in the prefaces to his 1966 and 1979 books, where the proximal-distal distinction has been abandoned and replaced by the ambient optic array. In contrast, Holt was not among those acknowledged as influences in J. J. Gibson's (1950a) psychophysical book where the proximal-distal distinction is retained.

DIRECT PERCEPTION

Gibson's claim that perception is direct and unmediated virtually stands alone in 20th-century psychology. All other recent theories assume that between stimulus input (sensations, sense data, stimulation, etc.), and psychological outcome (perceptual experience, response, action, etc.) are mediating processes that enrich or otherwise transform this input. The overwhelming dominance of this viewpoint testifies to the profound influence that Helmholtz's writings in the 19th century has had on 20th-century psychology.

Helmholtz's theory, with its intellectual roots in Berkeley's analysis of visual perception, is fundamentally an associative theory.[5] A classic problem that this theory was developed to address is that of distance perception. Berkeley and later Helmholtz (and legions of others) argued that distance in the third dimension, extending away from the perceiver, is not an immediate quality of visual experience owing to the two-dimensional character of the retinal image. Given this limitation, distance and any quality implicating the third dimension (as already seen in the case of shape perception) must be something added to visual experience (perception) beyond what is conveyed by processes involved in detecting stimulation (sensation). For this reason, Helmholtz argued that an individual must learn to detect distance through the intervention of mediating perceiving processes—that distance or depth is not an immediate quality of visual experience.

At least three prominent contemporaries of Helmholtz—Ewald Hering, Carl Stumpf, and William James—did not accept this empiricist account of distance perception. Instead, they argued that visual experience of a three-dimensional world is immediate, and that the experience of distance is an inherent quality of vision. If this is so—if distance is perceived immediately—then there is no need for intervening, mediating processes that add this quality to visual experience. This debate over the inferred versus the intrinsic nature of distance perception at a deeper level may turn into a debate over direct versus indirect perception.

In *The Principles of Psychology*, James offered a lengthy chapter on the "Perception of Space," which includes a detailed examination of the historical treatment of perception of distance or depth. James also dealt with this topic in the chapters on "Sensation" and on "The Perception of Things." He drew heavily on the writings of Hering and Stumpf in these sections. His approach to the perception of "space" is an intellectual antecedent to Gibson's argument for direct perception.[6] Moreover, it offers a compelling logical argument for why perception of depth must be direct.

---

[5]Cutting (1986) argued that the associative aspects of Helmholtz's and Berkeley's theories, respectively, have been overemphasized by 20th-century theorists, whereas other features of their treatment of visual perception have been neglected. See Hatfield (1990) for a detailed study of Helmholtz's account of perception.

[6]I need to explain why the term "space" appears in quotes here. In many writings on perception, Gibson's early writings included, 'space' is used interchangeably with the term *environment*. However, these terms have very different connotations, and accordingly, it is important to employ them consistently (as Gibson later did) in ways that reflect these differences. Use of the term 'space' in theories of perception derives from Cartesian thinking. It was the genius of Descartes to recognize that position could be mathematically expressed in relation to three orthogonal axes. With this framework, one can talk about position or location with a high degree of precision and objectivity. Within the universe of Cartesian coordinates, objects are located in empty container space. The application of mathematical specificity to object location is a critical discovery underlaying much modern technology and physical science. *(continued on next page).*

Sensation and Perception According to William James

It is useful to begin a consideration of James's approach to 'space perception' by examining how he used the terms *sensation* and *perception*. This is an important place to start because James's usage differs from that of standard uses of these terms in perceptual psychology, and for this reason, he can be easily misread. Moreover, clarification of James's intentions here sheds light on Gibson's theory.

With few exceptions, the standard use of sensation refers to elementary deliverances from the sensory receptors. A corollary to this definition is the claim that there is a stage following sensation called perception during which these elementary sensations are utilized in the construction of the individual's experience of the world. So, for example, sensations that themselves provide no information about space or distance are collated or cross-referenced associatively with sensations that do (e.g., tactile sensations) so that a three-dimensional world is constructed in perception.

James (1890/1981) viewed sensation and perception in a very different way. For James, both terms refer to "processes in which we cognize an objective world" (p. 651). That is, each refers to a relation that an individual establishes with the world. Sensation and perception are "names for different cognitive *functions*, not for different sorts of mental *fact*" (p. 651). Knowledge of the world is conveyed by both sensation and perception.

These claims anticipate the kind of approach James would later develop in detail in his radical empiricist philosophy; and, in retrospect, knowledge of radical empiricism clarifies James's intent for these concepts in *The Principles*. Radical empiricism seeks to establish the metaphysical grounds

---

[6] *(continued from previous page)* Central to the ecological position is a recognition that, unlike space, the environment is not an empty expanse in which objects are located. The environment is comprised of inanimate and animate objects, events, and so on. The latter are not in the environment, as objects are *in* space; they *are* the environment. A description of the environment is a description of the layout of surfaces and of the location and movement of objects relative to that surface layout (J. J. Gibson, 1979).

This difference in terminology matters because using the term 'space' synonymously with environment can affect how the environment is conceptualized. As a case in point, consider the recent literature on 'spatial cognition.' Researchers interested in studying children's and adults' knowledge of environments, and stimulated by Piagetian theory (with its intellectual roots in Kantian philosophy), have formulated research problems in terms of an abstract, geometric conceptualization of the environment-as-space. There is reason to believe, however, that performance on tasks assessing spatial knowledge (e.g., Euclidean relations) may not be strongly related to performance in environments. This possibility is reflected in the fact that the skill in children's everyday environmental activities exceed what might be expected from estimates of geometrical reasoning (see Heft & Wohlwill, 1987).

for a theory of knowing built on a foundation of an immediate relation between the knower and the object known. For James, perceiving is not a mental event occurring apart from the world. In his essay "Does Consciousness Exist?" (James, 1912/1976), he rejected this view of mind. Instead, perceiving is a relation between perceiver and the world. It is in this vein that he suggested considering sensation and perception both as relations or "functions for cognizing the objective world."

If sensation and perception are both relations between knower and known, then how do they differ? Unlike the empiricist theory that has percepts being constructed out of sensations, in James's view sensations and perceptions are integral processes in their own right, differing in the degree of complexity of their content. This qualitative difference turns on James's distinction between "knowledge by acquaintance" and "knowledge about." Knowledge by acquaintance is a "dumb way" of knowing, a mere exposure to a quality:

> I am acquainted with many people and things, which I know very little about, except their presence in the places where I have met them. I know the color blue when I see it, and the flavor of a pear when I taste it ... but about the inner nature of these facts or what makes them what they are, I can say nothing at all. (James, 1890/1981, p. 217)

Sensations are the basis for knowledge by acquaintance: "The nearer the object cognized comes to being a simple quality like, 'hot,' 'cold,' 'red' ... the more the state of mind approaches pure sensation" (James, 1890/1981, p. 651). As for *perception*, the richer in relations the cognized object is, such that it can be perceptually "classed, located, measured, compared", that is, the more that its function is "knowledge *about* a fact" (James, 1890/1981, p. 651), the more is the experience one of *perception*. But in either case, experience is a relation between the perceiver and the world. Importantly, "in both sensation and perception we perceive the fact as an *immediately present outward reality*, and this makes them differ from 'thought' and 'conception,' whose objects do not appear present in this immediate physical way" (p. 652).

As this passage makes clear, James distinguished between sensation and perception, on the one hand, and thought, on the other, with reference to how these phenomena appear in experience; and he concluded that they differ in terms of whether the cognized object is present. This demarcation differs from Helmholtzian accounts, where the conceptual "break" among these three terms is drawn between sensation, on the one hand, and perception and cognition, on the other. In Helmholtzian theories, perception is viewed as operating along the lines of cognitive processes, being inferential or "ratiomorphic."

James did not agree with the view that percepts are constructed out of sensations because the introspective (phenomenological) evidence does not support it. An individual can perceive, and by extension, think about an entity without any familiarity with the entity's qualities *qua* sensations:

> A blind man may know all *about* the sky's blueness, and I may know all *about* your toothache, conceptually; tracing their causes from primeval chaos, and their consequences to the crack of doom. But as long as he has not felt the blueness, nor I the toothache, our knowledge, wide as it is, of these realities, will be hollow and inadequate. (James, 1890/1981, p. 656)

"Knowledge by acquaintance" and "knowledge about" are distinct; the former is not a part of the latter. An elaborate knowledge about X will still lack certain qualities about X in the absence of sensation. Thus, if blueness or pain is not already part of an individual's immediate experience, perceptions will not be able to supply them.[7]

This same argument applies to the experience of distance. If distance is not already an intrinsic quality of experience, then subsequent processing cannot put it there.

> Retinal sensations are spatial; and were they not, no amount of "synthesis" with equally spaceless motor sensations could intelligibly make them so (p. 907). [And further] ... how it may be asked, can association produce a space-quality not in the things associated? How can we by induction or analogy infer what we do not already generically know? Can "suggestions of experience" reproduce elements which no particular experience originally contained? ... No theory is worthy of the name which leaves such a point obscure. (pp. 908–909)

On these grounds James argued that "space" must be an intrinsic quality of all experience: "*In each and every sensation, ... is the original sensation of space*, out of which all exact knowledge about space we afterwards come to have is woven by processes of discrimination, association, and selection" (p. 777).

Directly Perceiving Distance

In his development of "higher-order psychophysics," J. J. Gibson (1950a) gave considerable attention to problems concerning space perception, in-

---

[7] In contemporary philosophy, a similar kind of argument has been offered by Nagel (1974). He argued that we are unable, in principle, to fully adopt the point of view of an animal with different perceptual systems than ourselves.

cluding the perception of distance, of absolute and relative location of objects, and of shape constancy. He attempted to provide an empirical account for how these phenomena could be conveyed in the patterns of retinal stimulation. That is, he tried to show how it might be possible that distance was inherent in perceptual information, and thus that perception of distance was direct and unmediated. Principally, Gibson pointed to "texture gradients" as conveyors of such information. With this idea, it is argued that space, in the sense of the third dimension or distance, is perceived as recession along a textured ground surface that is "projected as a *gradient* of the decreasing optical size and increasing optical density of the features of the ground" (J. J. Gibson, 1979, p. 117).

The concept of texture gradients has become a staple of the perception literature. It is noteworthy, however, that in the mainstream literature a texture gradient is most often treated as a distance cue, i.e., as something to be used to infer distance, rather than as a basis for immediate experience of distance, which was what Gibson intended. In this fashion, Gibson's notion of texture gradients becomes assimilated to the dominant Helmholtzian theoretical point of view.

Although in his later work J. J. Gibson (1966, 1979) shifted his approach from looking for the basis of space perception in retinal stimulation to looking for its basis in the array of reflected light surrounding the perceiver, at both points in the development of his thinking he is exploring the Jamesian hypothesis that distance is directly perceived. In the later work where he has abandoned the proximal-distal stimulus distinction, texture gradients are not viewed as patterns of retinal stimulation but rather as projected structure from surface layout available to be perceived in the ambient optic array.

There is a difference between James's and Gibson's account of the nature of the immediate experience of 'space', however. James proposed that 'space' is an intrinsic quality of sensation, whereas Gibson claimed that it accompanies the detection of information about environmental layout, that is, it is a quality of perceptual awareness. This difference is probably little more than hair-splitting. Lacking the analytical tool of ecological optics, James reasonably viewed this property as a primitive quality of sensation. For Gibson, perceiving is a process of information pick up, and if 'space' is specified by, for example, properties of surface layout in the available information, then 'space' would be an intrinsic quality of perceiving. For Gibson, sensations—although also experienced in an unmediated fashion—do not carry information. Here J. J. Gibson (1966) explicitly acknowledged the influence of Thomas Reid's distinction between sensation and perception on his thinking, and he supported the validity of this distinction by arguing that "*detecting* something can sometimes occur without the accompaniment of sense impressions" (p. 2). He cited Michotte's "tunnel effect" as a clear example of the latter phenomenon (J. J. Gibson, 1966, p. 205).

On logical grounds, Gibson offered the same kind of argument that James did for the claim that distance is an intrinsic quality of visual perception. Parallel to James's claim that visual sensations originally lacking in spatial qualities could not be made to have them, J. J. Gibson (1979) stated in more general terms: "The fallacy is to assume that because inputs convey no knowledge they can somehow be made to yield knowledge by 'processing' them" (p. 253). If it is argued that spatial knowledge must come from somewhere, rather than being intrinsic to visual experience, then to claim this knowledge comes "magically" from ratiomorphic processes or from innate knowledge[8] is question begging. It only offers the appearance of an explanation: "Knowledge of the world cannot be explained by supposing that knowledge of the world already exists. [This is to] … imply cognition so as to account for cognition" (J. J. Gibson, 1979, p. 253).

Gibson may have picked up this Jamesian line of argument from Holt, who argued:

> To pretend that an organism *knows its environment* by means of a "soul" inside the organism knowing sensations and ideas which are also inside the organism, is, in the first place, to explain the process of knowing as being the process of knowing. This tautology does not attack the problem. (Holt, 1937, p. 35)

Instead, what James and Holt supposed from the perspective of radical empiricism is that perception of 'space' is intrinsic in the relations between the knower and the environment, and accordingly, this quality like many other perceived qualities can be found in immediate experience—it need not be added to experience. Indeed, it cannot be so added, in principle.

But, doesn't the claim that "space qualities" are intrinsic in the relations between knower and known merely relocate the tautology from the mind to the perceiver–environment relation? It does not because from a radical empiricist perspective there is structure in immediate experience that conveys this quality. Gibson took this Jamesian supposition further by exploring what this structure might be. He did so by developing ecological optics, which is certainly one of his most significant theoretical contributions.

---

[8]Gibson sometimes was misinterpreted as advocating a nativist theory. This error demonstrates the power of the nativist-empiricist fallacy. With this dichotomy as the only set of options, a rejection of empiricism would seem to imply an embrace of nativism.

If it is assumed that perceiving begins with a pattern of stimulation projected on the retinal surface, then perceiving depth or distance becomes a special problem that needs to be explained. Arguing as Gibson did that apprehension of distance is an intrinsic characteristic of perceiving surface layout suggests that distance is not a special case in perception after all, but instead that it is continuous with other perceptual phenomena. If perception begins with information about surface layout instead of perception of two-dimensional retinal patterns, then "there is no special kind of perception called depth perception, and the third dimension is not lost in the retinal image since it was never in the environment to begin with" (J. J. Gibson, 1979, p. 148). Indeed,

> [depth] is a loose term. If *depth* means the dimension of the object that goes with height and width, there is nothing special about it. Height becomes depth when the object is seen from the top, and width becomes depth when the object is seen from the side. ... The theory of depth perception is based on confusion and perpetuated by the fallacy of the retinal picture. (p. 148)[9]

Looked at in this way, the problem of depth perception as a special puzzle for perceptual theory is generated by contestable assumptions concerning the nature of vision.

Arguably, Gibson's stance on this issue shows the influence of Koffka and the Gestalt approach, with its roots in Hering's nativist views of 'space' perception. There is no question that Koffka was a major influence on Gibson (see chap. 6). However, Gibson's approach was more in the Jamesian than the Gestalt tradition, particularly when it comes to this issue. An important difference between the Gestalt view and the Jamesian–Gibsonian view is that for Gestalt psychologists, who were profoundly influenced by Kantian philosophy, qualities such as 'space' are attributable to inherent properties of brain processes. For a radical empiricist, however, space is an inherent quality of pure experience, residing in the relation between a knower and the world. In a related vein, because in James's and Gibson's accounts 'space' or distance resides in the perceiver–world relation, both theorists allow for perceptual learning from an initially primitive experience (E. Gibson, 1969, 1994). In contrast, the Gestalt approach, with its roots in Kantian transcendental philosophy, greatly underappreciates the place of perceptual learning in an individual's experience of the world.

---

[9]Gibson (personal communication, 1977) gained this insight from Merleau-Ponty's (1942/1963) writings on the phenomenology of perception.

THE ECOLOGICAL SOLUTION TO JAMES'S "TWO MINDS" PROBLEM

The final section of this chapter takes up a significant philosophical difficulty James faced in developing radical empiricism. The following discussion may seem like a departure from the preceding examination of Gibson's ecological theory, focusing as it does on a somewhat narrow philosophical problem. But, it is warranted at this juncture, for the following reasons: The viability of radical empiricism as James initially envisioned it, and on which (as this volume argues) the ecological program rests, may require an adequate resolution of this difficulty. (A second philosophical problem with the same potential consequences is examined in the next chapter). Moreover, and importantly, it appears that particular features of the ecological program can be applied reflexively to push radical empiricism in the very direction it needed to go in order to shore up this problem. In short, specific features of the ecological program that were examined earlier in this chapter may be the very tools James needed to resolve what was for radical empiricism a critical conceptual problem. This contribution of ecological psychology to radical empiricism further attests to their theoretical compatibility.

There has been some debate among James scholars about the nature of his metaphysical position. On the one hand, there have been those who have claimed that fundamentally James was a direct realist, or at least desired to be one, and that he sought to develop a *monistic metaphysics* that was compatible with this epistemology. Accordingly, he claimed that the ground of immediate experience existed independently of a perceiver and it could be experienced directly, and this ground was neither physicalistic nor idealist—the "stuff" of immediate experience is neither material nor ideational—but an ontologically neutral monism. As pointed out earlier, with radical empiricism James claimed that experience was fundamentally of a common primordial stuff ("pure experience") that can be known directly (without intermediaries) and out of which all the varieties of what is known are differentiated. Principal among the individuals holding this view were the New Realists, including Holt and Perry, James's early biographer.

On the other hand, some have claimed that a discontinuity exists between the neutral monism of James's epistemology and his metaphysics. Flanagan (1997), for one, argued that although neutral monism may hold for James's phenomenology (i.e., the world may fundamentally be experienced as being made of "one stuff") "such phenomenological primacy carries no ontological weight" (p. 45). Accordingly, James's neutral monism may be limited to his treatment of knowing or epistemology, and "being right about that has no consequences whatsoever for what is metaphysically basic" (p. 45).

Kuklick (1977), among others, went further to argue that toward the end of his life James embraced a metaphysics of pluralistic panpsychism as a means of addressing some conceptual difficulties. If so, James would be giving up neutral monism, in a metaphysical sense, for a form of idealism. This move is problematic with respect to James's realistic inclinations, as is discussed shortly.

I am reluctant to weigh in on this technical and complex philosophical debate. However, I believe that I can contribute to this discussion in a manner not yet considered. At least with regard to the theoretical problems that pushed James in the direction of panpsychism, I believe that some of the concepts of ecological psychology can head off this move. Whether the proposed ecological resolution to these problems (one to be taken up next and a second to be examined in chap. 5) can address the full gamut of reasons why James is read by some as advocating in the end this form of idealism, I cannot presently judge. But I do believe that the conceptual tools of ecological psychology can reflexively strengthen the possibility that a realist epistemology and a metaphysics of neutral monism can be reconciled.

Must Radical Empiricism Capitulate to Idealism?

What is this problem that vexed James so? This is the problem of how two perceivers ("two minds") can simultaneously experience the same thing; and it stems from the need to reconcile some essential claims in his psychology and philosophy. In his treatment of the nature of thought in *The Principles*, James identified several of thought's characteristic features, one of which is that the experiences of individual minds are personal and separate:

> My thought belongs with my other thoughts, and your thought with your other thoughts. ... Each of these minds keeps its own thoughts to itself. There is no giving or bartering between them. No thought even comes into direct *sight* of a thought in another personal consciousness than its own. Absolute insulation, irreducible pluralism, is the law. (James, 1890/1981, pp. 220–221)

The self-evident nature of this seemingly irrefutable assumption masks a deeper concern for James at the time. If, as the Idealists claimed (and recall that Idealism was the primary philosophical alternative to empiricism in late 19th/early 20th century), the relations in individual experience are provided by a transcendent Absolute, then ultimately all minds are connected via the Absolute. If this is true, then individual consciousness is not personal. As was discussed in chapter 1, Idealism was unacceptable to James for several reasons. First, it was inconsistent with the empirical fact of separate, insulated consciousnesses. Second,

James sought a naturalistic philosophy in which individuals inhabit and gain understanding about a common natural world, and any version of idealism would hinder this goal:

> James's own hope was to place different minds in a common world by giving them the possibility of directly experiencing the very same things. Only thus, he sometimes felt, can radical empiricism escape the snares of absolute idealism, for which contact between different minds can only occur within a universal consciousness. (Sprigge, 1993, p. 148)

Third, this "block universe" view offered by Idealists, where everything was interconnected via its relation to the transcendent Absolute, was incompatible with the possibilities for novelty and open-ended change that accompany an evolutionary perspective. Moreover, possibilities for change are essential for James's commitment to individual choice and action, and central to his ethics (H. Putnam, 1990). Thus, it was important for him to reject Idealism.

However, one common phenomenon of everyday experience appeared to be an obstacle to radical empiricism's fundamental claim that perceiving is a direct relation between a knower and an object, and seemed to leave him little option but to adopt a version of idealism. This is the phenomenon of two perceivers experiencing the same thing simultaneously.

Here is the problem. James wanted to maintain the following:

Perceiving is a direct relation between a knower and an object (the fundamental principle of radical empiricism).

The thoughts of individuals are insulated from one another (a primary attribute of consciousness that sustains individual choice and action).

Two (or more) individuals can experience the same object at the same time (the phenomenon to be explained).

James saw that it is difficult to maintain that all three claims are valid, for if knowing is a relation between an object and a knower, then how can two individuals—that is, two independent consciousnesses—simultaneously experience the same object directly? If perceiving is a direct relation between knower and object, and if two individuals can perceive the same object, it might seem that the assumption of the personal nature of consciousness cannot also be true. For if perceiving an object is a functional relation I establish with this object in my field of experience, how is it that you can also perceive the same object when I do? If James claims, as is consistent with naive realism, that we can both experience the same object at the same time, then he seems to place a central tenet of his psychology in jeopardy because, as he revealed in a 1905 note to himself, "in my doctrine that the same [object] may be known by two knowers I seem to imply that an identical part can help to *constitute* two fields [of experience]" (Perry, 1935, p. 750). That is, when you and I perceive the same object, "an identical part" of the world would be a facet of both of our experiences. This possibility presents a problem for James's position, because if an identical part of the world can simultaneously be an aspect of two knowers' experience, then each individuals' experience is not personal, rather they overlap at least partially with one another. This outcome would breach the autonomy of individual consciousness and would lead James down the path of *Idealism* by providing a connection between separate minds and ultimately a connection to the transcendent Absolute.

But this possibility simply does not square with the facts of daily life. If an individual's experience is not insulated and personal, but can overlap with that of another when they both are perceiving a common object, then at such times each individual would also have access to additional contents of the other's conscious experience (through the lines of relation that connect an individual's percepts and concepts). As a result, the claim that one part of an individual's field of experience (the perceived object) can simultaneously be a part of another individual's field of experience must be rejected. But how then can this common phenomenon of two perceivers experiencing the same thing be explained?

Rejecting the possibility that two individuals' fields of experience can overlap, there is a second avenue open to James, but one that is equally objectionable. It could be assumed that the experience of different individuals is separate and distinct and that two individuals can experience the same object if one rejects the immediacy of experience claim. Following this avenue of reasoning would require James to accept "the ordinary dualistic philosophy of insulated minds each knowing its object representatively as a third thing" (James, 1912/1976, p. 63). Thus, it is possible to claim that minds are insulated from one another, and that two (or more) individuals can experience the same object, if the object each mind is experiencing is in fact a representation of the object and not the object itself. In other words, the problem can be resolved by accepting *representationalism*, or indirect realism. The object would be part of both fields of experience not in any direct sense, but only as a token or a representation of a real physical object, the latter being located outside of both minds. For James, the solipsistic possibilities that follow from this dualistic position were to be avoided at all costs.

James initially sought to avoid these difficulties by proposing a different alternative: Direct experience of an object is quickly supplanted by a more indirect experience. In his essay, "How Two Minds Can Know One Thing," James stated the need to ask, "more precisely how the unit enters into either one of the streams of consciousness alone. Just what, from being 'pure' [experience], does its becoming 'conscious' *once* mean" (James, 1912/1976, p. 63). In reply to this question, he suggested that when the object of thought becomes part of conscious thought, it has been selected out of the stream of pure experience and is now a different, unique, and personal experience of the object:

> The [object], realized in this retrospective way as my percept, thus figures as a fact of "conscious" life. But it does so only so far as "appropriation" has oc-curred; and appropriation is *part of the content of the later experience* wholly additional to the originally "pure" [object]. ... To be "conscious" means ... to have awareness of one's being added to that being; and this is just what hap-pens when appropriative experience supervenes. (p. 64)

How adequate is this alternative? Following this line of theorizing, it appears that when "appropriative experience supervenes" direct experience, the object of consciousness is now "insulated" in separate minds. But he has salvaged personal consciousness at the cost of potentially reintroducing indirect perception into the position.

A remaining possibility also has undesirable consequences for radical empiricism, but in the end it appears to be the only avenue James viewed as left open to him. He wanted to follow Berkeley's dictum that "to be is to be perceived" in order to avoid physical world–mind dualism. Thus, knowing is a direct relation between a knower and an object in a field of experience. However, holding onto Berkeley's dictum while trying to account for how two (or more) individuals can experience the same object, and simultaneously avoiding Berkeley's and Royce's Idealism, requires that James posit the co-existence of two (or more) separate fields of knower–object experience wherein direct perception occurs. This circumstance is only possible if somehow there is a doubling (or more) of the object:

> [A] fact of consciousness exists but once. ... Its *esse* is *sentiri*; it is only so far as it is felt; and it is unambiguously and unequivocally exactly *what* is felt. The hy-pothesis under consideration would, however, oblige it to be felt equivocally, felt now as part of my mind and again at the same time *not* as a part of my mind, but of yours (for my mind is *not* yours), and this would seem impossible without doubling it into two distinct things. (James, 1912/1976, p. 63)

Under this account, there would be as many existing objects as there are individuals experiencing them at a given time. This solution is only avail-able if James adopts a metaphysics of *pluralistic panpsychism*. In such a world, there can be multiple realizations of an object in reality as gener-ated in relation to knowers. A significant difficulty with this solution is that (arguably) James's initial intention for radical empiricism was to develop a neutral ontology in order to avoid a metaphysics of either physicalism or idealism (see chap. 1, especially fn 9). With this pluralistic panpsychic alternative, "neutral experience was now not neutral, but throbbing, alive, constantly coalescing and re-coalescing" (Kuklick, 1977, p. 333). It is, in another words, a type of idealism, whereby reality is not ontologically neutral but mental.[10]

Among these three responses to the "two minds" problem—idealism, representationalism, and panpsychism—the latter ultimately appeared to James to be the least undesirable of three undesirable choices (Kuklick, 1977; Moller, 1997; Sprigge, 1993). By adopting this panpsychic resolution to the two minds problem, if not abandoning radical empiricism entirely, James was significantly retreating from his initial realist hopes for it.

Must radical empiricism in the end capitulate to panpsychism and hence become a variation of idealism? Apart from the difficulties it raises for radical empiricism, if panpsychism is the necessary outcome of the problem of two minds, then this book's claim that radical empiricism can function as an adequate metatheory for ecological psychology would be seriously weakened because the naturalistic status of radical empiricism would be undermined. For ecological psychology is a psychology of *realism* (the world that individuals experience is what it appears to be) and as such it cannot countenance idealism. At best, I could only maintain that a naturalistic reading of radical empiricism provides the foundations of ecological psychology. But I want to go farther and argue that a "natural realism" was what James himself was striving for. To accomplish this, he needed to reconcile the claim that individual knowers have separate minds (that consciousness is personal) with the apparent fact that individuals can experience the same thing.

The Ambient Optic Array and the Problem of Two Minds

James lacked the necessary conceptual tools to resolve the two minds problem in a manner satisfactory to a realist perspective. Radical empiricism rests on the empirical claim that relations between objects of perception are intrinsic to experience; but James had no means of even speculating how this could be so and therefore how direct perception is possible. In the absence of a conceptual framework that might offer insight into how perception can be direct, a problem like "how two minds

---

[10]Noting that the Idealists have called their position *"Identitatsphilosophie,"* which reflects the view that ultimately the object of thought and thought are a unity in the Absolute, James wrote: "The pure experiences of our philosophy are, in themselves considered, so many little absolutes, the philosophy of pure experience being only a more comminuted *Identitatsphilosophie"* ((James, 1912/1976, p. 66).

can perceive the same object" does indeed threaten the viability of radical empiricism.

Both the preceding and the present chapters (and the next) show that Gibson's ecological psychology is an offspring of radical empiricist philosophy. The present discussion intends to demonstrate how the conceptual framework of ecological psychology can be employed reflexively to place radical empiricism on firmer ground with respect to this problem of two minds.

As discussed earlier, ecological optics provides an account of how reflected light is structured by surface layout, and how higher order, relational structure in the ambient array of reflected light can function as information specifying environmental features. More specifically, unchanging or invariant structure revealed in the context of change—typically generated by the perceiver's exploratory actions—can specify objects and events. That is, constant properties of objects are preserved in invariant structure in the ambient array. This information does not need to be supplied by mind, but rather it is detected in the environment by an active perceiver. Moreover, because the ambient array is comprised of reflected light intersecting in a highly dense set (and, practically speaking, in an infinite set) of observation points, an object is *multiply specified* in the ambient array.

Consider the case of perceiving a single object, where there exists a multitude of *different* paths of observation in the ambient array from which an individual can perceive that object. In other words, the invariant relations specifying that object can be detected from any number of positions in the environment. The object is multiply specified in the reflected light filling the environment. For example, as a perceiver walks around a rectangular table, the invariant specifying the table's constant shape across transformations of perspective views is detectable at innumerable phases or moments in this circumnavigation. And, if it is the case that a single individual can pick up the relevant invariant from more than one position, then it follows that multiple perceivers can detect the same invariant when they are positioned at different locations. What they cannot do is occupy the same location at the same time. But this rarely makes any difference. It would only matter if the invariant information in question is, for some reason, most readily detected from a few select vantage points, and this is rarely the case.[11]

Therefore, if the ecological concept of the ambient optic array is adopted, it can reasonably be argued that two minds can directly perceive the same object simultaneously because that object is multiply specified

---

[11]This may be true, for example, with certain anamorphic paintings, Holbein the Younger's "The French Ambassadors" (1533) perhaps being the best known example.

in the reflected light filling the environment. That is to say, the invariant specifying the object can be perceived simultaneously from multiple positions. This analysis provides grounds for the claim that each perceiver directly perceives the same object, and it does so without resorting to panpsychism. In this way, two (or more) perceivers' experience of an object can be both independent and shared. Ecological optics makes intelligible the claim that direct perception of the identical object from different places is possible for different perceivers.

The conceptual tools of ecological psychology, and the program of ecological optics in particular, accordingly provide a way for a radical empiricist to resolve the two minds problem without retreating either to dualism or idealism. And most interestingly, the avenue of resolution it offers grows out of the radical empiricist framework itself. This framework proposes that most fundamental is the relation between knower and object known. Immediate experience of objects has this relational quality, and it does not reduce more basically to an environment–perceiver dichotomy. Information specifying objects is directly perceived through the pick up of invariants—that is, it needs no intermediary. And the analysis of how information specifying objects is present in the ambient array of reflected light reveals how objects can be multiply specified. By identifying this possibility, ecological optics, as an outgrowth of radical empiricism, has the potential to remove a roadblock long impeding the initial realist impetus for radical empiricism.

As I mentioned at the outset of this discussion, the intention here is to contribute to the ongoing discussion concerning the relative continuity or discontinuity between James's epistemology and his metaphysics. It seems clear that what must be preserved in any discussion of these matters is James's overall commitment to the possibility of open-ended growth and change. The possibility for knowing ever more *about the world* depends on, at bottom, immediate relations between knower and known where the boundless field of potential structure awaits discovery. And the possibility that the universe itself is a source of novelty, and it could be changed through individuals' actions ("meliorism") may depend on a continuity between individual experience and what is (Levinson, 1996).

The Concepts of the Ambient Array and Information

Before turning to the next chapter, the previous discussion may have itself raised a new question that needs to be addressed. Is it the case that the two minds problem has been resolved at the cost of creating a different problem? By invoking ecological optics, which after all is a physical analysis of light (albeit one dealing with higher order structures rather than physical optics as such), has a dualism been reintroduced between a physical world and a psychological domain? In order to save radical empiricism from the Scylla of idealism, has ecological psychology in its analysis of ecological optics sacrificed radical empiricism to the Charybdis of metaphysical dualism by positing a physical world over against experience?

In order to clarify this question, and prepare to respond to the dilemma it raises, reconsider an issue only partially examined in chapter 3. There it was claimed that, according to Gibson, what is directly perceived are affordances. Affordances, in turn, are perceived through the pick up of information in the ambient perceptual array. That being the case, what is the status in a metaphysical sense of information in the ambient array and of affordances? If it is affordances that are directly perceived, and if affordances are specified by information of an optical, auditory, tactile, and so on, nature, then isn't there a dualism lurking in ecological psychology between a world of experience and a physical world? If so, any attempt to merge ecological psychology and radical empiricism would undermine the latter, as well as point out a fundamental problem in ecological psychology's claim of direct realism (Fodor & Pylyshyn, 1981). These are important issues to examine because in doing so Gibson's framework and its relation to James's radical empiricism can be further clarified.

Recall that for James perceiving involves an immediate apprehension of aspects of the world; it is direct experience without mental intermediaries. In contrast, *conceiving* is a process of abstraction from this immediate experience; it involves a "substitution of concepts and their connections ... for the immediate perceptual flow" (James, 1911/1996, p. 39). This substitution does not displace immediate knowing, however; rather, concepts leaven percepts, and vice versa. "Percepts and concepts interpenetrate and melt together, impregnate and fertilize each other" (James, 1911/1996, pp. 52–53).

With the use of this distinction between percepts and concepts, it can be seen that affordances are percepts, whereas the ambient perceptual array is a concept. The latter is an abstraction from the flow of immediate experience, proposed to offer a way of accounting for the structure that is present in immediate experience. Like any concept, scientific or otherwise, to the extent that the concept of the ambient array claims to articulate and deepen our understanding of the coherence of immediate experience, it requires validation, pragmatically speaking, in the context of or in relation to the facts of immediate experience.

This Jamesian distinction between percepts and concepts provides deeper insight into the nature of Gibson's research program. Working from the phenomena of immediate experience (percepts), most notably affordances, Gibson posited structures via ecological optics (concepts) that are not present in immediate experience but help to account for immediate experience. These concepts are intended to refer to processes operating at a different level of analysis than immediate experience (see chap. 6). For example, the reflective properties of surfaces play a critical role in Gibson's analysis of vision. These properties give rise to an ambient array of structured light. However, scientists cannot directly see the reflective properties of surfaces, as light interacts with the microstructure of an object's surface; nor can they see the ambient array. What can be seen are only the consequences of these conditions in the character of immediate experience. In other words, affordances are perceived, not information.

The invariant information carried in reflected light (and detected by a perceptual system) is part of the conceptual framework of ecological optics. It is an abstraction derived from immediate experience that is offered in an attempt to explain how direct perception is possible. Much of the ecological research program is an effort to test possible informational invariants against the phenomena of immediate experience. Given some perceived event, for example, an approaching surface, the information that accounts for this experience is hypothesized, and then attempts to demonstrate its effective role in some environment–behavior circumstance are carried out experimentally. Under such circumstances, the concepts are valid (pragmatically true) to the extent that a display of the posited information produces behavior congruent with that event.

Viewed in this way, the ambient array and information have the same metaphysical status as the notion of wavelengths of light. Neither are facts of immediate experience, but they are concepts derived from immediate experience. This discussion should help clarify what Gibson was up to. Often starting from phenomenological observations, such as affordances, Gibson offered a conceptual framework for understanding perceptual experience. Of course, this is ultimately what all scientific theories do. Scientific theories are abstract, conceptual systems that are proposed to explain our everyday experience.

5

The Stream of Experience and Possible Knowledge

> We live, as it were, upon the front edge of an advancing wave-crest, and our sense of determinate direction in falling forward is all we cover of the future of our path. ... Our fields of experience have no more definite boundaries than have our fields of view. Both are fringed forever by a *more* that continuously develops. (James, 1912/1976, pp. 34–35)

An essential quality of psychological experience is its temporally extended character: Each of us experiences a suffusion of perceptual events, thoughts, and feelings *over time* in the course of our daily existence. This claim is among the most distinctive and central features of William James's *psychology*. It is ironic, then, that whereas James is generally celebrated as one of the more important early influences on psychology, scant attention has been given by psychologists to this most essential feature of James's approach to psychology. It is no exaggeration to say that what was utterly central for James's psychology has remained marginalized in most post-Jamesian psychology. Recognition of the temporally extended character of experience has far-reaching implications for the development of psychological theory; and until this facet of James's thinking is incorporated into psychology, the full impact of his ideas will not be felt.

This chapter examines the ways in which this significant feature of James's work is expressed in Gibson's ecological psychology and explores some of the implications of this issue for an analysis of knowing. In advance of the following discussion, the contention is that Gibson's approach to perceiving, and knowing generally, is a rare expression in experimental psychology of James's insight about the continuous nature of experience.

In his chapter in *The Principles* "The Stream of Thought," James argued that conscious experience is a flux, always in the process of change. This claim is ultimately rooted in James's phenomenology of experience, and it stands against the elementaristic tradition that conceptualizes the content of experience in discrete, static, and isolable units. By adopting the elementaristic approach:

> the continuous flow of the mental stream is sacrificed, and in its place an atomism, a brickbat plan of construction, is preached, for the existence of which no good introspective grounds can be brought forward, and *out of which presently grow all sorts of paradoxes and contradictions, the heritage of woe of students of mind.* (James, 1890/1981, p. 196, emphasis added)

We contemporary "students of mind" need to keep the continuous flow of experience at the center of our analyses. In doing so, we can circumvent some of the self-created "paradoxes and contradictions" growing out of our intellectual history and can break new ground exploring the theoretical and research implications of this perspective.

PERCEPTUAL SYSTEMS AND THE DETECTION OF INFORMATION OVER TIME

The source of the flow of experience, according to James, is the activity of the body. Lived experience is "the experience of activity" (James, 1912/1976; see chap. 1). At the simplest level, it is possible to get a feel for what "the experience of activity" means by imagining what it is like to run a hand over a variously textured surface. Over time one texture is felt, replaced by another, and then another, and so on. There is a flow of felt textures as the body engages these features of the world. The surface textures are felt through action. It is not the case that actions mediate experience, in the sense of their coming between the world and experience. At the most basic level, perceptual experience *is* the action of the body on features of the world.

More meaningful and complex perceptual experiences than that of textures can arise from this activity. To remain with the example of tactile perception, imagine handling an object presently out of sight. By turning it around in one's hand and feeling its surfaces, contours, and edges, invariant properties of the object are revealed that specify its shape and quite possibly its identity. The superiority of active over passive touch in shape recognition is a robust experimental finding (e.g., E. Gibson, 1969; Heller, 1984; Klatzky & Lederman, 1987). Perceiving the world tactually occurs most effectively through self-directed exploration over time (see D. Katz, 1925/1989).

Because the relative superiority of active touch is so evident and so readily demonstrated, if tactile perception were the dominant perceptual modality in human experience rather than vision, perceptual theory might well have taken on a very different look historically than it did. In that case, a perceptual theory might have developed that takes the temporally extended character of perceiving as primary. But, in fact, the temporally extended character of touch has had little influence in shaping perceptual theory, and this has been so for three reasons: Touch has been relegated historically to "the minor senses"; the perceptual modalities have historically been treated as separate channels of sensation; and picture perception has structured most of the thinking about perceiving. As a result, it has been mistaken beliefs about vision, originating in modern Western thought, that have dominated theories of perceiving.

The Picture Theory of Vision

Contemporary theories of vision have been shaped by the discovery, made at least as early as the 16th century (Lindberg, 1976), of an image of the world optically projected onto the receptor surface (the retina) of the eye. The existence of this retinal image, or picture, suggested to early theorists (e.g., Kepler and Descartes) that vision begins with a still picture impressed on the eye. This notion was reinforced by the discovery and subsequent development of the *camera obscura*[1] in the visual arts, which itself was a precursor to the modern camera. This idea, in conjunction with Descartes' mechanistic account of bodily processes based in part on his observations of automata (Jaynes, 1973b), has had a profound influence on the developing ideas about human knowing. Together, they offered a view of a passive organism functioning as a receptacle for static sensory impressions originating in the environment.

With this picture theory of vision as the central idea behind perceptual theory—as opposed to the kind of active process suggested by the description of tactile perception earlier—lived experience becomes the experience of receiving images rather than "the experience of activity." The perceiver is conceptualized as a spectator, as a recipient of impressions, rather than as a participant in the world. The perceiver stands detached from the world, rather than being actively immersed in it. In the picture theory of vision, the body does not play a facilitating role in vision

---

[1]Steadman (1995) presented a fascinating and persuasive argument suggesting that Vermeer's much admired interior portraits were created with the aid of a camera obscura located in the artist's studio.

as it does in tactile perception,[2] quite the opposite. Bodily produced movements would seem to impair seeing because they would have the effect of blurring or smearing the projected image on the retina unless they were controlled in some way. In contemporary theory, a common way of dealing with the problem of potential blur is to assume that the saccadic movements of the eyes, operating analogously to a shutter in a camera, capture static projections or snapshots, which in turn are accompanied by some sort of transsaccadic integration (e.g., Irwin, 1996), or a cognitive integration (Hochberg, 1968, 1974) of these separate images. Here is a case of a certain way of conceptualizing a phenomenon generating a new problem, namely, the integration of discrete inputs, that itself requires explanation.

As discussed in the previous chapter, another set of problems produced by holding a "picture theory of vision" concerns explaining how properties of experience of a three-dimensional world are recovered or reconstituted from the presumed starting point for vision, which is a two-dimensional retinal image. Problems stemming from this account, which include the perception of distance, the perception of relative size and size constancy, and the perception of shape constancy, have generated an enormous body of research, as anyone familiar with the study of vision over the past two centuries knows. If, however, instead of assuming that the first step in seeing is a static retinal image, it is assumed that seeing like touching is a continuous process of information pick up by an active perceiver engaging the world, these research problems become transformed and, in so doing, they may become more tractable (J. J. Gibson, 1962, 1966, 1979).

Perceiving as a Mode of Activity

Gibson's ecological approach inverts the view of perceiving just described. Instead of adopting a picture theory of vision, and consequently considering movement as creating a problem for perceiving processes, Gibson proposed that movements of the individual actually promote perceiving. From the perspective of ecological optics, movements facilitate the detection of the unchanging or invariant structures that serve as information specifying environmental features (chap. 4).

In the ecological approach, perceiving is not the reception of sensory stimulation; it is a mode of activity by which the individual becomes aware

---

[2]There have been, of course, various motor theories proposing that the products of movement (e.g., reafferent signals) can enrich visual input (Held, 1965). In these accounts, which are progeny of Berkeley's theory of vision, movement adds additional information to that provided by visual stimulation. Such theories typically assume something like a static image on the retina and therefore should be distinguished from the account of perceiving-acting offered by Gibson. As already noted, Holt's account of perceiving was a motor theory, and here Gibson parted company with his mentor.

of environmental features. Seeing is normally a collaborative process of acting and of detecting structure, and for this reason, visual experience, like tactile experience, is rooted in the activity of the body. The world is revealed though perceiving–acting processes.

With the idea of a *perceptual system*, J. J. Gibson (1966) proposed a radical reformulation of the standard view of sensory processes. 'System' is a critical term employed here to underscore the synergism and reciprocity of perceiving and acting. That, for example, vision or touch (or better seeing or touching) is a *perceptual system* calls attention to the fact that perceiving is more than the stimulation of a sensory channel, but a systemic act of the whole animal—a claim central to Holt's view of perceiving (see chap. 2). Perceiving is not the passive reception of sensory input, but it is a function of a dynamic, exploratory system. As such, it subsumes both information pick up (detection) and acting, which are mutually supporting processes. Although sensory (afferent) and motor (efferent) processes may be distinguishable at a neuroanatomical level, when considering the whole organism, separating perceiving and acting is artificial in most cases (Dewey, 1896). Although Gibson's term "perceptual system" has been gaining currency in the psychological literature in recent decades, regrettably it has often been misused as a label for receptive and passive descriptions of perceiving, and not as it was intended to refer to perception–action processes.[3]

James's description of psychological experience as a temporally extended stream or flow and Gibson's approach to perceiving as a perception–action system fit hand in glove. James's emphasis on this characteristic of psychological experience clearly influenced Gibson's thinking about perceiving. Perceiving, like the stream of thought, is continuous and ongoing, and this quality is attributable to the fact that perceiving is a function of an action system. J. J. Gibson (1979) explained:

> The act of picking up information, moreover, is a continuous act, an activity that is ceaseless and unbroken. The sea of energy in which we live flows and changes without sharp breaks. ... Hence, perceiving is a stream, and William James's description of the stream of consciousness applies to it. Discrete percepts, like discrete ideas, are "as mythical as the Jack of Spades." (p. 240)

In turn, Gibson's account of perceiving as involving the animal moving around the environment, exploring and inspecting features, generating changing patterns of stimulation through its movements and thereby iso-

---

[3]Moreover, perceptual systems are often, and erroneously, treated as separate channels of input. This view of separate sensory and perceptual pathways was formalized with Johannes Muller's law of specific nerve energies proposed in the early 1800s. In contrast, J. J. Gibson (1966, 1979) argued for the *cross-modal* nature of perceptual systems. For a recent discussion of these and related issues, see Stoffregen and Bardy, (in press).

lating invariants, provides a *foundation* for James's phenomenological observation of the changing nature of conscious experience (see chap. 3). As action systems, perceptual systems occasion a continuous stream of experience as the individual explores features of the world. James anticipated this point in his preliminary discussion of the experience of activity (chap. 1), where he suggested that the flow of conscious experience, even the flow of concepts, has its origins in the activity of the body.

Looking Ahead and Looking Back: The Problem of Temporality[4]

From the vantage point of the received picture theory of vision, what is impressed on the retinal surface is an image of the environment that is in front of the perceiver "now"—in the present. In this case, what is perceived is the field of view at "this moment," at "this instant in time." As James pointed out, however, there is a fundamental difficulty with this claim. He argued that if we adopt an empirical attitude and carefully attend to our own immediate experience, it seems that most fundamentally perceiving, and psychological experience generally, is temporally extended and continuous. If that is the case, when precisely is "now"?; when is "the present"? If psychological experience is continuous, then the notion of the "present" as an instant in time is muddled, for experientially there is no instant in time, no temporal "razor's edge." James (1890/1981) wrote, "The practically cognized present is no knife-edge, but a saddle-back, with a certain breadth of its own on which we sit perched, and from which we look in two directions into time" (James, 1890/1981, p. 609). For this reason, James described the "now" as "the specious present."

This provocative characterization of the present is in need of clarification. In turn, its implications for perceptual theory, as well as how cognitive processes are defined, need to be explored. Gibson's account of perceiving helps to carry forward this Jamesian commentary on the "present." If, as the ecological framework proposes, perceiving fundamentally involves the detection of invariants that are typically revealed over time in the context of change,[5] then "the present" takes on a more extended meaning than the

---

[4]A version of this and later sections of the present chapter appeared in Heft (1996).

[5]If the preceding hypothesis strikes the reader as implausible, consider the alternative view. If perceiving is based on fixing brief temporal slices of input, how brief in duration is each slice? Is it the length of time between saccades? If so, is the "present" or "now" less than 50 milliseconds in duration? And, if experience is based on the collation of these separate very brief slices of "present" stimulation, the experience of environment is *a fortiori* indirect. That is, what we take to be the world is in fact a mental construction experienced "in the projection room of the skull" (J. J. Gibson, 1979). Thus, Gibson's approach cannot reasonably be rejected in favor of a constructionist view merely on the grounds of the latter's greater plausibility. Constructionist views are just as susceptible to that criticism, if not more so. The resolution of this difference will hinge on their predictive power, the internal coherence of the account of perceiving they each offer, and their coherence to accounts of other cognitive processes.

usual sense of that term. Perceiving an invariant includes the possibility of being aware of what *will be* perceived when taking up a new observation point or when watching an event unfold, as well as the possibility of being aware of what *was* already perceived from a prior observation point or earlier in an unfolding event sequence. That is to say, perceiving shades off into what will be experienced and what was experienced: It is both *prospective* and *retrospective* (E. Gibson, 1991; E. Gibson & Pick, 2000). Under these circumstances, when precisely the present is becomes an abstraction at best.

If the notion of the present is not a "knife-edge," if it is extended in time, then just how extended is it? James struggled unsuccessfully with this question in *The Principles*, trying to resolve it partially within the constraints of the introspective data of his day (James, 1890/1981, chap. 15). He considered how extended in a subjective sense the present moment of experience is, and it appears that the boundaries of the present moment are exceedingly difficult to pin down introspectively. The question of boundaries becomes hopelessly tangled, and the suspicion arises that the problem rests with how the matter is formulated to begin with. The ecological approach liberates this question from the intractable difficulties of looking introspectively for fixed temporal boundaries by considering instead what perceiving means.

First consider the case of visually inspecting a small object, say a cube, as it is turned in one's hand. Drawing on the previous discussion of ecological optics (chap. 4), it can be claimed that the invariant specifying the object's shape can be detected over a brief interval of time, on the order of seconds. The invariant specifying object shape is the information that is revealed to be constant over time, that which does not change, as the object is viewed from different vantage points. Awareness of the cube is not a snapshot in time (it is not a two-dimensional projection of surfaces), because an invariant is detected over time. In the present example of perceiving the cube, it may be reasonable to say that the "present" extends over those few seconds as the invariant is detected.

What if the object in question is not something that can be held in the hand but must be walked around in order to be seen? The invariant information specifying a large free-standing object, such as a statue, might require as much as a minute of exploration before it is fully revealed. And the information specifying the layout of a building might require hours. And information specifying the layout of a city might require days or months. One might grant the possibility of perceiving, as with the case of the cube, extending a few seconds in time. But a few hours or longer? Surely that is implausible. It is true that it is not common to speak about perceiving in such an extended way; but if perceiving involves the detection of information over time, then what temporal criterion should be employed to distinguish perceiving from other cognitive processes? It seems arbitrary to choose a priori where to draw such a time limit.

Moreover, as already noted, having detected the invariant, and being aware of the whole object, including surfaces presently hidden from view, perceivers can anticipate what the object would look like if they returned to a prior observation point, and what it would look like from some observation point not yet adopted. That is, individuals can perceive retrospectively as well as prospectively by anticipating the object's appearance from a different observation point in the setting. (Anticipating means an awareness that is coupled with the intention of picking up information, as discussed later). To refer to the retrospective and prospective character of perceiving is to deviate from standard ways of conceptualizing psychological processes.[6] Retrospective awareness is not typically considered to be an act of perceiving, but of memory for moments past; and prospective awareness is not typically viewed as an act of perceiving but of imagining possible moments to come. Why then take the step of adopting such a nonstandard approach to the already difficult task of how to adequately conceptualize cognitive processes?

In truth, the matter is in large measure definitional. But to say this is hardly to minimize its significance—quite the contrary. Definitions of concepts go to the heart of psychological theory. Continuing to have the definitional differences between remembering, perceiving, and imagining hinge on when the present begins and ends will maintain the conceptual confusion that attends the current treatment of these psychological processes. How, for instance, can a distinction be made between perceiving and remembering if it is claimed that perceiving involves receiving static retinal snapshots followed by the assembly of these inputs based on prior experience? This view would suggest that when individuals are perceiving, they are in fact largely engaged in a process of remembering; that memorial processes provide the glue for assembling snapshots of the present. Where then does perceiving end and remembering begin? And if perceiving is so dependent on memorial processes, then we give up the possibility that the environment is experienced directly. This leads back to the difficulties of representational knowing from which James struggled to free himself and the field of psychology.

To claim that perceiving deals with present experience and remembering the past is useful only to the extent that present and past can be clearly distinguished. But if the merits of James's critique of the specious present are accepted, drawing such distinctions may be a hopeless task. The ecological approach suggests an alternative way of

---

[6]Phenomenologists working in the Husserlian tradition, which has some of its roots in James's thought, claim that experience has a "horizon" (e.g., Carr, 1986).

drawing these distinctions, and it is an alternative that permits avoiding the difficulties tied up with the false problem of determining the fixed boundaries of the present.

From an ecological perspective, perceiving is a process of picking up information that is available in the environment and, as we have seen, that information is typically detected over time in the context of change. To pick up information is to be aware of the environment's features. Perceiving can be prospective when the individual is aware of what would be experienced in the environment with appropriate action; and it is retrospective when the individual is aware of what was already experienced in the environment, for example, if she retraced a prior set of actions. In both cases, it is awareness of what would accompany the pickup of information (i.e., it is awareness connected to the intention of information pickup).

As such, this intentional awareness does not involve having a mental image of what would be seen or was previously seen. How does perceptual awareness and imagining differ? Because a mental image is derived from prior experience, it possesses a preexisting degree of definition. It is not open to the discovery of new information, only to noticing features of the image itself. For example, a mental image can be scanned and features already present can be noticed (Kosslyn, 1994). In contrast, the possibility of discovering new information is the defining characteristic of perceiving. That is, perceiving is a more open-ended process than experiencing a mental image because with perceiving there are new possibilities that may accompany further exploration. As J. J. Gibson (1970) pointed out, imagining and hallucinating can be readily distinguished from perceiving in that only in the latter case will further exploration reveal new information not already present.

Along these lines, Reed (1988) distinguished between perceptual awareness and nonperceptual awareness. He proposed that *remembering* is a mode of nonperceptual awareness in that it is awareness of what something looked like in the absence of the possibility of picking up or detecting more information. For example, I can remember the house I lived in that has since burned down; and indeed that is all I can do in this case because perceiving the house is no longer possible (J. J. Gibson, 1976). Consequently, my awareness of its various details is limited to what I have previously experienced, and I cannot learn anything more by examining its remembered appearance. *Imagining* is another form of nonperceptual awareness by which an individual can experience what something looks like in the absence of any possibility to pick up information because the imagined object had never been directly experienced. Obviously, this does not mean that the imagined object cannot change; it can be elaborated cognitively through reflection.

However, nonperceptual awareness in both cases is not open to the discovery of new information in experience, only to noticing features of the imagined experience itself or elaborating existing imagined features.

In short, a critical difference between the cognitive process of perceiving and the cognitive processes of remembering and imagining does not rest on a temporal criterion: namely, what is perceivable "now" in this instant of time versus that which is presently out of sight. Instead, it rests on the possibility or impossibility of picking up information. Perceiving is a temporally extended process, and as long as that which is presently out of sight can be brought into sight by changing one's vantage point, then *perceptual* awareness is possible.

Taking this analysis of perceiving one step further, once the invariant specifying an object or place has been detected, in a sense the individual can *perceive* the entire object or place. That is, the appearance of the object or place can be anticipated from any observation point in the intentional process of picking up further information. Such an argument follows from the previous discussion because in detecting an invariant, an individual is perceiving the object or place from no particular point of view, because that which is invariant, by definition, is not tied to one observation point but is common to all of them. Discussing the perceiving of places in the environment, Gibson wrote that when the invariant structure of a place is detected, "the whole habitat will be apprehended. The hidden and the unhidden become one environment. ... One is oriented to the environment. It is not so much having a bird's-eye view of the terrain as it is being everywhere at once" (J. J. Gibson, 1979, pp. 198–199).

Claiming to be aware of an object from all sides at once or a place from everywhere at once may seem like an odd assertion, but as noted, it follows from the claim that perceiving involves the pick up of invariant information. And Gibson was not alone in making such a claim. Merleau-Ponty (1962), for one, independently argued that although it is possible to intellectualize that perceiving is limited to the projected surfaces presently in view, in fact it is "none of these appearances; it is ... the flat projection of these perspectives *and* of *all possible perspectives*, that is, the *perspectiveless position from which all can be derived*" (p. 67, emphasis added). In other words, objects, environmental layout, and so forth are perceived both prospectively and retrospectively.

This discussion was intended to clarify James's claim that the *experienced present* is temporally extended, but its abstract nature may not have advanced things much closer to this goal. Carrying over aspects of this discussion to consideration of a particular research area may help to achieve greater clarity. The research area in question is navigation and environmental cognition generally. An examination of some theoretical issues concerning this topic also facilitates the consideration of some ways in which a radical empiricist framework can be applied to contemporary psychological theory.

Navigation and Event Structure

Environments are extended; and with rare exceptions, they are populated with diverse features. Because of the diversity of features present, any view of the layout of the environment from a particular vantage point will be distinctive and unique, and in turn, so will any path through the environment. When a perceiver moves along a path of travel, in effect he or she generates an optical flow of information in relation to the environmental layout. Gibson called this flow of environmental information generated by actions of the perceiver *perspective structure*. To the extent that the features along different paths differ (which they almost always do, the rare exception being repetitive designed patterns in buildings and neighborhoods, and even here subtle differences exist), different paths of travel will give rise to distinct flows of perspective structure specific to each route.

In a series of experiments, I have tried to articulate the nature of this perspective structure based on ideas offered by J. J. Gibson (1966, 1979), and also to demonstrate, if only in a preliminary way, that perceiving can be prospective. (For a more detailed examination of this work and its theoretical underpinnings, as well as the research program as a whole, see Heft, 1996.) To present briefly the conceptual framework, there are two distinguishable types of features present in the flow of perspective structure: *vistas* and *transitions*. A vista is an expanse—an extended layout of surfaces presently visible from a particular observation point. As the perceiver travels within a given vista, there will be local changes, such as motion parallax as well as the occlusion and disocclusion of features (i.e., previously seen features being concealed behind others present in the view of view, and new features being revealed from behind others). At certain places along the path of travel, changes of a greater degree than these within-vista events occur in the flow of perspective structure. At these points, a new vista gradually comes into view, and that just traveled goes out of view. Perhaps the most prominent event in the field of view is disocclusion as the succeeding vista is gradually revealed at an occluding edge, such as a stand of trees, (as well as an accompanying occlusion of the just traversed vista), as the perceiver makes a turn. These more momentous changes can be considered *transitions* in the perspective flow, and they are especially distinctive and are associated with high levels of interest among perceivers (Heft & Nasar, 2000).

In short, as a perceiver travels along a path through the environment, he or she experiences a continuous series of vistas connected by transitions which is generated by his or her actions in relation to environmental structure. This is a self-generated event, owing to the actions of the perceiver in relation to the environment, and it is structured over time by the layout and the features of the vistas. Most important, path information is an event that is structured over time; and owing to the path's temporally extended structure, navigation entails looking ahead or prospectivity. In this regard, it may share some of the characteristics of other temporally extended events, such as music.[7]

Jones and Boltz (1989) offered a valuable analysis of the temporal structure of music and, in so doing, have explored some of the implications of this analysis for an account of perceiving. A melodic structure typically can be described as a sequence of temporal units, and the perceiver detects the structure of this sequence as it unfolds over time. There is an awareness of temporal structure through the pick up of information, and reciprocally, perceptual awareness is carried along by or *entrained* to this temporal structure. In the case of a familiar melody or in the common case of a melody with a recurring structure, perceivers experience more than the present moment; they also anticipate the coming structure. That is to say, perceiving a melody has a prospective quality. Jones and Boltz (1989) referred to this prospective awareness that rests on the perceiver's "tacit use of an event's dynamic structure" (p. 473) as "dynamic attending." Attending to the unfolding of the temporal structure of music affords looking ahead. It is a perceptual awareness of knowing what is to come, an awareness of the event as temporally extended.

This notion of dynamic attending differs from standard uses of attention. In the present framework, attending is not conceptualized as an intra-organismic process distinct from perceiving. Perceiving is intrinsically a selective activity of information pickup, and dynamic attending highlights this selective quality. For this reason, to a considerable degree, the structure of *environmental information* controls attending. In a recent statement of this approach to event perception, Large and Jones (1999) commented:

> The approach maintains that external rhythms drive attending, permitting enhanced selective attending in time. It also assumes that attending can be 'tuned' in that it adapts over time to changes in event structure. This implies that the temporal structure of events governs the ability to attend. (p. 149)

---

[7]A striking example of the how temporal structure in music can be viewed similarly to the temporal structure of visual information is Chatwin's (1987) account of the use of song for navigational purposes by Australian aborigines. "Dream songs" recall the paths followed by mythical beings across the landscape, and as such offer an intermixture of mythology with navigational guidance. Accordingly, the melodic structure and the imagery of the song correspond to the topography of the landscape. Although Chatwin's fascinating book is not, strictly speaking, an ethnography, it is generally consistent with existing ethnographic data (Morphy, 1996).

The character of the temporal structure of events can be further elaborated. Events are rarely a mere simple sequence of distinct event units or phrases stacked end to end, like a train of box-cars. Typically, events have a temporally extended hierarchical structure, with some event units nested within a particular higher order event unit of structure, and other event units nested within a different higher order event unit. These higher order units each may be nested within still higher order units, and so on. The nesting of event units between levels and the overlap of event units within levels gives rise to a discernible hierarchical structure that makes looking ahead, i.e., *prospectivity* in the context of this complex event, possible.

There is evidence that some temporal structures afford more extended prospectivity than do others. Jones and Boltz (1989) showed that highly coherent time structures (i.e., time structures with a recurrent periodicity) enable perceivers to anticipate the occurrence of rhythmic accents and changes in tempo most readily; that is, enable them to "look" ahead in anticipation of the structure to be revealed. However, if the time structures are not very coherent or regular, then the perceiver has more difficulty anticipating coming structural change. As already noted, the prospectivity of perceiving is directly tied to structural qualities of the event, such as its coherence and regularity considered over time. In short, dynamic attending is an entrainment of awareness by events, with discernible temporally extended structure making looking ahead possible.

This framework developed by Jones and Boltz in relation to musical structure has been applied to navigation and the perception of the event structure of a path of travel (Heft, 1996). In one experiment, individuals were asked to segment (by pressing a button) a videotape of a walk through a complex environment during its second viewing into "its smallest meaningful and natural units" (the fine grain condition) or "its largest meaningful and natural units" (the large grain condition). In the fine grain condition, participants' responses tended to cluster at the transitions between vistas in the path (the locations of which were independently established), as well as at numerous other places (e.g., at distinctive landscape features) within these transition boundaries. The response patterns in the large grain condition were more selective (i.e., they had a greater degree of economy) with participants marking almost exclusively these same transitions along the path of travel, but omitting within transition features marked in the fine grain condition. These results suggest that perceivers can reliably identify transitions in the path as units of structure as they are revealed over time. Further, the findings in the fine grain condition by comparison suggest that some features are experienced as being nested within the units demarcated by these transitions.

A second experiment provided evidence that perceivers detect increasingly higher order structural units with increasing experience, a pattern of findings consistent with the claim they are better able to look ahead (i.e., engage in prospective perceiving) with continued experience. Participants were asked to segment the route into "its largest meaningful and natural units" either on first, second, or third viewing of the videotape. The results indicated that with greater exposure to the route, but especially between the second and third exposure, participants segmented the route into increasingly inclusive structural units; and there was substantial interobserver agreement as to where these unit boundaries were located. Thus, with greater familiarity with the route structure, individuals were able to detect larger temporal chunks of event structure, a claim consistent with E. Gibson's (1969) analysis of perceptual learning.

These findings indicate in a preliminary fashion, at least, that the structural units of a path can be distinguished at different degrees of inclusivity, with small units nested within larger units. Whether, in fact, the sensitivity to increasingly higher order units of structure along a path of travel enables the participants to anticipate ever greater or more extended units (i.e., whether there is prospective perceiving) remains to be directly examined. This interpretation seems likely, however, when these data are viewed in conjunction with those of Jones and Boltz (1989), who directly examined perceivers' anticipation of structure of musical events.

Cognitive Maps: Being Here Is Being Everywhere at Once.   These consider-ations, as well as others such as von Hofsten's (1982) demonstration that infants can anticipate through reaching the trajectory of a moving object, offer grounds for claiming that perceiving is prospective, that it involves the detection of temporally extended structure. The discussion preceding the prior section went further than this, however. It was also proposed that prospectivity can lead to comprehension of structure independent of the successive pick up of information—that, for example, having de-tected the invariant over time specific to an object, one is aware in princi-ple of what the object looks like from any vantage point. Consider this possibility again in the domain of navigation, with the intention of making this claim clearer. In doing so, the vulnerability of our thinking in this area of research to the "psychologist's fallacy" can be seen. In this regard, take the concept of cognitive map.

Environmental psychologists employ the term *cognitive map* in both broad and narrow ways. Broadly, it refers to any knowledge of place, particularly that supporting navigation, such as knowledge of the relative location of features, knowledge that certain paths lead to particular destinations, and knowledge of the overall layout or configuration of a place. More narrowly, cognitive map tends to be used in the latter vein, referring to knowledge of configuration, by which is meant roughly a "bird's eye view" of a place. On phenomenological grounds, it is apparent that we can imagine what a place looks like from "above." Besides, there is much behavioral evidence from solving detour problems to map drawing, indicating that individuals acquire knowledge of configuration of a place. What is most unclear in this literature, however, is what the nature of this knowledge is, and especially, how it is acquired.

The standard account of cognitive maps as configurational knowledge follows the constructivist line of thought discussed previously. It goes as follows: Cognitive maps are developed to overcome the limitations of perceiving. What is perceived is the immediately visible environment, what can be seen "from here now." From a series of these momentary views along a path of travel, supplemented by prior experience in that place usually in the form of a mental representation, the perceiver cognitively constructs an image of the remaining layout that is presently out of view. Consequently, awareness of paths and configuration is assumed to require an underlying mental representation of a setting that mediates perceiving and acting. Given the temporal limitations of perceiving, awareness of configuration cannot be based on direct experience.

This view rightly claims that a conceptual process like constructing an image is required when the information to support extended perceiving is not available. But from an ecological perspective, the constructivist approach errs in assuming that this circumstance is always, or even usually, the case. Rather, perceiving is not limited to what is presently visible, but it is prospective; and the information specifying the extended layout may be available as the perceiver travels through the place. With this conceptualization of perceiving and the information that supports it, acquiring knowledge of the configuration of a place may be viewed as a process of perceiving information over time, not necessarily constructing an image of environmental layout.

How might a perceiver's growing knowledge of extended path structure develop into an awareness of *configuration*? That is, if perceiving in a temporally extended sense is viewed as a process based on the discovery of information that is available in the environment, then what information results in an individual becoming aware of the *configuration* of a place? Previously, I proposed that the information specifying a path of travel constitutes, what Gibson called, *perspective structure*, which in the present case is a nested sequence of transitions connecting vistas, a flow of information generated by a perceiver moving through the environment. The perspective structure concurrently specifies movement of the self through the environment (chap. 3). Further, a place such as a neighborhood, a town, or a city has an *invariant structure*—and typically a rather complex one, at that. The invariant structure of a place is established by the *fixed relative positions* of prominent natural features, buildings, roads, and so on. Is it possible that this invariant structure is revealed to perceivers as they travel through that place? That is, when traveling around a city, perhaps the perceiver detects fixed relations among some subset of the city's features. By analogy, just as perceivers can, in principle, detect invariant relationships (e.g., cross-ratios) specific to a particular object while turning it in a hand or while walking around it, so they can detect the invariant relations among the locations of a place's features while walking around or through it—or at least, so I hypothesize. In doing so, what is perceived is that which is invariant about at least some of its structure.[8] To perceive the invariant structure of a place is to be aware of the positional relations among some of its features, as well as to understand one's current location in relation to environmental features. Such knowledge allows one to be *oriented* in that place. It is an awareness of configuration in the absence of mental representation.

This latter claim needs further elaboration, but let us first take up an anticipated criticism of the argument thus far.

Inaccuracies of Cognitive Maps. Because an ecological approach claims that perceiving is direct rather than mediated, this view would seem to be easily dismissed when it is applied to knowledge of environmental configuration. This is because clearly individuals' knowledge of the layout of a place, except in the simplest cases, is almost always incomplete and frequently contains some inaccuracies. The limitations in individuals' configuration knowledge are readily apparent in their drawn maps of places (e.g., Milgram & Jodelet, 1976).[9]

As discussed in chapter 2, however, the claims that perceiving is direct and that errors and omissions can occur in perceiving are not contradictory. The proposal that perceiving is direct rests on the assumption that perceiving involves the detection of properties of the environment, not on the assumption that perceiving is always veridical. Considering the complexity and expanse of many places, it is to be expected that configurational knowledge at any moment will be

---

[8]The cases of perceiving an object versus a place differ in two respects, however. First, and most obviously, the length of time required for exploration and the complexity of the relations is surely greater in the case of place perception. The second difference between these two cases is that while one walks around (literally) an object, one walks "around" a city by walking through it. What both cases share is the assumption that individuals have the potential to extract invariant structure over time.

[9]It should be added that drawn maps are notoriously poor indicators of an individual's knowledge of environmental layout for several reasons. The most obvious problem with this method of assessing environmental knowledge is that it is confounded by an individual's drawing skills. Even so, the shortcomings of drawn maps cannot be completely attributed to this fact. Configurational knowledge is partial.

incomplete. Knowledge of the layout of a place can almost always be sharpened, as new invariant relationships and new features are discovered in the course of exploration. Further, errors can be made when the demands of navigation (or the demands of an experimenter) require individuals to go beyond what they have directly experienced to make inferences. But errors of this nature do not invalidate the claim that an awareness of configuration can emerge from directly perceiving invariant relations in the environmental layout—only that the process is ongoing in relation to the complexity of the layout.

As discussed earlier, direct perception and veridicality *seem* to be linked as long as veridicality of knowledge is considered to be a matter of *correspondence*—that is to say, if it is assumed that the accuracy of knowledge about something "in" experience is assessed against the way that something "really is" in the world. This way of formulating the issue assumes a comparison between what is truly "out there" and the knowledge represented "in" the mind. Recall, however, that radical empiricism and its allied theory of pragmatism—what I submit are the foundations of ecological psychology—reject the dualistic correspondence of "inside to outside" as an assessment of "truth," and in its place emphasize coherence within experience. A facet of immediate experience is veridical or not in terms of its coherence to other facets of experience: "[Truth] is not, in particular, a matter of relating experiences to a reality *external* to experience, but rather a matter of the relations which *certain* experiences bear to *others*" (Scheffler, 1974, p. 103). In short, truth (or accuracy) of experience is revealed within experience.

Consider this viewpoint in the case of environmental cognition. What is known about something, say a route in the environment, at any given time is an interweaving of structure revealed through detection of relations in immediate experience and of structure generated through reflection (i.e., abstraction) on this immediate experience—what James called "percepts" and "concepts," respectively. (Note that there is an interweaving of percepts and concepts in immediate experience, not a mediation of percepts by concepts; see chap. 1.) The validity of the intermixture of percepts and concepts that comprises immediate experience can only be assessed with respect to their mutual coherence, and especially with respect to how consistently concepts cohere with percepts. Such an assessment of coherence occurs in relation to the immediacy of perceiving and acting.

Take the simple case where an individual knows the path of travel from *a* to *b*. On some occasion when following that path, the individual may discover that the familiar route is blocked, and for this reason, an alternative route (a detour) that will lead to *b* needs to be chosen. Abstracting from what is known, the individual sets out on an alternative route c to reach b. Whether or not the detour is accurate is to be established in experience by its result. A choice that leads to b via another route is coherent with respect to what is already known.[10]

As already stated, because of their complexity, it is to be expected that knowledge of places will be partial and facets of it will prove to be inaccurate when assessed for their coherence in relation to the rest of experience. The claim that perception is direct does not insure veridicality; but ongoing evaluation of the coherence of concepts in relation to percepts holds out that possibility.

Having said this, why does a correspondence approach rather than a coherence approach probably seem like a more natural way of thinking about environmental cognition? This is the case for most of us because of the salience of maps and other pictorial representations in our culture. We typically view the cartographic map as being the "correct" description of the environment. What is on a map is taken to be what is "really" out there—the "world according to Rand McNally," as Wohlwill (1976) once put it. But, of course, maps are particular abstractions from immediate experience, and as such have characteristic idiosyncrasies, if not inaccuracies. In fact, particular mapping techniques introduce very specific distortions (Downs, 1981). Maps no more (and no less) indicate what is really out there than any other product of reflection on immediate experience. This is not to diminish the value of maps; they are most impressive intellectual and cultural products. What makes maps so valuable is that maps have been tested against immediate experience and refined across generations of individuals. They are exemplars *par excellence* of collective public knowledge (see chap. 9). It is important to bear in mind, however, that a map of the world is not the world, but rather a highly refined representation of it.

Finally, taking an individual's drawn map or model of a place as an adequate account of what an individual knows is an instance of committing the psychologist's fallacy, as identified by James (chap. 1). Maps and models are products of what individuals know rather than what is known as such. And as products of knowing processes, they may only partially reflect what is known.

Moreover, they are susceptible to errors stemming from task demands. For example, as already noted, in the process of drawing a map, a person may incorrectly connect two areas because the task itself may elicit an effort to produce a unified representation. In the act of navigating, the person may never have needed to consider how these two areas are

---

[10]This analysis indicates, of course, that sometimes a facet of experience may only prove to be incoherent (nonveridical) at some later time; and in some cases, concepts that are never tested against immediate experience may remain uncorrected indefinitely.

related. Such an error is generated by the task, and it can be corrected with subsequent direct experience. It is critical to always bear in mind that an individual's drawn map, verbal directions, and even mental image of environmental configuration are all abstractions from what is known through perceiving-acting.

Configuration Knowledge Without a Mental Representation. In some instances in which the actions of an individual might seem to be supported by a mental representation, other simpler explanations are available. For example, H. L. Pick (1993) cited the example of those children in the study by Hazen, Lockman, and Pick (1978) who were unable to make directional inferences among a series of rooms previously walked but were able to construct a model of the room layout. The former results suggest the absence of a mental representation of configuration, whereas the latter reflects its presence. How can these different outcomes be reconciled? Pick observed that the children appeared to have built the model in the order and position of the rooms as they walked through them, which suggests, according to Pick, that "they did not seem to have the configuration in mind from the beginning" (p. 35). This possibility indicates that "the simple production of the external model may not necessarily imply configurational knowledge" (p. 35).

Moreover, awareness of configuration does not necessarily require an underlying mental representation. Pick went on to show by way of a thought experiment how awareness of configuration of a place can stem from perceiving-acting processes. (His account is modified slightly here.) Suppose an individual is moving through a city and has noted in particular two distinctive buildings. As the person continues along a path of locomotion, one of those buildings becomes temporarily occluded by some other feature. To quote H. L. Pick (1993):

> As movement continued in the same direction down [the path of travel] …
> the relative change of direction of the occluded object would be mirrored by
> the relative change of direction of the object which has remained in view. In
> short, there could be *concurrent perceptual information* for the location of
> out-of-sight objects, provided one had registered certain kinds of relations
> when the objects were in sight. (pp. 35–36, emphasis added)

In this example, the relations between features as specified by visual information detected when moving through the setting can be utilized to update the location of one of these features when it is out of sight. Pick cited a study by Rieser, Guth, and Hill (1986) as preliminary evidence that the location of a feature that is not presently visible can be updated. Rieser et al. demonstrated that when individuals walk without vision between locations on a path, they are able to "update" the relative positions of features, as compared to when individuals are asked to imagine walking the path. Because individuals have considerable experience calibrating optical flow patterns with biomechanical information when walking, presumably when walking without vision (but not when solely imagining walking) the participants in this study were able to update the position of previously seen features. These findings suggest that awareness of the relative positions of features can be maintained even when some of those features are temporarily out of sight. And an underlying configurational representation cannot be persuasively invoked as an explanation given the performance differences between the two conditions.

The question might still be raised: Why is this not an enrichment account of perceiving? Isn't it the case that motor sensations via walking are furnishing needed supplemental cues for vision? But this is not an adequate account of the processes involved here. Information specifying movement through a particular setting can be detected in multiple ways. In fact, if we give up the notion of separate channels of stimulation, and instead view perceiving as the pick up of information by perceptual systems attuned to different kinds of information all specifying a common feature or event, then visual information and biomechanical information can specify the same event. As a result, in sighted individuals, vision and biomechanical processes are tightly coupled such that awareness of one's relative position through one source of information can update awareness via the other coupled source, even when the latter is temporarily unavailable. Support for this viewpoint is provided by evidence that visual and biochemical information can be recalibrated (H. L. Pick, Rieser, Wagner, and Garing, 1999; Rieser, Pick, Ashmead, and Garing, 1995).

The perspective emerging from this work suggests a way to think about what it means to know the invariant structure of a place without presupposing that such knowing is built on a configurational mental representation. Knowledge of the structure of a place, including those features presently out of sight, can be derived from discovering the relative positions of its features and by continually updating their relative locations, even when some of those features are temporarily out of sight, through other available information. In this way, individuals could develop knowledge of relations among features over some environmental extent, and they can utilize this knowledge to perceive in a prospective fashion some features that are not presently in sight; and even to generate an image of configuration or to draw a map. But what the individual knows in such cases is not configuration per se; rather, what has been acquired is an awareness of a set of invariant relations of features in the environment. Importantly, the discovery and the updating of relational information occurs through direct experience in the process of perceiving and acting.

Finally, that the updating in the Rieser et al. (1986) research occurred when participants were walking with blindfolds, but not when they imagined walking, is consistent with a robust finding in the environmental cognition research literature: self-directed exploration leads to more accurate knowledge of environmental configuration than does passive exposure (e.g., when one is being conveyed on a vehicle or is led by the hand through a setting; e.g., Feldman & Acredolo, 1979). But why this is the case has never been adequately explained employing the standard constructivist approaches to environmental cognition. The most common approach in the perception literature for this sort of finding is that action enriches visual experience—an argument traceable to Berkeley's writings on vision. But the nature of this enrichment is not clear. The ecological perspective offers a fresh insight into this pattern of findings. Perceiving and acting collaborate in the detection of invariant information. Because invariants are most readily detected by the perceiver moving with respect to environmental structure—thereby causing what is invariant to separate off visually from what is not—control over one's movements will most readily result in detection of this information. Being passively exposed to an environmental layout can also result in the invariant being revealed, but in the absence of control over movement this structure is considerably more difficult to isolate perceptually. Controlling movement through the detection of environmental structure will highlight this structure in ways that passive (or even imagined) exposure will not.

The preceding somewhat lengthy discussion of navigation was undertaken as an effort to clarify through an example the Jamesian claim that perceiving is temporally extended. When traveling in a familiar place, an individual is typically aware of the structure of the path of travel as it unfolds over time, its structure emerging from the perceiver–environment process of navigation. In this way, the individual can look ahead and is aware of the path to be encountered to varying degrees. Further, an awareness of the configuration of place begins to emerge as invariant relations are detected among fixed features of the setting. As J. J. Gibson (1979), has written: "Visual perception is panoramic, and over time the panorama is registered" (p. 112–114). From a Jamesian perspective, panoramic vision is a type of direct knowledge. The structure of the environment has an immediacy, an extended "thereness."

AN ECOLOGICAL APPROACH TO THE PROBLEM OF POSSIBLE KNOWLEDGE

Let us return briefly to some philosophical matters. In the previous chapter, a problem that deeply troubled James because it threatened the consistency of radical empiricism was examined: This is the problem of how two minds can simultaneously experience the same thing. That discussion attempted to demonstrate how Gibson's ecological framework potentially provided James with the conceptual tools he needed to resolve this problem. This resolution, in addition to addressing a problematic issue in radical empiricism, provided further evidence for the interconnectedness between radical empiricism and ecological psychology. As reiterated throughout Part II, Gibson's ideas are a direct outgrowth of James's philosophy, and indeed each framework can enrich the other.

Another issue presents the same opportunity. The preceding portrayal of perceiving as looking ahead reveals a distinguishing characteristic of both radical empiricism and ecological psychology: namely, the assumption that *possible knowledge is real*. However, in trying to confront the status of possible knowledge, James again found the viability of radical empiricism threatened, potentially compromising his initial objective to develop a metaphysics of neutral monism. With this issue, too, Gibson's analysis of perceiving aids in fulfilling James's original intentions.

Possible Knowledge and Radical Empiricism

In James's radical empiricism, possibilities are real, and the world is filled with possibilities. There is a latent structure to the world, a structure that is potentially knowable by a perceiver. For James, that latent structure is present in the objects and relations of pure experience (chap. 1). Pure experience, "the instant field of the present ... is only virtually or potentially either object or subject as yet" (James, 1912/1976, p. 13). The relations in pure experience offer opportunities to the knower for identifying structure: "In this naif immediacy [pure experience] ... is of course *valid*; it is *there*, we *act* upon it" (p. 13). And our action leads knowing processes on further to trace out lines of connections in the field of experience. In other words, knowing involves a "leading-towards, namely, and terminating-in percepts, through a series of transitional experiences *which the world supplies*" (p. 14, emphasis added). What the world supplies are objects of experience and their relations, and *"the known is a possible experience either of that subject or another, to which the said conjunctive relations would lead, if sufficiently prolonged"* (James, 1912/1976, p. 27, emphasis added).

Because this is a difficult point, additional commentary on it might be useful. Sprigge (1993) explained this notion of possible knowledge as follows:

> What exactly are those appearances which are merely possible and which constitute things insofar as they are not perceived ... ? Clearly, they are not merely logically possible. Presumably, they are possible in the sense that they could occur, or could have occurred, as the termini to acts of exploration which might have been undertaken by various conscious subjects. Thus their existence as possibilities consists in the fact that there would have been

actual experiences of the relevant sort if subjects of experience had given themselves certain experiences of going to certain places, etc. (p. 132)

The viewpoint of possible knowledge as virtual or inherent in experience portrays knowing as an ongoing, open-ended process, as the knower discovers more richly connected, inexhaustible relations in the knowable. This is an important feature of James's perspective (and Gibson's also). However, left as such, this analysis is insufficient. James, for one, recognized that he needed further grounds for claiming possible knowledge is real.

For James, that which is presently experienced is real by virtue of its being experienced—here Berkeley's influence is evident. But what about that which is not presently experienced? How is it possible to talk intelligibly about the reality of latent structure in experience? Take, for example, the pen that is located on the desk in the next room and that I am not presently experiencing. In what sense is it real? James only saw two philosophical options for answering this question, and one was only slightly more desirable than the other.

First, there is the commonsense view that objects presently outside of our experience are real because they exist in a material world. This avenue is not open to a radical empiricist, however. If radical empiricists were to adopt this materialist view, then they would be acknowledging from the outset a distinction between a real, material world "out there," and a separate world of experience. This dualistic viewpoint was the very approach James wanted to overturn through radical empiricism.

Alternatively, radical empiricists could maintain greater theoretical consistency by claiming that only objects that are experienced are real. However, by adopting this idealist position, they would be suggesting that as objects enter and then leave conscious experience, they go in and out of existence. In this case, theoretical consistency might be preserved at the cost of abandoning realism.

Kuklick (1977) claimed that this problem of the status of possible knowledge was of deep concern to James, and of the two avenues he contemplated for addressing this problem, James gravitated toward the following variation of the latter idealist view: If only that which is experienced is real, then if the pen in the next room is real—which James wants to claim—it must be experienced by someone or something other than me. Assuming that no one is in the room, the only things that could experience the pen are other objects in the room or the pen itself. This position that Kuklick suggested James entertained would lead radical empiricism to a form of idealism, namely, pluralistic panpsychism (see chap. 4). He quoted James as stating: "The beyond must, of course, always in our philosophy be itself of an experiential nature. If not a future experience of our own or a present one of our neighbor, it must be a thing in itself ... that is, it must be an experience *for* itself" (James, quoted in Kuklick, p. 325).

Such a solution would bring James close to adopting the position held by the Idealists like Royce and Bradley, although here he would be advocating a pluralistic rather than a monistic idealism—a distributive collection of minds rather than minds unified in the Absolute. As already discussed, this position would undermine the realism James otherwise sought and bring with it some of the concerns he had with idealism (see chaps. 1 and 4).

Possible Knowledge in Ecological Optics

James needed a way to make the claim that possible knowledge is real without invoking either dualism or idealism. Gibson's ecological psychology, and his concept of the ambient optic array specifically (i.e., a concept in the Jamesian sense, see chap. 4), provides a basis for the *realist* position James desired. Recall that the ambient array is constituted by reflected light from surfaces of the environment. Consequently, the structure that is the ambient array is there to be perceived. Indeed, it offers "the permanent possibilities of vision—that is, the set of all places where a mobile individual might be" (J. J. Gibson, 1966, p. 191).[11] He continued: "There is an infinite number of vantage points from which an observer could look at his surroundings. The most indefatigable tourist could only sample them. But they all exist as permanent possibilities for vision" (p. 192). Here then is a way to conceptualize possible experiences in a way that is compatible with a realist epistemology. J. J. Gibson (1979) was clear that what is there as permanent possibilities for vision are affordances, and *they exist as such because they are specified by information in the ambient array*: "The observer may or may not perceive or attend to the affordance, according to his needs, but the affordance, being invariant, is always there to be perceived" (p. 140). Turvey (1992) made this point in a slightly different way. Because the prospectivity of perceiving is lawfully controlled by informa-

---

[11] The claim that there are "permanent possibilities for vision" is another interesting convergence between Gibson's ideas and those of James. Gibson was attracted to John Stuart Mill's idea of the "permanent possibilities of sensation." According to Reed (1988), Gibson learned about this idea from H.H. Price during a sabbatical year at Oxford. Price was attempting to apply this aspect of Mill's work to the then current idea of sense data. Gibson commented briefly on the similarities and differences between his views and those of Mill in *The Senses Considered as Perceptual Systems* (1966, p. 223). James had great admiration for John Stuart Mill (he dedicated *Pragmatism* to him) and was significantly influenced by his writings. The influence of Mill's "permanent possibilities of sensation" and the development of James's claims about potential experience warrant careful study (see Perry, 1935, chap. 23, for some preliminary remarks).

tion specifying affordances, and because "real possibility is identical with lawfulness" (p. 177), possibilities are real.

This conceptualization of an ambient array of potential information has significant implications for the problem of epistemological relativism. If information is available to be perceived, then it is available in principle as potential information for anyone present. Said in other words, an individual's experience in the environment is in principle public rather than private in the following sense. Although two individuals cannot occupy the same point in the ambient array at the same time, and in this way, their experiences at any "moment" are unique or private, they can adopt one another's vantage point and thus have access to the same ambient structure as the other. Consequently, the notion of the ambient array extends the prospect that two (or more) individuals can have the same experience of the world (J. J. Gibson, 1979, p 43). By extension, this framework proposes that the ambient array continuously offers new information at vantage points and along paths of observation for a particular individual; and the information at these points extends opportunities for new discoveries—that is, they constitute possibilities for knowing.

Certainly there are no guarantees that an individual adopting the same position in environment will experience the same world as a previous occupant. After all, their different histories may have differentially sensitized each individual to alternative facets of the abundant information available. But the important point from the perspective of social relations is that Gibson's analysis extends the hope of achieving common ground, or at least common understanding. Nor are there guarantees that an individual will detect new structure along newly explored paths of observation. But because an array of potential information is available to be detected, that possibility always exists. This argument becomes clearer with a few comments about processes of perceptual learning.

The Discovery of Structure

The claim that possible knowledge is real can be further developed from an ecological perspective by briefly considering the role of the individual as agent in perceptual learning, as well as the manner in which others assist in the discovery of affordances.

As discussed previously (chap. 3), the affordance possibilities of a place for an individual are established by the structure of the environment taken with reference to that individual. Which affordances could be perceived depend minimally on characteristics of the individual's body (e.g., weight, leg length, arm reach), and that individual's potential for action. The affordances that are presently perceived depend on the individual's current purposes or intentions. Selectivity is the hallmark of a knowing agent from a radical empiricist/ecological point of view.

The contribution of agency to the awareness of an affordance can be illustrated by the fact that environmental features often have multiple affordances for a person. For example, I am not typically aware that the stapler on my desk can serve to hold a book flat to a certain page until I have a need for such an object and look on my desk for something that will serve this purpose. That particular affordance remains as a latent property of the object until it is realized in experience through selectivity.

This example also clarifies the previous claim that possible properties are real. The stapler can be used to hold open a book because of its weight and dimensions. This affordance is a property of the object. And when I learn that the stapler can be used as a paperweight, I am not imposing this property on the object; that is, I am not mentally constructing a new way of representing the object. Rather, I am discovering through perceptual learning new properties of the object taken with reference to my purposes and action possibilities. Importantly, the object has this potential function with reference to a perceiver even if it is not presently being experienced. In other words, this possible function is real, even if it is not yet realized.[12]

That potential affordances are real properties of objects, and not properties imposed on them, can also be seen by the fact that other persons often aid in the discovery of these properties. The knowledge that others have about object properties, and the actions they can employ to demonstrate these properties to us, vastly enlarge our knowledge. Writing in the 1930s, Vygotsky (1978) may have been the first to call attention to this important function that more experienced individuals play for novices. In recent years, Cole (1996), Rogoff (1990), Wertsch (1985), and Valsiner (1987), among others, have helped to revive and to explicate his ideas. One of Vygotsky's important insights was that the possible actions for a developing child are established not only by the level of the child's skills at a particular time, but also by the ways those skills can be enlarged by more experienced collaborators involved in the child's learning. Vygotsky called this extended range of possibilities for a child's actions the "zone of proximal development." The zone of proximal development is a further indication of how properties of objects are discovered, not imposed or mentally constructed. The knowledgeable person demonstrates to the novice the "new" properties of the object, or guides the novice's actions so that these new properties are revealed. At other times, these properties are revealed to the novice by observing models, without the teacher

---

[12] An examination of the claim that affordances are both relational and independent of perceivers is offered in chapter 4.

intentionally engaged in guiding a child's actions (Tomasello, Kruger, & Ratner, 1993). In either intentional guidance or incidental teaching, what is possible concerning object properties becomes actualized for the learner.

These considerations lead back to the point that opened this examination of James's and Gibson's ideas and, further, provides some closure to Part II. Both radical empiricism and ecological psychology begin with the assumption that the essential unit of analysis is the perceiver–environment relation. Within the context of a particular perceiver–environment relation, possible knowledge exists—although it may not be experienced by an individual at a given moment—because the properties of relationally specified features of the environments are real properties.

Unlimited Knowing

Arguing along Jamesian lines, attaining knowledge of the world is a process of discovering latent structure in the relation between the knower and the known. Owing both to the perceptual richness of the world and the dynamic nature of knowing, such a process has no limit. As J. J. Gibson (1979) put it "The information in ambient light, along with sound, odor, touches, and natural chemicals, is inexhaustible. A perceiver can keep on noticing facts about the world she lives in to the end of her life without ever reaching a limit" (p. 243). James (1912/1976) made the same point about knowing in commenting on the dynamic character of the natural world: "When the whole universe seems only to be making itself valid and to be still incomplete (else why its ceaseless changing?) why, of all things, should knowing be exempt" (p. 37)?

Knowing is an ongoing transaction between a knower and the world. The psychological activity of the individual is ceaseless until loss of sentience; and through the activity of perceiving in a world of boundless structure, heretofore unknown information and meanings are continually discovered. More refined and differentiated structures, as well as more inclusive, higher order, and temporally extended structures are revealed through continuing exploration (E. Gibson, 1969; E. Gibson & Pick, 2000). Furthermore, the results of reflective examination of these direct experiences—i.e., the generation of concepts—enormously expands the scope of the known.

What can be perceived is certainly limited in part by our biology. But these biological boundaries have been extended through the invention of devices that make otherwise unavailable structure available to be perceived. Devices such as telescopes and microscopes have for centuries extended our range of perceiving, and their modern counterparts have greatly augmented our perceptual grasp of what was once inaccessible. Ongoing processes of knowing, augmented or not, put the individual in closer contact with the fabric of the world—an open-ended process both for the individual and for the culture as a whole. This perspective is central to James's pragmatic vision of truth; and Gibson's ecological theory provides a way of realizing this vision.

III

Ecological Psychology
and the Psychological Field

Prologue: Field Theory and Collective Social Processes

The discussion up to this point has been somewhat narrowly focused in at least two respects: First, by locating the metatheoretical foundations of Gibson's ecological psychology in the radical empiricist tradition, I have neglected other substantive influences on the development of his thought. Second, by exploring ecological psychology from a radical empiricist perspective, my attention has been restricted for the most part on the individual, in keeping with James's focus. In the process, however, the place of sociocultural structures in psychological analyses has been largely ignored. Part III broadens the discussion in these two ways.

To take each of these points in turn, the theoretical base of Gibson's ecological psychology is enriched by considering another prominent influence on his thought, namely, Gestalt psychology. In addition, the discussion considers the ways that Gestalt thinking inspired the independent development by Roger Barker of an ecological psychology of collective, dynamic social structures. Examination of this ecological analysis of social structures leads more generally to a consideration of the place of sociocultural processes in ecological psychology. Further, examining the influence of Gestalt psychology on Gibson's and Barker's programs provides an initial step toward a possible synthesis of these two ecological programs.

Some preliminary remarks relating to these goals are needed. The most far-reaching influence on Gibson's thinking after radical empiricism was Gestalt psychology. And it becomes evident that William James's psychology and Gestalt psychology have much in common from a historical viewpoint. The *bete noire* for both James and for the Gestalt psychologists was *psychological reductionism*. They both had deep reservations about any psychology that takes discrete elements of consciousness or discrete elements of behavior to be the most fundamental units of analysis in the study of human phenomena. For both, a reduction of psychological phenomena to a collection of elements transforms the character of these phenomena.

A central aim of Gestalt psychology, and especially its founder Max Wertheimer (1880–1943), was to restore meaning as a central and intrinsic quality of psychological experience. In his view, meaning had been relegated to a minor role in experimental psychology by reductionistic and mechanistic theories: first by those working from Wundt's experimental framework, and especially structuralists like Titchener who developed selected features of Wundt's thinking; and then by Watsonian-style behaviorism. The Gestalt psychologists wanted to place meaning, and more generally structure, at the center of psychology.

Likewise, both James's psychology and Gestalt psychology opposed *physiological reductionism*—the claim that ultimately physiological explanation alone could provide an adequate account of psychological phenomena. This is not to say that they refrained from physiological theorizing per se. Physiological processes, and most especially dynamic brain processes, played an essential role in their accounts of many psychological phenomena. But both James and the Gestalt psychologists felt that an account based solely on a physiological analysis, either of a reductionistic or holistic nature, suffered from the same shortcoming that psychological reductionism did: Neither approach captured the essential qualities of "what it is to be human."

In short, they worried that any psychology adopting either psychological or physiological reductionism was bound to present a distorted view of human experience. And such a distortion was more than merely inaccurate; it was also morally perilous. For through it, in effect, the science was offering up for our adoption an authoritative view of ourselves stripped of many of our distinctive qualities. Instead, by taking immediate experience as the starting point for psychological inquiry, both James and the Gestalt psychologists placed the distinguishing qualities of human experience at the heart of their psychologies.

Gestalt psychology is a label that can be applied narrowly or broadly. Narrowly, the founding core group of Gestalt psychologists were Max Wertheimer, Wolfgang Köhler (1882–1967), and Kurt Koffka (1886–1941), and its institutional center prior to World War II was the Psychological Institute at the University of Berlin. Several other prominent and influential psychologists throughout Europe were allied more or less closely with this group, sharing their commitment to holistic, dynamic theory, while developing ideas along somewhat different lines than they. Among this second group, two individuals who played a formative role in ecological psychology are Kurt Lewin and Fritz Heider. Lewin and Heider, along with Egon Brunswik (who was closer intellectually to logical positivism than Gestalt psychology) were among the first psychologists to give careful consideration to the nature of the environment.

Kurt Lewin's (1890–1947) interests were more developmental and social psychological than those of his Gestalt colleagues at Berlin. In brief, he applied the field-theoretical perspective of Gestalt psychology to analyses of individuals' actions. Lewin (1951c) took the critical step of viewing a psychological event, such as an action, as being situated in a constellation of co-occurring environmental influences, as well as being influenced by the individual's personality dispositions and developmental constraints. It was Lewin's conviction that actions are rarely understandable as being triggered by a single environmental precipitant or personal disposition; instead, converging influences from multiple sources are the rule. Moreover, an action is not caused by a stimulus; rather, an actor is situated in a field of multiple environmental and personal influences, and the observed pattern or direction of action is an outcome of their mutual convergence. With this field-theoretical framework, Lewin challenged psychologists to think about psychological processes and the psychological environment in more complex ways than they ever had before.

Fritz Heider (1896–1988) is best known in contemporary psychology for *The Psychology of Interpersonal Relations* (1958), which helped to invigorate the cognitive dimensions of social psychology. Specifically, it was an impetus for the development of attribution theory, which was perhaps social psychology's dominant theoretical framework in the decades of the 1970s and 1980s.[1] But his most significant contributions from the standpoint of ecological psychology come out of his early work on perception (1926/1959, 1930/1959). As already discussed in the Introduction and in the Prologue to Part I, Heider focused on a relatively unexamined, yet absolutely central problem in perceptual theory, namely: How can objects be perceived that are located at a distance from an individual? Heider sketched a template for addressing this problem that rested on the crucial distinction between an object (thing) and a medium. This conceptualization is examined in detail later, but for now it should be noted that not only is this distinction central to Gibson's perceptual theory, but it is foundational for the ecological account of collective social processes developed by Roger Barker. The Gestalt influences on both Gibson's and Barker's thinking are examined in chapter 6.

Chapter 7 is an explication of Barker's ecobehavioral perspective. Barker was a postdoctoral student with Lewin at the University of Iowa, and this contact with Lewin had a lasting effect on him. Moreover, consideration of Barker's ideas returns the discussion to an issue raised earlier; namely, the importance of recognizing a hierarchy of nested levels of analysis among naturally occurring phenomena. Barker and his

---

[1] Malle and Ickes (2000) argued that Heider's *The Psychology of Interpersonal Relations* "became a classic in part through the selective attention and resulting misunderstandings of its interpreters." In making this assertion, they are not judging that acclaim associated with this book is undeserved, but rather that Heider's contributions have yet to be fully appreciated.

colleagues discovered through their empirical work in psychology a dynamic ecobehavioral structure, the *behavior setting*, that operates at an extra-individual level of analysis. This dynamic social structure goes a long way in helping to account for much of the order and regularity we observe in daily social life. Its value in this regard pushes the present analysis in the direction of considering collective social structures that are sustained by individuals' actions and that reciprocally constrain these actions. Importantly, in this respect, it expands the ecological perspective developed by Gibson, recognizing the significance of higher order extra-individual structures in everyday life. Reciprocally, Gibson's account of animal–environment reciprocity at the level of individual functioning shores up a problematic feature of Barker's framework (chap. 8).

Beyond the specific merits of the concept of behavior setting, more generally this discovery demonstrates the critical role that social *context* plays in individual action. Accordingly, the behavior setting invites a fuller consideration of the role of contextual factors in psychological processes; and, in turn, it calls for an examination of a wider range of sociocultural influences and their psychological significance (chap. 9). Finally, an ecological consideration of sociocultural influences on human functioning will once again bring to the forefront of the discussion the central place of meaning in human experience.

Fritz Heider
(University Archives, Kenneth Spencer Research Library,
University of Kansas)

6

Gestalt Psychology
and the Ecological Approach

In considering the environment in its relation to perception, one has to analyze its macroscopic structure. (Heider, 1930/1959b, p. 30)

Without retreating from the claim that radical empiricism lies at the core of
ecological theory, it must be said that radical empiricism was not the only
substantive influence on Gibson's thought. Among other influences (see
Reed, 1988), there is no doubt that facets of Gestalt psychology played a
major role in the development of Gibson's ecological program. It is not
simply the case, however, that Gestalt psychology constitutes a second independent influence on Gibson's thought because James's psychology
and philosophy and Gestalt psychology are not wholly independent bodies of work. It becomes evident that the roots of Gestalt psychology are inti-
mately tied to some of James's ideas.

This chapter examines some of these Gestalt influences on the
development of Gibson's ecological psychology, particularly those
stemming from the work of Kurt Lewin, Kurt Koffka, and Fritz Heider. This
discussion of Gestalt psychology serves more than a historical function; it
also sets the stage for examining another notable ecological program in
psychology, that of Roger Barker (chaps. 7 and 8). Identifying the common
Gestalt roots shared by the frameworks of Gibson and Barker provides the
basis for conceptually linking these two programs. To date, these two
programs have received separate treatment in the literature, but conjoining
them greatly expands the range of phenomena that an ecological
framework built on a radical empiricist perspective can encompass.

WILLIAM JAMES, GESTALT PSYCHOLOGY, AND THE ORIGINS
OF ECOLOGICAL PSYCHOLOGY

There is much compatibility between James's psychology and Gestalt psychology. Several features of Jamesian psychology and Gestalt psychology are rooted in the Continental philosophical tradition. Although it is true that much of James's thinking derives from and is a reaction to the British Empiricist tradition, the bases for many of his quarrels with the British Empiricists have Continental roots. James's emphasis on the active nature of mental experience, his desire to treat mental phenomena holistically, and his intentional claim that selection is a hallmark of mental processes are just a few of the more obvious reflections of the Continental tradition on his thinking.

James's work itself contributed in a very fundamental way to the emergence of Gestalt psychology in the early decades of the 20th century. As discussed in chapter 5, James is widely cited as a primary intellectual precursor to the philosophy of phenomenology formally developed by Husserl (e.g., Edie, 1987), and the Gestalt psychologists embraced this sort of phenomenological attitude as the starting point for all psychological studies. Moreover, Stumpf, one of James's closest European colleagues and mentor to several of the core group of Gestalt psychologists, was an early proponent of experimental phenomenology. Indeed, it was Stumpf who initially drew Husserl's attention to James's *The Principles* (Edie, 1987). Thus, the phenomenological strain running through Gestalt psychology can be traced back through Husserl to James.[1]

Early on in his training, Gibson was exposed to Jamesian and Gestalt psychology by his two Princeton mentors Holt and Langfeld, respectively. Holt's relationship to James was explored in detail in chapter 2. Langfeld received his Ph.D. with Stumpf in Berlin and was a colleague of Holt's at Harvard before moving to Princeton. (Recall that he subsequently recruited Holt to Princeton.) With this training, Langfeld was one of the earliest American psychologists to advocate phenomenological description in experimental psychology. Gibson would have also been somewhat familiar early on with Jamesian and Gestalt psychology through the work of Tolman. Tolman studied with Holt and Langfeld at Harvard and spent a year with Koffka in Germany in 1912. Because of these experiences, when the newly minted professor Gibson met Koffka as a senior faculty colleague at Smith College, he would have brought to these encounters a greater measure of appreciation and sympathy for the

---

[1]With this generalization, this discussion glosses over several subtle, yet notable differences between James's view of intentionality and that of Husserl and his teacher Brentano (see Sprigge, 1993).

Gestalt position than many others who, like himself, considered themselves to be behaviorists. This is not to say, however, that there was an absence of tension between Gibson's views and those of Koffka.

For the most part, the influences of Gestalt psychology on Gibson's thinking are in those areas where the Gestalt perspective does not clash with James's radical empiricism, but instead where it reinforces and in some cases extends its themes. I have in mind here the Gestalt psychologists' commitment to phenomenology as a starting point for psychological analysis, their emphasis on relations and structure in perceptual experience, and their efforts to locate meanings and values in experience. Among those points where a conflict does arise and where Gibson parts company with Gestalt theory (and many phenomenologists) is their seeming acceptance of some version of metaphysical dualism.

GIBSON'S EARLY EXCURSION INTO FIELD THEORY

Gibson's *The Perception of the Visual World* (1950a) set the stage for his transformation from an S-R behaviorist to an ecological theorist, and the influence of Gestalt psychology is evident in this work. Most obviously, Gibson's search for structure in patterns of sensory stimulation, resulting in his concept of a texture gradient, stems from the Gestalt emphasis on structure in the perceptual field and without question reflects Koffka's influence. J. J. Gibson (1950a) wrote that the Gestalt psychologists

> were aware of the problem of *some kind* of correspondence between retinal stimulation and our awareness of things. Koffka, in his *Principles of Gestalt Psychology*, spoke of a "more comprehensive correspondence between the total perceptual field and the total stimulation" (p. 25).

However, whereas Koffka attributed much of this correspondence to dynamic laws of sensory organization—that is, it was partially imposed via brain processes—Gibson claimed that the order was present in "the total stimulation" itself. In spite of this difference, clearly Gestalt psychology helped to direct Gibson's attention to the structure of the *perceptual field*, which had a lasting impact on all of his subsequent work.

Gibson's interest in the Gestalt notion of the perceptual field can be found before the publication of *The Perception of the Visual World*. It can be seen in a remarkable paper written many years earlier where he adopted a Lewinian perspective for an examination of movement through the environment (J. J. Gibson & Crooks, 1938). Before exploring features of this paper, consider in more detail the previous introductory comments concerning Lewin's approach.

Lewin proposed that the actions of an individual are best understood as the joint outcome of several factors: multiple environmental determinants in the individual's perceptual or *phenomenal field;* personality and motivational factors; and developmental level. An individual's present phenomenal field, or *life space*, consists of the self and the various features of the environment as experienced by the individual at a particular time. The property of an environmental feature in the life space that figures most prominently in Lewin's framework is its *valence*. An object may be experienced by an individual as being attractive or repellent as a consequence of its features as experienced by the person at a particular time. Clearly, the notion of an object's valence rests on phenomenological and relational considerations. When multiple objects are admitted into the analysis, the life space can be viewed as a field comprised of lines of force between the individual and the perceived character of those features present. These forces can be described as vectors of potential movement from the point of view of the individual. A collective analysis of the vectors in the life space at any given moment provides the basis for predicting the person's actions. In other words, behavior can be viewed as a multiply determined vector, a vector of vectors, in the psychological field (Lewin, 1951c).

Gibson employed this Lewinian framework in "A Theoretical Field-Analysis of Automobile-Driving" (J. J. Gibson & Crooks, 1938). At first glance, this work appears to be an anomaly among Gibson's published works as regards its topic and its theoretical perspective. However, a close reading indicates that it anticipates a number of the perceptual issues that would concern him in the development of ecological theory. Gibson selected this problem primarily for what it reveals about the *visual character of movement*. As Gibson and Crooks pointed out, because the motor movements involved in driving are relatively simple, an analysis of this activity predominantly involves understanding the complex and multiple *visual* features that accompany driving.

When driving, individuals experience themselves at the controls of a vehicle—which is a tool for enhancing locomotion—and moving in relation to a field with both positively and negatively valenced features. It is a *"field of safe travel* [and] it consists at any given moment of the *field of possible paths which the car may take unimpeded.* Phenomenally, it is a sort of tongue protruding forward along the road" (p. 120). The field of safe travel at any given moment is configured by the features that have a positive valence, such as the flat, obstacle-free surface of the road, and the features that have a negative valence for this activity, such as the guard rail and other vehicles. It is a field *"within which certain behavior is possible.* When [such fields] are perceived as such by the driver, *the seeing and the doing are merged in the same experience.* ... The field must be shaped in accordance with the objective possibilities for locomotion" (p. 125, emphasis added).[2]

From the vantage point of this Lewinian-inspired analysis, behavior is multiply influenced; these influences are ascribed to the psychologically meaningful properties of features; and the meaning of features are to be understood in relation to the perceiving-acting individual who is phenomenally co-present with these features in the psychological field. The kind of analysis Gibson and Crooks offered here differs from the standard behavioristic analysis in several interrelated ways: First, action occurs within a field of objects and can only be adequately understood when examined with respect to their combined influences. As such, action in everyday settings requires more than a linear S-R causal analysis. In fact, it involves more than simply moving from single to multiple causation; it entails a somewhat different take on the notion of causality itself. A field theoretic approach proposes that environmental features constrain and channel goal-directed behavior rather than provoke or elicit it (see chap. 8).

Second, the standard distinction between sensing and behaving is brought into question. Instead of being distinct occurrences, "seeing and doing are merged in the same experience." With its emphasis on action, this viewpoint has closer ties to Holt and Dewey's critical analysis of the reflex arc than to Lewin.

Third, an important difference from the standard behavioristic approach toward explaining action is that the Lewinian framework recognizes the intentional character of behavior. One consequence of this view is that the purposes of the individual contribute in some fashion to how a feature is experienced. As Gibson and Crooks claim:

> The valences of objects with respect to locomotion may be quite different ones from their valences with respect to eating or esthetic enjoyment when the individual is not simply propelling himself between them. For instance, a hot-dog wagon has a negative valence with respect to locomotion, but a positive one with respect to appetite. (p. 121)

The valence of the object can only be specified with respect to the psychological field at a given time, which includes the individual. A hot dog wagon along the road neither promotes avoidance nor approach behavior per se. Rather, the motivational state of the individual influences the valence of the object, and this valenced object combines with others also present in the field to channel action in a certain direction.

---

[2]In order to simplify the discussion and also to keep it on track, Gibson and Crooks' distinction between "the field of safe travel" and "the minimum stopping zone" is ignored.

Because valenced objects are to be understood in the context of an intentional consideration of action, the stimulus object exists within the psychological field, not outside of it. Yet notice that Gibson and Crooks claimed that the field consists of "objective possibilities" for action. That is, objects in the psychological field are claimed to present objective properties. Were Gibson and Crooks making an internally inconsistent claim here? How can object properties exist within the psychological field and also be objective? There would appear to be some inconsistency, but in asserting the objective character of valences there is a foreshadowing of Gibson's controversial position on the dual status of affordances (chap. 3). It is with regard to this question of the independent versus person-dependent character of meaning, and more generally, the objective versus subjective status of the psychological field, that the tension between Gibson's mature system and the position of Lewin and other Gestalt psychologists becomes most apparent. It is a problem that will need close examination, and to do so I turn to an examination of Koffka's (1935) influential distinction between the "geographical" and the "behavioral environment."

THE GEOGRAPHICAL AND THE BEHAVIORAL ENVIRONMENT

On a winter evening amidst a driving snowstorm a man on horseback arrived at an inn, happy to have reached a shelter after hours of riding over the wind-swept plain on which the blanket of snow had covered all paths and landmarks. The landlord who came to the door viewed the stranger with surprise and asked him whence he came. The man pointed in the direction away from the inn, whereupon the landlord, in a tone of awe and wonder, said: "Do you know that you have ridden across the Lake of Constance?" At which the rider dropped stone dead at his feet. (Koffka, 1935, pp. 27–28)

With this tale, Koffka illustrated the difference between the environment considered independently of behavior and the environment as experienced by a behaving individual. From the former point of view—that of the *geographical environment*—the primary environmental feature of the preceding story is a body of water, albeit in a frozen state. Its properties as a body of water exist independently of any perceiver. From the point of view of an individual on horseback, the lake as a *behavioral environment* is a surface supporting locomotion. The actions of the rider (prior to dying of fright) are explainable in terms of the perceived properties of this behavioral environment.

Clearly, the behavioral environment does not exist independently of the geographical environment. The possibilities in the behavioral environment rest on the existence of certain properties of the geographical environment. The surface is real and its existence is attributable to the co-presence of water and subfreezing temperature. Reciprocally, actions by the individual in the behavioral environment can change conditions in the geographical environment. The rider on horseback could have broken through the ice while crossing the lake—the dread possibility that the rider realizes in retrospect. The behavioral and the geographical environment, although distinguishable, are interrelated. But how?

The Behavioral Environment as a Mediator

According to Koffka, the behavioral environment is the more immediate "cause" of behavior. It is "a mediating link" between the geographical environment and behavior. Viewed in this way, "the relation between the geographical environment ... and behavior ... is thus broken up into two different relationships, that between the geographical and behavioral environment and that between the latter and behavior" (Koffka, 1935, pp. 33–34).

Consider, first, the relation between the behavioral environment and behavior. Using Koffka's terminology, the relations among features of the behavioral environment and the Ego comprise the phenomenal *behavioral field* within which behavior is experienced to occur.[3] By situating action in a behavioral field rather than in the geographic environment, such historically problematic notions as consciousness and meaning become properties of the behavioral field, residing in the relation between the actor and the behavioral environment, not within the actor. Given Koffka's phenomenological orientation, it makes little sense to talk about "a behavioral, or experienced, within" (p. 35). There are not experiences occurring within in contrast to those outside of ourselves. There is a phenomenal field at a particular moment, which includes experiences having referents to the Ego or the environment portion of the phenomenal field. Köhler (1938) put it this way: "Percepts are, of course, not ghosts belonging somehow to the phenomenal 'self.' ... Their place is not in the 'self'—why should these percepts be localized inside another particular percept (i.e., the 'self')" (p. 63)?

By considering the immediate effects of the geographical environment on action within the behavioral field, "every *datum* is a behavioral datum" (Koffka, 1935, p. 35). The significance or meaning of an environmental feature for an individual resides within the relation between the

---

[3]Koffka's behavioral field and Lewin's life space are similar, both reflecting the phenomenal experience of the environment and including the self. However, Lewin's conceptualization was more formalized, intended to offer precise predictions as a result of the topological system and vector analysis he developed.

geographical environment and the individual, as a property of the behavioral environment. The behavior environment is a mediator between the geographical environment and behavior; and consequently, the behavioral environment "must not therefore be considered as something *within* the animal" (Koffka, 1935, p. 35).

Koffka's discussion of the behavioral environment can be seen, in part, as an attempt to address the criticism by behaviorists that Gestalt psychology proposed a mentalistic psychology. By locating phenomenal experience in the relation between the behavioral environment and the Ego, he hoped to avoid the accusation of ascribing subjective states to processes within the person. Apart from whether this line of argument was convincing to most behaviorists, Koffka's couching of Gestalt psychology in this sort of relational language probably made it more appealing to Gibson than it might otherwise have been. Such a proposal viewed in general terms bears some broad resemblance to the relational approach developed by James and Holt (in spite of their differences when examined closely).

The relation between the geographical and the behavioral environment is a different matter. From the Gestalt perspective, it is a relation mediated by physiological processes of the brain. The isomorphism between the physical domain and the brain field provides the bases for correspondences between physical reality and psychological experience. This hypothesis of psychophysical isomorphism was the most controversial part of the Gestalt proposal (and has yet to find much empirical support). The appeal to physiological processes appeared to be a necessary step from the point of view of Gestalt psychology because visual experience apparently could not be explained with reference to retinal stimulation alone. Structure in the geographical environment projected to the eye would be broken down at the level of the proximal stimulus into distinct elements among visual receptors, and organizing processes in the cortex would seem to be needed in order to reconstitute the initial structure.

This claim, of course, is a decisive point where the Gestalt psychologists and Gibson part ways. As has been pointed out, Gibson's program of ecological optics (chap. 4) offers grounds for the claim that the structure of environmental features is preserved in reflected light and thereby available as stimulus information for the active perceiver to detect.[4] A critical step

---

[4]In view of this difference between the Gestalt program and Gibson's subsequent ecological optics, a curious footnote can be found in Köhler (1938). Critically examining the Kantian claim that mind imposes order on experience, thereby providing our known scientific principles, Köhler wrote: "There remains the other possibility that, to some degree, at least, they are inherent in the 'material.' The validity of Kant's theory depends altogether upon his assumption that, in the 'material,' there is no intrinsic principle of order" (p. 44, f. 4). Here Köhler appeared to be gesturing in the direction of a claim that Gibson later made vis-à-vis stimulus information.

here is Gibson's abandoning an analysis of perceiving that gives a role to the proximal stimulus, and instead, taking up Holt's notion of the "recession of the stimulus," locating structure "distally" where it is preserved in reflected light. In adopting this approach, Gibson's account of perceiving operates solely at an ecological-psychological level of analysis, instead of turning to a physical-physiological level of analysis (as the Gestalt approach does) to explain order in experience. In short, a crucial difference between these approaches is Gibson's conceptualization of a medium for perceiving, which has no counterpart in Koffka's and Köhler's work.

Two Environments or One?

Although Gibson equivocated somewhat in J. J. Gibson and Crooks (1938), in his later writings it was clear that he rejected Koffka's geographical environment–behavioral environment distinction (J. J. Gibson, 1971). The problem for him was that this distinction, maintained by Koffka and by Lewin in a slightly different way (see chap. 7), suggested that there are two worlds pertinent to the analysis of psychological phenomena, a phenomenal world and a physical world. As such, the Gestalt framework preserves the ontological dualism that radical empiricism so firmly rejected. By maintaining this distinction, Koffka came close to saying that each individuals' experience is subjectively encapsulated in so many private worlds. J. J. Gibson (1971) pointed out:

> Now the assertion that behavior is regulated by phenomenal experience is, to say the least, debatable. And to say that behavior occurs "in" a phenomenal world leads to difficulties. If this means that each animal and every man behaves in his own private world, as it can be taken to mean, it is surely mischievous. Koffka did not go so far, but he nevertheless persisted in believing that there are two distinct meanings of the basic notion of an organism-in-an-environment. With two kinds of environment, behavioral and geographical, he could hardly avoid muddle and confusion. (p. 7)

For Koffka, meaning is viewed as an intrinsic object property in the behavioral environment that changes with the needs of the individual. But how could meaning be an *object* property under such circumstances? Such a claim would seem to maintain a physical world where the object exists value-free and a phenomenal world where the object takes on various meanings in relation to the individual. Gibson wanted to assert with Koffka that meanings are properties of objects, but this position can only be sustained without contradiction by rejecting the two environments viewpoint and claiming that "the affordance of something does *not change* as the need of the observer changes" (J. J. Gibson, 1979, p. 139).

Gibson's resistance to Koffka's two environments distinction is indicative of the radical empiricist roots of his thinking, and it points to an important difference between the Jamesian and Gestalt traditions. Whereas for the Gestalt psychologists there indeed are two worlds, the physical world and the phenomenal world, and "we are each confined to our own perceptual world" (Henle, 1974, p. 42), for James at the bottom there is but one world, the world of pure experience.

This is not to say individuals do not experience the world differently and understand it in different terms. As discussed previously, from a Jamesian perspective, the possibilities for selection in immediate experience are vast, and what different perceivers select from the "quasi-chaos" of pure experience may (and usually does) result in different perceptual experience. To this basis for differences between perceivers, add James's distinction between percepts and concepts, where the latter are abstractions from that ground of immediate experience, and the possibilities for differences between individuals' experiences grow even larger. But it is important to recall that for James, concepts collectively compose an intellectualized domain derived from immediate experience, and as such are never wholly separate from immediate experience. It is a hypothesized system interwoven with, and difficult to separate from, the reality that is immediate experience (see chap. 1). But it is not an alternative reality or an alternative environment.

In truth, the Gestalt psychologists are a bit inconsistent on this issue. On the one hand, it is beyond dispute that they give primacy to immediate experience and like James treat scientific concepts as derived from that. According to Koffka (1935), "Physical reality is not a datum but a constructum" (p. 35). Köhler (1947) also offered this kind of claim repeatedly, asserting that the data of psychological experience are primary, and that knowledge of the physical domain is always mediated by perceptual experience. At the same time, however, Gestalt psychologists, and Köhler in particular, wrote as if the world of the physical sciences was a domain that stands behind experience and is more fundamental than it. While giving primacy to the perceived world, they still treated it as the veneer of a more fundamental physical world (see Henle, 1974). In this regard, it is worth noting that Gestalt theory was informed by developments in field physics.[5] As such, Gestalt psychologists shared a tendency with standard approaches of behaviorism in acceding foundational metaphysical status to the physical world (although obviously the model of physics underlying each was different).[6] The physicalism in the Gestalt

---

[5]Einstein was a colleague and friend of Wertheimer's at the University of Berlin (R. W. Clark, 1971).
[6]This assertion may be more accurate with respect to Köhler's views than Koffka or Wertheimer, however. I am not trying here to identify the subtle differences among the three.

viewpoint creates an odd tension in relation to its claim that direct experience (phenomenology) is primary.

Radical empiricism, and ecological psychology by extension, side steps this tension by treating the physical world as a "concept." This physical world is a conceptual, hypothesized domain, whereas the phenomenal world is immediately there. What is real are the qualities of immediate experience.

This is not to say that radical empiricism denies the physical world—to do so would be absurd. Moreover, stating this in no way diminishes the analytical value of the "physical world." Indeed, as shown in chapters 4 and 5, an analysis of some features of the physical world, namely, the ecology of reflected light, helps to shore up apparent problems in the radical empiricist approach. But recognizing the physical world as a conceptual system makes it intelligible how views of the physical world can be (and have been) overthrown. In contrast, immediate experience cannot be; it can only be described differently by noting inherent structure that was previously overlooked, that is, previously unselected.[7]

These differences between Gibson's approach and the Gestalt perspective come down to a deeper issue than has been examined so far. For Gibson, and for James before him, what is known reflects the ongoing process of an organism attempting to come to terms with the demands and possibilities of its environment. That is, it is an ecological theory all the way up from its evolutionary foundations. Gestalt psychology has very different roots. It is grounded in Kantian philosophy, which took the foundational concepts of the physical sciences as a priori categories. Accordingly, space, time, causality are not concepts derived from experience; they structure experience a priori and are inseparable from it. Like the Gestalt "laws," they reflect the structuring processes of mind. Gibson, however, reminded us repeatedly that these categories have their origins in the physical sciences and mathematics, not in the ecological domain, and although derived as concepts from perceptual experience, are not constitutive of it.

PERCEIVED MEANING

The Gestalt psychologists' claim that the meaning and value of objects are perceived by the individual was a view that had great appeal to Gibson. However, as can be anticipated from the preceding, he developed a somewhat different stance on this matter than they did with his concept of

---

[7]In view of this discussion, it should be clear why I would disagree with Epstein and Hatfield's (1994) assertion that "Gibson's distinction between ecological reality and physical reality parallels the Gestalt distinction between the behavioral and the geographical environment" (p. 174).

affordance. Gibson's concept of affordances was examined earlier (chap. 3) in relation to radical empiricism. Here its relation to the Gestalt literature is considered.

Aufforderungscharakter

J. J. Gibson (1979) traced the origins of the concept of affordance to the writings of Lewin and Koffka (J. J. Gibson, 1979, pp. 138–140). In Lewin's case, the term is tied to valence (discussed earlier), which is an English translation of Lewin's German neologism *Aufforderungscharakter*. According to Lewin's biographer Marrow (1969), the English connotations of valence may result in it being taken more narrowly than Lewin intended (pp. 56–57). Valence in its older sense of "value, worth, power, strength, and significance," rather than the more limited "attracting versus repelling" connotations, is probably closer to his intentions. Considering the dominant contemporary connotation of valence, Henle (1974) suggested that Gibson's affordance is more apt: "It brings out the qualitative variety that the word 'valence' conceals, and thus eliminates the danger of reducing behavior to approach and avoidance" (p. 54). Still, Gibson appeared to have had something a little bit different in mind than did Lewin.

Affordance also has its roots in Koffka's (1935) brief comments about the perceived meaning of an object. He explained that in naïve experience, "each thing says what it is and what [the perceiver] ought to do with it: a fruit says, 'Eat me'; water says 'Drink me'; thunder says, 'Fear me,' and woman says, 'Love me'" (p. 7). These comments are reminiscent of James's discussion of "affectional facts" in experience (chap. 3). Koffka's observations about perceived meaning are more global than Lewin's, for whom valence was part of a formal system.

For Köhler, too, meaning and value are qualities of the phenomenal field. Köhler grappled with this issue in *The Place of Value in a World of Facts* (1938).[8] His core concept in this study is "requiredness." Requiredness connotes the appropriate outcome under particular circumstances. Immediate experience is described as having a "geography of requiredness" (p. 86), which in any instance is referable to the "vector-aspect of phenomenal contexts" (p. 87). To illustrate requiredness, consider the Gestalt "law of closure." An incomplete figure is typically perceived as a whole figure, with the completed form being a continuation of what is implied by the visible partial form. It is not the case

---

[8]It would appear that James' work was an important influence on this book, although this remains unstated. This influence can be seen, first, in its theme, which was of great concern to James; second, in its dedication to R. B. Perry, James's student; and third, in the title itself. *The Place of Value in a World of Facts* is a variation on the title of James's 1905 essay, "The Place of Affectional Facts in a World of Pure Experience," which explores similar issues.

that the incomplete figure could not be completed in any number of ways; but there is one resolution that seems "right," that fits best, that is "required." Requiredness refers to a *determining tendency*, not a determining cause. Importantly, requiredness for Köhler has this quality of "appropriateness" taken in the widest sense possible. Indeed, for him "truth ... is a case of intrinsic requiredness" (p. 51). As in his early discussions of physical Gestalten, he tried to show how requiredness is not just a property of the phenomenal world, but also of physiological processes and physical systems generally.

Gibson's concept of affordance attempts to capture the same phenomenological quality that the Gestalt psychologists highlighted in these ways. Developing this claim was for all concerned more than a narrow psychological matter. Although meaning and values in immediate experience were a central concern for Gestalt psychology from the outset, this was a topic that took on increasing importance by the early 1930s when the values of the German social order were turned inside out.[9] At this same time, Gibson was exploring in his social psychology the possibility that values are "objective as well as subjective," that there is a requiredness surrounding many aspects of our phenomenal world. Writing about this period, Reed (1988) stated that Gibson wanted to explore the possibility that "human action is motivated by values whose source lies outside the individual, values as basic as food or sex, and as abstract as freedom" (p. 55). In such a world, there is an objective basis for determining what kinds of action are appropriate, and what actions fly in the face of reasonableness and decency.

An essay written by Gibson at this time reflects this point of view. In "The Aryan Myth," J. J. Gibson (1939) explored how psychological meaning can be warped by political ideologies fostering social stereotypes (see Costall, 1989). Indeed, the possibility that meaning is a feature of the environment, and for that reason a property that could be manipulated by social processes, was an important concern in the social psychology course that he taught for many years at Smith College (Reed, 1988). Even after his social psychological interests became a less central feature of his writing,[10] the question of perceiving meaning does not abate. He devoted a chapter to the topic of meaning in *The Perception of the Visual World*

---

[9]It is interesting to note that Lewin's earliest writings on the meaning in the behavioral field come out of his experiences as an soldier in the trenches in World War I. Perhaps the meaning and value that is a property of environmental features even under mundane conditions become most apparent in extreme circumstances. A detailed examination of Lewin's "Kriegslandschaft" (the landscape of war) can be found in Heider (1959). I draw on some of Heider's comments later.

[10]Gibson's views pertinent to social psychology are most explicitly addressed in J. J. Gibson (1939, 1950b, 1953).

(1950a). Therein he wrote that whereas perceptual theory emphasizes such things as surfaces and shapes,

> this description leaves out the fact that the surfaces are familiar and the shapes are useful. No less than our primitive ancestor, we apprehend their uses and dangers, their satisfying or annoying possibilities, and the consequences of action centering on them. ... The visual world, in short, is meaningful as well as concrete: it is significant as well as literal. (p. 198)

This chapter is filled with ideas that become more fully developed in his work several decades later. Criticizing the concept of stimulus as being inadequate "to explain why behavior is a function of objects," J. J. Gibson (1950a) noted that "the theory of patterned stimulation or *Gestalten* arose to reintroduce the notion of intrinsic meaning in a new fashion" (p. 206). His further explorations of patterned stimulation or *structure* through the development of ecological optics, and the concept of affordances more specifically, enriched his analysis of meaning.

Affordances and Ecological Optics

There are some subtle but significant differences between Gibson's concept of affordance and the Gestalt treatment of meaning, and these differences lie along the same lines that led Gibson ultimately to reject Koffka's geographical-behavioral field distinction. Where Gibson and the Gestalt psychologists part company concerns how to explain perceived meaning. In a certain sense, Gibson wanted to think of meanings as part of the "physical" world, that is, as independent of a perceiver. But, as he emphasized, "no one, not even gestalt theorists could think of them as physical and, indeed, they do not fall within the province of ordinary physics" (J.J. Gibson, 1979, p. 138). Unlike familiar physical properties, object meanings seem to be impermanent properties of objects (like secondary qualities of objects for the British Empiricists). For example, the property of the stapler on my desk to hold open a book, as it is doing now, seems to be an impermanent property; that is, it is a property I experience only at certain times. Doesn't this kind of example (which could be easily multiplied) indicate that object meanings are not real, independent properties of the environment? Koffka and Lewin argued that the meaning of an object changes as the needs of the individual changes. Cases such as this, along with the lack of any suitable physical framework for describing them, seem to indicate that object meanings issue from the perceiver, not the object. As such, meaning would seem to be part of a subjectively perceived world, not an independent property of objects.

Lewin recognized that objects have some independent properties (e.g., mass), what he called revealingly "nonpsychological properties," which are present beyond the boundaries of an individual's life space (i.e., outside of immediate experience) at a particular time (also see chap. 7). It is when objects are perceived that they take on a valence (a psychological property) in relation to the individual's needs at a particular time. Lewin (1943b/1951a) asserted: "I do not consider as a part of the psychological field at a given time those sections of the physical and social world which do not affect the life space of the person at that time" (p. 57). This being the case, the meaning of objects, in a psychological sense, would appear to go in and out of existence as they affect and cease to affect the life space at different moments.

One reason why this kind of view would be disagreeable to Gibson exposes his radical empiricist roots. William James sought a philosophical basis for a common ground of experience in order to avoid the skepticism—indeed, the solipsism—which attends representational accounts of mind. In such a view, individuals' meaningful existences would be consigned to so many separate worlds. If meanings arise only in individuals' private experience, and are not traceable to properties of objects, then the possibilities for a common ground of meaning become elusive, if not miraculous. Psychological encapsulation becomes the norm; common, shared experiences are rare.

In order to provide the grounds for shared experience of meaning, a framework is needed that offers the independent quality of a physical description, but unlike a physical description appears capable of conveying meaning. Gibson believed he had the beginnings of such a framework in ecological optics: "The values of things seem to be perceived immediately and directly ... because the affordances of things for an observer are specified in stimulus information" (J. J. Gibson, 1979, pp. 139–140). Meanings are independent properties of objects because they are directly tied to characteristics of those objects.

To return to the example of the stapler as a paperweight, it is not the case that any object could serve to hold open the pages of my book—that is, I cannot impose that meaning on any object because I have a need to do so at this time. An object can be used in this way only if it has particular characteristics: It must have sufficient mass to hold down the pages, and it must be a minimum length to sufficiently span the book when open. That is, it must have particular properties in relation to a goal of the individual. As such, "an affordance is not bestowed upon an object by a need of an observer and his act of perceiving it. The object offers what it does because it is what it is" (J. J. Gibson, 1979, p. 139). Such properties are perceptible properties of the paperweight; and accordingly, they can be specified by information in the ambient array. "To be sure, we define *what it is* in terms of ecological physics instead of physical physics, and therefore it possesses meaning and value to begin with" (J. J. Gibson, 1979, p. 139).

What does Gibson mean by an ecological physics? An ecological level of analysis entails a consideration of the features of the environment taken in relation to and at the scale of an animal (chap. 3). The concept of an econiche illustrates this kind of relational consideration. An ecological physics, among other things, would offer an account of how functionally significant properties of the environment considered at the level of animals are conveyed in stimulus information. In contrast to properties of the world taken in terms of "physical physics," which are lacking functional meaning, an ecological physics would preserve functional meaning. As Gibson (1979) stated: "Physics may be value-free, but ecology is not" (p. 140).

Perhaps another brief example is helpful here. A flight of stairs is not functionally neutral, and it has functional meaning for someone who has a need to reach another level in a building. Taken with reference to a given individual (or to a class of individuals), a flight of stairs has potential meaning. And importantly, it has this potential precisely because of its object properties; namely, it consists of surfaces of support of a minimal depth separated by risers of a minimal height. Those properties exist whether or not an individual perceives them because they are specified by stimulus information: "The observer may or may not perceive or attend to the affordance, according to his needs, but the affordance, being invariant is always there to be perceived" (J. J. Gibson, 1979, p. 139). Consequently, "The central question for the theory of affordances is not whether they exist and are real but whether information is available in the ambient light for perceiving them" (J. J. Gibson, 1979, p. 140).

From this vantage point, it can anticipated why Gibson would object to Lewin's term "nonpsychological" to refer to object properties not being experienced at a given time. The implied distinction here is between a nonpsychological or physical realm and a psychological one (e.g., the life space). In the former case, objects lack meaning and value; in the latter, they take these *phenomenal* qualities on. ("For Koffka, it was the *phenomenal* postbox that invited letter-mailing, not the *physical* postbox": J. J. Gibson, 1979, p. 139). With ecological optics, Gibson was proposing instead an ecological physics on the basis of which it is coherent to talk about meaning and value, that is, psychological qualities, in the environment. As an ecological physics, it is a relational physics of a different sort than the field physics embraced by Gestalt psychologists. Instead of being a physics of a relational field of physical objects, it is a physics of a relational field of animal and environment. Here the crucial distinction is not between the nonpsychological and the psychological, but rather between potential and actual (or realized) structure in experience (chap. 5). The functional properties of the environment are present because the environment, taken with reference to an individual, is what it is. And this claim cuts across the problematic dichotomy of the

natural and cultural worlds (see chaps. 3 and 9). In radical empiricism—
and by extension, ecological psychology—what is potential is also real.

THING AND MEDIUM

In 1926, Fritz Heider published a remarkable paper based on his dissertation. Heider's "Thing and Medium" is a landmark in the development of
ecological psychology. It profoundly shaped the ideas of Gibson and
Brunswik (see later), the two principal advocates of an ecological perspective, as well as the work of Barker (chap. 7). The Heider–Gibson connection is easy to trace historically. As noted in the Introduction, Heider
and Gibson were both faculty colleagues at Smith College and good
friends (Heider, 1983). It appears that Gibson was indeed fortunate early in
his career to find Koffka and Heider among his Smith colleagues.

Perhaps most remarkable about "Thing and Medium" was its exploration
of an insightful and yet simple question that apparently had received little
attention up to that time. Heider (1926/1959a) asked: "How is it possible that
the region of perception does not end with our skin, that we obtain
knowledge not only about the small narrow part of the world near us but
that we live in a wider world that extends far beyond us?" (p. 2). For
example, we do not see the proximal cause of visual perception, namely,
retinal receptors stimulated by light; rather, we typically experience objects
that are illuminated. How is this possible? Why isn't the proximal cause of
vision what is experienced rather than the more distant object? Heider was
drawn to this problem by his mentor Meinong, who questioned the
adequacy of the causal theory of perception (Heider, 1983).

Heider (1930/1959b) placed his concerns in a broader context, and
herein his anticipation of an ecological as opposed to a physical analysis of
the environment is apparent. He explained (and part of the following was
quoted earlier):

> Everybody will concede that the perceptual apparatus belongs to an organ-
> ism which is adapted to the environment; nevertheless, in discussion of per-
> ception the structure of the environment is often completely neglected, and
> only the proximal stimuli (for instance, the wave length of the stimuli imping-
> ing on the organs) are taken account of. ... The description of the environ-
> ment to which the perceptual apparatus is adapted is a problem of physical
> science and as such not part of psychology. The fact that it has been ne-
> glected is due to the present state of physics, which so far does not offer suit-
> able concepts. (p. 35)

Heider pointed out that psychologists have relied on physical descriptions
of sensory stimulation for the study of perceptual questions to the exclusion of an analysis of the environment that is perceived. What is required

to meet this need of a "description of the environment to which the perceptual apparatus is adapted" is an ecologically relevant physics. Whether such analysis falls outside of the province of psychology, as Heider claimed, or requires a redefinition of psychology, is another matter.

Heider made a start at developing an ecological physics by drawing a distinction between the object of perception and that which mediates the object of perception being perceived. Take the problem of perceiving objects located at a distance. Perceiving objects at a distance is possible because of the structural differences between objects and media. The object and the medium are the two components, or "substrata" of the environmental side of perceiving. The object has a "strong individuality"; its elements are coherent and interconnected, and the object will "respond" as a whole entity. As a result, "external influences affect it only to a small degree" (Heider, 1926/1959a, p. 3). For example, a kinetic force such as a vibration applied to an *object* produces a vibration in the object that is shaped or transformed by the properties of the object itself. That is, the subsequent vibration will be affected by the object's composition and shape.

However, the parts of *media* are not as interlinked or coherent as are those of objects. They function relatively independent of each other. Hence, by comparison, a medium (e.g., air) does not substantively transform that which is conveyed by an external influence, but instead is transformed by it, carrying its structure as a *composite* event: "Everything is taken over and carried on by [this] substratum. Many different events are possible in it. External rather than internal conditions determine possibilities which are realized" (Heider, 1926/1959a, p. 3). Because of the relative independence of the elements of the medium, they can function as "spurious units," thereby conveying the structure of an external influence through its extent. It is the case that external influences are better preserved in some media than in others as a function of the degree of coherence existing among the elements: "The more independent [each part] is from its neighbors, the less is the message altered in the course of transmission" (Heider, 1926/1959a, p. 6).

In short, media can convey the structure of an external force in a relatively unaltered fashion. Significantly, because structures of external influences are carried by properties of media, they exist "*whether or not [they] are used by an organism as such*" (Heider, 1930/1959b, p. 36, emphasis added). Structure conveyed by media is a property of the environment.

Another way to distinguish things and media is that they exist at different levels of analysis. Objects (things) are structured at a level commensurate with perceptual experience and have direct significance for our actions. In contrast, at the level of our actions, the medium itself is lacking in intrinsic structure—it is "transparent" and insubstantial—and its constituents typically have little bearing on objects: "Much occurs in our physical surroundings which is irrelevant for our behavioral world. The media are filled with units of a lower order, but empty as regards [thing] order. Only thing events are of importance for us" (Heider, 1926/1959a, p. 13).

These points are especially relevant to matters taken up in the next chapter.

The Perceiving Function

With this view of the nature of things and media, how did Heider conceptualize perceiving? For him, the process of perceiving involves reconstituting the object as a psychological entity from the spurious units of the medium. This function of restoring, as it were, objects at a distance to a percept at a comparable level of complexity as the object, permits the perceiver to be affected by objects. Heider summarized this viewpoint as follows:

> The light rays proceed from the things; they form a composite event, which, although it is coordinated to the unit of the thing, is not itself a true unit. The organism gathers these effects together and thus they become effective in the region of things; for instance, the organism moves around in a way which conforms to the solid bodies of the environment. The effect of the things remains latent and physically unreal in the medium. It appears again in the organism. Thus in the brain there is again something which is coordinated to the thing and which at the same time is physically unitary. (Heider, 1926/1959a, p. 24)

The function of perceiving, then, is "to reconstruct the coordinated core event [i.e., the object] from the offshoots [i.e., the medium]" (Heider, 1926/1959a, p. 25). He went on, "And if we want to construct an apparatus which would react to distant things through a medium in a coordinated way, we would have to build one that gathers into units *the composite effects which have their source in the distant units*" (Heider, 1926/1959a, p. 25, emphasis added). Heider continued: "In this sense the synthesis is *conditioned by* the structure of the physical world" (p. 25, emphasis added).

The terms *synthesis, reconstruct*, and the like are apt to be somewhat misleading to the contemporary reader. Taken alone, they might suggest that the sensory system imposes organization on the spurious units of the medium. Taken in context, it would seem that this is not what Heider had in mind. As the last sentence in the aforementioned quote indicates, perceiving processes are such that they can take on structure conveyed by the medium that corresponds to "things." He viewed the object and the perceiver relation as being a coordinative one. Owing to its dynamics, the perceiving "apparatus" can "react meaningfully to many different stimulus configurations" (p. 27). That is, "two different manifolds of stimuli would have as their effects two different central processes, not because they set into action two different fixed apparatuses, but because the same apparatus reacts in two different ways" (p. 27). He stated the point more clearly later when he explained that "a process can belong to a system Y but be centered, or have its source, in system X. This is possible if system Y has a great range of possibilities, while X determines which one of these possibilities will be actualized in a concrete case" (Heider, 1930/1959b, p. 48). The perceiving apparatus does not need to restore structure to the data provided by the medium because the structure is already latent in the medium and can be realized by the perceptual function. It gathers the structure up such that the distant object is realized in experience.

The conceptualization of perceiving that Heider was suggesting looks much like the kind of model Gibson had in mind of a perceptual system resonating to structure, in contrast to a constructivist type account whereby structure is imposed on input. Further support for this reading, and a clearer sense of Heider's perspective, can be found by considering his assessment of Brunswik's use of the "thing and medium" formulation.

Differing Views Concerning the Nature of the Medium

Brunswik's probablistic functionalism, and the lens model that was its core idea, was perhaps the first perceptual theory that explicitly called for a detailed ecological analysis of the stimulus environment. Apart from historical interest, it is useful for present purposes to consider Brunswik's ideas here because of the light they shed, by way of contrast, on Heider's position, and, by extension, on Gibson's.

Brunswik (1966) acknowledged that an initial impetus for his lens model was Heider's "Thing and Medium." Taking up Heider's suggestion, Brunswik drew a distinction between distal and proximal causes of perception. However, the proximal influences in Brunswik's theory were quite a departure from what Heider proposed. Brunswik assumed that the proximal cues, that is, stimulation on the receptor surface, bear a probabilistic relation to their distal sources. That is, proximal cues are imperfect predictors of distal conditions, and the degree of correspondence between the two is something that an individual learns through experience in the environment. Thus, proximal cues acquire predictive weights as a result of experience. What the perceptual system has to go on are cues that are, at best, probabilistically related to distal conditions, and these probabilities or weights can then be employed in the process of perceiving, which Brunswik conceptualized as a ratiomorphic (i.e., reason-like) process. Accordingly, Brunswik followed Helmholtz's assumption about the basis for perceiving: What is perceived is the object that most likely would give rise to the particular pattern of stimulation presently on the individual's receptor surfaces. Hence, what is perceived is a mental construction based on these cues, with perceptual experience of things being indirect.

Brunswik recognized the importance of the problem Heider had brilliantly articulated. He agreed that theorists had not paid much attention to how objects distant from receptor surfaces could be perceived, and he was perhaps the first psychologist to attempt a detailed analysis of this problem identified by Heider. In fact, Heider (1939/1959b) asserted: "Without a doubt, the most imposing system using distal determination is Brunswik's psychology in terms of objects" (p. 75). However, although Brunswik appeared to have accepted the broad outline of the framework Heider had sketched, he had not adopted its more radical implications.

Central to Heider's analysis, and contrary to Brunswik's position, is the claim that the structure of the distant object is preserved in the medium. Commenting on Brunswik's theory, Heider (1939/1959b) wrote: "However, we find that the role of the stimuli in mediation and their place 'between' objects and the organism is more or less disregarded" (p. 76). In his published notebooks edited by Benesh-Weiner (1988), Heider offered this more pointed criticism of Brunswik's work, which also reveals a great deal about the position Heider proposed: He "took the lens model from my Thing and Medium, but he cheapened it—and he did not use the concept of the 'spurious unit' … Brunswik treats coaction of part cues statistically, while for me it contains a grammar" (pp. 125–126).

Viewed as a "grammar" the parts of the medium, although independent, when considered collectively can convey *structure.* Brunswik took the parts of the medium in far too molecular a manner from Heider's perspective, which undoubtedly reflects Brunswik's logical positivist training.[11] But as Heider revealed in his notebooks, "As long as you find only probabilities, you have not yet got hold of the *relevant variables*" (p. 420). And where can the relevant variables be found?: "In considering the environment in its relation to perception, one has to analyze its macroscopic structure" (Heider, 1930/1959b, p. 35). It is precisely this claim that Gibson explicated in *The Perception of the Visual World* (1950a); and despite the changes in his position following that book, it is one of the constant themes in Gibson's perceptual theory through its evolving phases.

Finally, Heider noted a problem in the Helmholtzian–Brunswikian position that both James and Gibson identified in another context (see chap. 4). If some quality, such as the third dimension of space, is not

[11]Brunswik trained under Karl Bühler at the University of Vienna, and there was influenced by the philosophers of the Vienna Circle (Tolman, 1956).

somehow already present in a pattern of stimulation, how can it possibly be inserted into it? In his notebooks (Benesh-Weiner, 1988), Heider asked: "How does Helmholtz come from proximal to distal? When distal is never given in experience [in Helmholtz's formulation]?" (p. 420). He could have asked the same kind of question about Brunswik's view. If what is conveyed in proximal stimulation is only the probability of some perceptual quality being present but not the quality itself, then where does experience of the quality come from?

Heider diagnosed the source of these difficulties as a result of the properties of the medium for perceiving having been neglected. Once these properties are recognized, the qualities of the distal object can be conceptualized as being preserved in the spurious units of the medium. Consequently, constructive processes in perceiving, such as Helmholtz's unconscious inference and its various 20th-century progeny (including Brunswik's lens model), are unnecessary as well as illogical. Perception of the structure of objects in the environment is a much more direct process than these theories permit.

Is Heider advocating a direct theory of perception along the lines Gibson conceived? The answer to this question is not altogether clear. One passage of the Heider notebooks contains this reflection: "The differences between Gibson and me are not very great" (p. 318). Presumably, he offered this judgment because Gibson, like himself (and unlike the Gestalt psychologists and certainly unlike Brunswik), claimed that the structure of distal objects is conveyed in the medium. However, judging from most of his writings on perception, it would seem that Heider is not embracing the same position as Gibson. At times, his perceptual theory seems to more closely resemble the Gestalt position where there is some kind of object–psychological process isomorphism. But it would be incorrect to assimilate Heider's views in any simple way to the Gestalt camp. For one thing, he distinguished two lines of thought concerning the "distal stimulus" beginning with Brentano (cf. Notebooks, p. 330). One line comes from Brentano through Stumpf to the "Berlin School" of Wertheimer, Köhler, and Koffka. The other leads from Brentano to the "Graz school" of Meinong, Heider's principal teacher, and Benussi. The Berlin Gestalt psychologists were rather critical of aspects of Meinong's work (see Heider, 1983).

A difference between Heider and the Berlin School is apparent in Koffka's *Principles of Gestalt Psychology*. He made only one reference to Heider in this book, referring to Heider's analogy between a distal object and pattern of stimulation at the receptor level and that of an object and a photographic plate. Koffka emphasized the independent character of each point on the plate relative to the others. As on the photographic plate, "The immediate cause of our vision of any object is just such a *mosaic* of stimulation" (Koffka, 1935, p. 75, emphasis added). How then can the question "why do things look as they do?" be explained? Koffka's answer was, "Things look as they do because of the field of [neural] organization to which the proximal stimulus distribution gives rise" (p. 98). From the preceding discussion of "Thing and Medium," it is obvious that Heider would not describe proximal stimulation as a "mosaic." It would contain structure because of the properties of the medium. Moreover, Heider did not attribute the structure of experience to neural organization generated, instead (as quoted earlier) he (1926/1959a) proposed that "the synthesis is conditioned by the structure of the physical world" (p. 25). That is, in contrast to the Gestalt psychologists, Heider gave considerably more causal weight to the world itself.

What is clear from his Notebooks is that Heider struggled with the process by which structure in the world is reconstituted in experience, and other implications of "thing and medium" for perceptual theory, for a half century after he first insightfully formulated the framework. There is no mistaking the fact that Heider wanted to establish some theoretical distance between his views and those of the Gestalt psychologists, and some of his ideas come close to the relational views of Gibson, and by extension, James. Consider Heider's (1959c) critical assessment of Koffka's distinction between the geographical environment and the behavioral environment, which appears in a discussion of Lewin's early paper on the phenomenology of the war landscape. After restating that the geographical environment is the environment as described by a physicist or geographer, in contrast to the phenomenal features of the landscape that are experienced by the soldier ("it is dangerous place"), Heider pointed out that these *phenomenal features* give the landscape "a certain kind of *objective existence*" (p. 114, emphasis added). That is,

it contains the *functional possibilities* of the environment which do not vary according to the personal needs and biases of a subject in a particular situation. It refers to what a typical soldier can do and what he may suffer in this environment. These functional possibilities are objective in the sense that they are more or less valid for all persons in this environment. (pp. 114–115)

Where can these "functional possibilities" be located in Koffka's geographical–behavioral environment distinction? Heider wondered: "Could it be that this description of the war landscape does not after all describe the behavioral environment or life space, but something between the behavioral environment and the geographical environment?" (p. 115). He proposed the notion of a "geo-behavioral environment," which refers to "everything that persons have in common in the interactions with the environment" (p. 115). This proposal led to a surprising conclusion:

In a way, the average person is then attributed to the outside. In this way we can enter more and more on the accounts [i.e., on the side of] the environment until *the person shrinks to an undifferentiated point*: the environment is then characteristic for one particular person at one particular moment. ... And we have not given up entirely the attribution of the person. We have to characterize these environments by saying: this is the *environment for this group, or for this person*. (pp. 115–116, emphasis added)

Thus, in describing the functional character of the environment, the dualism of geographical–behavioral environment distinction vanishes. Heider appeared to arrive at a *relational view of person and environment* that accords with that of Gibson and, more fundamentally, with radical empiricism.

The question then is how is it possible to talk intelligibly about an environment that individuals have in common? Or, put differently, how can we talk about their perceiving a common world, described relationally, such that the Brunswikian move toward constructivist processes that produces so many separate, subjective worlds is avoided? The analysis of "thing and medium" seems well suited for that task, and even more so does one of its conceptual offspring, ecological optics.

CONCLUSION: GESTALT PSYCHOLOGY AND ECOLOGICAL PSYCHOLOGY

In spite of their various commonalities, Gestalt psychology and ecological psychology remain opposed. Ultimately, what separates these views is that ecological psychology grows out of radical empiricism, with its rejection of a physical realm–mental realm distinction, whereas the Gestalt psychology retains this traditional dualist formulation through its Kantian roots. Moreover, ecological psychology rests on a biological foundation rooted in evolutionary theory, whereas Gestalt psychology rests on a physical science foundation.

Gestalt psychology offers essentially a psychophysical framework (as did Gibson in his 1950 book, which predated the development of his ecological approach). Its concern is with the correspondence between the world described by physics, in this case field physics, and psychological experience. It is the relation between these different worlds that needs to be resolved.

From the perspective of James's radical empiricism, and Gibson's ecological extension of it, the problem of correspondence between the physical world and psychological experience arises from a dubious and mischievous way of framing the problem of perception. In this regard, Gestalt psychology is in the same philosophically tenuous position as other theories that accept the mind–world distinction, including otherwise divergent views such as those coming out of the British Empiricist tradition. Instead of following this route and conceptualizing the physical world as a parallel domain to which the psychological domain must be aligned, it may be better to follow James's approach of viewing the physical world as a conceptual framework that is derived from immediate perceptual experience and continually tested against it. From the standpoint of radical empiricism, there is but one reality, the world of immediate experience.

This rejection of dualism for an emphasis on immediate experience does not also entail rejection of a world independent of an individual's experience. At a psychological level of analysis, the world that exists independently of the individual is an ecological world, not a physical world. Unlike a physical domain, the ecological world encompasses those functionally significant properties of the environment in relation to which perceptual systems have evolved, as well as those that have been created as a result of sociocultural processes (chap. 9). As such, the ecological world stands in a more immediate relationship to the individual than does the physical domain.

This ecological domain has been heretofore insufficiently investigated in psychology, and Gibson, and Heider before him, pointed out this deficiency in the science and provided some signposts in the attempts to develop an understanding of it. Such an analysis requires a consideration of the environment in terms appropriate to psychological experience and action. Heider saw the absence of such a framework as being attributable to "the present state of physics, which so far does not offer suitable concepts" (Heider, 1930/1959b p. 35). Gibson would agree, although he would probably argue that psychologists bear some of the responsibility for providing the needed "ecological physics." The ecological turn that his writing and research took around 1960 was intended to do just that.

Roger G. Barker, 1930s
(Courtesy of Louise Barker)

7

Ecobehavioral Science: The Ecological Approach of Roger Barker

"Life is a series of locations, as the body traces its paths through space."
(McGinn, 1999, p. 106)

A science of psychology requires a way of conceptualizing the environment that is adequate both to standards of science and to the qualities of human phenomena. This is a rather tall order to fill. In order to do so, psychology needs to have at its disposal a way of thinking about and describing the environment that is independent of any particular perceiver; and, at the same time, it needs a descriptive language that captures the qualities of environments that individuals experience. Typically, the traditional framework of the physical sciences has been appropriated into psychology because it meets the first criterion, objectivity. However, this physicalist framework falls rather short when it comes to conveying the qualities of psychological experience.

Of course, there have been long-standing objections to undue physicalism in psychology, but usually these protestations take a form that raises the opposite kind of problem. Such protests elevate the subjective, taking the qualities of individuals' psychological experience as primary. But then these subjectivist positions are faced with explaining how individuals' psychological experience can be connected to a common world that stands independently of each perceiver.

These two problems are mirror images of one another, and they arise because the discipline lacks a psychologically adequate description of the environment in the first place. Psychology has been handicapped historically because of the absence of such a framework. To make matters worse, it has not often recognized its need for one. On the one hand, so-called physicalists in effect either treat *qualities* of human experience as epiphenomenal or as matters to be swept under the rug; and on the other hand, so-called subjectivists take the environment as so many individually experienced cognitive constructions.

It was out of an attempt to address certain aspects of this dilemma that Gestalt psychology arose (see previous chapter); and the early work of Fritz Heider in particular was an invaluable step in this direction. Heider called for the development of an "ecological physics," and he provided the foundation for such a physics in "Thing and Medium." Unquestionably, Gibson was deeply influenced by this work. Gibson agreed with Heider that describing the environment in terms of physical stimuli does not adequately capture the properties of the environment an animal perceives and to which it is functionally adapted. Along the lines laid out by Heider, Gibson developed ecological optics.

In the late 1940s, and contemporaneous with Gibson's early work on the stimulus information for vision, Roger Barker began exploring research questions that would also lead him to apply Heider's "thing and medium" distinction, but in this case to phenomena of a very different sort than Gibson. Barker and his colleagues, working outside of the mainstream of developmental and social psychology, patiently and painstakingly developed an ecological psychology of everyday social behavior. In this endeavor, Barker gradually came to realize that the shortcoming Heider identified in the domain of perception applied to the domain of social behavior as well—namely, that there is needed an objective and psychologically meaningful description of the environment that, in this case, would be adequate to the phenomena of behavior in everyday social settings. This work led Barker to call for an ecological psychology, later renamed ecobehavioral science, that would provide concepts and methods for understanding the lawful ways in which environmental contexts structure the social actions of individuals and groups. With this stance, Barker began to study the higher order structures that emerge from collective social actions and contribute to some of the social order present in everyday life.

This chapter and the next examine some of the principal features of Barker's ecological approach with an eye toward linking this program to the tenets of Gibson's ecological psychology developed in the previous chapters. Gibson's and Barker's programs have been treated in most writings as being independent, although sympathetic with each other's goals. This discussion is intended to show that the connections between the two run, in fact, quite deep with their commonalties being rooted in shared antecedents in Gestalt psychology, and in Heider's early writings in particular. By articulating their connections, it is possible to indicate how they can contribute jointly to a more encompassing ecological psychology than either offers alone.

LEVELS OF ORGANIZATION AMONG NATURAL PROCESSES

Before examining Barker's ecological approach and its structural similarities with Gibson's work, it is useful first to consider a feature of their shared metatheoretical perspective. Both theorists assumed that natural processes are structured in a hierarchy of nested levels of organization. The assumption that the phenomena of nature are ordered and that this order can be described as a hierarchy of nested units is a recurrent theme in the ecological sciences (Allen & Starr, 1982). This conceptualization has been treated in passing in various places in the preceding chapters, and here it is explored in more detail. By doing so, the differences as well as the relations between Gibson's ecological psychology and Barker's ecobehavioral science can be more readily understood.

Locating Nature's Joints

The dynamic and structured processes that are natural systems, including physical systems, biological systems, and sociocultural systems, can be conceptualized as operating at various scales of order in the natural world. This conceptualization assumes a nested hierarchical structure across natural systems, with distinctive functional properties characterizing each of the various levels. So, for example, a nested series of functions are found at ascending levels of organization in the human body, functions associated with the operations of, successively, individual cells, individual organs, interconnected organs systems, and the individual organism considered as a whole (Weiss, 1969). More broadly, a varied but ordered distribution of functions, from a subatomic level of analysis to a cosmic level of analysis, reflects the presence of diverse types of natural systems of differing functional character.

The natural system of most obvious interest for the study of psychology is the environment–animal system. Environment–animal relations result in a level of functional organization in nature that is distinguishable from other natural systems. The defining functional operation of this type of system considered from the point of view of the history of the species in question, is *natural selection*. The outcome of selection pressures up to any particular point in a species' history is reflected in its functional attributes. Perceiving, for example, refers to an ensemble of activities that has evolved as a response to selection pressures, fostering a functional fittedness between individual animals and the properties of their surround. From the point of view of the history of an individual animal, the defining functional operation is *adaptation*. The ongoing detection by an animal of functionally significant properties in the surround over the course of a day, year, and lifetime enables it to maintain an adaptive attunement to these features.

What is distinctive, then, about environment–animal systems operating against a background of natural selection and adaptation is that they reflect biological/behavioral systems organized in relation to *environmental regularities* that are functionally significant for an animal considered as a whole. Wimsatt (1976) offered:

> Suppose that systems, which are relatively changeable ... are left to do so. One feature that quickly emerges if we take biological organisms as an example is that *under pressure of selection, organisms are excellent detectors of regularity and predictability.* ... To the extent that this is so, one would expect to find the greatest density of organism-types at the places of greatest regularity and predictability. (pp. 238–239)

Other natural systems operate under different selection principles:

> What natural selection does for organisms, other selection processes do for entities at other levels, both physical and mental. Atomic nuclei and molecules constitute two other levels of organization and foci of regularity. They are so because they are the *most probable* states of matter under certain ranges of conditions. (Wimsatt, 1976, p. 239)

As a result, different natural systems are operating at various levels of organization. Owing to different selection processes (broadly defined) at different levels of structure, these levels are marked by shifts in the functional properties of distinctive, but interrelated, systems. In short, there appear to be "joints" in nature, which are transitions in the operations characterizing natural processes at various levels of organization.

With a shift in functional properties at different levels of organization, each level can be expected to have a characteristic and discernible *functional coherence*:

> In picking out a level of organization (which we generally do by naming a few characteristic entities and interrelations) we are doing so on the basis of something like a gestalt—a recognition that these entities and these [within level] relations hang together more strongly with one another (in terms of frequency and density of connections) than they do with other units and relations. (Wimsatt, 1976, p. 242)[1]

---

[1]Wimsatt's claim that individuals make level of organization distinctions by attending to structures in experience ("gestalts") is consistent with the radical empiricist perspective that the conceptualization of the natural world emerges from immediate perceptual experience. Similarly, Allen and Starr (1982) wrote:

> We do not mean to imply that that reality, independent of our cognizance, is in its nature hierarchical; in fact we are not sure what that could mean let alone what it does mean. What we are trying to say is that somewhere between the world behind our observations and human understanding, hierarchies enter into the scheme of things. (p. 4)

Because of this functional coherence, each level of organization tends to retain certain essential properties; that is, these are *quasi-stable systems*. Any natural system can maintain its integrity in the face of some degree of perturbation, although there are limits to any system's resiliency. Beyond such a limit, the defining functions of the system cease to operate (Simon, 1969; Wimsatt, 1976).

Significantly, these varying levels of organization are not functionally insulated from neighboring levels of functional organization. There are ongoing interactions among adjacent functional systems. These cross-level interactions occur precisely because "the same system will be found at a *number* of levels, if it has any reasonable degree of complexity, though it will of course be *a* system at only one level" (Wimsatt, 1976, p. 242). At any given level of complexity (e.g., level M), a natural system will interact not only with others of the same system *type*, in a network of within-level [M(1) ... M(n)] interactions, but at the same time, it will be implicated in between-level interactions as well. Systems at one level (level M) function as constituents of a higher order natural system (level L); and working in the other direction, for any given natural system operating at level M, there are constituent systems comprising it that function at a lower level of organization (level N).

The interconnections across levels of organization are especially apparent in biological systems. These interconnections are manifested in a positive way as system organization, but not only in that way:

> It is sometimes advantageous, however, to view organization not positively as a series of connections, but rather negatively as *a series of constraints*. Ordered systems are so, not because of what the components do, but rather because of what they are not allowed to do. (Allen & Starr, 1982, p. 11, emphasis added)

The dynamic configuration of a system at a particular level of organization is generated by the mutual interrelations of its constituents, and in turn this *overall configuration constrains* the range of functioning of these constituents. This hierarchical organization is indicative of the dynamic properties emergent upward from relations among constituents, and also of the presence of *control processes* in place exerting downward between-level influences (Pattee, 1973). That is, the degrees of freedom of the individual constituents of a system are constrained by the dynamic configuration of the system considered as a whole. Pattee (1973) summarized the preceding view thusly, "*[H]ierarchical controls arise from a degree of internal constraint that forces the elements into a collective, simplified behavior that is independent of selected details of the dynamical behavior of its elements*" (p. 93).

The existence of hierarchical controls at successive levels of organization is especially critical in light of the likely role they play in the evolution of complex systems such as biological systems. Simon (1973) argued:

> One can show on quite simple and general grounds that the time required for a complex system, containing k elementary components, say, to evolve by processes of natural selection from those components is very much shorter if the system is itself comprised of one or more layers of stable component subsystems than if its elementary parts are its only stable components. (p. 7)

With the emergence of subsystems, natural processes consolidate the gains of selection over time, producing a "ratcheting effect" at successive levels of development. Simon offered the example of two watchmakers assembling watches comprised of thousands of parts. The strategy of one watchmaker is to build successive, and in some cases ever-more inclusive *subsystems*, whereas the approach of the other is to assemble the watch component by component with a single cumulative assembly strategy. Assume in both cases that the assembly processes are not smooth, but are frequently interrupted (akin to shifts in climate or landform in geological time and their attendant effects). Because the component-by-component assembly at any given moment is likely to be unstable, interruptions would continually bring down most of the structure, impeding all but the most modest progress. By contrast, construction by subassemblies would insure that interruptions would have a more limited effect, with the existing set of subsystems functioning like a ratchet wheel, preventing appreciable backsliding. This ratcheting effect is manifested because the subsystems as a whole limit the degrees of freedom of its components and preserve some measure of the achieved stability. For this reason, "hierarchies will evolve much more rapidly from elementary constituents than will non-hierarchic systems containing the same number of elements. Hence, almost all the very large systems will have hierarchic organization. And this is what we do, in fact, observe in nature" (Simon, 1973, p. 8).

Two features of hierarchical control, mentioned already, demand particular emphasis. First, hierarchical control results in quasi-stable equilibria such that collections of entities, owing to their dynamic interrelations, can withstand some measure of perturbation. Second, hierarchical control results in a measure of freedom within constraints among the constituent entities. Consequently, hierarchical control does not mean a severely limited determinism imposed on constituents as a result of their place in the dynamic configuration. It lends order to natural systems while preserving possibilities for variability among constituents within constraints (Weiss, 1969).

Related to this latter point, it is most significant that the constraints imposed on lower level processes create possibilities for change that would not occur in their absence. Commenting on cell development,

Pattee (1973) wrote: "Although each cell began as an autonomous, 'typical' unit with its own rules of replication and growth, in the collection each cell finds additional selective rules imposed on it by the collection, which causes its differentiation" (p. 77). In other words, the paths of later differentiation become possible because of the convergence of particular prior constraints. One way this process may occur, which will have some value for later discussion, is as follows. The collection of components as a whole operates to maintain its dynamic structure in the face of perturbations from variability of constituents. In some cases, these perturbations in relation to existing dynamic constraints present problems to be solved, and their resolution can produce novel outcomes in the form of a differentiation of the previous configuration. In short, hierarchical control simultaneously constrains and creates conditions for invention that otherwise would not exist. Creativity and novelty grow out of constraints.[2]

Viewed comprehensively, a hierarchical systems framework offers a *pluralistic* account of natural systems, and this is so in two related respects. First, no single level of organization is any more causally fundamental than any other. The continuing function of any particular system X depends on the following: conditions residing among other within-level processes, the satisfactory collective operation of X's lower level constituent conditions, appropriate support from higher level conditions within which system X itself is a constituent, and the absence of new higher order constraints that would threaten the integrity of X.

Second, it follows that this pluralistic stance asserts that no particular level of functional organization is any more real than any other, if "real" is taken to mean more fundamental in a functional sense. Instead, what is "real" means what is functionally meaningful, in the sense of what is "reliably detected" by a system at a given level of organization. As Wimsatt (1976) suggested, "we might take as real at a given level those properties which are reliably detected by an appreciable proportion of the entities at that level" (p. 242). In psychological analysis, concern is with the functioning of whole organisms, and what is reliably detected is reflected in action. On these grounds, among what is real for human perceivers are affordances of the environment.

Finally, if the notion of hierarchical organization and control processes is considered generally, there has been a tendency historically to assume a linear structure to the hierarchy and the existence of an executive level of control operating at the most comprehensive level of organization—that is, a single master control unit at the top of a particular nested hierarchy.

---

[2]"The more constraints one imposes, the more one frees one's self of the chains that shackle the spirit" (Stravinsky, quoted in Pattee, 1973, p. 74).

Over recent decades there has been growing criticism of such a conceptualization in relation to the operations of complex systems from such diverse fields as cognitive science and robotics to developmental psychology and the analysis of motor behavior. For one thing, such a system would seem to be nearly unworkable. A single central control unit exerting "downward" influences would need to manage information about the state of all constituent processes. Within a complex system, the monitoring, control, and coordination of all the multiple subsystems would be close to an overwhelming task. Instead, a decentralized control structure seems more likely, and this view is in keeping with the developing view that information is distributed in systems rather than being channeled serially through a centralized hierarchical structure. (These issues are discussed further in the next chapter.)

Between-Level Influences from a Psychological Perspective

Distinguishing various levels of dynamic structure among natural phenomena is important because the properties of systems are likely to differ across different levels of structural complexity. For this reason, it is mischievous to ascribe functional properties to one level of organization that instead are characteristic of processes operating at a different level of organization.

It was this concern that prompted Gibson's and Heider's call for an "ecological physics." In doing so, both were claiming that what psychology is lacking is a description of the environment at a level of complexity that is commensurate with the level of complexity of the functioning individual. This kind of framework would permit within-level accounts of psychological phenomena.

The traditional psychophysical perspective, which undergirds conceptualization in most of those areas of psychology that consider the environment at all, attempts to explain psychological phenomena in terms of their relation to environmental processes operating at a lower level of organization than those psychological phenomena. It is for this reason that certain problems in the analysis of perceiving have historically seemed so difficult to solve. In fact, with this formulation, the explanations offered have often created new, even greater problems (e.g., the mind–body interaction) than the ones they were intended to address. Although these lower levels of analysis of the environment might be appropriate for explanations of organismic functioning at a commensurate level (i.e., at the level of neurophysiological processes), they would not often be very useful for explaining higher level functions. Indeed, progress in psychology has been hampered precisely because we have often tried to account for psychological phenomena only in terms of environmental conditions operating at a lower level of analysis.

This is not to say that lower level environmental phenomena are irrelevant to an analysis of higher level psychological functioning. Such a claim would fly in the face of volumes of data. However, whereas environmental conditions taken at a lower level of analysis (i.e., the physical level) do affect psychological functioning, these effects are best understood in relation to the biological processes of the organism—that is, at a level of analysis commensurate with these physical environmental conditions. Physical conditions can affect psychological functioning indirectly through their impact on biological activity precisely because these biological processes are constituent functions of an organism considered at a psychological level.[3] So, for example, exposure to high quantities of lead in the environment can produce movement and speech disorders and a variety of cognitive deficits because lead has specific toxic effects on the central nervous system. Indeed, as this example demonstrates, adequate understanding of certain problems is only possible after including consideration of lower level of relationships.

Thus, although much of the preceding has been intended to emphasize the importance of drawing distinctions between different levels of organization and functioning of natural systems, and to recognize the importance of including in psychological analysis factors operating at a level commensurate with the phenomena to be explained, it is not the case that an analysis limited to within-level considerations is complete. An appreciation of between-level influences is critical as well. An ecological perspective, which emphasizes the multiple and interdependent within-level influences of the animal–environment system, needs to be embedded ultimately in a multilevel, hierarchical framework of natural systems.

Up to this point in discussion, the individual–environment relation has been taken as the *higher order* system or unit of analysis. But does the analysis stop there? With the conceptualization of a natural order of nested hierarchical relations, it follows that the individual–environment relation might also operate as one constituent part of a collective that is functionally embedded within a yet higher order, extra-individual system. If such a higher order dynamic structure exists, then it would be expected to exert downward influences on the individuals that comprise its constituents. In other words, it would function as a control system with respect to a collection of individuals.

As a predictor, it would be expected that a higher order system operating at an extra-individual level, like any higher order system, "captures the effect of significant variations in lower level or less abstract

---

[3]Wimsatt (1976) stated: "To interact causally with a system X is just to produce an effect on it at its own level, Lx. (Effects produced primarily at lower or higher levels will be interactions with sub or supersystems of X, and only indirectly with X.)" (p. 259).

variables" (Wimsatt, 1984, p. 149). For this reason, such a higher order unit of analysis would identify extra-individual structures that account for some of the order we see among the actions of individuals that, at the same time, is not explainable at the level of individual functioning. This structure, like any higher order unit of analysis, would bring with it a measure of imprecision when it comes to describing the functioning of any individual component. It would offer, as Weiss (1969) put it, *"determinacy in the gross despite demonstrable indeterminacy in the small"* (p. 31).[4] That is, what it would offer is a description of collective processes and the identification of the source of some of the regularity that is seen among constituents.

With a few exceptions, the possibility that such extra-individual processes exist has been ignored in the disciplines that are concerned with human phenomena. Within psychology, little attention has been directed at extra-individual processes. And although there are entire disciplines devoted to social structures, these structures typically operate at levels too remote from the individual either to shed light on how properties of social structures can emerge from constituent, individual action, or to identify lawful relations between social structures and individual actions.

Are psychological functions influenced by dynamic structures operating at a more superordinate, extra-individual level? In retrospect, in view of the fact that discussions of hierarchically structured natural systems have been relatively commonplace for some time, it is surprising that this question has rarely been raised. At least three reasons can be pointed to as the basis for this neglect. First, and most obviously, the strong reductionistic orientation of psychology in the 20th century was   an obstacle to higher order analysis of environmental conditions. If the tendency is to look for reductive explanations of psychological phenomena, why even contemplate possible higher order influences? Second, if such influences do exist they may be considered beyond the domain of psychology. But, as becomes evident, the location of upper level boundaries of the discipline are no more clear than its lower level boundaries. Third, psychology lacks a conceptual framework for thinking about such dynamic structures. What might be the nature of such higher level structures? How might such structures exert an influence on lower level psychological processes? These questions lead the present discussion to a consideration of the significant work of Roger Barker and his associates.

---

[4]Weiss (1969) refers to this property of systems as *macrodeterminacy*:

> "If physics has had *the sense of realism* to divorce itself from microdeterminism on the molecular level, there seems to be no reason why the life sciences, faced with the fundamental similitude between the arguments for the renunciation of molecular microdeterminacy in both thermodynamics and systems dynamics, should not follow suit and adopt "macrodeterminacy." (p. 30)

THE NEED FOR AN ECOBEHAVIORAL SCIENCE

In an autobiographical essay written toward the end of his career, Roger Barker (1903–1990) described an epiphany he experienced 30 years earlier during a train ride through rural Illinois:

> In short, I had an overwhelming *negative* "Aha!" experience. Here I was, a native of the culture and an expert on child behavior (and especially on frustration) who knew no more about the everyday behaviors and environments of the children of the towns than laymen know. I was aware, too, that other child psychologists knew no more than I did, and furthermore, that we had no means of discovering more. (R. Barker, 1990, p. 67)

Barker compared the position of psychology in this regard with that of other areas of study:

> I thought of how different the position of an agronomist might be. He would know or could determine the kinds, yields, and qualities of the crops we were passing, the properties of the soils in which they were growing, and the relations between soil conditions and output. This was the beginning of a growing conviction that a science that knows no more about the distribution in nature of the phenomena of which it is concerned than laymen do is a defective science. (p. 67)

This observation is a rather serious indictment; and it is difficult to refute. Why has psychology found itself in this position of ignorance concerning the natural occurrence of many of its basic phenomena?

As R. Barker (1968) pointed out, psychology may be unique among the sciences in that it began explicitly as an experimental discipline and, unlike other natural sciences, never experienced a descriptive phase. And as an experimental discipline, psychology focused its efforts in attempting to discover "if x, then y"causal laws of explanation (see chap. 8). In contrast, other sciences such as astronomy, botany, zoology, and geology all began with active naturalistic description of its basic phenomena, and they continue to pursue this kind of work even in their mature, experimental phases. However, "the descriptive, natural history, ecological phase of investigation has had a minor place in psychology, and this has seriously limited the science" (R. Barker, 1968, p. 1).

This state of affairs is especially surprising because it demonstrates a rather limited view of the very sciences that psychology has often attempted to emulate. R. Barker (1968) explained:

> In these sciences, the quest for the phenomena of science as they occur *unaltered* by the techniques of search and discovery is *a central, continuing task*; and the development of techniques for identifying entities ... without

altering them (within organisms, within cells, within physical systems, and within machines) is among the sciences' most valued achievements. (p. 145, emphasis added)

A detailed examination of the historical basis for psychology's neglect of descriptive, naturalistic research would be a worthwhile undertaking.[5] What do "descriptive, natural history, ecological" investigations provide, and accordingly, in what way has psychology been limited by their absence? First, they enable one to develop a systematic *taxonomy* of psychology's basic phenomena.[6] In doing so, it is possible to begin to establish, for example, what kinds of psychological phenomena occur in everyday settings beyond the laboratory. This kind of information might seem rather obvious, but in view of the possibilities of generating psychological artifacts in unrepresentative experimental situations, such an endeavor is far from trivial. As R. Barker wrote 30 years ago:

> Although we have daily records of the oxygen content of river water, of the ground temperatures of cornfields, of the activity of volcanoes, of the behavior of nesting robins, of the sodium iodide absorption by crabs, there have been few scientific records of how human mothers care for their young, how teachers behave in classrooms (and how children respond), what families actually do and say during mealtime, or how children live their lives from the time they wake in the morning until they go to sleep at night. (p. 2)

Although this situation may have improved slightly since the time Barker initially made these assertions, (and perhaps, in part, as a consequence of his writings), improvements in these regards have been minimal at best.

Second, descriptive, natural history, ecological investigations provide information as to the frequency of these psychological phenomena. Having identified some of the classes of entities, it is necessary to determine how common or representative of the population these classes are. Surely it is important, for example, that a geologist, having identified a particular mineral, know whether it is rare or common. Barker was particularly aware of the need to determine the representativeness of any given phenomenon. Somewhat to his embarrassment, he discovered in his naturalistic research that a laboratory phenomenon that brought him considerable attention early in his career was in fact a relatively rare occurrence in the public lives of children. The phenomenon in question is the developmental regression of a child's behavior under frustrating

---

[5]Danziger's (1990) study of the development of experimental methodology in psychology is an excellent beginning for this much needed historical work.

[6]In this respect, the historically sensitive reader would point out that an early area of psychology, structuralism, attempted to do just that. Unfortunately, the phenomena structuralists (e.g., Titchener) focused on proved to be elusive, at best.

conditions (R. Barker, Dembo, & Lewin, 1941). Based on observational data, Barker found that events of this nature do indeed take place, but the fact is that their occurrence appears to be relatively infrequent. The only way of knowing their incidence was through the kind of naturalistic research that is largely absent in psychology as it has developed.

Third, descriptive analysis informs the researcher as to the context in which particular phenomena are to be found. That is, it provides information about the distribution of basic phenomena: Under what circumstances is one likely to find a particular phenomenon? Commenting on the lack of understanding psychologists have about this matter, R. Barker (1968) stated:

> It is different in other sciences. Chemists know the laws governing the interaction of oxygen and hydrogen, and they also know how these elements are distributed in nature. Entomologists know the biological vectors of malaria, and they also know much about the occurrence of these vectors over the earth. In contrast, psychologists know little more than laymen about the distribution and degree of occurrence of their basic phenomena: of punishment, of hostility, of friendliness, of social pressure, of reward, of fear, of frustration. (p. 2)

This is a rather dramatic and sad indictment of psychology—and one that seems difficult to contest. These three types of information— identification of naturally occurring entities, estimates of their frequency of occurrence, and a description of the context of their distribution—are sorely lacking in the discipline.[7]

The Beginnings of Ecobehavioral Science

Lewin's "Psychological Ecology."   Barker may have started on the road to these ideas in a moment of clarity, but in fact their seeds were planted years earlier in his postdoctoral work with Lewin at the University of Iowa. As seen in the previous chapter, Lewin (1946/1951c) conceptualized behavior as being a function of the constellation of factors present in the phenomenal field (i.e., the life space) at a particular time. It is this multifactor *psychological environment* as experienced by the person that is critical, according to Lewin, for an analysis of behavior.

Lewin also recognized that environmental features outside of the individual's life space at a particular time, comprising what he called the "*ecological environment*," have significant, if indirect, effects on behavior. In his view, these so-called "nonpsychological" factors residing beyond

---

[7]Possible exceptions to this claim are the taxonomic work in the areas of personality and clinical psychology, and broadly in the study of individual differences.

the life space have their origins in physical environmental conditions and sociocultural processes. Analytically, forces that "reside beyond the life space" operate according to something other than psychological laws. In other words, psychological laws and those laws operating outside of the life space are incommensurate. However, these alien forces can still indirectly determine the possibilities and the limitations of the life space. For example, the social patterns of communication in a culture (i.e., who is normatively permitted to communicate directly with whom) establish certain possibilities in the life space. Because these communication patterns are not based on psychological processes, but rather perhaps on sociocultural, legal, and ideological grounds, they are not describable in terms of psychological laws. Consequently, they remain ecological influences beyond the life space as nonpsychological factors.

On what grounds did Lewin determine which phenomena fall within the boundaries of the life space versus those existing beyond it? The phenomena included in the life space are those that are *meaningful* in an individual's experience. In this regard, as in many others, Lewin revealed his close connections to the Gestalt program, which sought to restore meaning and values into psychological theory (see chap. 6). Meaning is a distinctive quality of psychological experience. Features of the environment considered from a psychological point of view are not neutral, physical objects, but intrinsically meaningful objects or events that may draw the individual toward them or may repel the individual. As a result, Lewin felt that properties of the environment considered from the point of view of physics or biology had to be excluded from the psychological field. Such processes serve as a backdrop for individual experience and set constraints at the psychological level (and hence may be manifested in behavior), but they themselves are not directly experienced. They may help to explain order in experience, but they are not part of immediate experience.

Consider from Lewin's perspective two additional examples of nonpsychological factors affecting the life space. During World War II, in an effort to help develop strategies for food rationing and substitution, Lewin (1943/1951b) tried to understand why the food habits of Americans were apparently so resistant to change. As it turns out, food preference choices are influenced by more than an individual's attitudinal tendencies. What food preferences an individual might express through actions are to a large extent determined, according to Lewin, by nonpsychological factors, such as availability of certain foods in a given locale, food distribution, and economic factors. As a result, it is non-psychological factors, rather than psychological processes per se, that set constraints on behavioral possibilities.

To take a second example, the furnishings and equipment in a classroom are nonpsychological factors that provide opportunities and set constraints on what activities are possible for the children in that room. Whereas these factors establish boundary conditions in the life space, and in that way have psychological impact, their genesis and their character is not a psychological matter.[8]

Because of their impact on the psychological field, the study of such nonpsychological factors is important. In fact, Lewin asserted in his later writings that an initial analysis of the field of behavior should begin with a determination of relevant boundary conditions. This type of analysis Lewin (1943/1951c) called "psychological ecology": "Only after these data are known can the psychological study itself be begun to investigate the factors which determine the actions of the group or individual in those situations which have been shown to be significant [by the initial ecological analysis]" (p. 170). Psychological ecology, then, is an attempt to reveal "what part of the physical or social world will determine during a given period the 'boundary zone' of the life space" (Lewin, 1943/1951a, p. 59).

Lewin did not, in fact, conduct any studies of psychological ecology, with the exception of the analysis of food preferences just described. Instead, he limited his attention to processes within "the psychological field." He sought to establish a science of psychology that operated according to principles specific to its domain of analysis.

The Psychological Field Station.   Barker and his colleague Herbert Wright, also a Lewin postdoctoral fellow, responded to Lewin's call for a *psychological ecology*, and in so doing they developed this component of psychology much farther than Lewin did.[9] In fall 1947, Barker and Wright opened a research office in Oskaloosa, Kansas (population about 700), which served as their base of investigations of life in a small town. In so doing, they established the first field research station in psychology for the study of human behavior. As R. Barker (1968) put it:

> The Midwest Psychological Field Station was established to facilitate the study of human behavior and its environment *in situ* by bringing to psychological science the kind of opportunity long available to biologists: easy access to phenomena of the science unaltered by the selection and preparation that occur in laboratories. (p. 1)

Both Barker and Wright were on the faculty at nearby University of Kansas. Thus, the selection of Oskaloosa afforded them the opportunity of a research site while carrying out their other academic responsibilities, as

---

[8]This claim, as well as the preceding one, may draw too sharp a distinction between cultural and psychological factors. This relation is reconsidered in the next two chapters.

[9]The other notable "neo-Lewinian" who also has contributed significantly to the development of "psychological ecology" is, of course, Urie Bronfenbrenner (see Preface).

well as having access to graduate students to enlist to work at the field station. Oskaloosa was also chosen for reasons other than its convenient location. Its small population size made a thorough investigation of the lives of the residents a possibility; it was a self-contained entity rather than being connected to other entities; and it seemed to possess a distinctive feeling of community. Eventually, Barker and Wright and their families moved to Oskaloosa, and they became full-time residents of the community under study. Oskaloosa was given the pseudonym "Midwest" for the purposes of published reports.[10]

Among the first data collected by the researchers of the Midwest Psychological Field Station were detailed written records of the observed activities of individual children over the course of their day ("specimen records"). One of these records was published as the book *One Boy's Day* (R. Barker & Wright, 1951). Several other daily records of children's behavior exist as unpublished manuscripts (see R. Barker, 1968, p. 231).[11] In each instance, an observer known to the child was present when the child under study awoke at home in the morning, and the child was followed by this observer (and replaced on a rotating basis by a round of observers) throughout all of the activities of the day until bedtime. The resulting written record of behavior was a detailed account of what the child did in the various circumstances encountered during the day.

One Boy's Day is a remarkable document. Just on technical grounds alone, and from the vantage point of the present day with the ready availability of palm-sized video and audio recorders, the prodigious and meticulous effort required to collect these data is astounding. Even in later years when such technology was available, however, Barker felt that a written record extends possibilities that electronically recorded records do not offer. Its primary advantage is that it provides a narrative account "in the language of laymen [that] provide excellent coded descriptions of ongoing behavior" (R. Barker, 1987, p. 1415). That is, it can better preserve the content of the action and the social climate of the settings than a decontextualized photographic record or an abstracted behavioral analysis. Barker's goal was to record observed events without transforming them (see R. Barker, 1968, pp. 139–145), but recording psychological events while preserving their content entails more than a head count or a tally of responses. Some qualitative descriptors are needed for a faithful transcription. To take a simple case, recording what an individual says without also including the tone of the comment could

---

[10]A valuable collection of reflections by many of the central participants in the Field Station has been assembled by Bechtel (1990).

[11]The data generated by the Field Station over a 25-year period, including 16-day records of behavior, are stored and indexed in a special collection in the Spencer Research Library at the University of Kansas.

distort the nature of a social exchange. Barker became convinced of the value of developing narrative accounts from his work with Lewin. He felt that such narrative records are invaluable research tools: "When the narrative record is used by a skilled observer with a facility in language, it is extraordinarily effective for describing multiple attributes of behavior and the immediate situation" (R. Barker, 1989, p. 18).

The initial functions of the field station were primarily to collect naturalistic data (i.e., data minimally altered by scientists) and to serve as a repository for these narratives. Subsequently, behavior setting surveys (see later) became an important addition to this endeavor. Apart from the handful of research centers that administer longitudinal psychological studies, such data archives are unusual in psychology. To date, the records of the Midwest Field Station have not been heavily been used by investigators outside of this project.[12]

The Structure of the Behavior Stream

The account of the ongoing activities of individual children consists largely of "unprocessed" data. At first glance, what these records appear to be are a string of events in the form of narrative sequence of observable actions by a single child and the environmental features and persons with which this child interacts. However, when analyzing the records of these "behavior streams," patterns and structures begin to appear.

Behavior occurs in episodic *units*. These units are marked by a goal-directed activity that has a beginning, a directionality, and an end. These behavior episodes or events can occur successively or simultaneously, and they often overlap, in the sense that one episode may begin before a previous one has concluded. Further, behavior episodes can be hierarchically nested (see R. Barker & Wright, 1955, chap. 7).[13] (The hierarchically nested structure of events was discussed in chap. 5).

In addition to the structure of behavior episodes, Barker and his colleagues were concerned with identifying the environmental antecedents of behavior episodes. That is, what environmental occurrences account for the observed behaviors? They began examining this question by analyzing the behavior records to determine if events in the environment just prior to or simultaneous with the initiation of a behavior episode accounted for a particular episode. This was done by assessing whether there was congruence between a contiguous environmental

---

[12]One exception to this claim is a study by Heft (1988a), in which the record in *One Boy's Day* was utilized to examine the child's environment in terms of Gibson's concept of affordances (see later).

[13]Other useful resources for examining the analysis of these behavior records can be found in R. Barker (1963, 1978) and Wright (1967).

event, such as an action by another person (e.g., a verbalization, such as a request) and an ensuing behavior episode.

Their findings were disconcerting and humbling. Overall, they found greater inconsistency between environmental occurrences and behavior episodes than a scientist looking for lawful relationships in natural phenomena would hope for. In the best of cases, behavior episodes were congruent with social occurrences in the environment only 50% of the time. And most often, congruence occurred less frequently than that. Barker (1968) described the reaction of the research group to this initial finding:

> This finding was discouraging to us; it seemed to foreclose the possibility of discovering lawfulness between ecological inputs and behavior episodes within the behavior stream. Although it is true according to Brunswik that the prediction of behavior from input can only be made "probabilistically," predictions with only 50 percent accuracy are not impressive. (p. 150)

Pressing on from this initially discouraging conclusion, however, Barker had an important insight: Children's behavior over the course of their day did appear to be structured and indeed was even predictable if instead of looking for proximate causes of actions, such as immediate social inputs, characteristics of "the more remote environment" were examined.

BEHAVIOR SETTINGS: HIGHER ORDER ECOLOGICAL UNITS

A comparison of the day-long activity records of children in Midwest revealed three notable behavior patterns:

1. "The characteristics of the behavior of a child often changed dramatically when he moved from one region to another, e.g., from classroom, to hall, to playground, from drugstore to street, from baseball game to shower room."
2. "The behavior of different children within the same region was often more similar than the behavior of any one of them in different regions."
3. "There was often more congruence between the whole course of a child's behavior and the particular locale in which it occurred than between parts of his behavior and particular [proximal] inputs from the locale." (R. Barker, 1968, p. 152)

These comments may be summarized as follows:

> We found that some attributes of behavior varied less across children within settings than across settings within children. We found, in short, that we could predict some aspects of children's behavior more adequately from knowledge of the behavior characteristics of the drugstores, arithmetic

classes, and baseball games they inhabited than from knowledge of the behavior tendencies of particular children. (R. Barker, 1968, p. 4)

These patterns of action pointed to a higher order environmental structure with respect to which behavior of different children was congruent. Barker called this environmental structure a *behavior setting*. The functional nature of behavior settings and their psychological significance are the most significant theoretical contribution of Barker's research program.

Conceptually, evidence for behavior settings suggests that the environment considered independently of an individual's experience is structured and ordered. To the extent that psychologists considered environmental conditions at all, they tended, as Brunswik did, to assume that the environment at best had a probabilistic regularity. Even Lewin, who in many other ways differed from Brunswik, agreed that the relations between what he called the "non-psychological factors" and the "psychological environment" were at best probable. Barker, however, found evidence to indicate that the environment could be described in terms of identifiable higher order structures that influence behavior in predictable ways: "I found not only that the nonpsychological environment affects the lifespace at the boundary, but also that the distal environment has consequences" (R. Barker, 1989, p. 19).

As pointed out earlier, if it is assumed that the structure of the environment is at best probabilistic, then it is necessary to view psychological processes as operating to impose order on this semi-chaos. This assumption underlies the dominant constructivist metatheory (Part I). Barker began to adduce evidence contrary to this assumption. His work demonstrates that the extra-individual environment has a regularity and structure that constrains behavior in predictable ways.

Defining Behavior Settings

The term "setting" is rather broad and can refer to any number of environmental features that have varying degrees of influence on behavior. To be useful as a scientific concept, a behavior setting must be more precisely defined than that.[14] Following R. Barker (1968, pp. 16–17), behavior settings include the following properties:

Behavior settings occur *naturally* as a function of the collective actions of a group of individuals. (They are not constructions of a scientist.)

---

[14]*Behavior setting*, like Gibson's terms *perceptual system* and *affordance*, is often used (or rather misused) in the literature in diffuse and imprecise ways.

Behavior settings have a *specifiable* geographical location. (Where a setting transpires can be stipulated.)

Behavior settings have temporal *boundaries* that are self-generated and maintained by the dynamics of its occupants. (Settings have understood beginning and end points.)

The boundaries of behavior settings are *discriminable*; that is, they can be perceived. (One is typically aware of entering/leaving a behavior setting.)

Behavior settings are *quasi-stable*; they manifest mechanisms in response to perturbations, and in so doing, within limits they preserve their integrity.

Behavior settings exist *independently* of any single person's experience of them. (They are identifiable by independent observers; accordingly, they meet the essential scientific criterion for being real in an objective sense.)

Individuals who occupy a particular behavior setting are to an appreciable degree *interdependent*. (This means that actions by one person in a behavior setting are likely to affect others in the same behavior setting.) Indeed, interdependence of actions is the primary criterion used in identifying a behavior setting.

Although this list of behavior setting properties is not exhaustive, it is sufficient to begin considering the dynamic properties of these ecological entities.

Drawing on this chapter's earlier discussion of nested hierarchical structures in nature, behavior settings should be viewed as occupying a higher order position in the natural order than the position of a functioning individual. To employ Barker's terminology, behavior settings are "circumjacent" to (i.e., they surround) individual behavior. Conversely, individual behavior is one component part of a behavior setting. Individuals, as well as behavior objects ("milieu"), are "interjacent" components of a behavior setting.

The circumjacency of behavior settings and the interjacency of individuals in the setting produce an important set of dialectical properties. On the one hand, a behavior setting is comprised of a particular pattern of relations generated and maintained by its occupants. It is the relation among the interjacent components (i.e., persons and objects) that generate and maintain the circumjacent setting. It is in this sense that a behavior setting is self-generating. On the other hand, and reciprocally, as a higher order dynamic structure, a behavior setting constrains action possibilities of its occupants. It is this property of behavior settings that led to their discovery in the first place, as already noted.

An Example of a Behavior Setting

At this point, offering a concrete example of a behavior setting should help readers who are unfamiliar with Barker's research program get a firmer grasp on this concept. For this purpose consider an example Barker effectively employed, namely, that of a baseball game. Viewing a baseball game as a behavior setting means taking a specific instance or occurrence of a game, not the game generically. So, for example, on April 26, 1995, between 1:55 pm and 4:12 pm, the Baltimore Orioles played the Chicago White Sox at the Camden Yards in Baltimore, Maryland. In short, this behavior setting, like any behavior setting, has a *specifiable geographical-temporal locus*. It is a real ecological event.

This game occurred at that place and that time because a requisite number of individuals assembled and, in effect, agreed to interact in accordance with a set of consensually shared rules. Further, in order for the game to be played, certain minimal materials (e.g., bats and balls) and structural supports of the environment (e.g., baseball diamond, foul lines, outfield boundaries) were required. These components are the behavior setting's "milieu." This equipment and other aspects of the milieu, as well as the players and umpires, are the interjacent components to the setting considered as a whole.

The circumjacent entity, the baseball game, is generated by the actions and relations maintained among its components. What is established is a "quasi-stable equilibrium," to borrow a Lewinian term. Reciprocally, in maintaining its quasi-stability, a behavior setting constrains or limits the degrees of freedom of the participants. That is, in contributing to the creation and maintenance of the behavior setting, the participants in turn are limited by its consensually defined meaning. Accordingly, they engage in a game of baseball.

An individual's violation of game rules or the expected decorum—actions that exceed the proscribed degrees of freedom allowed an individual—can, of course, result in ejection. This occurrence, in fact, reflects one way in which behavior settings are quasi-stable entities: Typically, some participants are given the power to remove threats to the setting's stability.

What about the other defining criteria cited earlier? In what sense are behavior settings objectively real properties of the environment? They are objective and real because they do, in fact, occur. That particular baseball game mentioned did happen; its outcome is a matter of record. ("You can look it up.") In what sense is it an extra-individual phenomenon? It is because I do not need to know which specific players participated in the game to understand its character and outcome. That is, its occurrence did not depend on specific individuals, but instead on specific roles (which are part of the defining attributes of the setting) filled. Indeed, if any particular player was unable to participate, then a substitute would have stepped in. (This is not to say that who the participants were did not affect its character and outcome, but rather that the occurrence of the behavior setting was not person specific.) Finally, how is the interdependency of components revealed in this example? As the game transpires, actions by one participant lead to actions by another. If, for example, the secondbaseman accidentally allows a ground ball to roll between his legs, two of the outfielders may converge to field the ball. An endless list of examples can illustrate this point. To a discerning spectator, the interdependencies are in evidence on every pitch. In fact, it is this interdependence that is especially interesting to a baseball aficionado. The game as a behavior setting is a dynamic, interdependent system.

The interdependencies and the resulting quasi-stability reflect the presence of hierarchical control. What actions are possible by individual players are constrained. But also note, as discussed previously, it is the existence of these constraints that create opportunities for invention and creativity. No two baseball games are identical. Throughout the unfolding of each game, the participants are presented with problems to address and ways available within the rules for addressing them. In the context of the constraints operating, there are seemingly endless ad hoc choices to be made by each participant as the circumstances of the game keep shifting. As discussed previously, by identifying a higher order circumjacent phenomenon, the functioning of any individual interjacent component is not being described with a high degree of precision. Instead, this is a description of collective processes. Behavior settings do not determine individual behavior; they constrain it. And by limiting possibilities, they create opportunities for individual choice, even individual invention, within its framework.

Behavior Settings as Ecobehavioral Resources

Barker and his colleagues devised rigorous methods for identifying behavior settings (see R. Barker, 1968, chap. 4). Equipped with these procedures, the behavior settings present in a given locale over a particular time period can be enumerated. What is to be gained by making such a determination? If, for example, one were to engage in a "behavior setting survey" of a small town, like Midwest, and catalogue the occurrence of behavior settings over some period of time, such as a month, what would be learned? Such a survey would reveal something about the *ecobehavioral resources* of Midwest during that time period; it would chronicle what options individuals had available to them in public settings over this period of time. This is because "persons outside of their homes were always inhabitants of behavior settings; there were no interstitial areas" (R. Barker, 1987, p. 1429). Just as a hydrological survey provides information about the availability of a community's water supply, and a geological survey provides information about a community's soil types, minerals, and topography, a behavior setting survey offers information about the community's resources from a psychological standpoint. A profile of the behavior settings in Midwest reveals the behavioral opportunities that were available at the community level over a particular time span.

To illustrate this point using Barker's data, in Midwest over the course of the year 1963–1964, there were 71 organized baseball games that cumulatively lasted for 167 hours, and 124 organized basketball games that lasted for a combined 272 hours. There were no instances of games of lacrosse or cricket; therefore, if there were devotees of either sport in Midwest during that year, they would have no opportunities to engage in the activity. There were 10 dances (12 hours total), 1 carnival (3 hours), 137 meetings among 7 different lodge groups (325 hours), the fire station was open 309 days (1,009 hours total), 2 hardware stores were open for a combined total of 610 days (5,060 hours), and so on. Looking at the data at a more aggregate level, the behavior setting survey for 1963–1964 lists 220 types of settings available to residents at least once during that year.

By examining the types of settings available and the extent to which they were in operation, it is possible to determine what community activities were possible for residents of Midwest during that year. In addition to being valuable in offering a picture of the psychological resources in some place over a specifiable time period, such data can also be compared to other behavior setting surveys of the same locale at other times in order to track community changes (R. Barker, 1968). It can be compared to surveys in other places in order to compare different communities. The most detailed instance of a comparison of communities is Barker and Schoggen's (1973) analyses of Midwest and a comparably sized town in England (Yoredale) both assessed at two different times.[15] Obviously, this approach extends endless possibilities for cross-locale comparisons.

To take but one example, R. Barker and Schoggen (1973) reported that in 1963–1964 Midwest and Yoredale had roughly a comparable number of behavior settings operating and the population size of Midwest was

---

[15]The data Barker and his colleagues painstakingly collected are far richer than this discussion indicates. For example, they examined the kinds of people (by age, race, gender, social class) who participated in various settings and their relative position of power in these settings. Thus, for example, one can see that Midwest offered adolescents few settings in which they could hold positions of responsibility relative to adults. But in comparison to adolescents in the comparison English town, Midwest adolescents had far more opportunities for holding responsible positions in community settings.

smaller. Bearing in mind that behavior settings are dynamic, self-regulating systems (i.e., the set of processes that constitute a behavior setting operate to preserve and maintain the setting), these data open an avenue for some insights about the nature of community life in both places. To put it simply, for a comparable number of behavior settings to have operated among a smaller number of town inhabitants means that individuals in Midwest (vs. Yoredale) participated in a greater number of settings and were pressed into positions of responsibility more often. (This pattern of results was confirmed by a more fine-grained analysis as well; see R. Barker & Schoggen, 1973, and Schoggen, 1989, for more details). What emerges from this kind of analysis is a picture of the quality of community life in each place; and such an analysis can be illuminated in more detail by consideration of the kinds of settings, and thus, the kinds of opportunities, that are operating. As already noted, the resulting account does not offer predictions at the level of any particular individual. Instead, it provides an analysis of the ecobehavioral resources of a place at an extra-individual level.

Behavior Settings and Heider's Analysis of Thing and Medium

In seeking to uncover lawful explanations of behavior, Barker was led to ecological structures—behavior settings—operating at a higher level of organization than the actions of individuals. That is to say, these ecological structures affect actions of individuals en masse, unlike ecological entities such as affordances, whose relation to action is to be understood at the level of an individual. Indeed, potential behavior setting influences are typically considered in the absence of any particular individual (Schoggen, 1989), with individuals usually being replaceable. A question, then, that Barker needed to confront was how to understand the relation between behavior settings and the actions of individuals. How should the relation between these dynamic entities that operate at different levels of complexity be conceptualized? Barker drew on Heider's analysis of thing and medium in order to conceptualize their relationship (chap. 6).

Behavior settings are higher order behavior-milieu entities operating circumjacent to the activities of any single participant in the setting. Following Heider, Barker claimed that behavior settings possess "thing-like" characteristics. They are ecobehavioral entities consisting, by definition, of a high degree of coherence or interconnectedness among their constituents. The coherence and stability of a behavior setting is attributable to "a balance between many independent forces that bear upon them" (R. Barker, 1968, p. 161). The kinds of "forces" that contribute to their stability and maintenance stem from various factors, including the following: sociopolitical processes in the community that maintain the need for certain settings (e.g., government offices) and social traditions that perpetuate some settings (e.g., fraternal lodges); factors intrinsic to the milieu of the setting (e.g., presence of a dedicated structure, such as a Courthouse); and factors related to the occupants of the setting, as in the case of individuals with particular skills, talents, and interests (e.g., a community band). These various influences converge to maintain in a dynamic fashion the integrity of the behavior setting. Behavior settings have quasi-stable equilibria.

The occupants of the setting collectively possess characteristics of "media." That is, considered apart from a behavior setting, they do not possess a particular form or coherence among them—they are a "loose aggregate." Accordingly, occupants *qua* media have the property of being able to take on collectively the dynamic structure of the circumjacent behavior setting. As an ensemble, and within limits, media are *malleable* (in Heider's terms, they are "spurious units") with respect to functional properties of their context. A medium can be structured by extrinsic influences because its constituents are relatively independent, as compared to "things" whose constituents are highly coherent. For example, the frequency of the vibration of a tuning fork (a coherent thing) is carried in the adjacent medium because molecules of air react somewhat independently. In interaction with the object and each other, these molecules collectively take on the resonating frequency of the vibrating object, although individually they are not changed in substance. That is to say, the constituents of the medium are relatively "docile" with respect to contextual influences. In this way, the medium can take on the structure of the circumjacent entity without being changed in its substance:

> The thing-medium relation ... refers to the transmission and maintenance of pattern between thing and medium, not to the transformation of thing-phe-nomena into medium-phenomena. ... Knowing that A and B are related as thing to medium makes it possible to predict something about B from infor-mation about A, and vice versa; the prediction tells us nothing about the sub-stance behind the pattern. Nevertheless, when the thing-medium connection obtains, *certain consequences with respect to pattern follow with complete certainty.* (R. Barker, 1968, p. 188, emphasis added)

When individuals are considered as *media of behavior settings,* they take on its dynamic structure. As R. Barker (1968) wrote:

> People conform to a high degree to the standing patterns of the behavior set-tings they inhabit. ... While it is possible to smoke at a Worship Service, to dance during a Court Session, and to recite a Latin lesson in a Machine Shop, such matchings of behavior and behavior settings almost never occur in Mid-west, although they would not be infrequent if these kinds of behavior were distributed among behavior settings by chance. (p. 164)

But, of course, these behaviors are not distributed by chance. That is the essential point of Barker's discovery of behavior settings. There is order in the environment considered independently of any particular individual.

The docility or malleability of a collectivity of individuals with respect to behavior settings—that is, a reason why they can function as media under such circumstances—can be explained largely by the fact that humans are fundamentally social beings, attuned from the outset of life to information from social sources and social processes (chap. 9). Viewing psychological processes as *person–environment* functions (as opposed to taking individuals as isolated units of analysis) means the character of the immediate setting will be reflected in individual action in psychologically fundamental ways. This relation between settings and individual actions is possible because of a functional reciprocity: "People, en masse, are remarkably compliant to the forces of behavior settings" (R. Barker, 1968, p. 164). Said differently, behavior settings operating as extra-individual, quasi-stable ecological entities maintain their dynamic structure by limiting the degrees of freedom of their participants. To reiterate, the collective actions of individuals, along with supportive milieu features, generate behavior settings, and reciprocally, behavior settings structure the actions of those individuals who participate in them.

There is recognition here that entities at each level of analysis—the circumjacent behavior setting and its interjacent components—are different. This is not a system reducible to a single kind of entity. Note, however, that these are not completely incommensurate levels of analysis, as Lewin suggested. Because the differences between levels is *structural* and not substantial, and the relation is one of thing to medium, the *transmission* of structure is possible. Under these circumstances, univocal predictive relations of collective action, not merely probablilistic estimates, become feasible.

By emphasizing the structural differences between settings and individuals en masse, Barker is offering a pluralistic perspective in the sense of requiring psychologists to be sensitive to processes operating simultaneously at more than one level of analysis. It is by adopting a more encompassing psychological perspective than usual that the discovery of lawful relations between the environment and social behavior becomes possible. This results in a different vision of psychology than has typically been expressed, but one that brings with it considerable gains. As R. Barker (1968) put it:

> On the one hand, the sublime but millennial goal of developing a single con-
> ceptual system incorporating psychological and ecological phenomena is
> detoured, [but] on the other, the discouraging prospect of mere empiricism
> and probabilism is avoided. (p. 187)

A lawful account of individual action requires typically consideration of processes occurring at more than one level of analysis.

THE REALIZATION OF ECOBEHAVIORAL SCIENCE

Barker came to appreciate more fully in later years that what he was developing was not, in fact, an ecological psychology, but instead an ecobehavioral science inasmuch as he was not attempting to predict the actions of any individual, but the actions of individuals en masse. In prefatory comments to a collection of papers from the Midwest Psychological Field Station, R. Barker (1978) offered some remarks that clarified in retrospect the direction of much of his earlier work:

> We were slow to discover that psychology is not enough when one seeks to explicate behavior that occurs in reading classes, grocery stores, and worship services, that *an extraindividual behavior science is essential* [emphasis added]. We resisted the evidence of our data. Our prolonged use of the term *ecological psychology* is an indication of our recalcitrance. In fact, one book (Barker, 1968) that dealt with what we now see as eco-behavioral science was entitled *Ecological Psychology*. But at last the data triumphed, and we saw that to fully elucidate behavior and its environment both ecological psychology and ecobehavioral science are required. (p. 2)

Although Barker and his colleagues were unable to find reliable ecological predictors of individual behavior, working from the perspective of the higher order ecological structures that are behavior settings, they were able to make reliable predictions about behavior en masse. With this discovery, the goal of his enterprise was transformed: "The environment in terms of behavior settings opens up the more modest and hopeful possibility of discovering general principles of eco-behavioral organization and control without a comprehensive theory of the phenomena that are regulated" (pp. 187–188)[16]

So although Barker's framework had its roots in Lewinian theory, his approach evolved into something quite different in at least one important respect. Although Lewin sought a means of predicting individual behavior as it is mediated by that individual's experience of the environment at a particular time, Barker offered no such predictions. Instead, he described

---

[16]Barker's comments here raise the question of what a science of complex phenomena can hope for. Hayek (1952, 1967) argued, for example, that there are limitations in our understanding of complex systems phenomena. Unlike the univocal predictions possible vis-à-vis simple phenomena, where only a few variables are operating and one can reasonably apply a *ceteris paribus* proviso, complex systems at best allow "an explanation of the principle ... [whereby] explanatory value is claimed for theoretical models even though they do not enable us to ascertain precise values of the variables involved" (Weimer, 1974, p. 242 ff.).

collective effects of settings on its participants' actions: "Only total medium manifolds are regulated by the control systems of behavior settings; individual inhabitants as unique entities are not regulated" (R. Barker, 1968, pp. 194–195). This framework, then, is at best a partial fulfillment of Lewin's goal to develop a "psychological ecology" that elucidates the relation between nonpsychological conditions—conditions at the boundaries of the life space—and individual behavior.

From the point of view of psychology, it is clear that Barker's framework is deficient. Although he has discovered and articulated an essential extra-individual ecological structure, little has been said about what has been traditionally psychology's primary focus—the individual. What still remains, then, is an account of *psychological* processes. And if what is being sought is a coherent, multilevel ecological theory, then it must be an account that is compatible with this ecobehavioral framework and its commitments.

The Individual in an Ecobehavioral Science.

In some of his last writings, R. Barker (1987) reflected on how his program had considered the environment for an individual. He identified two different, although necessarily related, paths of analysis of the individual through the data. One path leads to the environment "independent of a person's psychological system but that, nevertheless, affect[s] the system and, therefore affect[s] behavior" (p. 1416). He described this path as exploring the *ecological environment*. A second path leads to "the surround that is part of a person's psychological system with direct effects on behavior" (p. 1416). This he called the *psychological environment* (and in earlier writings, the "psychological habitat"). This distinction is consistent with Lewin's treatment of environmental factors outside of the boundaries of the life space and those within its boundaries, respectively.

As for the "ecological environment," some behavior episodes are initiated and terminated by attributes of the behavior setting (if only probablistically). As an example, Barker cited the behavior episode "writing in a copybook" by 8-year-old Clifford Matthews, which was an episode initiated by a directive of his teacher. This initiating event is a feature of the ecological environment because it is observable by anyone in the setting and thus has the potential to affect others' actions in the setting as well. Moreover, this event "causally regresses" into more remote layers of the ecological environment that are not directly experienced by the individual in question. For example, the teacher's initiating the writing exercise may be rooted in more distal factors, such as the actions of the principal of the school and the actions of the curriculum committee of the educational authority.

However, other of Clifford's behavior episodes were more autonomous and did not typically extend into more remote layers of the setting. Two of these episodes were "watching Miss Culver deal with Philip Butley" and "wiping nose, resting, stretching, and playing with pencil" (p. 1417). The former incident was not necessarily directed to the group, but was observed by Clifford; and the latter event although observable by others could only be fully experienced by him. What is distinctive then about these events is that they were solely *selected* by Clifford and were not features of behavior setting operations. As a result, they were part of his psychological environment, but not necessarily part of the ecological environment considered extra-individually.

As we have seen, Barker and his colleagues, for the most part, abandoned the study of the "psychological environment" for an extra-individual, ecobehavioral focus. They did not pursue that path very extensively except in the early years in the life of the Field Station and incidentally in the course of later studies: "After reaching the fork in the trail and realizing the difference between the [psychological environment] branch and the [ecological environment] branch, we devoted most of our effort to exploring the latter branch, while recognizing the importance of both to the new discipline" (R. Barker, 1987, p. 1419). The work that was developed explicitly along the lines of the psychological environment can be found in some of the published work of Wright, especially *Recording and Analyzing Child Behavior* (1967), which is restatement of portions of R. Barker and Wright (1955). Although it ostensibly deals with methodology, the reader can find therein the beginnings of the kind of analysis of the psychological environment Barker, Wright et al. were considering. Other publications that examine some of the records of individuals' behaviors include R. Barker (1963, 1978). Also, data collected concerning individual students' satisfaction with high school settings explore this line of inquiry (R. Barker & Gump, 1964). Further, some limited predictions of the impact of behavior setting attributes on individuals were possible, such as some effects of having less than optimal number of participants in a setting. But the study of individuals per se, and the character of the "psychological environment" was limited.

Why did Barker and his colleagues focus almost exclusively on the ecological rather than the psychological environment? It could be, as Barker suggested, that the considerable efforts required for the analysis of the ecological environment left little time and energy for the study of the psychological environment. Without discounting that explanation, there may also be another reason. It could also be that Barker was unable to envision how the Lewinian approach to analyzing the psychological environment could fit compatibly with his ecobehavioral science.[17] Chapter 6 tried to show how a Gestalt approach stands in tension with a realist perspective. Perhaps Barker's program, which I view as seeking a realist psychology, all the while being anchored in aspects of Gestalt thinking, could not wrest itself free from this tension.

In order to explore this possibility, and to set the stage for considering *a realist approach to the individual* that is compatible with Barker's program, consider a proposal explicitly intended to shore up the neglect of the individual in the ecological program.

The Individual in the Behavior Setting: One Proposal

Retracing the history of Barker's program, Wicker (1987) pointed out that Barker and Wright's initial goal was to describe the "psychological habitat" of the child (i.e., "all of the things and events with *meaning* for the child that go to make up *his* environment"; R. Barker & Wright, 1955, p. 12). However, they were soon led away from this goal. After establishing that the structure of the environment shared by children determined their actions more fully than did more idiosyncratic aspects of their environmental experience, Barker and his colleagues directed their work toward aspects of the extra-individual surround. In several papers, Wicker attempted to resume the initial focus of the Barker program on the individual.

Wicker was critical of Barker for underestimating the contributions of individual participants in behavior settings. One reason for this neglect, according to Wicker, is that Barker limited his attention to established behavior settings, and hence settings whose operations reflect mostly maintenance functions. In such cases, unique contributions of individuals will not be very apparent because the dynamic, collective forces in established settings are comparatively stable. Wicker suggested a broader consideration of behavior settings, examining these ecobehavioral entities at different points in their life cycle.

Wicker importantly expanded Barker's initial conception of behavior settings by recognizing that settings undergo cycles of change over time, from growth ("convergence"), to maintenance ("continued existence"), to modification, to dissolution ("divergence"). A factor precipitating many of these changes is contributions by particular individuals. Actions of individuals are especially critical, according to Wicker, at those points in

---

[17]According to Barker's colleague Paul Gump (personal communication, 1998), one possible reason why Barker came to direct most of his attention to the "ecological environment" rather than "psychological environment" was that the approach of identifying episode units and looking for their environmental antecedents, while leading to the discovery of behavior settings, did not readily lend itself to uncovering psychological habitat variables. The suggestion here that the relative neglect of the psychological habitat reflects an underlying tension between the realism of the ecological analysis and the phenomenalism of the Lewinian approach is consistent with this explanation.

the cycle when behavior settings initially develop, are modified, and dissolve. It is at these points that special skills and talents of particular individuals become most critical; and as a result, it is at these points analytically where treatments of individuals as anonymous participants in a collective become insufficient. In Wicker's view, the changes behavior settings undergo cannot be fully understood without examining contributions of specific individuals:

> If one begins with an image of settings as mature, stable entities, then that stability needs to be explained. If, on the other hand, one regards settings as *social constructions* that are continually being built and rebuilt through the deliberate actions of individuals, then explanations are needed for the organizing and operating processes. (Wicker, 1987, p. 623, emphasis added)

How then does one conceptualize the distinctive psychological processes associated with these individuals who play a central role in constructing behavior settings? Wicker proposed that individuals' contributions to behavior settings are best understood in terms of the *cognitive representations* they bring to settings. His "sense-making model of person–environment relationships" draws on the writings of Weick, who proposed that individuals rely on cognitive representations called "cause maps" in their interaction with others in social settings. Cause maps refer to the knowledge individuals' have about how specific organizations—or for Wicker's purposes, settings—operate, and how different settings are connected.[18] Why are cause maps necessary as explanatory tools? According to Wicker (1992):

> The social/physical could be acted upon and interpreted in numerous ways. Cause maps are a means for *reducing the uncertainty in the environment* by providing a template of variables, classifications, and relationships through which events can be *filtered* and *made sensible*. ... Cause maps are subjective residuals of past transactions with the environment... The ecological environment is therefore highly screened or filtered—only a small portion of the events in behavior settings are attended to by any occupant, and what is attended to is greatly influenced by the occupant's cause map. (p. 175, emphasis added)

It is true that Barker's work gave insufficient attention to individuals' experience of the environment, as Barker acknowledged. However, in my estimation, his ecological approach is not well served by a psychological framework such as this one, which relies on the existence of cognitive

---

[18]Wicker's extensions of Barker's ecological framework go beyond the sense-making model examined here. Refer to Wicker's (1987, 1992) fuller statements.

representations to explain individual action. The primary problem here is that this approach makes the goal of developing a realistic psychology unattainable.

This problem has come up in earlier chapters. Briefly reconsider the difficulties here in the context of Wicker's proposal. The approach Wicker suggested proliferates environments. There is the ecological environment of ecobehavioral science, that is, the environment considered independent of any specific person; and, added to this, in the "cause map" account, are the multitude of private or subjective "environments" represented "within" each person. Such maps are constructed by "filtering" some set of possibilities out of the range of all possible interpretations an individual could make of the ecological environment in an effort toward "sense-making" for the purpose of uncertainty reduction. As discussed in Part I, where the focus was on the writings of James, efforts toward realism in psychology are impeded by viewing environmental experience in this constructivist way. This is the very problem identified earlier that keeps the Gestalt perspective in tension with an ecological approach. Perceivers are viewed as being insulated in their idiosyncratic, subjective worlds, (e.g., a life space); and as a result, the possibilities of connecting with a common environment are rendered exceedingly difficult. Thus, the considerable clarity Barker shed on the nature of the environment seems to be compromised by this proposal. Instead of offering a view in which individuals construct private worlds, which then must somehow intersect if social actions are to be coordinated, why not assume that individuals inhabit a common world, which includes behavior settings?

Of course, individuals do differ in terms of the behavior settings they know. And even in the case of a common behavior setting, individuals may only have a partial understanding of its operation, sometimes being aware mostly of the role they play and remaining largely ignorant of what responsibilities others in the setting have. But these differences need not be accounted for by positing differing private worlds based on so many cause maps. Individuals may differ with respect to the settings or facets of settings they have been exposed to and, hence, are familiar with and sensitive to. In this domain, as in all aspects of environmental experience, there is considerable perceptual learning that goes on; and perceptual learning viewed as a process of differentiation (E. J. Gibson, 1969; J. J. Gibson & E. J. Gibson, 1955) results in awareness of some features of the environment rather than others. Thus, instead of being viewed as inhabiting separate, insulated, subjective domains, individuals are viewed, from this perspective, as encountering a common, shared world but perhaps differing with respect to some of the facets of that world each individual is aware.

These points can be clarified by considering alternative interpretations of the notion of "social construction," which Wicker employed somewhat ambiguously. One interpretation of this idea—and by far the most common one in psychology—is that the social domain is subjectively constructed by each individual. That is, each person surmises what the social domain is like by arriving at one possible interpretation of the setting rather than some others, and then projecting that one idiosyncratic view onto the world. In this case, what settings mean becomes solely an individual matter. A notable problem social groups would face if this viewpoint is valid is how to negotiate a common social order with common meanings. Under such circumstances, the grounds for a shared, meaningful world of thinking and action are elusive (Heft, 1998a).

An alternative interpretation of "social construction," and one more in keeping with behavior setting theory, is that social structures are *publicly constructed* by individuals sometimes intentionally, perhaps coming together to create these structures for common purposes, and sometimes producing these structures adventitiously. I agree with Wicker (1992), when he writes, "The coordinated activities of setting occupants [are] reflections of *the consensual meanings that characterize the setting* at any given time ... [as] continually evolving social constructions" (p. 173, emphasis added). Stated in this way, the consensual meaning of a setting, arising out of the "coordinated activities of setting occupants," resides publicly in the setting as individuals establish (or re-establish) that meaning through their coordinated activities. As Barker insisted, behavior settings are objective features of the environment and their properties are discriminable.

Wicker's claim that individuals create and alter settings, not merely act in conformance with them, is certainly correct and, as he claimed, is in need of further explanation. His argument that individuals' contributions to behavior settings may be best understood by considering settings at different stages of their life cycle is an important insight. But, if behavior settings are viewed as the product of subjective representations, such as cause maps, then it is difficult to conceptualize how so many subjective worlds can eventuate in a common ecological realm.

These comments need to be placed in a broader context. In fairness to Wicker, the tension between his conceptualization of individual processes and the conceptualization of behavior settings is present to some extent in Barker's theoretical writings. As explained earlier, Barker seemed to hold onto the Lewinian distinction between the ecological environment and the psychological environment even after discovering that the only environmental variables he found useful as predictors of action were those that were independent properties of the environment. He retained the "psychological environment" (i.e., the environment as experienced by the person) for understandable reasons. The first-person dimension of experience is salient to each of us; it is impossible to deny its presence, and hence it must be addressed from a psychological perspective. The question is what to make of immediate experience, and in what ways it can be connected to environmental variables.

With radical empiricism, James proposed that most fundamental for an adequate ontology underlying human phenomena (and Lewin's ecological/psychological environment distinction reflects an ontological position) is the relation between a knower and the known that is apparent in first-person experience. Said differently after closer examination, most fundamental is the relation of selecting agency and latent structure. The subsequent distinctions between a person and the world, the physical domain and the psychological domain, objectivity and subjectivity, and so on, are derived from that fundamental, ontological relation (chap. 1). This conceptualization can lay the groundwork for an account of a common world ultimately tied to immediate, individual experience (chap. 4).

With the discovery of behavior settings, Barker identified a structure in the environment that was a correlate of actions considered collectively. However, was the inability to discover a correlate of individual action in the environment due to the fact that the "ecological environment" does not include such correlates? Or was the conceptualization of the environment in relation to the individual insufficiently developed? Absent of apparent ecological correlates of individual action, it is an understandable tendency to posit subjective control processes, like cause maps, that direct individual behavior. Perhaps, though, just as extra-individual structures could be identified existing independently of individual experience, so too independent environmental structures considered relative to an individual can also be identified.[19]

The next chapter returns to this theme with the goal of integrating these ideas with Gibson's approach. At the heart of this integration is a common metatheory underlying Gibson's and Barker's program. Before doing so, it is useful to consider one further matter. Why are efforts to identify environmental structures that are correlates of individual action preferable to positing the existence of underlying mental representations that control actions in social settings? Debating the relative merits of ontological frameworks is not readily resolvable on empirical grounds. Can some logical argument be offered? It seems so, with its outcome demonstrating that the mental representation approach is unworkable.

---

[19]The apparently contradictory claim that environmental structures can be relative and in-dependent of the individual was addressed in Part II.

ENVIRONMENTAL STRUCTURE OR SCRIPTS?

In addition to the problem of connecting idiosyncratic subjective worlds to a common public world, there is another problem with a claim that individuals' experience of specific settings is mediated by cognitive representations of those settings. This problem can be identified by contrasting Wicker's comments about *scripts* with those of Schoggen (1989) in his revision and extension of Barker's *Ecological Psychology*.

Briefly put, a script is a cognitive representation of the actions appropriate in a particular setting (Shank & Abelson, 1977). More generally, it is "the subclass of schemata that are used to account for generic (stereotyped) sequences of actions" (Brewer, 1999, p. 729.) As such, a script reflects an individual's knowledge of behavior appropriate in certain settings. As a cognitive representation, it is a compatible with the notion of a cause map. The paradigmatic example of a script is that representation guiding thought and action in a restaurant. For example, a restaurant script might entail waiting to be seated by a host or hostess, accepting a menu from a server, examining a menu, making a selection, placing an order with a server, eating the meal, paying for the meal, and leaving a gratuity. Wicker (1987) considered the script to be directly comparable to Barker's notion of the "program" of a behavior setting, the latter of which refers to requirements and goals of a setting that individuals in the setting function to maintain. The program operates like a set point in a negative feedback loop (although arguably, it most appropriately refers to the collective actions of the setting's participants; see chap. 8). Wicker wrote, "In some ways, the script appears to be a rediscovery of behavior setting programs from a quite different approach than Barker's" (p. 624). In spite of the person-centered roots of the script notion, he continued, the approaches are "sufficiently similar that further cross-fertilization of ideas is possible" (p. 625).[20]

Compare this view to Schoggen's (1989) comments on scripts. He clearly distanced himself and Barker's ecological psychology from the notion of script because it is exclusively a subjective construct. Schoggen explained:

> What clearly differentiates the two approaches is that all of the concepts of script analysis represent cognitive structures in the head of a particular perceiver or actor; script analysis deals only with the entities used by the memory of a particular person. ... [I]t seems to us that script analysis would be greatly strengthened by including a more systematic representation of the objective physical and social world, such as provided by behavior set-

---

[20]In this discussion, Wicker also included consideration of Forgas' (1979) concept of social episodes.

tings. ... *If the ecological environment were not so organized ... script analysis would be impossible.* (pp. 320–321, emphasis added)

The last sentence in this quoted passage is emphasized because it is reminiscent of the arguments reviewed earlier by both James and Gibson (as well as Heider) about a fundamental problem with any account emphasizing mental representation: If environments were not already organized in certain ways, then they could not be experienced in the ways that they are.

To see why this is so in the present case of scripts, consider that a restaurant script would be close to useless in guiding action in everyday life. There exist settings consensually agreed on as restaurants that violate each action in a standard restaurant script like the one offered previously. In some restaurants, customers are not seated by an employee of the restaurant, rather they find their own seat. In some restaurants, customers do not even sit, but instead they stand at a counter or bar. In some restaurants, customers are not handed a menu; they need to know to look at a menu posted in a single location. In some restaurants, customers do not order, but instead they select among preserved dishes. In some restaurants, customers pay before eating the meal rather than after. In some restaurants, the gratuity is included in the price of the meal, and in others, gratuities are not appropriate. For individuals to be prepared to take into account these variations and many more, either the number of different scripts they must know would need be increased many-fold, or the notion of a script must be pared down to include only the minimal steps for operating in this kind of setting. The former possibility is simply implausible, if not downright unworkable, especially when it is recognized that this same problem holds for *every type* of setting with which an individual is familiar. As for the latter possibility, when the script notion gets sufficiently pared down so that it can cover all permutations, it becomes vacuous as a representation that can control, and thus explain, behavior. This is so because to be effective in a sufficiently wide range of settings, the representation cannot control very much behavior. In order to effectively control actions, the representation would need to be highly specific to a particular setting; but the result would be a limited sequence of stereotypic behaviors, and hence an inflexible repertoire. In short, scripts are inadequate concepts for use in ecological psychology because such cognitive structures would be of a little use given the variability of everyday circumstances. The needed flexibility in action rules out the utility of a mental representation such as a script.[21]

---

[21]Fuhrer (1990) saw schemas or plans fitting readily into this framework, but he also acknowledged the improvisational character of actions in behavior settings and approved of Suchman's (1987) critique of such representation-driven control systems (discussed in chap. 8). But there is a tension in juxtaposing these two conceptualizations.

What then does control behavior in such settings? Much of the needed structure for controlling actions is built into the setting itself, considered relationally. One's knowledge of a restaurant is always an unfolding event that is concretely expressed in the transaction between an individual and the structure of a specific place. Perceiving and acting are not based on abstractions or representations disconnected from environmental structure. Instead, perceiving and acting involve the selective detection of structure over time in the environment (see chap. 5). In the case of settings, the information that is being detected is of social structures that have been publicly constructed through the coordinated actions of individuals. It is in this sense that behavior settings are social constructions. In the context of perceiving–acting relations, this perceived structure sets constraints on actions (chap. 8).

At the center of this objection to conceptualizations like Wicker's sense-making model is the view of the environment it holds. As one of the earlier quotations indicates, Wicker assumed ambiguity and hence uncertainty in the environment, and causal maps are needed to reduce that uncertainty. But to paraphrase Schoggen (and echoing James and Gibson), 'if the ecological environment were not *already* organized, sense making would be impossible.' One identifies structure present *in the environment* rather than imposing order on disorder. Said otherwise, environments are meaningful. The cognitive activity that Wicker referred to as sense making does not entail cognitively imposing social constructions on the world; instead, it involves the selective detection of information that is already present in the world. This information arises out of the collective actions of individuals.

In order to undertake an analysis of such information, an initial step is to focus on patterns of action that are public in nature, such as patterns of collective, setting-specific actions,[22] and the construction and culturally sanctioned use of particular tools, artifacts, and representations. That is, the goal should be an account of the *ecology of social life*. To achieve this end, shared social meanings need to be identified as they are realized in the patterns of daily activities with objects and in settings, and in the sharing of those actions—that is, in social practices (Heft, 1998a). These issues are taken up in chapter 9.

Before turning to those matters, however, an important set of issues deferred until now—namely, the interrelation between Gibson's ecological psychology and Barker's ecobehavioral science— needs to be considered.

---

[22]An excellent example of a research methodology that identifies these patterns of activity is Barker's behavior setting survey.

Roger G. Barker, 1958
(Courtesy of Louise Barker)

8

Ecological Psychology and Ecobehavioral Science: Toward a Synthesis

> If we ask the "What is it" question of an item in our experience, one thing we are asking is, what changes can that item endure and still remain what it is? ... Matter might look at first like the most enduring substrate, in that it persists through ... birth and death ... [But in] general, no list of particular materials will give us a substrate as stable and enduring as ... form or organization. ... That is the nature of living things—to be forms embodied in ever-changing matter. (Nussbaum & H. Putnam, 1992, p. 29)

Gibson's ecological psychology and Barker's ecobehavioral science can be shown to be compatible and mutually reinforcing programs. Numerous features in each are strikingly similar, despite differences in focus of the two frameworks. At the root of their theoretical compatibility is the fact that Gibson's and Barker's approaches are representative of the same kind of psychological theory. They adhere to a common metatheory, and it is a perspective markedly different from that underlying the received view of psychology. Holding in common broadly similar theoretical commitments, but adopting different levels of analysis, their integration broadens the scope of each program in theoretically coherent ways.

The first part of this chapter is a metatheoretical consideration of the kind of approach the two programs embody. This discussion shows how both theories share a nonstandard conceptualization of *causality*, although it is nonstandard only from a contemporary vantage point. This commonality separates them from much 20th-century empirical psychology, even while it provides a basis for bringing these two positions together. Their common perspective provides grounds for both approaches to tackle the elusive problem of perceived meaning, and further, it serves as a bridge for the beginnings of their synthesis.

CAUSALITY AND THE ECOLOGICAL APPROACH

There may be philosophers or theologians who derive comfort from the idea of a Laplacian universe made up of a mosaic of discrete particles, operating by laws of micro-causality. I submit, however, that modern science cannot deliver such a picture in good faith, least of all life science. (Weiss, 1969, p. 28)

A key to understanding the metatheoretical commonality between Gibson's and Barker's programs resides in Heider's analysis of "thing and medium." As previously discussed, Heider's position is central to both programs. Working on different problems—Gibson on perceiving and acting, and Barker on behavior in everyday social settings—both theorists needed to find a way of conceptualizing how properties of one entity (affordances and behavior-milieu synomorphs, respectively) are shared with or transmitted to other entities (perceivers and setting occupants, respectively). Gibson developed a way of conceptualizing how functionally significant properties of environmental features are available in stimulus information for active perceivers; and Barker developed a framework for understanding how the dynamic functioning of a social setting exists among the inhabitants of that setting considered en masse. What ultimately became clear to both theorists, and what Heider's framework served as a vehicle for conceptualizing, was that what is shared in both cases from environment to individual in Gibson's case, and, from environment to individuals in Barker's case, is structure.

Gibson and Barker are offering causal accounts of how structure can be conveyed between two entities. What is critical for understanding both positions is recognizing the kind of causal account they offer. It is not the kind of causal view reflected in much 20th-century psychological theory; but it is a causal account with a well-established pedigree nonetheless. It is a view traceable to Aristotle's metaphysics and psychology. In order to understand Gibson's and Barker's approach to the problem of how structure is shared between entities, a brief philosophical digression is necessary.

Aristotelian Causality

An Aristotelian analysis of cause has a considerably wider scope than the treatment of causality in contemporary psychology. In modern times, for readily identifiable, historical reasons (including the displacement of a narrow Aristotelian tradition by scientific materialism), "cause" has taken on a restricted meaning. It is employed in one of two related ways: First, cause is used to refer to antecedent–consequent relations, such as the consequences of the impact of one entity on another—colliding billiard balls being paradigmatic in classical physics, the stimulus–response relation being the paradigmatic example in psychology. Second, cause is used to refer to the underlying material basis for some observable occurrence, such as the neurobiological processes underlying psychological phenomena.

As a result, when one is asked in contemporary psychology to provide a causal explanation of some event, what is expected is either an account of the circumstances that led up to or resulted in the event to be explained, or a reductive description of the more fundamental correlates of that event. From an Aristotelian perspective, both explanatory accounts are variations of the same type of explanation, namely, "efficient cause." This type of explanation seeks to identify causal factors either in precipitating conditions occurring prior to the event to be explained or in conditions occurring simultaneously with the event to be explained.[1]

However, "cause" meant much more than this for Aristotle. The question of cause addresses the broader question of "why something is the case"(Barnes, 1982). This question goes beyond asking "why something happened" because why something happened depends not only on antecedent or concurrent events, but also on factors such as what is (are) the nature of the entity (or entities) in question. That is, "why something is the case" requires more than the identification of efficient causes, although the latter certainly are part of that explanation. Two other types of cause are classically called "material cause" and "formal cause."[2]

In Aristotle's metaphysics, all natural things are comprised of *matter* and *form*. That is, two properties that constitute any natural entity are, first, what it is made of (its material substance) and, second, its form or structure. That these two properties are analytically distinguishable can be illustrated as follows: Two natural things such as a bowl and a sculpture may be made of the same material (i.e., clay), but they may differ in form. In contrast, a clay bowl and a bronze bowl have different material properties, but may be identical in form. This form–matter distinction is incorporated into Aristotle's analysis of cause.

---

[1]Of the two, Aristotle claimed that simultaneity is the more common type of efficient cause (Barnes, 1982).

[2]Modern experimental psychology has also eschewed Aristotle's fourth kind of cause, *final cause*, because of its recognition of an intrinsic teleological or goal-directedness tendency in natural things. Such a quality has traditionally been seen as explainable only with reference to nonmaterial processes. With the advent of purposive machines, the once controversial nature of final cause in scientific circles has been (or should be) dispelled.

Metaphysical analysis of "why something is the case" is attributable, in part, to the nature of the composition of the thing in question: its material cause. The reason why a clay bowl is a clay bowl rather than a bronze bowl is explainable with respect its material composition; and these different properties can be discerned in various ways (e.g., relative hardness, melting point, etc.). Further, natural things differ with respect to their form. What distinguishes a clay bowl from a clay sculpture is, in part, their respective forms or structures. Whereas their material cause is identical in this latter case, they have different formal causes. The commonality between a clay bowl and a bronze bowl is explainable with reference to the same formal cause.

From a contemporary perspective, there is a tendency to under-estimate the significance of formal cause. Most modern scientists would claim that because all natural things are material, surely their material nature is most fundamental. This modern claim is traceable to Democritus, and it was precisely this position that Aristotle, via Plato, sought to overthrow. Aristotle, who like Democritus (and unlike Plato) was concerned foremost with natural things, argued that a natural thing is the kind of thing it is as much because of its structure or organization (i.e., its form) as it is because of its material composition. Formal cause, no less than material cause, contributes to a thing being what it is.

This form–matter distinction plays a central role in Aristotle's *psychology* (Grene, 1963; MacLeod, 1974; Nussbaum & H. Putnam, 1992; Robinson, 1989). Aristotelian psychology offers an analysis of the form properties of *living* things. What sets living things off from nonliving things is their formal differences. Living things have distinctive animate/biological functions. Furthermore, it is what sets off particular living things from other living things, such as humans from plants and animals.

Consider two functions that Aristotle claims are shared by animals and humans: a nutritive function and a perceiving function. These functions are possible because the structure or form of animals and humans is what it is. Both of these natural functions involve the interaction between objects in the world and organisms. Insight into how the nutritive and perceiving functions differ rests on the distinction between material causes and formal causes.

Nutritive processes involve the interaction of living things with the material aspects of food, but not their form. When eating an apple we incorporate the material character of the apple into the material character of our body without incorporating its form. In his explanation of the perceiving function, Aristotle in effect brilliantly inverts this analysis of the nutritive process: In perceiving, organisms incorporate the form of natural objects, but not their matter. The organism as perceiver has the potential to take on the form of a natural object without taking on its matter. An apple is perceived because its form, but not its matter, is assimilated by the perceiving function. Aristotle's well-known analogy of perceiving to a seal and wax clarifies this claim. When a bronze seal is impressed onto wax, what is shared between entities is form or structure. The wax takes on the structure of the seal, that is, its imprint, but not its metallic composition or matter.

What is important about this analysis of perceiving for present purposes is its proposal that perceiving fundamentally involves the transfer of structure from object to perceiver. This is an account of perceiving that emphasizes formal cause. By distinguishing form and matter in this analysis, an Aristotelian account of perceiving is resistant to a reductionistic explanation, although it does not deny the material features of perceiving processes. Rather, it is arguing for the necessity of including a consideration of structure distinguishable, but never existing independent of, the material.[3] In this regard, this analysis differs from most modern accounts of perceiving, which for historical reasons are often collectively referred to as causal theories.

Causal Theories of Perception

To invoke the expression causal theory of perception is to refer to a number of different accounts of perceiving that all share a common viewpoint. The "cause" in all causal theories of perception is—to use an Aristotelian category—efficient cause.

In causal theories, perception is viewed as the outcome of essentially a linear chain of events. A prototypical causal explanation of visual perception proceeds as follows: The first event in the chain of occurrences is a physical stimulus making contact with a receptor surface; this contact initiates a succession of neural impulses in the sensory receptors, followed by a volley of impulses along receptor tracts to a series of brain sites; and the resulting pattern of neural activity gives rise to a perceptual experience. This kind of an account of visual perception should be readily recognizable to the modern reader—indeed, to any scientist or philosopher from the 17th century to the present. This is the framework

---

[3]It would be a mistake to interpret Aristotle's resistance to reductionism as an embrace of some type of mind–body dualism. Aristotle's form–matter distinction sidesteps this problematic distinction—predates it actually. The form-matter distinction draws a contrast between structure and composition, not between mind/spirit and matter. Natural things are both form and matter. Thus, resistance to reductionism does not entail rejection of materialism per se, but to a reductive materialism (or previously referred to as physicalism; see Introduction, footnote 2). Nussbaum and H. Putnam (1992) wrote: "The functional essence of a living being like an animal (whose essence it is to be a perceiving creature) *does* require mention of material embodiment [i.e., form], in that its essential activities are embodied activities" (p. 46). (Also see Cohen, 1992.)

attributed, in broad outline, to Descartes and repeatedly reworked since then to keep pace with ongoing discoveries in neurobiology. This causal account of perception reflects Descartes' more general application of "push–pull" models to explain all bodily functions—an overall approach in keeping with, or rather foundational to, *mechanistic* explanations of natural occurrences.

A mechanistic explanation assumes the interaction among material entities with their effects being conveyed through the exchange of some property from one entity to another. Moving object A makes contact with stationary object B, propelling B along some determinable path and at some determinable velocity as a result of the transfer of inertial energy. This sort of mechanistic analysis of natural phenomena revolutionized Western thinking beginning approximately in the early 17th century, and contemporary psychology continues to function in the wake of this stunning shift in thinking.

A "cottage industry" in the area of philosophy of mind subsequently developed that wrestled with the numerous problems arising from this approach as it is applied to perception and cognition (Hamlyn, 1961, 1990). A principal problem presented by this approach is that of *correspondence* (discussed previously in Part I). If cause is conceptualized only in a mechanical manner, then how are the perceptible properties of an object, such as its size, shape, or color, conveyed to the perceiver? That is, assuming there is some degree of resemblance between that which is the initiating stimulus and the resulting experience, how can this correspondence be explained? How do object properties transfer from the "outside" world to "inside" the perceiver? Following Locke, causal theorists typically have agreed that the "power" in the object to cause an experience cannot be substantively the same as the experience itself because objects are material and mind is not. Putting the problem in this dualistic way, and hence drawing the differences between world and mind so sharply, has led some theorists to join Hume, among others, in abandoning the possibility of knowing the material world itself. At best, it is only possible to know some "internal" mental representation of it.

In its modern neurobiological incarnation, the correspondence problem can be restated as follows: environmental stimuli are in fact various types of physical energies (e.g., electromagnetic, chemical, thermal, mechanical), and these energy types are transduced by receptors into the bioelectrical energy of the nervous system. This more sophisticated statement of the processes involved at the neurochemical level appears more manageable than Lockean mind–world dualism (and its offshoots) because physical and neurochemical concepts are of a common currency. However, relying solely on neurobiology leaves the correspondence problem untouched because most *perceptual* properties are not locatable in this framework. Consider this point further.

From the point of view of the historical treatment of perception, only "like things" can affect each other mechanically. This is the central problem with Descartes' mind–body interaction: How do two unlike substances, matter and mind, make contact and have the potential to induce changes from one to the other? By translating this problem into physical–neurobiological terms, apparent "unlike things" (stimuli and sensations) can be seen to interact at a level of common like things. In such cases, a mechanistic causal account works well.

However, the problem presented by the Cartesian dichotomy is not skirted by taking this reductive turn. It is only transformed until it is no longer the same problem. The question still remains as to how properties in the world are experienced by a perceiver. Short of treating psychological experience or awareness as epiphenomenal—whereby only neurophysiological processes are to be considered significant and efficacious organismic events—this question cannot be addressed in a satisfactory manner as long as it is couched solely with respect to mechanism or efficient cause. If psychological experience is to be treated as a natural phenomenon—that is, as an occurrence in the natural world (which, indeed, it must be in a science of psychology)—then accounts of psychological processes must broaden the conceptualization of causality.

Formal Cause and the Distinction between Things and Media

Heider's "thing and medium" analysis can be most fully appreciated in the context of the preceding discussion. Recall (chap. 6) that the question prompting Heider's analysis concerned how perceivers can detect a world distant from receptor surfaces. What was unique about his approach to this problem is the claim about what is shared between world and perceiver. In Heider's analysis, what is shared is not physical properties per se but structure. What makes this possible is the presence of a medium that preserves structure with a minimum of distortion.

To review briefly the earlier discussion, thing and medium are distinguishable in terms of the relative coherence of their constituents. Because objects (things) have high internal coherence, when extrinsic events interact with them, what results are unitary effects; consequently, an object transforms the precipitating event in ways consistent with the object's composition. A drum stroke on a drumhead results in the transformation of mechanical energy into acoustical energy. The kinetic properties of the stroke are not simply preserved, but transformed owing to the "thing-like" properties of the drumhead. In contrast, media lack coherence; their components are relatively independent from each other. As a result, external influences produce in media composite effects; and consequently, media preserve the structure of external influences rather than transform them. The air surrounding the drum carries the structure of the vibration of the drumhead. With the aid of this framework, it is possible to conceptualize how structure can be shared between two different kinds of entities.

Heider was proposing here how structure or form can be conveyed in a world that is comprised of matter. In so doing, he is tacitly invoking a distinction between the material composition of a natural entity and its structure; that is, he is invoking the Aristotelian distinction between matter and form. Objects and perceivers are both matter and form, and what is shared between them is structure, not matter. To reiterate an earlier point, to claim that structure and not matter is shared does not mean that these are nonmaterial processes under consideration. The sharing of structure must be "realized in the matter" (Nussbaum & H. Putnam, 1992, p. 37). What is being emphasized here, however, is structure rather than matter, and how structure can be conveyed via a material medium, while not being reducible to it. Causal theorists working only with the notion of efficient cause do not have available to them this valuable Aristotelian insight. Heider's analysis, intentionally or not (for Heider makes no reference to Aristotle), resuscitates it.

Ecological Theories and Formal Cause

Following Heider, both Gibson and Barker are concerned primarily with structure rather than with mechanisms. Because most psychological theories are mechanistic at their core, for this reason many psychologists have difficulty evaluating Gibson's and Barker's programs on anything other than mechanistic grounds. But these programs are not offering mechanistic explanations, and to evaluate them along these lines is not to take them on their own terms.

To ask, for example, "What causes (mechanistically) a particular percept?" or "What causes (mechanistically) behavior to conform to a particular setting?" is to ask the wrong question vis-à-vis these frameworks. Instead, questions like the following are more appropriate: "Why does perceptual experience have the characteristics it has in a particular instance?" And, "why does behavior in a social setting have the characteristics it has in a particular instance?" The key to understanding environmental perception in the case of Gibson, or the effect of settings on the collective actions of its occupants in the case of Barker, is in seeing these problems as requiring an account of how structure is shared, and thus preserved across different entities. That is, in seeing these problems primarily in terms of formal cause.[4]

---

[4]Some theorists erroneously take Gibson's account of stimulus information as the first step in a series of information-processing stages, the latter which Gibson fails to provide. Barker, on the other hand, has been embraced erroneously on occasion by operant theorists who greatly simplify the operations of behavior settings by viewing the coercion of action as operating through contingencies of reinforcement.

Consider each of these ecological programs in turn. Central to Gibson's ecological approach is the idea of animal–environment reciprocity (chap. 3). Adaptive behavioral functioning requires that the animal detect functionally significant properties of the environment. How are such properties detected? First, these properties are carried by structure in the various media for perceiving. Gibson's program of ecological optics is an attempt to demonstrate how this is possible in the case of vision. Second, the biological substrate of a perceptual system is such that it can "take on" this available structure given relevant prior attunement—that is, given relevant phylogenetic history and ontogenetic experience. To borrow on the Aristotelian analogy, just as the wax has the potential to take on the structure of the seal without taking on its matter, so too perceptual systems have the potential to take on, or (using Gibson's metaphor) to "resonate" to environmental structure without incorporating physical properties of stimulus input. That, in essence, is what perceptual systems do. In effect, no-*thing* crosses the environment–body boundary. Stimuli do not cause percepts the way that inertial energy of a moving object is mechanically transferred to another object. Instead, structure is shared between environmental features and perceiver because this structure can be preserved as information in the medium and because perceptual systems are uniquely designed to pick up information specific to these features in the surround. In short, perceiving environmental features is most readily understood in terms of *formal cause*.

Behavior setting influences on individuals en masse can be conceptualized in a similar manner. Behavior settings are dynamic structures comprised of standing patterns of behavior and milieu (chap. 7). Their dynamic structure is a property of collective, purposive actions in conjunction with supportive (i.e., synomorphic) milieu features. This higher order pattern is generated by setting participants; reciprocally, it structures their shared actions because individuals in social settings readily take on a constituent role in relation to a collective function. (This is possible, in part, because humans are fundamentally sociocultural beings, with propensities to function in groups; for this reason, social dimensions of the environment are especially salient to us; see chap. 9). The relation of behavior-milieu structures and the actions of its occupants is one of shared structure or form. Barker employed Heider's terminology, stating that settings have thing-like properties and occupants have medium-like properties, and as the medium can take on the structure of things so occupants take on the dynamic structure of settings in their collective actions.

In spite of their similarities, Gibson and Barker employed the thing–medium distinction in different ways precisely because they offer somewhat different theories. Gibson's is a *within-level theory*, examining as it does perceiving within the ecological level of perceiver–environment reciprocity. That is, the source of structure (the environment) and that which takes on structure (the perceiver) are located at a common level of organization, the ecological level, with the medium constituting a part of the perceptual surround for a perceiver. Barker's is a *between-level theory*, with its concern being how higher order structure imposes constraints on the constituents of that structure. In this case (and unlike in perceiving), the medium is not functioning as the surround of the setting at a common level of organization; instead, the medium (individuals and milieu) is interjacent to the behavior setting. What the two theoretical positions share is a recognition that the answer to their central questions (i.e., "Why does perceptual experience have the characteristics it has at a particular time?" and "why does behavior in a particular social setting have the characteristics it has?") rests in understanding how structure is preserved across entities.

Without minimizing these differences (indeed, they require more extensive examination), the focus at present is what does a structural analysis bring to these psychological theories that cannot be provided by mechanistic accounts? Surely there are mechanistic processes involved in perceiving (e.g., physical energies causing receptors to fire), and in behavior in social settings (e.g., a disruptive occupant of a setting exiting at the request of the setting's leader). Why isn't a mechanistic analysis alone sufficient for a psychological account of either type of phenomenon? The reason is because mechanistic accounts cannot adequately address the question of *meaning*. Referring to the previous examples, what specifically is perceived at present cannot be understood by examining only physical stimulation and its neurobiological results; and why the occupant's behavior was disruptive in the setting cannot be understood by merely its effects. Mechanistic explanations are not up to the task of accounting for meaning in either perceiving or in social settings. This is hardly a minor shortcoming for psychological theory because meaning is the central feature of psychological experience.

ENVIRONMENTAL MEANING AND ECOLOGICAL THEORY

Phenomenological description of environmental experience—from the most informal and unsystematic efforts to the most formal and exacting—all give a central place to meaning in our perceptual life. From a first-person perspective, objects, persons, and places comprise a manifold of meaningful contexts within which we act, the common, interpersonally shared world within which we live. In view of its centrality in human experience, it is striking how little attention has been paid to meaning in 20th-century perceptual theory. Why has this been the case?

This situation is traceable in large measure to the dominance of the mechanistic viewpoint in psychology. If the sciences are narrowly defined as areas of inquiry that employ mechanistic explanations (and for much of last century psychologists have tended to think they are), then meaning falls outside of the domain of the sciences. And if psychology aspires to be a science in that somewhat narrow sense (which in most cases it has), then meaning is not properly an issue for a science of psychology to address on its own terms. In that case meaning in human experience can largely be left to the humanities to worry about, while it is addressed in the very limited ways that mechanistic science is able. However, a psychology that has so little to say about such a central feature of human existence, without distorting it beyond recognition of everyone outside of the field, is a rather limited psychology.

The problem may rest in narrowly viewing science, and psychology in particular, as solely mechanistic enterprises. Recognizing the contribution of accounts of formal cause in science opens up the possibility of incorporating meaning into a science of psychology.

The Vicissitudes of Mechanistic Approaches

Critics of mechanistic approaches to psychological phenomena from the 18th-century philosopher Leibniz to the 20th-century Gestalt psychologist Max Wertheimer have argued that the inability of such theories to address meaning is inherent in their very nature.[5] As Wertheimer pointed out, meaning is carried among relations in the psychological field, that is, meaning is primarily a matter of intrinsic structure. (Perhaps the simplest and most familiar example of this point is that the identity of a melody is preserved when playing in a different key as long as the relations among the notes are maintained.) In contrast, a mechanistic treatment of psychological phenomena, which treats relations as being imposed on a set of elements, creates enormous problems for an account of meaning.

To explore these ideas further, from a mechanistic perspective, pattern or order among entities is attributable to adventitious connections produced most commonly through *contiguity*. In such cases, connections are established solely because two or more entities occurred closely in time or closely in spatial proximity. Temporal and spatial contiguity are the only bases on which patterns take shape; there are no intrinsic qualities—

---

[5]Leibniz (1765) recognized that application of the then new mechanistic approach to psychological phenomena would leave untouched the qualities of psychological experience:

> Moreover, it must be confessed that *perception* and that which depends upon it are *inexplicable on mechanical grounds*. ... And supposing there were a machine, so constructed as to think, feel, and have perception; it might be conceived as increased in size, while keeping the same proportions, so that one might go into it as into a mill. That being so, we should, on examining its interior, find only parts which work upon one another, and never anything by which to explain a perception. (quoted in Robinson, 1981, p. 274)

no qualities specific to the entities themselves—that account for their relatedness. Contiguity, then, is an *extrinsic* ordering principle.

As Hume argued, however, if order or patterns arise from extrinsic relations, then they would have an underlying and undeniable arbitrariness about them (chap. 1). If the meanings that we experience in the world are based on relations established in this contingent manner, then it becomes difficult to understand how the meanings arising from our experience of the world can be anything more than idiosyncratic and capricious. They would be based on whatever set of contiguous relations happened to have been experienced previously by each individual, with another set of experiences creating a different set of meanings. And of course, differing sets of experiences are likely given any two individuals. How anything close to shared understanding can emerge from such an account is difficult to imagine.

This viewpoint stands in contrast to an alternative that views the meaning in our experience as being grounded in relations reflecting how the world is itself structured, rather than how we happen to have experienced its bits and pieces. But before discussing this viewpoint further, let us return to the received view.

Following Humean thinking, order or pattern is something imposed on experience. If B follows A, and C follows B, the "belief" is acquired that A, B, C naturally go together in sequence; that is, individuals believe that is the way the world is. However, when meaning is construed in this inductive way, individuals can never know what meaning things actually have (if they have any meaning at all) because meaning is an *inferred property*. Contemporary theories of perception and cognition commonly make such a claim, if only implicitly. Identity and meaning are qualities imposed on the world by perceiver's *constructions*, rather than being qualities discovered in or about the world, even though they may naively hold the latter viewpoint.

Theories in the empiricist tradition posit that these constructions are products of prior experience, commonly a set of cognitive expectations. An isolated perceptual "moment" in the present (a stimulus) gives rise to a network of previously built up associations functioning as a *hypothesis* or *inference* about what the world, extended spatially and temporally beyond this perceptual moment, is probably like.

Theories in the rationalist tradition may argue, as did the Gestalt psychologists, that there is an intrinsic structure of the physical world; but typically in these views, this physical structure is broken down at the stage of stimulus input, only later to be *reconstituted* in perceptual or cognitive experience. In this case, the perceived structure is not provided by contingent relations among prior happenings, but by dynamic processes inherent in the individual. However, as with empiricist theories, there is a sharp distinction drawn from a psychological perspective between the world as such and the world as experienced by a perceiver.

Because this world-experience bifurcation is inescapable according to both of these approaches, they both diverge sharply from an ecological account that seeks to locate meaning in the environment, relationally considered. Both are *constructivist* approaches, putting psychological meaning and the experience of environments in so many private individual minds. At best, there is only a tenuous connection between separate individual experiences and the world shared by these individuals.

Progress has been slow in those areas of study that have attempted to examine psychological phenomena in everyday settings, such as environmental psychology and certain aspects of social and developmental psychology, precisely because their practitioners tend to adopt some variation of a constructivist perspective. In a prescient essay entitled "The Environment Is *Not* in the Head!," Wohlwill (1973) pointed out the irony of environmentally oriented social scientists locating experience of the environment in the heads of individuals, in the form of schemas, cognitive maps, personal constructs, and so on. Presumably, a primary aim of environmentally oriented psychologists should be articulation of the character of the *shared environment* within which psychological actions and the psychological development of individuals occur. Among other things, this kind of project would clarify the relations between environmental conditions and psychological phenomena, and in an applied vein, would guide environmental decision making for the promotion of psychologically adequate environments. But how can either of these goals be achieved when the essential qualities of environments, including their meanings, are attributed to processes located in private, intrapersonal domains? Wohlwill pointed out that if environmental psychologists construe environmental experience as a private, intrapersonal phenomenon, then an unbridgeable gap exists between the common world that perceivers share and co-exist in, and the idiosyncratic, intrapersonal "worlds" they inhabit.

How then can the meanings of environmental features that different individuals share be accounted for? Put differently, how is it possible to experience a common world—which individuals surely do, as is evidenced by the coordinated nature of interpersonal life in the face of enormous complexities and subtleties? If an exclusively mechanistic (efficient cause) approach is adopted, then "you can't get there from here." Similarly, if a rationalist approach is adopted, then the world as such is inaccessible or "noumenal," and individual experiences are forever isolated. Better possibilities in explaining perception of a common meaningful world are afforded by structural (formal cause) approaches.[6]

As James argued, perceived patterns do not typically have a structure imposed on them from without. Their structure has an integrity that is *intrinsic* to the pattern in question. To put it in Jamesian terms, relations are to be found *in* experience—this is a central tenet of radical empiricism. Meaningful patterns are intrinsic to particular relations among features.

What then is the origin of these patterns or structures in perceptual experience? Instead of making the move that the Gestalt psychologists did and assume that this intrinsic structure arises out of dynamic brain processes, we can adopt James's and Gibson's positions that structure, and hence meaning, is intrinsic to the structure of the environment considered in a relation to a perceiver. Further, we can suppose, following Heider, that the structure of the environmental features is preserved in the medium to be detected by a perceiver. If it is assumed that the potential meaning of environmental features is carried in the intrinsic, structural relations in environmental information, and these relations are available in principle to any perceiver, then an account of detecting this environmental structure that uses formal cause as a conceptual vehicle may help to clarify how individuals perceive a common, meaningful environment.

How does viewing the relation between environment and perceiver as a sharing of structure—that is, viewing the relation from the perspective of formal rather than efficient cause—help make the problem of perceiving shared environmental meaning more tractable? This is an avenue of inquiry well worth exploring. Both Gibson and Barker argued that the perceived meaning of environmental features is central to an individual's experience of the environment. Examining aspects of their proposals will help to make the preceding comments more concrete and open a potentially fruitful avenue for conceptualizing the problem of perceived meaning.

Formal Cause and Ecological Meaning: Affordances and Behavior-Milieu Synomorphs

Two classes of meaningful environmental features in Gibson's and in Barker's frameworks are affordances and behavior-milieu synomorphs,

---

[6]It might be argued that Gestalt psychology, with some of its roots in Kantian philosophy, does indeed utilize formal cause in its analysis (Slife & Williams, 1995). However, this seems only partially correct. Consider the case of vision: Patterns on the retina are broken down as a result of the mosaiclike of the receptors, and thereby, the initial pattern is reconstituted by dynamic brain processes. This account presents a mixture of efficient and formal cause, and because it retains aspects of the former, environmental perception in the Gestalt view is representational rather than direct.

respectively. The concept of affordances most basically highlights the congruence between structural features of the environment and functional possibilities for the perceiver (see chap. 3). When an individual perceives this congruence, there is awareness of a fit. Environmental features are experienced as having a functional meaning for the individual. The features afford some action or extend some potential functional consequence.

Consider the simple example of a step: An arrangement of surfaces will be perceived as affording stepping-up-on if particular structural relations obtain between the features and the perceiver. There must be an environment–perceiver fit. For instance, there must be a fit between riser height and a determinate proportion of leg length (W. H. Warren, 1984). In the absence of this relation, the surfaces do not extend the possibility of stepping-up-on. Awareness of this affordance is not a contingent affair. That is, perceiving that a particular feature can function as a step is not merely the outcome of previously successful attempts at stepping up on that feature. It cannot solely be the case that an individual has tried to step up on countless features, and those features that proved successful are subsequently perceived as steps. Even admitting some experimenting of this sort, the range of possibilities attempted is surely restricted to a considerable extent from the outset. What an individual chooses to even try as a potential step in the first place is a function of perceived relational structures. The functional meaning of this feature, its affordance, resides in intrinsic environment–perceiver relations, not between the extrinsic relations of behavioral outcomes superimposed on particular features. In short, a mechanistic analysis does not explain this relation.

This sort of analysis applies to any type of affordance, such as grasp-able objects, lift-able objects, passable apertures, surfaces that afford concealment, and so on. A feature or set of features must have a particular intrinsic structure for any of these properties to be even possible. Moreover, a particular relation—namely, an environment–person congruence—must exist between the feature and an individual for that feature to be realized in experience as a particular affordance. Meaning resides in this congruence of environment–person; and in doing so, it dissolves the putative environment-person boundary.

In Barker's framework, the term synomorphy refers to the presence of congruence between topographic and designed features of the setting, on the one hand, and the activities that take place in the setting, on the other. Structurally, behavior settings are behavior-milieu synomorphs. The meaning of a behavior setting—that is, what kind of setting it is and thus what kinds of activities are appropriate in that place—resides in perceived synomorphic relations between milieu features and action. For example, functionally adequate classrooms possess synomorphy between, on the one hand, furnishings and lighting, and on the other, the planned educational activities. As for its meaning, the kind of setting a classroom is, that is, the kinds of activities that normatively go on there, are posited to be perceivable in its structure (R. Barker & Wright, 1955, p. 60):

> The structure of the behavior pattern and the structure of the milieu in a behavior setting are seen to be congruent, to fit, to be synomorphic. The criterion of this synomorphism is *perceptual*; it is *directly seen* (p. 46). ... The meaning of a behavior setting, that is, what kind of setting it is and thus what kinds of activities are appropriate in that place, resides in *perceived* synomorphic relations between milieu features and behavior. (p. 53, emphases added)

As with affordances, a mechanistic analysis does not adequately capture these phenomena. A critical set of relations must obtain among the milieu features of the setting. A mere aggregation of milieu features, irrespective of certain within-setting relations among them, does not give rise to particular action possibilities. A classroom and a large storage room, for instance, may both contain desks and chairs, but these features need to be arranged in some suitable configuration for this interior space potentially to function as a classroom. Suitable arrangements will be those congruent with the collective actions intended normatively for the setting. The relation between milieu and behavior is not contingent. It is not the case that because this room worked well as a classroom on previous occasions that it can be used for that purpose again. Rather it worked well on previous occasions (or not) because of its structure or form.

Because the meaning of the setting resides in the congruence between behavior and milieu, this relational structure has the potential to bring actions of individuals entering the setting into line with its functional character. The structure (or form) of the behavior-milieu synomorph is detected by the perceiver; and in the process of becoming a participant in the setting—that is, by contributing to its overall structure through his or her actions—the individual becomes part of its structure in a functional sense. Such a conceptualization is compatible with the notion of formal cause. In Barker's terms, settings "coerce" behavior:

> The children of Midwest appear to see a smooth, level area which is free from obstructions, such as the football field, the Courthouse lawn, the school gymnasium, or the American Legion hall, as places for running and romping in unorganized, exuberant activity. The milieu features of such behavior settings appear *via perception to demand this kind of behavior*. Open spaces seduce children. The behavior settings of Midwest are loaded with these perceived, seductive characteristics. The displays and arrangements of the stores, the order of the church services, the ceremony at weddings, the guide lines painted on streets, the furnishings of homes are all calculated to coerce behavior *to the pattern appropriate for the setting*. (R. Barker & Wright, 1955, pp. 55–56, emphasis added)

Viewed in this way, the synomorph and the action of the individual come to share a common structure, and as with affordances, the putative environment–person boundary in effect is dissolved.

The concepts of affordances and behavior-milieu synomorphs have much in common. In fact, in some cases they may nearly overlap.[7] What distinguishes affordances and synomorphs at a conceptual level is that synomorphs refer to milieu features that define settings and functionally support collective actions of individuals. Affordances, by definition, do not support collective actions, but instead are identified relative to the actions of specific perceivers. But the boundary between these two concepts is not sharp (as will be seen later). They both refer to publicly accessible, meaningful features of the environment specified relative to the behavior(s) of an individual(s).

The assertion that the perceived meaning of environmental features is carried in relational structures, such as in body-scaled affordances and behavior-milieu synomorphs, requires considerably more clarification. Part of this effort involves continuing the line of affordance research, which attempts to identify stimulus information that can carry such functional meanings, and extending this kind of approach to the study of behavior-milieu synomorphs. Obviously, there is a great deal of work that needs to be done on this problem.

In spite of the very preliminary nature of our understanding of affordances and behavior-milieu synomorphs, these concepts identify some ways in which that much neglected aspect of experience, perceived meaning, can be incorporated into accounts of psychological phenomena. Admittedly, these are fairly simple cases of meaning, but they offer a starting point for viewing meaning as arising out of action. Further, explicating these concepts helps to demonstrate why a conceptualization of environment–person relations along the lines of formal cause rather than efficient (mechanical) cause is essential.

Selecting, Discovering, and Creating Environmental Meaning

There is a crucial piece of the ecological framework missing from the preceding account of meaning. The affordances, behavior-milieu synomorphs, and other meaningful features of the environment are one facet of a dynamic individual–environment transaction. The other facet is intentional actions of individuals; and this attribute of the individual–environment rela-

---

[7]For instance, from the perspective of an individual, a desk and chair in a room afford writing and studying. Considered in the context of a setting in which these objects may be located, such as an office, a desk and chair are synomorphic to the intended overall functions of the setting.

tion becomes most apparent in the selection, the discovery, and the creation of meaningful environmental features.

Individuals selectively engage particular affordances in their surround and selectively seek out certain behavior settings. As for affordances, individuals typically make choices from among the range of potential affordances in a setting to support some activity. The same can be said for individuals' relations to most behavior settings. Usually, the occupants of a behavior setting are self-selected. Which setting individuals choose to enter is based in part on the psychological possibilities that the setting offers to them.

However, in the case of both affordances and behavior settings, individuals do not have unconstrained choice. Factors outside of their control may limit the range of socially sanctioned choices. For example, within a given cultural context, individuals may be prohibited from using particular affordances (e.g., sitting in a chair with specific social significance or "ownership" through prior use). Similarly, behavior settings "sort and select occupants regardless of their wishes" (R. Barker, 1989, p. 29). For instance, age can often be a restriction in determining who can be admitted to certain settings. In short, there is self-selection of the affordances and behavior settings engaged, but often within constraints.

Intentionality in actions is also apparent in the processes through which individuals learn about and discover the affordances and behavior-milieu synomorphs in their surroundings. Individuals learn about affordances and synomorphs primarily by actively engaging these features of the environment. Moreover, as discussed in the previous section, this is not a process of randomly engaging objects to discover their effects. Rather, which objects (and settings) are selected in the first place is delimited by the perceived congruence between a feature's or a setting's properties and the individual's functional capabilities and intentions. This reciprocity gives rise to exploration and discovery within constraints. Finding novel uses for familiar objects is a particularly satisfying way for new affordances to be discovered. In the case of behavior-milieu synomorphs, individuals can discover the meaning of a setting through participation.

There is a different source of influence often present as well. Actions involving the learning about environmental properties are frequently guided by others (Rogoff, 1990). Throughout life, but perhaps most apparently during childhood, individuals are explicitly taught, often in very subtle ways, to recognize and utilize the functional properties of objects and the resources of settings. Guided learning requires activity on the part of the learner, and for this reason, Rogoff (1993) aptly described these actions as "guided participation." Obviously, individuals also learn about the meanings of objects and settings by observing the actions of others, and the act of observation is itself an instance of selectively engaging the environment (Tomasello, 1999a).

Finally, affordances and synomorphs are sometimes created when the range of possibilities available in the environment are insufficient to meet certain goals. The sociocultural world is comprised of perceptually meaningful features and places that were created by an individual or a group of individuals at some time. This ubiquitous fact about the world is one manifestation of the fundamental reciprocity of individuals and environment. Individuals do not merely take the world as they find it. The environment is continually being modified as new tools, artifacts, paths, settings, and sites for activities are created (see chap. 9).

J. J. Gibson (1979) saw many of these activities in modifying natural features as efforts to create new affordances in order to address specific individual and sociocultural needs. Barker also recognized that behavior-milieu synomorphs are created by intentional human activities. According to R. Barker and Wright (1955):

> The synomorphy of milieu and behavior arises, too, from the explicit de-
> mand of behavior for a particular milieu. The boys of Midwest want to play
> basketball. This requires a particular milieu, including special behavior ob-
> jects. Midwest boys have therefore, created the necessary milieu and as-
> sembled the necessary behavior objects, and in consequence the behavior
> setting. (p. 57)

In fact, much of the behavior in Midwest is "concerned with creating new milieu arrangements to support new standing patterns of behavior, or altering old milieu features to conform to changes in old patterns of behavior" (p. 57). The creation of new behavior settings has only recently begun to receive much attention, however (Wicker, 1987, 1992).

Sometimes, too, affordances and behavior-milieu synomorphs are unintended. For example:

> This can occur as an incidental resultant of the behavior. The path from the
> south entrance of the Midwest school house to the corner of the yard is a
> prominent behavior-milieu synomorph; a great part of the going to and com-
> ing from the school is associated with this path. In this case the milieu was
> created by the feet of many children taking the shortest way home (p. 56).

The ubiquity of affordances and synomorphs that are explicitly created by individuals points to an important issue that is addressed in the next chapter. In many cases, meaningful features of the environment that are created reflect individuals' knowledge, individually or collectively, about environment-behavior relations. Viewed in this way, it can be said that a great deal of what is known is embodied in the environmental structures and settings individuals create. Such a perspective opens the way for recognizing that we live our lives in environments rich in what might be called *ecological knowledge*. An ecological perspective proposes that the meanings of objects and places reside in the environment. It is there where meanings are discovered, and there where they are created.

AFFORDANCES IN PLACES AND AFFORDANCES OF PLACES

Up to this point, some commonalties between Gibson's and Barker's programs have been examined. In particular, aspects of the shared metatheoretical context for their ideas have been considered, as well as how their approaches to perceived meaning grow out of this common context. The remainder of the chapter explores some ways in which different aspects of their two positions can be brought together while retaining their distinctive contributions. Because of their common metatheoretical roots, such steps are possible without significantly sacrificing the commitments of either.

This section of the chapter examines Gibson's concept of affordances and Barker's concept of behavior-milieu synomorphs. Each concept brings into a joint ecological framework qualities that are distinctive and vital. At the same time, each concept can enrich the other. The purpose here is to explore some ways the conceptualization of the meaningful ecological entities stemming from these programs can be both broadened and made more focused.

Sources of Affordances and Behavior Settings

Sources of the varieties of affordances and behavior settings available in a community can be identified with the aid of Gibson's and Barker's writings. J. J. Gibson (1979, pp. 36–42) offered a broad classification of affordance types. An examination of these categories in relation to R. Barker and Wright's (1955, pp. 55–57) discussion of sources of behavior-milieu synomorphy points to at least three broad sources of functionally significant environmental entities, and in turn offers the beginnings of a framework for identifying the origins of affordances and behavior-milieu synomorphs. Certainly, there is by necessity some overlap among categories.

"Terrain features" (Gibson) or "physical forces" (Barker & Wright) refer to *topographical features* that give the layout of surfaces particular functional possibilities. Among the features Gibson included here are paths, obstacles, barriers, and slopes. Existing topographical characteristics of the landscape are exploited, making certain activities possible while limiting others. For example, natural features such as slopes afford coasting for children, but make it difficult for activities such as building playhouses or forts. Likewise, an open, smooth expanse affords certain types of games, such as baseball, but are incompatible with others such as hide and seek.

Topographical features, such as tools, paths, barriers, and so on, are also built or constructed, as are the milieu features that support collective behaviors. The structure of an elementary school classroom (as already discussed), or the interior furnishings of a library reading room, support some activities of individuals, but also make other activities inconsistent with the location's intended use more difficult.

Although their effects are less pervasive than topographical features, *climatological properties* of settings, or what R. Barker and Wright (1955) called "physiological forces," also operate as sources of affordances and milieu. These properties refer to such things as prevailing climatic conditions that can have a functional impact on human activities. Places in parks and plazas that are well-lit and sunny are sought out for reposing and reading on cool days (Whyte, 1980). Windy places, such as particular beaches and cliff edges, by contrast, are often not ideal for reading, but are frequently sought out for kite flying and gliding. These examples illustrate that places may be selected for use because their climatic conditions extend opportunities for specific activities to individuals and to groups. The functional influences of climatic properties are most obvious in somewhat extreme circumstances.

As with topographical features, climatic features can be intentionally designed. The control of interior temperatures is an obvious example of providing climatic conditions that support particular activities. At times, such control can take on a somewhat specialized focus, as in the following example from Barker and Wright (1955): "In Kerr's [Meat] Locker, where the temperature is maintained near zero, behavior is brisk, and movements are stiff and ungraceful" (p. 55).

Cutting across the previous two categories is a factor demanding particular attention as a source of affordances and of behavior-milieu synomorphy, namely, *sociocultural practices*. The relation between sociocultural influences and affordances has received some attention earlier (chap. 3) and is considered further in the next chapter. The functional meanings of a place, like the meanings of affordances considered individually, are often established by sociocultural practices. For example, cultural groups sometimes identify certain existing places in a landscape as special in some way, as in the case of sacred places. In many cases, these sites are selected partially because their topography is perceptually distinctive, with beliefs developing in relation to these landscape features. In other instances, places are constructed with their intended symbolic significance and function in mind at the outset (e.g., churches, temples); and these places too are invariably distinctive perceptually, conveying a shared symbolism.

In the domain of place perception, as in other areas of perception, individuals need to learn to detect the information that is distinctive of particular places. This information would identify these places as particular sites where certain activities can be engaged in and other activities are prohibited. When the meaning of a place arises more out of sociocultural practices rather than topographical or climatological features, the relevant information may be especially difficult to discern by young children being socialized into the practices of a culture as well as by newcomers to a culture. The psychological processes by which cultural neophytes discover the meaning of places have received little attention to date, and it is a topic ripe for investigation.

The identification of culturally derived place meanings can be especially difficult because behavior settings have both geographical and temporal boundaries. A particular place may afford some activity for an individual or a group only at specific times. For instance, the selfsame building can function as a worship sanctuary and as a hall for social activities at various times of the day. Individuals who participate in these settings need to be aware of such temporal boundaries. It is not known when in the course of development children become aware of the fact that the same place can have functionally different meanings at different times.

These three sources of affordances and behavior settings do not exhaust the possibilities. Other categories mentioned by Gibson, and either not mentioned earlier or mentioned in passing, include water, fire, other animals, objects, tools, and representations; and each could readily be discussed in conjunction with behavior settings. Objects, tools, and representations are examined in the next chapter.

Specifying the Milieu from an Affordance Perspective

The description of behavior-milieu synomorphs can be made more precise in light of affordances. Recall that behavior settings are generated by the collective actions of individuals, and these actions occur in relation to synomorphic (supportive) milieu features. Unlike affordances, which are specified relative to a particular individual, the milieu properties of behavior settings are considered collectively across individuals. However, this collective focus of behavior settings limits the preciseness of a description of milieu properties. Milieu features described for no one in particular lack a measure of specificity. In order to provide something other than a very global description of supportive milieu features, shared characteristics of the participants in the setting could be considered, and the affordance approach can help in this regard.

Approaching the notion of behavior settings with affordances in mind can lead one to think about the kinds of individuals who would participate in particular settings. If the shared functional attributes of the likely participants in a setting can be identified, then synomorphic properties of the setting that are functionally congruent for that group of individuals can be specified.

How can one begin to specify what the shared functional attributes of participants in a particular behavior setting are like? As noted in the previous section, there are factors operating to determine who the participants in a setting will be. In some cases, only individuals who meet certain criteria will be admitted to a setting, as is the case, for example, in age-graded school classes. At other times, the participants are self-selected as a function of the kinds of functional opportunities or affordances a setting extends. Such factors control to a degree the normative characteristics of the individuals in a behavior setting. Identifying the normative functional attributes of behavior setting participants in turn makes it possible to describe the synomorphic milieu properties of the setting with some specificity.

To illustrate this point with a simple case, knowing that a particular classroom is intended for 5-year-olds permits a greater measure of precision in the description of its milieu properties than simply identifying it as a classroom. For the milieu features of a classroom for 5-year-olds to be synomorphic to their activities, these features need to be scaled relative to physical characteristics typical of this age group. As a result, this classroom should differ in specifiable ways from a classroom for 14-year-olds. The scale of the furniture will differ, as will possibly the size of writing implements and tools, the position of door knobs, light switches, sinks, and so on. Although these sorts of differences are quite obvious, what this example illustrates is that it is possible to move toward greater precision in describing the appropriate milieu structure of a place by adopting an affordance perspective and thereby bearing in mind the functional needs of kinds of individuals in the setting.

Note that we are still not, strictly speaking, dealing with affordances in this example because there may well be some children in the class who the milieu scaling does not accommodate. The functional character of a behavior setting is specified relative to shared or normative characteristics of a group of occupants or intended users, but not in relation to any single individual; affordances are specified relative to a particular individual. Affordances are not synonymous with the milieu considered extra-individually (see later).

However, with affordances in mind, the description of extra-individual character of a behavior setting can be sharpened considerably. It is a setting considered independently of any particular individual, but only up to a point. By identifying some of the normative characteristics of participants in the setting, properties of the milieu can be broadly specified.

In short, the affordance perspective prompts a consideration of the *group-specific milieu properties* of a behavior setting, and in doing so it adds a measure of precision to behavior setting analyses that they otherwise do not have.

Affordances as Components of a Behavior Setting

Affordances are invariably treated as independent entities, considered apart from their relation to other environmental features. The notion of a behavior setting as a behavior-milieu synomorph encourages the recognition that in many cases affordances should be conceptualized as part of a higher order ecobehavioral entity. Moreover, a particular behavior setting can be thought of as a place where features with particular affordance properties are likely to be found. This nested relation provides a way of examining how affordances are distributed in the environment.

Recall that an inventory of the behavior settings available in some locale (a behavior setting survey) can serve as a basis for predicting the occurrence of extra-individual behaviors in that community (chap. 7). Behavior settings highlight the fact that the actions individuals are observed to engage in are not randomly distributed throughout a community, but are organized in relation to the particular settings present. These patterns are attributable to the fact that "[p]eople conform to a high degree to the standing patterns of the behavior settings they inhabit" (R. Barker, 1968, p. 164). Hence, an assessment of the availability of behavior settings provides a great deal of information about the distribution of behavior in a community. The results of a behavior setting survey offer a description of the ecobehavioral resources of a community.

If it is recognized that certain affordances are typically constituents of the milieu properties of a particular behavior setting, then a behavior setting survey will also provide some insight into the affordances that are available for individuals in a community. These observations merely point to a source of the distribution for affordances in the everyday environment, namely, behavior settings.

In addition, recognizing that specific affordances are often embedded in particular behavior settings points to some characteristics of what individuals know about their everyday environments. Specifically, not only do individuals learn the affordance properties of various environmental features, as discussed earlier in the chapter, but they also come to know where those affordances are likely to be found. To rephrase a passage previously quoted from Barker about how behavior settings structure the distribution of activities (but in this case substituting objects [in brackets] for behavior): While it is possible to [find a screwdriver] at a Worship Service, [a paintbrush] at a Court Session, and [an easel] in a Machine

Shop, such matchings of [objects with affordance properties] and behavior settings almost never occur (R. Barker, 1968, p. 164). An individual who is informed about the structure of the environment and who is searching for any one of these objects would not choose these settings to look for them. Individuals' knowledge that particular affordances are typically located within particular behavior settings, and rarely within others, is a facet of the claim that affordances are among the milieu components of behavior settings. It also indicates a way in which knowledge of the environment is hierarchically structured.

At present there is very little understanding about how knowledge of this hierarchical structure is acquired, but it clearly forms a part of the kinds of information individuals learn about their everyday environments. Knowledge about where affordances are to be found will often reflect a facet of cultural learning, because in most instances the presence of a particular affordance as a component of a specific behavior setting type is culturally normative.

Affordances of Places for an Individual

In addition to affordances being present as components of the higher order ecobehavioral entities that are behavior settings, it is also the case that behavior settings considered globally have affordances for individuals.

By definition, behavior settings are places with functional properties when considered as dynamic structures of collective behavior. It is reasonable to claim, by extension, that behavior settings as places afford certain possibilities for an individual. For example, the behavior setting "the regular Wednesday night pick-up basketball game" affords an activity for an individual that rests on a specific extra-individual behavior-milieu synomorph. In this example, the activity is a property of the setting as a whole, not a property of one milieu component of the setting. In other words, there is an affordance of place.

Considering affordances of places provides an avenue for clearing up one source of confusion in Barker's writings. There are some examples of behavior settings Barker cited that do not strictly adhere to the standard definition. For example, among the behavior settings reported in the 1963–1964 survey in Midwest are bus stops, parking lots, hallways, telephone booths, staff lounges at the school, and sidewalks. Although these are extra-individual features in the sense that they are not specified relative to a particular individual, they are not features of ongoing collective activity. Barker called these features behavior settings; and yet they obviously differ from the dynamic, collective behavior-milieu structures that are paradigmatic of behavior settings. The confusion can be avoided by viewing such functionally significant milieu features as affordances rather than behavior settings.

Summary

Joint consideration of the concepts of affordances and behavior-milieu synomorphs has suggested several ways in which the conceptualization of each can be enriched.

Two environmental sources of the functional properties that contribute to the makeup of affordances and behavior settings are topographical features and climatic conditions. A third source of functional meaning crosses the preceding two, namely, sociocultural practices. Among the ways that sociocultural influences can be expressed is through the role that objects and tools play in social practices (chap. 9), thereby establishing the social significance of certain existing environmental features, and through the design of built features with their social significance in mind. Often, the perceptual distinctiveness of functionally significant features needs to be learned, and such learning is a vital part of acculturation.

The synomorphic properties of behavior settings can be described with a greater degree of precision than they usually are once the shared characteristics of the group of individuals participating in the setting are recognized. In this case, the concept of affordance helps to sharpen the analysis of behavior setting properties with the recognition that behavior settings have group-specific milieu properties.

Reciprocally, to consider affordances from the perspective of behavior settings leads to the recognition that affordances are often components of a behavior setting. This has value because it provides a means of thinking about how some affordances are distributed in the environment. It also leads to recognizing that learning about affordances can entail both understanding their functional properties and understanding where in the environment they can be found. This indicates, in turn, a way that knowledge of everyday environments is hierarchically structured.

Finally, as affordances can function as components of behavior settings, so too behavior settings considered globally afford particular actions for an individual. These latter place affordances that arise out of collective activity should be distinguished from individual affordance features of the environment that are engaged by a person.

The preceding discussion should be seen as a preliminary effort to explore the proposal at the root of these two concepts—namely, that from a psychological perspective, environments are meaningful. The merits of these suggestions need to be evaluated in future research.

Conclusion: Should a Distinction Between the Two Ecological Programs Be Maintained?

With this examination of affordances and behavior settings in mind, one further issue needs to be explored here. In view of their commonalities, are there good reasons why a distinction between affordances and behavior settings should be preserved? For instance, why not subsume the concept of behavior-milieu synomorph under the broader notion of affordance? (Along these lines, the distinction between affordances and behavior setting cannot be sharply drawn. A sidewalk, for example, can be pointed to as having affordances for a particular individual, and yet Barker also used this feature as an example of a behavior setting.) Moreover, whereas behavior settings are usually generated by the joint actions of individuals, they do have affordances for any single individual entering the setting. Why not then extend the concept of affordance to include the phenomena designated by the behavior setting concept? In that case, behavior settings would be viewed as a particular category of affordances. A different way of raising this question is to ask why should an ecological psychologist working from Gibson's perspective be interested in behavior settings as distinctive entities in their own right?

It is the case that the concept of behavior setting cannot simply be assimilated to affordances without losing some of most distinctive properties of the former. To reiterate, unlike affordances, which are specified relative to an individual perceiver, behavior settings are functional properties of the environment generated by the collective actions of individuals. If the concept is consistently applied (and, in the process, marginal cases reevaluated, such as the sidewalk example), behavior settings only exist because of the interdependent actions of a group of individuals in relation to milieu. Both affordances and behavior settings point to objective properties of the environment, but these two properties operate at different levels of analysis. Affordances are a class of environmental properties operating at the level of an individual. Behavior settings are a class of environmental properties that reside among extra-individual relations, with the result that any individual in the setting can be replaced by another individual (admitting a few exceptions) and the setting will continue operating—that is, it will continue to exist. Behavior settings may afford particular opportunities for an individual, but they exist by virtue of extra-individual relations in which an occupant of a setting takes part. In short, affordances and behavior settings are both functionally meaningful properties of the environment; but they are environmental properties residing at different levels of environment–behavior processes—at the level of an individual and at the level of collectivities of individuals, respectively.

As a result, when operating from Gibson's framework, behavior settings bring into focus a set of psychologically meaningful features that would not necessarily be apparent if analysis were limited to individually specified environmental features. For this reason, the concept of behavior setting expands the scope of ecological psychology to include psychologically meaningful features that are best conceptualized if actions and supportive features of the environment are considered at an extra-individual level.

Now to turn the prior question around, why should a psychologist working from Barker's perspective be interested in affordances as distinctive entities? The reason is that affordances can sharpen the consideration of behavior settings in several ways. As discussed in the preceding section, the manner in which the notion of affordances is conceptualized leads to the consideration of the properties of behavior settings with a greater measure of specificity than is done otherwise. Given the psychological characteristics of the individuals typically participating in and therefore sustaining the setting through actions, it is possible to begin to describe the properties of milieu features required by these individuals considered en masse. In this way, the notion of affordances provides an avenue for making more precise an understanding of the ways in which milieu features are synomorphic to actions of setting occupants.

Along these lines, the experimental efforts to identify the perceptual information that specify particular affordances (see chap. 4) suggest a research agenda for future investigations of behavior settings. Barker claimed that the functional meaning of a behavior setting is perceivable—that its meaning is a physiognomic property of the setting. But there have been very few efforts to substantiate this hypothesis. Judging from the observation of individual actions, it seems apparent that individuals can detect the boundaries of a setting; that is, individuals appear to be aware of when they are entering and when they are leaving a behavior setting. Moreover, individuals apparently detect in a reliable fashion the meaning of settings, as is evidenced by the fact that setting-appropriate behaviors are commonplace in everyday life, and deviations are relatively rare. On these grounds, it is reasonable to expect that stimulus information specifying behavior settings is available to be detected and is the basis for these perception–action discriminations. But what the nature of this stimulus information might be is unclear. An analysis of the nature of information specifying behavior settings is needed, and the efforts along these lines with respect to affordances can serve as a useful template for such investigations. Identification of information specifying different classes of behavior settings would further support Barker's claim that behavior settings are objective features of the environment.

Apart from the ways in which the concept of affordances can enhance the analysis of behavior settings, Gibson's ecological approach can contribute at a deeper level to the theoretical formulation of Barker's ecobehavioral science.

THE FOUNDATIONAL ROLE OF ECOLOGICAL PSYCHOLOGY IN ECOBEHAVIORAL SCIENCE

Over the course of his career, Barker self-consciously chose to devote his time increasingly to what he called the "ecological environment" of extra-individual phenomena rather than the "psychological environment" of person–environment processes. Barker was clear in his later writings that what he was offering was not, strictly speaking, a psychological theory. He was proposing an "ecobehavioral science," and by this term he meant a focus on settings that serve as contexts for individuals' collective everyday actions rather than for individuals *qua* individuals (chap. 7). Following Lewin, Barker claimed that an ecobehavioral science can stand apart from an ecological psychology at the level of the individual.

A fully developed ecological psychology, however, requires an account of both ecobehavioral processes and environment–person processes. A focus exclusively on the dynamics of the environment at an ecobehavioral level, as surely as a focus exclusively on environment–person phenomena, will result in an incomplete ecological psychology.

In view of the fact that Barker and his colleagues devoted considerable attention to environment–person processes in the first decades of the Field Station, it might seem reasonable to pick up those threads in order to develop a complement to their ecobehavioral work. Such an approach would meet with only limited success, however. Barker's approach to person–environment processes, albeit in its preliminary form, appears in some respects to be inconsistent with his broader goals. This tension in Barker's program was addressed briefly in the previous chapter, and it is examined further here.

But why can't it just be stated that the processes operating at each level are incommensurate, and leave it at that? Although it is to be expected that the specific processes at work at each level of analysis will differ, because individuals are among the components of behavior settings, and because behavior settings provide the context for individual actions, there should be an essential compatibility reflecting the between-level influences that are apparent. A coherent ecological psychology describing processes working at both levels of analysis will require bringing Barker's ecobehavioral program and Gibson's ecological psychology into closer theoretical alignment. Consider some of the difficulties this task presents and how these difficulties might be met.

The Ecological Environment and the Psychological Environment

In the previous chapter, Barker's distinction between the ecological environment and the psychological environment was examined. To reiterate this view briefly, the ecological environment refers to features and events of the environment that can be considered independently of any individual and that can affect actions collectively (i.e., they are public). Behavior-milieu synomorphs are the principal entities investigated in the ecological environment, and they constitute the dynamic ecobehavioral structures that are circumjacent to individual behavior. The psychological environment refers to those events that are selectively experienced by a single individual and considered solely from the point of view of that individual. In contrast to the ecological environment, the psychological environment, according to Barker, does not exist independently of the individual experiencing it, but is private.

This distinction points to an important difference between Barker's and Gibson's thinking. With it Barker adopts the "two environments" perspective, which is characteristic of Gestalt psychology generally and that Gibson explicitly rejected (chap. 6). The ecological environment is an objective world "out there," independent of an individual, and the psychological environment is an autonomous, subjective realm. As argued earlier, this two worlds dichotomy is pernicious because it undercuts efforts to develop a realistic psychology. A world whose reality is dependent on an individual mind experiencing it is cut off from a world that exists independently of a knower and that serves as the common ground for interpersonal experience.[8]

Rather than positing two separate worlds, as the Gestalt psychologists with their Neo-Kantian roots were inclined to do, one can follow James in claiming that fundamental to all psychological experience is a knower in relation to a field of potential or latent structure. Particular aspects of this latent structure become actualized in the relation between a knower and the environment. In this framework, the features of the psychological environment are to be viewed as features in the environment that have been selected by an individual (i.e., a psychological agent). This selective action is, according to James, the hallmark of knowing. The features are selected by the individual-agent out of a ground (ecological environment) that is independent of an individual perceiver. Thus, instead of an objective-subjective dichotomy, James proposed a relational world of potential structure, and individuals' selective awareness of aspects of that world.

---

[8]This is not an attempt to deny private thoughts and experience. That would be absurd. What is being contested is the proposition that there is a private environment.

Is this a conceptual difference that makes a difference? Doesn't the distinction between potential and actual structure merely restate the distinction between the objective and subjective worlds? No, there is a subtle difference that carries with it far-reaching significance for a psychological theory. An account that begins with a domain of person–environment relations, and that views differences between how individuals' experience the world as being the *outcome* of selective processes (both percepts and concepts, in Jamesian terms), is an account that begins with direct experience of the environment. And with the grounds for direct experience in place, there is maintained an ongoing possibility for individuals to have common experiences through the discovery of structure in that world. In contrast, an account that begins with a dichotomy between the world "out there" and the world as individually experienced, nowhere allows for the possibility of direct experience of the environment. The environment from the start is "in the head." This ground of objective/subjective domains makes the possibility for common experiences across individuals precarious at best (see chap. 1).

Barker's goals for a realistic ecobehavioral psychology are best served by following, as Gibson did, the lines of radical empiricism rather than the Neo-Kantian tradition of Gestalt psychology, or (as is discussed later) other variations of the received view of knowing. Support for this claim can be found in some of the data from the Field Station. Consider these data and their implications.

Ecological Psychology and the E-O-E Arc

Recall what led to the discovery of behavior settings in the first place. When Barker and his colleagues tried to account for the actions of the children observed in Midwest, they found that the congruence between discrete ecological events and discrete actions was relatively low. However, when they "finally looked beyond immediate, discrete ecological inputs to the behavior streams of individual persons, it was not difficult to identify larger environmental units" (R. Barker, 1968, p. 152).

One of these larger environmental units, an "environmental force unit" (EFU; see Schoggen, 1963, 1978), was a reasonably good predictor of individuals' extended "behavior episodes." An EFU is "an action by an environmental agent toward a recognizable end state for [another] person" (R. Barker, 1968, pp. 152–153). An EFU is rarely a discrete action, but rather is a sustained set of actions whose "unity … comes from its constancy of direction with respect to the person upon whom it bears" (p. 153). An example of an EFU is the set of verbal promptings by an adult directing a child to complete some action. In a record of such an exchange, say, a parent prompting a child to put on a sock when dressing, a single prompt typically did not produce the desired action, but the series of promptings viewed as a unit did. The predictive value of EFUs is evidence that "conformity between the environment and behavior is more frequent over long than over short segments of the behavior stream" (p. 153). The conclusion that Barker drew from the concept of EFUs was "that the ecological environment *beyond* distal objects of the *E-O-E arc* is in some way causally implicated in behavior" (p. 152, emphasis added).

The expression "E-O-E arc" requires explanation. It is a concept Barker borrowed from Brunswik (1956) to describe the environment–organism relation. The arc spans successively the distal object, proximal stimuli, receptor processes, central organismic processes, motor processes, proximal behavior, and distal achievement (outcome). The model indicates that perception is of distal objects (one end of the arc), that responses are with respect to distal objects (distal achievements at the other end of the arc), and these end points of the arc are mediated by the intervening organismic process (Hammond, 1966). This is Brunswik's lens model.

Barker claimed that his data causally implicated events beyond the E-O-E arc. That places the critical variable (later found to be the behavior setting) outside of experience, in the ecological environment. When it enters the realm of an individual's experience (the psychological environment), the influence becomes part of the E-O-E arc.

But Brunswik's E-O-E arc is poorly suited for Barker's theoretical purposes, and it does not fit well with the behavioral data for which it was intended to provide order. The E-O-E arc is an input–output system, a variation of an S-R model. As such, it brings with it two related features that are problematic in the present context. First, it maintains the distinction between a world outside of experience and a world subjectively experienced. Second, instead of viewing perception and action as a coordinated, ongoing processes, it reduces them to a sequence of discrete acts, or in Dewey's (1896) critical assessment of an S-R model, to "a series of jerks, the origin of each jerk to be sought *outside the process of experience itself*" (p. 234, emphasis added).

Viewed in the context of Barker's overall framework, Brunswik's perceptual model is an anomaly. In every other respect but this one, Barker's theoretical approach is steeped in *systems thinking*. Barker did not view psychological processes, or ecobehavioral phenomena, as discrete chains of events. The "behavior stream" is continuous (R. Barker, 1963), and environment–behavior relations are a reciprocal, dynamic system.

Consider the example offered earlier of the parent prompting the child to put on a sock. The notion of the E-O-E arc led Barker to locate EFUs, such as these promptings, in the independent ecological environment (as quoted earlier, "the ecological environment beyond distal objects of the

E-O-E arc is in some way causally implicated in behavior"). And so they are. EFUs are independent of the child in the sense that they issue from the parent. But, in an important sense, the series of promptings are also not independent of the child. The parent's actions and the child's are clearly interconnected and reciprocal. For one thing, the parent's repeated promptings come from the noncompliance of the child, and they end with her compliance. Inversely, the child's actions (even the noncompliance) are reactions to the parent's promptings. This is a reciprocal relation; and part of the immediate context for the child's actions is the EFU. The observed events of the environment (the parent's promptings) and of behavior (the child's behavior) are not best viewed as a series of discrete stimulus–response events. Rather, they are ongoing and reciprocal. Moreover, and significantly, the parent's actions are not best viewed as being external to the actions of the child (and vice versa). The parent–child dialogue is a dynamic system, and actions of the parent and child occur within this system (see later). The actions of the parent in relation to the child (and vice versa) are independent, in the sense of being autonomous, and they are also relational and interdependent. These two sets of qualities need not stand in opposition, as they do when one embraces the objective–subjective dichotomy.

In short, Brunswik's perceptual model, being an input-output account, clashes with the overall systems orientation of Barker's framework, and it is not well suited to capture the reciprocal and dynamic character of person–environment processes that are revealed in Barker's data. Gibson's notion of a *"perceptual system"* is a far better choice for Barker as an account of environment–person processes. Perceiving from this point of view involves ongoing, reciprocal person–environment relations (chap. 3). This systems approach to perceiving is more consistent with the overall orientation of Barker's framework and with the dynamic, reciprocal character of actions revealed in Barker's behavioral records. As a result, it extends the possibility of an account of person–environment processes that will be congruent with Barker's conceptualization of extra-individual, dynamic patterns of behavior and milieu.

Behavior Settings, Ecological Optics, and Radical Empiricism

Although Barker's thinking was not shaped by the radical empiricist claims that influenced Gibson early in his training (chap. 2)—and there is no reason to believe from his writings that Barker was familiar with James's philosophy—it appears that he arrived at a viewpoint compatible in many ways with this perspective. Heider's writings were no doubt the impetus that moved Barker in this direction.

The realism of James's radical empiricism is grounded in the claim that experience from the outset is a relational field of potential structure, rather than being a formless chaotic swirl onto which structure must be imposed by cognitive processes. There is considerable prima facie evidence in Barker's writings to indicate that he would have been sympathetic with this viewpoint.

Barker pointed out an inconsistency between how psychologists typically viewed the nature of the environment and how the environment is conceptualized in other sciences. As for psychology,

> psychologists who have considered the problem [of environmental structure] have found the ecological environment on the afferent side of the person to be unstable, and to exhibit at best only statistical regularities. This has confronted students of the total E-O-E arc with the difficult problem of making precise derivations and predictions on the basis of unstable, disordered independent variables. In consequence, the selective and organizing powers of the intrapersonal segment of the arc—which to quote Leeper (1963, pp. 387–388), "yield relatively stable effects out of the kaleidoscopically changing stimulation they receive"—have claimed the greatest efforts of psychologists. It is here that the problems of perception and learning fall. (p. 151)

The view that Barker was describing here, whereby stability is imposed on experience of the environment by the "organizing powers of the intrapersonal segment of the arc," is precisely that adopted by Brunswik. In his lens model of perception, the relations among environmental (distal) features, and between distal features and proximal cues, are seen as, at best, probabilistic, and organismic processes provide the order otherwise absent in perceptual experience.

But in other sciences, R. Barker pointed out (1968), the environment is not conceptualized in this way:

> The environment as described by chemists, physicists, botanists, and astronomers is not a chaotic jumble of independent odds and ends, and it has more than statistical regularity. It consists of bounded and internally patterned units that are frequently arranged in precisely ordered arrays and sequences. ... [This] preperceptual world is not one system but many, and their boundaries and interconnections have to be discovered. (p. 154)

However, Barker recognized that not all psychologists hold to the view that the environment lacks structure. In a different passage, he wrote:

> When perception psychologists have turned away from the nature of perception to the preperceptual nature of light and sound, they have discovered something very important about the ecological environment of vision and

hearing: it is not random; it involves bounded manifolds of individual elements with varied and unusual patterns. The environment of vision and
hearing has a structure that is independent of its connections with perceptual mechanisms. (p. 15)

Although Heider was not named here, he must certainly be one of the psychologists to which Barker was referring. Whether or not he was also
thinking about Gibson is impossible to say. (There is no doubt that he was
familiar, if only superficially, with Gibson's work—see chapter coda).
Clearly, the claim that "the environment of vision and hearing has a structure that is independent of its connections with perceptual mechanisms"
is *inc*onsistent with the Brunswikian assumption that "the *ecological environment* on the afferent side of the person [is] … unstable, and … exhibit[s] at best only statistical regularities (emphasis added)."[9]

Importantly, the data that Barker and his colleagues collected in
Midwest accord with the view that the "preperceptual environment" (i.e.,
the ecological environment) is structured rather than disordered. Their
principal finding was that activities of groups of individuals in relation to
milieu features are regularly patterned; and, of course, the structural unit
here is the behavior setting.

It appears then that Barker felt the environment was structured, but he
was not always consistent in adhering to this point of view at the level of
person–environment analysis. Specifically, why did Barker accept the
E-O-E arc at the level of the individual, which assumes an unstructured
"preperceptual" environment, when the ecobehavioral phenomena he
investigated and the view of the environment in other sciences indicated
otherwise? This is a puzzle. The answer is probably threefold: First, Barker
was probably drawn to Brunswik's model because at the time Barker was
initially formulating his ideas, Brunswik was the only other psychologist
proposing an ecological theory, and the theory Brunswik proposed was in
keeping with mainstream theory in psychology.

Second, he may not have been particularly bothered by the differences
between an account of processes at the individual level and those at the
ecobehavioral level because he accepted Lewin's claim that there is an
incommensurability at different levels of explanation. Third, and related to
the preceding point, following Lewin (and as we have seen earlier),
Barker drew a distinction from the outset between the ecological
environment independent of a perceiver and the psychological
environment dependent on the experiencing individual. As a result, when
Barker's initial efforts to link discrete environmental events to discrete

---

[9]J. J. Gibson's (1957) review of Brunswik's *Perception and the Representative Design of
Psychological Experiments* (1956) is a particularly interesting comparison of these two perspectives.

actions at the level of individual processes failed, he did not press for the kind of order at the level of individual experience that Heider proposed. Instead, he looked to higher order units in the environment as predictors of action, and there he made significant discoveries. Acceptance of the two environments view, and their apparent incommensurability, encouraged him to leave unchallenged the claim that the environment at the level of the individual is unstable.

But if he had pressed on to see if there were other ways to conceptualize the environment at the level of individual processes, rather than abandoning this path for the study of extra-individual structures, he might have found that Gibson's program of ecological optics was congruent with his views.

The compatibility of Gibson's ecological approach to perception and Barker's ecobehavioral approach rests on three factors already mentioned, and they are offered as a summary here. First, both Gibson and Barker assumed the existence of structural regularities in the environment at the outset of experience. This assumption is fundamental to James's radical empiricism, and it is the primary reason why Barker's approach can be viewed as being broadly consistent with this philosophical program. Second, both Gibson and Barker were committed to a theoretical account that embraces *formal cause* rather than efficient (mechanical) cause as its dominant form of explanation. (Here is another difference between Gibson and Brunswik.) This view reflects the influence on both of Heider's analysis of thing and medium. Third, both Gibson and Barker adopt a *systems view* of psychological processes, and they applied this perspective to the phenomena of primary interest to each of them.

For these reasons, although the processes studied by Gibson (the dynamic system of perceiving and acting) and Barker (the dynamic system of behavior-milieu synomorphy) are distinct and operate according to different principles, with neither being reducible to the other, there is a fundamental compatibility between these two frameworks. The presence of this theoretical compatibility should not be altogether surprising. Person–environment processes are interjacent components of behaviors settings, and inversely behavior settings emerge from the relations among these processes. The view these two programs jointly offer of hierarchically nested natural systems and the operation of reciprocal within-level and between-level influences among them is, of course, a hallmark of an ecological perspective generally.

If the goal of formulating an ecological psychology that is both broad in scope and coherent is to be attained, then compatibility of the sort found between Barker's and Gibson's theories seems necessary. Moreover, because of this compatibility, Barker's ecobehavioral approach extends Gibson's ecological psychology in important ways that are in keeping with its essential claims (as already discussed); and reciprocally, Gibson's ecological psychology provides a psychological foundation for Barker's approach that is consistent with the latter's underlying assumptions.

THE STRUCTURE OF THE ENVIRONMENT AND DYNAMIC SYSTEMS

As a general framework for understanding behavior setting dynamics, Barker drew on systems theory circa 1960. In this regard, he was influenced particularly by Ashby's *An Introduction to Cybernetics* (1956).[10] This influence can be seen in the following comments about behavior setting dynamics: "The components of behavior settings are richly joined (Ashby, 1956) by a complex net, which produces a self-governing entity with attributes quite different from the psychological and mechanical processes that govern its interior connections" (R. Barker, 1968, p. 174). To reinforce this emphasis on the network of influences in a behavior setting, Barker asserted in a critical passage that "the reality and the nature of behavior settings as eco-behavioral entities *do not reside in* psychological processes of the inhabitants, but in the circuitry that *interconnects* behavior settings, inhabitants, and other behavior setting components" (p. 174, emphases added). By characterizing the operations of a behavior setting as being distributed across its participants and milieu components, Barker's conceptual treatment of his research findings is in accord with the sort of relational perspective found both in James and in Gibson.

A problem arises, however, when Barker explored the issue of the control processes of the behavior setting. The questions at hand are those that face any dynamic systems account: If the "reality and nature of the behavior setting" resides in the interconnections of the system, where does one locate that which controls the system and maintains its relative stability, and how does one conceptualize these control processes? To address these questions, Barker incorporated into Brunswik's perceptual model the TOTE concept proposed by Miller, Galanter, and Pribram in their highly influential book, *Plans and the Structure of Behavior* (1960). However, this choice does not seem to suit Barker's purposes very well. Perhaps more important for present purposes, it impedes the sought-after synthesis between his program and Gibson's.

In fairness to Barker, the attention devoted to this issue may be disproportionate to its role in his framework, and it probably reflects the conceptual resources Barker had available at the time. But this attention is

---

[10]This inference was confirmed by Jonathan Barker (personal communication, 1999), Roger Barker's son and a professor of political science. Jonathan Barker recently applied some of his father's ideas concerning behavior setting dynamics to the study of grassroots democratic processes (J. Barker, 1999).

warranted because it is a weak point in Barker's theory that can lead the approach astray in future applications. Perhaps most significant, this discussion provides a deeper appreciation for the systems perspective that the behavior setting approach embraces, and in doing so, it will tighten further the connection between Barker's and Gibson's programs.

Plans and the Structure of the Environment

What is critical in the operation of a behavior setting is the interconnections or "circuitry" among its components, as noted earlier. To this claim, Barker added: "the control unit [for any circuit of a behavior setting] is located *within the organism sector of the E-O-E arc*; it is, in fact, the mechanism of the TOTE unit identified by Miller, Galanter, and Pribram (1960) as *the fundamental unit of behavior*" (p. 171, emphasis added).

Although Miller et al.'s TOTE model has been superseded in the intervening years by many other control process models, it is a seminal idea whose imprint in contemporary psychology is pervasive. This model brought needed emphasis to the role of feedback loops in the consideration of psychological functions. A TOTE operation is posited to be a functional feature of intra-organismic processes. Individuals are assumed to operate in the environment by (T) testing current environmental conditions against some *plan* (i.e., desired state, set point) chosen by the individual; by (O) operating or taking appropriate actions if conditions do not match that desired state; by (T) testing the conditions again against the plan to confirm that the goal was met; and, if it was, by (E) exiting the operation.

In the context of Barker's theory, these TOTE processes are to be found in the inhabitants making up the circuits or interconnections of the behavior setting. Barker's application of the TOTE model is explained as follows:

> Within each of the circuits there is a control unit consisting of a behavior setting mechanism (S- MECH), which senses and transmits information about behavior settings; an executive mechanism (M-MECH), which tests information about settings against *inhabitants'* criteria of behavior setting adequacy and switches the appropriate goal program ... or [corrective] channel. ... [The state] of behavior setting components ... is sensed by S-MECH and transmitted to E-MECH where it is compared with the *inhabitant's* criteria of an adequate setting in view of his goal aspirations and program plans. If the state of the setting does *not* pass the inhabitant's test for these actions ... the eco-behavioral circuit is routed via M-MECH into maintenance channels. ... But if the behavior setting components pass the inhabitant's test within E-MECH, the circuit is routed via O-MECH [operating mechanisms] into operating channels, becoming goal or program circuits. (R. Barker, 1968, pp. 171–173, emphasis added)

In short, control processes are distributed across the circuits of a behavior setting, and within each circuit, individuals (to varying degrees as a function of their power in the setting) operate via TOTE mechanisms to monitor and maintain the program of the behavior setting.

Because Barker wanted to view behavior settings as complex systems, it is not unreasonable considering when he is writing that he drew on the TOTE model. It was the most visible systems account of psychological processes at the time. But Barker's selection of this account of psychological processes, like his selection of Brunswik's account of person–environment processes, was inconsistent with his overall goals and creates a tension in his position. Perhaps most problematically, it left Barker's approach susceptible to being deflected from its ecological intent and in the direction of a representational account of psychological processes.

This criticism needs to be elaborated. The problems associated with the TOTE model as a basis for explaining psychological processes derive from its central claim that a "plan" exists within the individual, or in Brunswikian terms, within the organismic portion of the E-O-E arc. What is posited is a plan that guides all actions and against which the effects of actions are tested recursively. The most general difficulty with this model is that when scrutinized carefully it does not amount to much of an explanation.

This is not to say that individuals do not have goals or plans. The purposive nature of individual action has been repeatedly emphasized in the preceding chapters. It is the *kind* of explanation of purposive action that is being questioned here. By pointing to an underlying, unseen mechanism—in the present case, a plan—to explain behavior, this type of explanation in reality mostly involves dressing the problem in a different form, while in fact adding little deeper understanding. In this respect, it is similar to a family of explanations that account for observable events by referring to unseen causes residing in one facet of what is in fact an interactive, multifactor system (Oyama, 1985). As a consequence, such a explanation offers only the illusion of advancing understanding by reifying into a mechanism a commonplace way of talking about some phenomenon. In the present case, because action is typically described as purposive, there is a tendency to posit a mechanism that accounts for this characteristic of behavior. Most problematic, with the illusion of understanding in place, efforts toward more adequate explanations are deferred:

To characterize purposeful action as in accord with plans and goals is just to say again that it is purposeful and that *somehow*, in a way not addressed by the characterization itself, we constrain and direct our actions. ... How we do that is the outstanding problem. Plans and goals do not provide the solution for that problem, they simply restate it. (Suchman, 1987, pp. 47–48)

But beyond offering little insight into the problem, psychological approaches like the TOTE model create new problems of their own. Serial processing computers, with symbolic codes and feedback loops, were the inspiration for TOTE. This kind of computer requires input that matches some symbolic code or representation already stored in its system. Thus, for every potential input, there must be a representation in the system that can recognize and process it. Another way of stating this point is that the system can only operate with respect to that which it already "knows." This operating characteristic of serial processing computers would seem to make them unworkable as models for human perception and thought for a number of reasons (Edelman, 1998).

Regardless of how detailed and complex its storage capacity, the fact is that this is a system that can recognize a finite number of inputs and possesses a finite number of operational routines, both of which are determined by the representations already in place. Considering the multiplicity of human phenomena (i.e., the enormous variety of what can be perceived, thought, performed, etc.), the number of representations or plans that would need to be in place in order to explain perceiving, thinking, acting, and so on, is simply staggering.

Complicating the situation further is that the conditions humans are responsive to cannot be specified in advance except in the broadest of terms—the environment is far too complex and far too dynamic for that. And the individual's active engagement of the environment over time as action unfolds only increases these complexities. In the normal course of performing some action, the individual will be typically faced with a series of multiple factors and conditions over time in relation to which actions must be adjusted. Learning and discovery are commonplace in everyday functioning. Do each of these adjustments constitute subplans or subroutines built into the system in advance? The complexities of such an approach are enormous:

> The big idea behind *Plans and the Structure of Behavior* also was the big mistake, that people operate on plans just as computers "run" on programs (Miller, et al., 1960, p. 197). It was this idea that led not only these authors but the whole cognitivist movement to suppose that behind the various verbal and nonverbal strategies and tactics by which we coordinate our own and each other's activities, there exists layer upon layer of increasingly minute plans exhaustively controlling our every move. (Leudar & Costall, 1996, p. 169)

The presence of seemingly endless plans nested within plans built into an organism who is prepared to respond to every contingency would be unwieldy, reminiscent of a Ptolemaic cosmos cluttered and tottering with epicycles.

But, in fact, the problem is even worse. It is more than a matter of accounting for how an organism adjusts to such complexities. Such a system would be maladaptive. If individuals engaged the environment with an established set of plans and subplans, their repertoire of responses would be limited to just those representations already in place. There may be a very large number of possibilities in place, but the system would have great difficulty handling any novelty. For example, it would be difficult to maintain some goal-directed action in the face of unanticipated events. If such unanticipated events were rare, those occasions—although problematic in themselves—would not matter too much in the bigger scheme of successful, anticipated sequence of events. But, in reality, unanticipated occurrences that arise and must be accommodated to in the course of goal-directed action are the norm.

Goal-directed actions typically unfold in a dynamic context of multiple opportunities and constraints presented by the environment and the body. A shorthand way of putting this fact of behavior is that actions are *situated*. And because actions are situated, the execution of plans are necessarily ad hoc, with adjustments and fine tunings being made "on the fly": "Plans are best viewed as a weak resource for what is primarily *ad hoc* activity. ... Stated in advance, plans are necessarily vague, insofar as they must accommodate the unforeseeable contingencies of particular situations" (Suchman, 1987, p. ix). Indeed, the vaguer a plan is, the better from the point of view of flexibility because it can cover an increasingly wide range of unforeseen possibilities. But, of course, as a plan becomes more vague it quickly begins to lose whatever explanatory power it might have offered in the first place because in covering so many possibilities it soon covers none. Thus, it would offer the appearance of explanation, but as an effective control process, it indeed offers little.

In addition to the dynamic character of situated action creating these problems for a representational model like TOTE, there is a further complication. The fact that the meaning of environmental features and events are highly context-dependent increases the number and layering of possible meanings in any given situation. This common characteristic of semantic comprehension places even a greater burden on a system that is assumed to have representations already in place for comprehension to occur. Suchman (1987) pointed out

The dependency of significance on a particular context, every particular context's open-endedness, and the essential *ad hoc*ness of contextual elaboration are resources for practical affairs, but perplexities for a science of human action. And ... it is an intractable problem for the significance of canonical descriptions—such as instructions—for situated action. (p. 48)

The cumulative weight of these challenges would appear to outstrip the capacities of any proposed representational system that would seek to account for flexible and meaningfully responsive action.[11] In short, recognition of the nature of the ordinary, everyday circumstances within which we live (i.e., developing an adequate conceptualization of the environment from a psychological perspective) rules out a representational model such as TOTE as a viable explanatory account.[12]

What such circumstances require of an agent is the capacity to articulate action and make choices in the ongoing, dynamic flow and rich context of environmental information. As is explored in the next section, for an agent to have these functional properties, perception-action phenomena need to be viewed as dynamically co-determined by a network of influences, instead of existing in any single component of that network as a set of fully formed alternatives (e.g., plans).[13] This alternative view locates psychological processes in the functional relations between the individual and the various facets of the environment, and in so doing, it is a view more in keeping with Barker's overall intentions for behavior setting theory than is the TOTE model.

---

[11]Some might argue that the preceding discussion has narrowly construed "representation," and it is a necessary part of even accounts where the cognitive system functions in a synergetic fashion with environmental and bodily forces and constraints (see next section). A. Clark (1997) indeed argued for a "minimal representationalism" where action-oriented representations (as opposed to structures that mirror the "external world") function as "partially programmed solutions" controlling the actions of an individual. A "partial program" specifies action while it simultaneously "cedes a good deal of work and decision making to other parts of the overall causal matrix" (p. 157). It may only amount to setting some organismic parameters in the interaction nexus of agent, body, and environment, but he argued, the contribution of even broad action specifications indicates that "internal representation" is playing an important role.

Resolution of this debate over the place of representations in dynamic, complex systems will hinge on an agreed on definition of representation, as well as future empirical studies demonstrating either that representations are necessary or expendable in accounting for complex psychological phenomena.

[12]An anticipated objection to this argument is that it sets up a "straw man" because no one intends terms like *programs, plans,* or *scripts* to be taken quite this literally. When program and the like are employed, they are meant to recognize the kind of flexibility mentioned earlier. But if they are not intended this literally (e.g., as algorithms), then what are they intended to refer to? The problem of "encroaching vacuity" lurks as one backpedals from the claim of literalness.

Debates around such matters have been swirling about in the artificial intelligence literature for some time. The central question is, "How can we begin to conceptualize a rule-governed system that is also flexible and adaptive in the face of novelty?" A dynamic system of mutual constraints seems to be a good starting point.

[13]It is noteworthy that recent advances in robotics and artificial intelligence have come about by approaching design problems as matters of establishing local, interacting constraints rather than devising a central control process (Brooks, 1995; A. Clark, 1997).

Recall R. Barker's (1968) assertion that "the reality and nature of behavior settings as eco-behavioral entities do not reside in psychological processes of inhabitants, but in the circuitry that interconnects behavior settings, inhabitants, and other behavior setting components" (p. 174). Juxtaposing this statement against his assertion that "the control unit is located within the organism sector of the E-O-E arc; it is, in fact, ... the TOTE unit" (p. 171), points to theoretical inconsistency. The source of this problem was identified in the previous section: the specific type of model of person–environment processes Barker selected. Barker adopted Brunswik's E-O-E model as a heuristic for conceptualizing person–environment processes, and the TOTE mechanism fits readily into this model. But the weight such an approach to individual processes places on a single component of a process, namely, intra-organismic processes, is inconsistent with the extra-individual environment–behavior system Barker so insightfully envisioned. The inconsistency can only be resolved by pleading for incommensurability of levels of analysis.[14]

In place of the representational model of person–environment processes, why not continue on the path Barker set for dealing with ecobehavioral phenomena? Doing so would maintain the focus on dynamic systems at the level of behavior settings and extend it to the level of person–environment processes.

In order to flesh out what this approach would look like, the next section considers the *dynamic systems approach* that has begun to receive considerable attention in recent decades. Replacing the TOTE model in Barker's approach with a more consistent dynamic systems analysis is in keeping with Barker's intentions for his approach, and further, it brings his program and Gibson's even closer together conceptually.

Dynamic Systems and Multiple Determination

Dynamic systems theory is an attempt to understand the time-dependent order that emerges from the complex interactions in physical and biological processes. Patterns and structures in the natural world are viewed as being multiply determined, and sustained and altered over time by the interplay of numerous factors. Control of dynamic processes is a property of

---

[14]If adamantly committed to a representational account, it could be argued that Barker hedged his claims by stating that the functioning of behavior settings reside in the interconnections of settings considered "as ecobehavioral entities." At the psychological level, the option would still open for a representational model, and the inconsistency can be chalked up to incommensurability of levels of analysis. This chapter claims that compatibility across levels (while maintaining their respective irreducibility) arising out of a more consistent application of systems thinking is preferrable from the standpoint of theoretical coherence. Moreover, as previously argued, representational models are unworkable as account of action in everyday circumstances.

the system considered as a whole. At a conceptual level, one attribute that distinguishes this perspective from what has long been called general systems theory is its emphasis on time-dependent processes.

The systems claim that patterns and structures are self-generated by the interaction of multiple contributing processes is to be contrasted with the standard account of the origin of structures that identifies their source as a latent property located in any one of the constituents.[15] From the point of view of dynamic systems theory, "The emergence of macroscopic order is *entirely* due to the dynamic interaction of the many microscopic degrees of freedom in the system" (Beek, Verschoor, & Kelso, 1997, emphasis added). Within psychology, this approach has been fruitfully applied to analyses of the dynamics of coordinated motor activity (e.g., Turvey, 1990) and motor development (e.g., Thelen, Kelso, & Fogel, 1987).

Thelen (1995) offered a helpful metaphor that captures the self-generated, time-dependent character of dynamic systems:

> An apt metaphor in this case is a mountain stream flowing over a rocky bed. Both the global course of the stream and its local whirls and eddies emerge from the architecture of the streambed and the force of the water flow, but are in no way programmed by those constraints. The pattern of a whirlpool may be quite stable as long as the water pressure and streambed do not change. Or a new pattern may form in response to a stray rock entering the bed or after a heavy rain. (p. 71)

The emergent pattern of water flow is not preprogrammed in any of the contributing influences that comprise the system. It is self-generated by the multiple, reciprocal influences at work. The resulting dynamic pattern has been described by Waddington (1971), who pioneered work in this perspective, as a "homeorhetic system" ("rhesis" derived from the Greek word *Rheo*, meaning to flow).

With this view in mind, if an attempt is made to understand the contribution of any single component of the system, then it is necessary to consider it in the context of the system as a whole as it operates over time. To excise and then isolate a component for closer scrutiny is in fact to examine that component in a different context. To isolate a component, say, in a laboratory is not to place it in a context-free setting, but to place it in a particular kind of setting. In doing so, the investigator will learn

---

[15]Paradigmatic of the standard view are claims about the genetic determination of particular phenotypic properties, as if the environment is not also a necessary co-determinant in *any* instance (Oyama, 1985). To make the latter assertion is in no way to deny that the expression of certain factors may be more or less resistant to modification. In Waddington's (1971) terminology, any given factor considered over time, that is, over the "epigenetic landscape," is more or less "canalized." But note that the canonical expression of any trait requires in place a certain range of other influences (see Elman et al., 1999).

something about how the component functions in that new context. But to take these characteristics that have been identified in one context uncritically as universal properties of the component itself is dangerously misleading. To do so ignores the context- and time-dependent nature of psychological phenomena. This is precisely the position that a great deal of experimental psychology has adopted in much of the 20th century by legitimizing one setting for the study of all manner of phenomena apart from broader contextual considerations (Danzinger, 1990). But this stance has greatly retarded understanding of psychological phenomena in a wide range of everyday contexts (Proshansky, 1976) and cultures (Cole, 1996).

To return to the preceding example, it is important to point out that the pattern of water flow in a river bed is a somewhat limited metaphor for dynamic systems including animate processes. A dynamical systems analysis that includes animate processes must recognize that at least one of the components (and usually more) contributing to the overall pattern is itself intrinsically dynamic and purposive. The component is not passive, like the water shaped by the river bed, but instead it has the capacity to operate selectively in a range of ways—it is an "agent."

It is agency operating within constraints, and the constraints contribute to the shape actions take over time. Taken in conjunction with the actions of an agent, constraints are not merely limiting, but they create possibilities. As Valsiner (1993) expressed it:

> In their relationship with the environments, these systems can adjust their existence to their contexts by way of selectively limiting the degrees of freedom at any given time and place, hence, making it possible for systems to participate in their own development in flexible ways. (p. 32)

The recognition that at least one facet of the dynamic person–environment system is an agent brings the discussion back to the problem identified earlier: How can the operations (e.g., control processes) of an autonomous agent in a complex system be conceptualized in a manner that is consistent with the operations of the broader, dynamic system with multiple determinants? A framework developed by Hayek (1952, 1967, 1969) offers a possible template. Hayek suggested that the operations of the individual be viewed themselves as emerging out of a confluence of "abstract rules" rather than a set of routines or subroutines that are in place. As for the notion of "abstract rules," emphasis should be placed on the word "abstract," and the word "rule" should be taken guardedly. This is because rule can suggest a prescription of steps, and taken as such it would be no different than a plan. Instead, these are abstract tendencies, each rule delineating a very broad class of actions, not one of which singly has very much definition; and it is only through the combination of multiple abstract rules that action has any degree of specificity. Moreover, the specificity that emerges from the confluence of abstract rules is not a prescribed plan or algorithm, but rather is a shifting pattern arising out of changing constraints. Abstract rules establish what is and is not possible, rather than particular steps to be taken. The superimposition of abstract rules results in possibilities for action within constraints:

> A disposition to act will be directed towards a particular pattern of movement only in the abstract sense of a pattern, and the execution of the movement will take one of many different concrete forms *adjusted to the situation* taken into account by the joint effect of many other dispositions existing at the moment. (Hayek, 1969, pp. 314–315, emphasis added)

Hayek's psychology, then, bears some resemblance to the dynamic systems account being explored here.[16] What does not receive sufficient emphasis in his account is the context of constraints established by the multiple and changing environmental conditions confronting the individual from moment to moment, although as the preceding quotation indicates, these factors are not ignored, perhaps only understated. Psychological functions at any given moment emerge from a confluence of multiple dispositions to act expressed in conjunction with the multiple and changing conditions of the environment confronting the individual over time. And considering the active character of animate processes and the changing character of environmental conditions, this is a dynamic, ceaselessly shifting process.

To further distance Hayek's position from those frameworks that posit plans and scripts as directing action, consider briefly how he approached what was identified as a significant problem for standard representational accounts, namely, the capability to deal with novel conditions. Because any instance of phenomenal experience or action is a result of the superposition of multiple dispositions, the system he was proposing is a generative one (Weimer, 1982). But this was not a rationalist position. Hayek (1969) is clear that the psychological outcome (phenomenal experience or action) is a product of the generativity in relation to environmental circumstances:

> The formation of abstractions ought to be regarded not as actions of the human mind but rather *as something which happens to the mind*, or alters that structure of relationships which we call mind, and which consists of the system of abstract rules which govern its operation. … Every appearance of a new rule (or abstraction) constitutes a change in that system, something which its own operations cannot produce but *which is brought about by extraneous factors*. (pp. 318–319, emphasis added)

---

[16]The common thread throughout Hayek's writings is the analysis of complex systems. See Weimer (1982) for a wide-ranging discussion of Hayek's often controversial contributions to the social sciences.

As discussed earlier (chap. 7), it is possible that a system of multiple constraints faced with a perturbation can produce novel outcomes through
differentiation of the system itself. Thus, he was envisioning a system of
multiple determinants operating simultaneously on both the individual
and the environment side of the person–environment relation that can
produce new ways of acting in an adaptive manner.[17]

The resulting conceptualization of psychological action and experience
over time can be viewed, to borrow a term from Holt (1912, see chap. 2), as
a "cross-section" of multiple environmental and organismic factors.
Arguably, Hayek's conception of mind broadly follows the same path
earlier blazed by James and Holt, whereby awareness and actions are
expressions of multiple influences in a field of environmental–person
processes. For James, experience was not an event "in" mind, over against
the environment; rather mind emerges from the interaction of person and
environment (see chap. 1). On these grounds, it is mischievous from a
psychological perspective to talk loosely about factors "in" the
environment and factors "in" the person. Recognizing that patterns of
action are co-determined through multiple, mutual influences and
constraints renders the "inside/outside" distinction meaningless (Oyama,
1985). Here again is a criticism of the "two environments" view
approached this time from a systems perspective. Although Hayek did not
fully explore these interactional claims, this appears to be a reasonable
reading of his proposal.

Moreover, it is important to underscore the fundamental Jamesian
point that what is being conceptualized here is a time-dependent process.
The confluence of environment–agent constraints is fluid and shifts over
time, making some actions possible and ruling out others.

These issues warrant further discussion, particularly from the point of
view of contemporary dynamic systems accounts of mind. However,
because the focus of this book is with conceptualization of the
environment, that exploration is left to others.

Dynamic Systems and Behavior Settings

Whereas some settings have criteria in place for who may be admitted to
them, to a large extent participants in behavior settings are self-selected.
Individuals choose to enter most behavior settings. In addition, part of individuals' participation in behavior settings is to contribute to the maintenance of its operations. It was in view of these latter efforts that Barker
invoked the TOTE model. Both choosing to participate in a setting and op-

---

[17]See Hayek (1952). Admittedly, with its primary focus on mental processes, some tension
may remain between Hayek's position and the one proposed here.

erating to maintain its functioning reflect the autonomous functioning of an agent. How can these actions be conceptualized in relation to the dynamic structure of the setting?

Individuals do not enter settings with a certain prescribed script in mind. For reasons already stated, because settings are highly complex, dynamic, and meaningful, the notions of plans, programs, or scripts are either unworkable (the sheer number required is staggering), maladaptive (a fixed number would preclude adaptability), or vacuous (adaptability might be explained at the cost of positing virtually empty "categories"). Further, a set of highly prescribed actions are not consistent with the experience from a first-person perspective: It seems, at least, that we enter settings in order to have the opportunity to operate within a range of activities and things, not to shackle ourselves to an algorithm. To choose to be a participant in the dynamic pattern of interactions of behavior and milieu that constitutes a behavior setting is to accept as operative a particular set of action constraints. That is, to choose to participate in a behavior setting is to choose to limit one's degrees of freedom in particular ways. But as mentioned earlier in the chapter, this is necessary to achieve certain ends because particular opportunities and experiences become possible only in a context of constraints.

There is openness in this context of constraints. For one thing, there is considerable uncertainty over time as to precisely how events will unfold. Moreover, the restriction of degrees of freedom allows for a certain range of variation, and this gives shape to action and development. Freedom and choice occur within constraints (see Reed, 1996, chap. 2).[18] And just as there is no uncertainty in following a program, there is no freedom either.

A mundane example may help at this point. If I want to play a game of baseball, I need to join a group of others who share this intention with me in a setting that supports this activity. By entering (and thereby contributing to) the geographical and temporal boundaries of this behavior setting, each participant chooses to operate within certain rule constraints. What specifically will transpire is unknown (and unknowable) at the outset. What is known is that there is a consensual (and usually tacit) agreement to operate within certain constraints. The constraints make certain kinds

---

[18]For this reason, the viewpoint that "anything goes" as being synonymous with freedom leads to a hopeless nihilism. As Dewey (1924) put it:

> To view institutions as enemies of freedom, and all convention as slaveries, is to deny the only means by which positive freedom in action can be achieved. A general liberation of impulses may set things going when that have been stagnant, but if the released forces are on their way to do anything they do not know the way nor where they are going. ... Not convention but stupid and rigid convention is the foe. (quoted in Reed, 1996b, p. 45)

of uncertainty possible by ruling out others. And it is the inability to anticipate the unfolding of the setting event within constraints that makes any particular occurrence (or game) appealing to both participants and spectators. Whereas it is true that an individual or a team may have a "game plan," that is only one factor among many operating in the setting; and an individual or team that does not adjust to conditions as they unfold does not usually prevail. What makes each game unique for participant and spectator is the ways participants react to the problem circumstances set for them over time.

In sum, behavior settings are best conceptualized as dynamic systems operating as contexts of constraint. They are time-dependent phenomena, with their boundaries established and maintained by the coming together of particular behavior-milieu components, and then subsequently dissolved when those relations no longer obtain. The "standing pattern of behavior and milieu" is self-generated by the dynamic interaction of these components. It is not preprogrammed in any one component of the setting, but emerges from a confluence of multiple influences. Thus, no one individual controls the operation of a setting (although individuals may differ in power to control the setting). Instead, the principal control process governing the operation of a behavior setting is consensus between individuals. In becoming a participant in a setting, individuals tacitly agree to accept the rule constraints of the setting. Behavior settings are quasi-stable systems in that they can withstand minor perturbations, often in novel ways, and their resiliency is due to the fact that the setting exists in the interrelations between its components. Likewise, the functional identity of behavior settings is distributed across a network of interdependent factors (chap. 9).

Of course, as anyone familiar with Barker's writings would be quick to point out, the preceding description in most respects is an elaboration of Barker's definition of a behavior setting. Where it differs is in the absence of a postulated control unit in any single component of the setting. In other words, it differs by attempting to preserve the systems character of Barker's framework at all levels of analysis.

To prepare the way for a central concern of the next chapter, consider one implication of the preceding paragraphs. A dynamic systems approach helps form a better understanding of why behavior settings and other similar, or even more complex, institutions are necessarily social structures. Particular higher order social structures are necessary because many complex problems cannot be addressed and many psychological opportunities cannot exist when individuals are operating alone. Indeed, some solutions and opportunities cannot even be envisioned in the absence of complex interactions arising out of a convergence of mutual constraints. Adopting a computationally oriented dynamic systems approach to cognition, A. Clark (1997) argued for just this role of contextual constraints operating at the level of groups:

> Our collective successes (and sometimes our collective failures) may often be best understood by seeing the individual as choosing his or her responses only within the often powerful constraints imposed by the broader social and institutional contexts of action. And this, indeed, is just what we should expect once we recognize that the ... nature of individual cognition is not ideally suited to the negotiation of certain types of complex domains. In these cases, it would seem, we solve the problem ... only indirectly—by creating larger external structures which can then prompt and coordinate ... episodes of problem solving. (p. 186)

The ubiquity of the varieties of these created environmental structures, and the implications for psychological theory of their presence in our everyday life, are considered in chapter 9.

Common Roots of Behavior Setting Theory and Dynamic Systems Theory

Barker's account of behavior settings is a remarkable early example of systems thinking applied to psychological phenomena. As noted earlier, systems thinking was very much in the air when Barker was formulating his theoretical framework. Significantly, Barker's training prepared him to be receptive to this approach. Recall that the roots of Barker's work rest in Lewin's psychology (see chap. 7), and at least one team of contemporary dynamic systems theorists have suggested that some of the roots of dynamic systems thinking can be found in Lewin's psychology (Thelen & Smith, 1994):

> Lewin was a true systems theorist. In order to understand behavior, Lewin claimed, "the person and his environment have to be considered as *one* constellation of interdependent factors" (1946, p. 793). A given physical setting has meaning only as a function of the state of the individual in that setting. Conversely, individual traits do not exist outside of the settings in which they are displayed. Thus, the goal in explaining behavior is to ... discover the function that links behavior to that life space. (pp. 320–321)

Lewin proposed that an individual's behavior can be predicted as a function of the combined influence of that person's motivational state and the perceived features of the environment. Behavior is the net effect of the set of vectors in the life space.

Moreover, Lewin's program was a dynamic theory not only in the sense that he adopted an emphasis on outcomes of multiple interactions, but also because he gave great emphasis to the individual's developmental history in determining how environmental features were experienced in the life space, and how the life space itself changes over time (see Thelen & Smith, 1994, pp. 313–314, 320–321). In so doing, the life space considered at any given time is but a momentary slice, or a cross-section, of a dynamic, developmental trajectory (see Lewin, 1946/1951c, pp. 244–248).

Because they share these common roots, recent work in dynamic systems thinking is a natural platform for further advances in behavior setting theory. Developments in ecobehavioral science can profitably continue on this course, while avoiding the blind alleys offered by representational concepts, such as plans, programs, scripts, and cause maps.

Conclusions

Explicating the dynamic systems framework in Barker's approach succeeds in bringing his work and Gibson's closer together. In addition to the nonrepresentational character of most dynamic systems models, this approach meshes quite comfortably with other aspects of Gibson's ecological psychology. Indeed, there is much fruitful cross-talk and collaboration among investigators with ties in each area (e.g., see Fogel, 1993; Goldfield, 1995; and the volumes edited by Dent-Read & Zukow-Goldring, 1997, and Port & van Gelder, 1995).

Although Heider's analysis of "thing and medium" accounts for much of the compatibility of two ecological programs from a historical vantage point, dynamic systems theory adds additional and valuable cohesion between the two programs in their mature forms. The operations of behavior settings, like perceiving-acting systems, involve the dynamic, reciprocal influences constituting a complex system. As such, behavior settings, like perceiving-acting systems, cannot be understood by looking within one facet of the system, but instead by considering dynamic structure distributed across and indeed, generated by the system in question.

The critical difference between the two ecological programs—and the difference that must be preserved—is their grain of analysis. Gibson's psychology takes the perceiver–environment relation as its unit of analysis; and it is Barker's unique contribution to have discovered an ecological structure that operates at an extra-individual level. Jointly, they offer a more complete view of the domain of ecological psychology than either does alone.

Finally, in fairness to Barker and his co-workers, it is important to restate that the goal here has been to bring his views and Gibson's together in a coherent, multilevel ecological framework. In doing so, some modifications are proposed in Barker's position that may not have been acceptable to him or to some presently working within his framework. For various reasons, they may prefer to retain some of the Gestalt and Brunswikian constructivist features that this discussion has attempted to eliminate. In the end, ecobehavioral scientists may prefer to align themselves with Lewin and Brunswik than with Gibson. If so, the synthesis I envisioned here may not be one that they find acceptable.

CODA: THE INTERSECTING CAREER PATHS OF GIBSON, BARKER, AND HEIDER

In the interest of drawing some historical connections, it is worthwhile to consider, if only briefly, parallels and intersections in the careers of Gibson and Barker. The two knew one another at a personal level (Sommer, 1994), and Gibson was familiar with Barker's work.[19] But curiously there are very few cross-citations to each other's writings, and there is no evidence that Gibson and Barker influenced each other to any degree. What then accounts for the striking commonalities among their theories? A partial answer to this question is the common intellectual link provided by Fritz Heider and, in a more general vein, the Gestalt tradition. Moreover, in the interest of the historical record, it is noteworthy that both of them knew Heider quite well both personally and professionally.

Gibson and Heider were faculty colleagues at Smith College for many years, and James and Eleanor Gibson and Fritz and Grace Heider were personal friends (Heider, 1983). The Gibsons left Smith College for Cornell in 1949. Around this same time, the Heiders were recruited by Barker to join the psychology department at University of Kansas, which he was hired to reorganize (Barker, 1979).

One further professional connection is significant to point out. In 1965, Heider was selected to receive the American Psychological Association's Award for Distinguished Scientific Contribution. The five-person selection committee was composed of previous recipients. Its chair was James Gibson, and three of the remaining four members included Roger Barker and Wolfgang Köhler (the other two were Henry Murray and Carl Pfaffman). The citation for Heider's award began and ended with the following statements, which Heider (1989, p. 153) attributed to Gibson:

> For his trailblazing thoughts about the fundamentals of perception, and for seeing problems that others did not recognize. Long ago he showed us the puzzle of the relations of things to their stimuli. ... Working within a long view

---

[19]I know from conversations with Gibson in 1975 that he was aware of Barker's work and thought highly of it.

of history and a wide view of science, he has provided grist for the mills of many experimenters and polish for the theoretical machinery of many thinkers. (American Psychological Association, 1965, p. 1080)

Gibson and Barker were two thinkers for whose work Heider evidently provided considerable "polish."

Ecological Knowledge and Sociocultural Processes

Any line drawn between organism and environment will have to be drawn elsewhere in terms of inquiry. For the purposes of inquiry [i.e., understanding the nature of knowing processes], the skin is not a very good indicator of where the organism stops and the environment begins. (Hickman, 1992, p. 43)

One of the goals of the chapters comprising Parts II and III has been to explicate within the context of Gibson's and Barker's ecological programs the radical empiricist claim that the environment considered relative to the individual possesses structure. It is now time to make a start at enlarging consideration of this claim beyond the issues explicitly treated by these two ecological programs. Doing so extends the analysis of the environment offered here, and it also provides a broader context within which to view ecological psychology.

One way to do this, while remaining consistent with the framework developed thus far, is to pick up a path of ideas that early on branched off from James's psychology and pragmatism. This is the path developed by Dewey and Mead, among others, emphasizing the fundamentally social nature of human existence. This path is followed for a brief distance here, but not by examining Dewey's or Mead's writings specifically.[1] Although doing so is a very worthwhile project, it would detract from the broader goals at this point. Instead, the focus is on more recent discussions in the

---

[1] Noble (1981) made a useful start in exploring the connections between Dewey and Mead, on the one hand, and Gibson's ecological approach to meaning, on the other.

psychological and social science literature in order to continue widening the scope of contextual factors that are essential to an ecological perspective.

The previous chapter explored some of the relations between Gibson's ecological psychology and Barker's analysis of behavior settings. This chapter considers these two ecological programs, and in particular the related issues of environmental structure and environmental meaning, against the broader backdrop of sociocultural processes. But first, some preliminary comments are needed to set the stage for that discussion.

ECOLOGICAL KNOWLEDGE

The environment is meaningful. We directly experience an environment of meaningful objects, of meaningful events, of meaningful places, of meaningful social actions, and of meaningful institutions.

The claim that the environment is meaningful might seem simple enough to some readers, but taken literally and with our intellectual history as a backdrop, it is loaded with difficulties. This is because from the point of view that has dominated psychology's intellectual past, the idea of a "meaningful environment" is an oxymoron.

To backtrack just a bit and cover some ground examined earlier (Part I), historically the environment has been conceptualized primarily from the Cartesian–Newtonian standpoint, and in that framework the environment is literally meaningless. This is because from that standpoint it is a material world, and just as there is no place for colors, sounds, smells, and tastes in the domain of matter, so too there is no place for meaning. Simply put, matter does not possess the quality of meaning. For this reason, the meaning that can be found in experience of environments, like sensory qualities, must by default be located in and limited to a subjective, psychological domain that is distinct and separate from the domain of the material world. In the Cartesian–Newtonian universe, meaning is, by definition, excluded from the world.

This perspective then leads to a view that the sensory qualities and meanings individuals experience are shut up in so many separate, isolated minds. Such a view brings to the foreground the differences between the experiences of individual perceivers, and indeed it offers an avenue for understanding some of these very real differences. But at the same time, it falls rather short in accounting for what is common in our experiences. And surely any analysis of social processes, and of culture more generally, requires coming to grips with the grounds for interpersonally shared experiences.

If individuals' experiences are as insulated from one another as the received view portrays, then collective actions become largely a matter of separate individuals' private constructions of social reality coinciding sufficiently to admit some minimal degree of social coordination. This kind of a picture is implicit in the social cognition approach of much contemporary psychology and social science. Individuals' social understanding would appear to run on so many separate tracks. Presumably there is sufficient commonality in these individual conceptualizations that when each is separately projected onto the world, a common social structure is realized.

Of course, no one puts the matter quite this baldly. But if a constructivist account is followed up to the level of collective social structures, this is the picture that emerges. And on its face, such an account of social processes should seem wildly implausible. (The extent to which it does not testifies to the influence of traditional physical science concepts on psychological thinking.) For could the order in our complex, shared environment rest on contingent relations arising from parallel but separate and individualized social constructions of reality? If so, cultural processes and social structures, requiring as they do social coordination and shared understanding, would then be a hit-or-miss affair being grounded in a multitude of separate psychological experiences that somehow come together in a reasonably coherent and consistent manner. From this view, the complex social coordination within human societies, not to mention the shared social knowledge, would be nothing short of miraculous.

As should be obvious at this point in the discussion, a dichotomy between a meaningless material world and a subjective, meaningful psychological realm is not the only way to conceptualize this array of issues. It may appear to be the only way to do so because of patterns of thinking growing out of our dominant intellectual heritage. An alternative to this approach was presented earlier—an alternative grounded in the relational metaphysics of Jamesian radical empiricism, and supplemented by Gibson's account of ecological optics. From this perspective, the problem of perceived meanings in experience takes on a different form, giving rise to a psychology that locates much that is meaningful for individuals in a relational, and yet independent, shared environment. In turn, the discussion of behavior setting theory in the immediately preceding chapters prepares the way for a consideration of shared, extra-individual psychological structures of the environment.

The present chapter expands this discussion of meaningful features of a common environment. These meaningful features, while being *products* of individual and collective action, are at the same time fundamental to and *constitutive of* individual knowledge. To put the point more simply, individual knowledge grows out of social processes and sociohistorical contexts.

As just suggested, one reason that it is justifiable to say that the environment is comprised of meaningful objects, meaningful events, meaningful places, meaningful social actions, meaningful social institutions, among other things, is because in large measure, collectively and historically, these features of the shared environment have been created by us. This is not say that meanings have been imposed on an otherwise meaningless environment. Rather we engage a meaningful environment of affordances and refashion some aspects of them. Some basic features of the terrestrial environment (e.g., ground surfaces, graspable and liftable objects, and water) have functional meanings for a perceiver apart from social processes (although this is not to say that these affordances are necessarily learned apart from social processes). By far the most abundant meaningful features of the environment are those shaped out of the materials of the environment and through coordinated social actions. In many of these cases, some of the things we have come to understand about the effects of certain actions on the environment we have subsequently built into environmental structures themselves. These latter constructed embodiments of what is known—which include tools, artifacts, representations, social patterns of action, and institutions—can be called *ecological knowledge*.

The various forms of ecological knowledge convey many individual and collective discoveries, and their production is an ongoing, cumulative process. Much of what we know, and what we need to know and need to share with each other, is woven into the public fabric of our sociocultural world. And it is well that this is so. For expanding what is taken to be knowledge to include its ecological embodiments—that is, recognizing the public nature of 'ecological knowledge'—significantly enlarges our potential as individuals and as societies of individuals. Indeed, ecological knowledge may be one of the factors that lies at the heart of what it means to be a cultural animal.

THE ECOLOGY OF CULTURE

The Historical Nature of Psychological Development

Cultural systems are ongoing, dynamic processes into which each individual is born. The environment individuals find themselves at the start of life is a product of the history of social activities preceding their existence. Each individual enters a world whose meaningful features have already been constructed and designed, and whose social meanings as expressed through individual and collective actions are already in place. As individuals learn about these environmental structures, they in turn (intentionally or not) sustain these products of prior generations' activities through their actions, and sometimes they contribute to their transformation.

This point of view itself has a history, traceable at least to the writings of Marx, as reflected in the often quoted aphorism, "Men make their own history, but they do not make it just as they please ... but under circumstances directly encountered, given and transmitted from the past" (quoted in McLellan, 1975, p. 43). This perspective has received considerable attention by many in contemporary sociological theory, perhaps most notably by Giddens (1984), who proposed the concept of "structuration" to refer to this feature of social processes. Structuration conveys the notion that collective social processes produce social structures, which themselves function as the context for and are constituent of ongoing social processes. There is a "duality of structure" (Shotter, 1983) in the sense that "the structural properties of social systems are both medium and outcome of the practices they recursively organize" (p. 25). Giddens emphasized that as a medium for social processes, social systems both constrain and enable particular social processes—and it should be added, they have the same bearing on psychological possibilities.

This perspective has also been explored by Bourdieu (1977), but in ways that differ somewhat from Giddens' analysis. Bourdieu conceptualized individual psychological functioning as a system of dispositions to act (*"habitus"*), which has been brought into existence by structures constituting the individual's "material conditions of existence" (p. 72). In spite of whatever differences exist between Giddens, Bourdieu, and others working in a related vein,[2] all share the perspective that individuals find themselves in a world that has been structured by their predecessors and they in turn tend to sustain.

It would be difficult to overestimate the psychological significance of this circumstance. It means that the environment into which each person is born is already highly structured, instead of being relatively formless or at best inherently probabilistic in character.[3] If either of the latter conditions were the case, psychological development would necessarily involve the development of cognitive processes that impose some order on what is otherwise a perceptual flux. Earlier chapters have already considered some of the difficulties this point of view poses for an account

---

[2]One of the critical differences between Giddens' and Bourdieu's analyses concerns the question of agency. Even while he stressed the routine or habitual nature of much social behavior ("practical consciousness"), Giddens admitted a place for individual agency in the context of participating in social structures. In contrast, Bourdieu's view of "habitus" as "systems of durable transposable *dispositions*" (p. 72) suggests a greater degree of automaticity and constraint.

[3]In truth, two separate issues are being conflated here for the purpose of emphasis. The claims that (a) the environment is there as a background for each individual from the start of life, and (b) the stimulus information for perceiving this environment is highly structured rather than probabilistically organized, are logically separable assertions. But, at the same time, it can be argued that the long-standing tendency for psychologists to assume perceiving is an inferential process based on probabilistic cues has had the reverse effect of obscuring the preexisting order of the environment from the point of view of individual processes.

of complex social processes. But if the psychological environment is already structured, then much of life would be a process of discovering meaning in our surroundings rather than imposing meaning on it. That is, if the environment "always already" has preexisting or latent structure, then much of our cognitive development would entail becoming attuned to these existing structures as we selectively engage some structures rather than others. Taken broadly, the claim that the environment has preexisting, latent structure that individuals selectively engage, of course, is one of the essential tenets of James's philosophy of radical empiricism.

This preexisting structure, considered from the point of view of sociocultural processes, has its own special complexities. Because histories are, in large measure, local (i.e., because structures in the environment tend to be localized to delimitable, geographical regions with their own historical course of events), the circumstances into which different individuals are born will differ in either small or substantial ways as a function of where and when their development transpires. Studies of psychological differences across cultures and the presence of cohort effects within cultures testify to this point. But, at the same time, local regions are not always sharply insulated from one another. Communication processes operate to diffuse information across geographical locales and across historical time, and design processes that blur regional differences are growing at unprecedented rates. Moreover, some universal properties of our common econiche, such as certain invariants in nature (e.g., the diurnal cycle, the horizon), are preserved in the design of settings and provide aspects of a common framework.

The preexisting structure of the environment is complex in another way. As discussed previously, structure within any locale or region is vast and rich, being multiple, layered, and dynamic. In principle, local structure is inexhaustible. So to claim that cognitive development entails, in part, becoming attuned to preexisting structures of the environment by selectively engaging those structures is not to describe a process with a terminus. It is open-ended, myriad in its branches, and lifelong. And through their actions, individuals can create new environmental structures while they transform or eliminate (through design or neglect) existing ones.

Evolving in the Midst of Culture

The preceding viewpoint differs from standard thinking in psychology in two ways: First, it presents individual cognitive development as a process of discovering environmental structure rather than of imposing mental structure on the everyday world. Second, it attributes greater significance than is usually done in psychology to the fact that from the outset of life,

each individual develops in relation to a background of sociocultural artifacts and processes. And more than this, it points to the possibility that the
human species evolved in the presence of sociocultural processes.

There has been a notable shift over the last half century in the social
sciences concerning how the relation between biological and cultural
evolution is viewed. This shift has been surprisingly slow in catching on in
psychology. For much of the previous century, if cultural factors were
considered at all in psychology, it was held that humans are first and
primarily biological creatures, and superadded onto this biological base
are the outcomes of cultural experiences. From this perspective, *Homo
sapiens* appeared as biological entities with expanded capacities for
development; and subsequently, the species extended its reach through
the development of culture. That is, the contributions of culture to human
psychological makeup have typically been viewed as a veneer atop a
constellation of biologically based tendencies, predispositions, and
instincts. Hence, culture is seen as a somewhat late happening in human
evolutionary history, being a product of humans' invention primarily
through the development of tools and language. In short, the evolution of
human's biological and psychological makeup is often seen as occurring
somewhat independent of and prior to the appearance of culture. In this
view, our common humanity derives from a shared biology, which in turn
is attributable to a shared evolutionary history.

The presence of a common biological foundation for psychological
processes is incontestable. What is at issue, however, is the relation
between biological and sociocultural processes. To put the matter in
perhaps a somewhat oversimplified manner, do sociocultural factors
essentially add a layer of sociality onto a fully formed biological being? Or
do sociocultural factors play a more constitutive, humanizing role than
that in development?

In recent decades, many in the field of cultural anthropology have
adopted an evolutionary perspective to argue strenuously against the
viewpoint that humans are foremost biological creatures and secondarily
social. The seminal analyses in this transformation are those of Geertz,
perhaps most notably his essay "The Impact of the Concept of Culture on
the Concept of Man" (Geertz, 1973). He identified the traditional approach
to understanding human nature as positing an underlying, common
biological core, whereas the differences found among individuals consist
of "mere accretions, distortions even, overlaying and obscuring what is
truly human" (p. 35). Such a view preserves the possibility of identifying, if
only through abstraction, some set of universal characteristics that is the
essence of human nature. Geertz argued, however, that such an exercise
of isolating a human core stripped of cultural influences is a logical
impossibility. Indeed, "to draw such a line [between human nature and

culture] is to falsify the human situation, or at least to misrender it seriously" (p. 36). This is because the human species evolved against a background of cultural processes and artifacts already in place. "What this means is that culture, rather than being added on, so to speak, to a finished or virtually finished animal, was ingredient, and centrally ingredient, *in the production of the animal itself*" (p. 47, emphasis added). For this reason, humans independent of culture are literally inconceivable. Rather than "noble savages," people would be "unworkable monstrosities with very few useful instincts, fewer recognizable sentiments, and no intellect: mental basket cases" (p. 49). Cultural and biological processes are functionally intertwined, as individuals' experiences in a particular cultural setting "finishes" them into encultured human beings with specific qualities. Absent of cultural structures, humans remain unconstrained, unchanneled potential. It is in interaction with these extra-genetic and extra-somatic structures that individuals' actions and thoughts take form:

> Undirected by culture patterns ... man's behavior would be virtually ungovernable, a mere chaos of pointless acts and exploding emotions, his experience virtually shapeless. Culture, the accumulated totality of such patterns, is not just an ornament of human existence but—the principal basis of its specificity—an essential condition of it. (Geertz, 1973, p. 46)

This viewpoint has been referred to as the "incompleteness thesis" (J. Miller, 1999), and it is supported by work in recent decades in archaeology and in the study of primate behavior and cognition.

Accumulating evidence from the archaeological record indicates that cultural processes were among the preconditions for the evolution of modern humans. It appears that the presence of some form of cultural processes preceded the emergence of *Homo sapiens*. Forms of cultural activity, or at least proto-cultural activity, predate human evolution and were pervasive features of earlier stages of hominid development. This claim is based on evidence of stone tool-making beginning with *Homo habilis* (beginning from 2.5 to 1.5 million years ago). The tools of this period have a degree of consistency in size, shape, and composition, often with one side flaked into a sharp edge for cutting or scraping. More advanced tool-making techniques are found in connection with *Homo erectus* sites (around 1.5 million years ago). These later tools are somewhat symmetrical with a double edge, thereby adding other functions, such as serving as a hand-axe or a spear when attached to a bone or wood. Further evidence of cultural processes among *Homo erectus* are indications of communal patterns of living (e.g., camp sites). Also, the widespread migration of *Homo erectus* throughout the Eurasian continent points to effective social communication and coordination among this ancestor of *Homo sapiens*. (See reviews by Cole, 1996, chap. 6; Diamond, 1992, chap. 2; Donald, 1991, chap. 6; Megarry, 1995, chaps. 6–7).

In addition to historical evidence, the documentation of tool use and social reciprocation among present-day chimpanzees of West and Central Africa, who share a nearly identical genetic makeup with humans, is evidence for the likelihood that proto-cultural patterns existed apart from and prior to human evolution (McGrew, 1992). Arguably, the observed activities can be appropriately called cultural or proto-cultural because they are not simply inherited species-specific traits. In many instances, geographically isolated groups of chimpanzees develop some distinctive tools and techniques reflecting adjustment to local ecological conditions that are transmitted across generations (McGrew, 1998).

In short, both the archaeological record of earlier hominid societies and contemporary field studies of closely related nonhuman primates suggest that forms of cultural processes were already in place before the appearance of modern *Homo sapiens* (around 40,000 years ago). This means the human species evolved with cultural processes as a backdrop. Or perhaps more accurately stated, humans co-evolved with cultural structures.

What does it mean to say that human beings co-evolved with cultural structures? In the emergence of the species, particular psychological functions, and their biological foundations, were selected for because they enabled individuals to function more effectively in the context of the proto-cultural processes already in place, and reciprocally, the actions of individuals sustained these social processes. In other words, culture is "not merely as a product of evolution but is itself a selective factor in the evolutionary process" (J. Miller, 1999, p. 87).

The specific psychological characteristics selected for, and consequently, the relation between biological and sociocultural factors during ontogenetic development, are the grounds for much current debate. The so-called evolutionary psychologists have proposed that domain- specific mechanisms evolved in support of particular adaptive demands. The result is a set of heritable cognitive modules dedicated to specific functions, such as face recognition and language acquisition (Buss, 1995; Pinker, 1994; Tooby & Cosmides, 1992). These domain-specific mechanisms are hypothesized to have evolved in relation to particular environmental features, they are highly canalized during ontogenetic development, and thus they are not constituted by environmental features over an individual's lifetime. The presence of appropriate environmental conditions are needed, to be sure, but these conditions contribute variously as triggering mechanisms, or as patterns needed to sustain responses present at birth, or by filling out surface details in what otherwise are biologically well-formed capacities.

This position can be criticized on several grounds. Most pertinent to the present context is the argument advanced by Tomasello (1999a, 1999b) that the comparatively short time period over which modern humans evolved (500,000 years by some estimates) makes the natural selection of so many distinct, domain-specific modules of cognition implausible. Alternatively, a viewpoint more congenial to the ecological approach proposed here is that cultural processes and products, in interaction with biological potentials, are constitutive factors in human ontogenetic development. Humans evolved as a species against a backdrop of culture, and humans develop individually over the course of their lives against such a backdrop as well. Humanity is only fully manifested in the presence of constitutive sociocultural factors.[4]

This viewpoint needs to be developed further. If the enormous phenotypic psychological and social differences plainly evident between humans and our closest nonhuman primate relatives are not due to something like highly canalized domain-specific mechanisms, then how are these differences to be explained? Consider a few of the factors that jointly have contributed to this gap, which has grown wider over time.

First, in light of the close genetic similarity, it is likely that the differences between human and nonhuman (proto-) cultures is more than solely the product of two different biological blueprints. Sociocultural factors themselves must directly contribute in a formative manner, both ontogentically and cumulatively through cultural evolution, to the enormous gap between the related species. This is not to deny biological differences, however. The question that needs to be addressed is what biologically based cognitive difference(s) between humans and nonhuman primates contribute(s) to these phenotypic differences?

Considering, as the evidence indicates, an increasing complexity in sociocultural processes among *Homo habilis* and *erectus*, subsequent

---

[4]This difference in viewpoint cannot simply be reduced to a disagreement between nativists and empiricists, respectively. Neither nativism nor empiricism offers more than a caricature of the respective positions. Indeed, it would be difficult to find any contemporary psychologist who does not embrace some form of interactionism. Virtually all psychologists are interactionists in this conceptual sense.But, in practice, the picture is a little different. In many discussions that recur throughout the past century and into the present one, following the opening caveats about environment-biology interaction, the environment is typically given far less emphasis as an influence on development than heredity. In part this is because comparatively little attention has been given to the nature of the environment from a psychological perspective. Redressing this shortcoming is, of course, one of the goals of the present work.

The complexity that is the dynamic interaction of biological and environmental/sociocultural factors over time must be fully recognized. Although all sides in these debates need to avoid creating "straw persons" through caricatures of others' positions, at the same time they need to beware of "the mirage of simplification and [embrace] the vision of complexity in biological reality" (Herrmann, 1998, p. 125).

selection pressures on cognitive skills accompanying the emergence of these sociocultural processes is possible. But if not numerous domain-specific modules (given the relatively short time period over which modern humans evolved), it might be expected that "a small difference that made a big difference—some adaptation, or small set of adaptations, ... changed the process of primate cognitive evolution in fundamental ways" (Tomasello, 1999a, p. 510). In order to take advantage of the existing (proto-) cultural structures, and in so doing promote the coordination and the sharing of acquired knowledge especially between successive generations, some general cognitive facility may have been selected for such that it became more readily available for humans in comparison to nonhuman primates.

What might this "small difference that made a big difference be"? Reconsider the overall conceptualization of knowing offered in James's radical empiricism. Recall that the starting point of an analysis of knowing from this perspective is an environment rich in potential structure that is available to a knower who engages this environment selectively. Selectivity is the hallmark of knowing processes, according to James. Perhaps contributing to the differences observed is a modification in the processes of selectivity such that the individual's potential for discovering functionally significant, environmental information is extensively enhanced.

Following Tomasello (1999a, 1999b), all primates (as well as other mammals) can be viewed as selectively engaging the environment in a "dyadic" fashion—that is, at any given moment as establishing a relation between self and an inanimate environmental object, or as establishing a relation between self and a conspecific. Humans, however, have a facility for establishing a "triadic" relation that includes the self, another person, and what that other person is selectively engaging. From this vantage point, the other can be understood as an entity with intentions. Thus, although we share with other nonhuman primates the property of being intentional agents, selectively engaging features of the environment, we may be distinctive in how readily we are able to perceive others as intentional agents.[5] In this way, the individual can begin to comprehend the purposes for which the other is engaging an object; and in turn and importantly, it becomes possible to learn about properties of the environment through another person's actions.

This development increases enormously the possibilities for learning about the environment. Through such "joint attention," the learner is directed by another's actions to attend to particular features of the

---

[5]Empirical support for this claim is provided by Povinelli (e.g., Povinelli, Bierschwale, & Cech, 1999; Reaux, Theall, & Povinelli, 1999) whose research suggests that although juvenile chimpanzees, like human children, will follow the gaze of an experimenter, the chimpanzees do not appear to understand the other's gaze as reflecting an intentional action.

environment, and through this means the functional properties of objects are exhibited (Fogel, 1993; Rogoff, 1990). Thus, certain features of the environment are identified as particularly pertinent to the conduct of some goal-directed action and the affordances of those features are revealed. Further, because more experienced others can also view learners as intentional agents, they can make explicit efforts to demonstrate how to skillfully engage features of the environment.

There is evidence that this quality of functioning is rather basic to human processes, as revealed by how early its precursors appear in development and how robust they are. Researchers differ as to precisely when joint attention appears (the differences probably being a matter of the criteria employed), but all agree that it is well-established by the end of the first year (Butterworth, 1995; Corkhum & Moore, 1995; Tomasello, 1995). Further, humans seem to be unique in their efforts to explicitly demonstrate and instruct others, especially the young (Tomasello, 1999b, chap. 2), although there remains some debate over this claim in the comparative psychology literature.

However, to reiterate, it is not simply a cognitive difference that distinguishes the learning patterns of humans and closely related nonhuman primates. As argued earlier, there are also significant differences in the typical sociocultural resources available in the human and the nonhuman primate environment. The availability of these sociocultural resources themselves may play a direct constitutive role in ontogenetic development. When chimpanzees are reared by humans, they engage in more acts resembling joint attention than mother-reared chimpanzees (Carpenter, Tomasello, & Savage-Rumbaugh, 1995). Further, the ability of these enculturated chimpanzees to learn object manipulation through imitation appears to be comparable to human children, in contrast to chimpanzees reared by their mothers (Tomasello, Savage-Rumbaugh, & Kruger, 1993). Most of these enculturation experiences involved extensive contact with humans and exposure to some kind of symbolic communication system in a laboratory setting. Thus, the presence of even a modicum of sociocultural resources makes a developmental difference. Add to these findings those few documented cases of the adverse consequences of children reared under conditions of extreme environmental and social deprivation, and it would seem that "a human-like sociocultural environment is an essential component in the development of human-like social-cognitive and imitative learning skills … [and] this is true not only for chimpanzees but also for human beings" (Tomasello, 1999a, p. 525).

One of the more compelling arguments for the biological determination of psychological functions, with environmental factors playing a relatively minor finishing role, is the presence of some common psychological attributes across cultures. What is often neglected in this position—and in fact, what has received little attention—is the possibility that there are common features of the sociocultural environment (i.e., "a human-like sociocultural environment") in place in all human cultures. Indeed, that is partially why they are recognizably human cultures. Thus, it is possible that the universal characteristics seen among humans in various domains are attributable to an interaction of biological and constitutive environmental factors.[6]

The earlier assertion that sociocultural processes are both a product of individuals' actions and serve as a background for the constitution of those individual actions (the "duality of structure") should be clearer now. From this starting point, what is especially of interest from an ecological perspective is a detailed characterization of the background sociocultural/ environmental resources.

The remainder of this chapter begins to illuminate some of the psychologically relevant features of this background of resources. In doing so, it considers in turn two of the distinctive characteristics of human cultures: the facility for transmitting knowledge across generations, and the potential for complex collective social actions. In each case, the primary focus is on the ways in which knowledge can be embodied in environmental features and the significance of these ecological manifestations of knowledge.

TOOLS, ARTIFACTS, AND REPRESENTATIONS

In order for the gains of any generation to be transmitted to successive generations, and thereby create the possibility for these gains to be developed further, some means of cross-generational sharing of knowledge must be available. The previous section pointed to a few processes that make this possible, such as learning through observing the intentional actions of others and the explicit demonstration of some knowledge or technique to a learner. One or the other (or both) of these means can be illustrated by Boesch's (1991) observation of young chimpanzees' learning from their elders to use a stone as a hammer to crack nuts. However, these means of cross-generational transmission, based as they are on the direct social exchange between two individuals, have significant limitations.

For one thing, if the sharing of acquired knowledge is possible only through direct social exchange between two individuals, this knowledge is very fragile. If, for example, one generation for some reason failed to learn a particular technique from its elders, the chain of transmission would be broken and the knowledge gains lost. In order for knowledge

---

[6]In the domain of language, Tomasello (1995) advanced this argument.

gains to have a better chance to survive over time in the culture, the exchange of knowledge must take forms that are not solely dependent on immediate social transmission. A solution to this problem is to develop techniques for preserving knowledge gains in "extra-somatic forms" that is, to develop embodiments of the knowledge among features of the environment itself apart from any individual. Such advances in knowledge exchange would have a "ratcheting effect" (Tomasello, 1995), promoting the possibility that any gains made could be maintained for a while, even in the face of the fragility of memory and the brevity of any individual life.

Moreover, the extra-somatic preservation of knowledge gains facilitates the accumulation and accretion of knowledge over multiple generations. If knowledge gains can be transmitted only through direct social exchange, then the possibility of the accumulation of knowledge over time would be remote. Only so much information could be communicated in this way. The development of techniques for preserving knowledge extra-somatically—that is, the development of forms of *ecological knowledge*—greatly enlarges the possibilities. No doubt this sociocultural factor contributes to the enormous gap between human and nonhuman societies.

Consider two cultural advances that drastically altered the possibilities of knowledge transfer, knowledge preservation, and knowledge accretion: first, the manufacture of relatively durable tools and artifacts that have information relevant to some task built into their structure; and second, the creation of means to express information symbolically in such a way that it can be preserved in some relatively durable form as a representation.[7] In both cases, what has transpired is that information becomes built into durable features of the environment. One result of these developments is that the background conditions of sociocultural information against which individual lives unfold become vastly expanded. Now individual development can transpire in relation to the gains of multiple prior generations, rather than relying solely on what one's immediate, living predecessors and cohorts can communicate.

Found Tools and Artifacts

Whereas it was once thought that humans are the only species to use tools, it is now clear that this is not the case. A variety of species utilize tools. Which species are to be included among this group will vary somewhat depending on what criteria are used to define a tool. Are the materials used in nest building by birds to be counted as tools? Are the branches used in lodge construction by beavers? What about the stones used by

---

[7]One category of processes being omitted here that plays an essential role in the transmission of some forms of knowledge across successive generations is ritual, broadly construed.

chimpanzees to catch ants or crack nuts? Or what about the branches used by elephants to swat flies? And so on. For present purposes, there is little to be gained by wading into such treacherous waters as to define what counts as a tool.

It will be more fruitful to employ a distinction offered by Ingold (1993) between *tools* and *artifacts*: "A tool, in the most general sense, is an object that extends the capacity of an agent to operate within a given environment; an artefact is an object shaped to some pre-existent conception of form" (p. 433). Ingold was proposing here a distinction between materials (tools) that have not been designed by an individual for a particular purpose, but instead have been selected for the purpose of extending action possibilities, and designed materials (artifacts) that have been explicitly fashioned with their role in carrying out some task in mind. "Found tools" might be an apt description of the former, and there are instances of the use of these by various species of animal. Dawkin's (1982) notion of "extended phenotype" might be appropriately applied to some of these cases. Artifacts, in contrast, are unique to human societies.

Tools, that is, found tools, are identified and selected because of the suitability of their affordance properties in support of some action. Long grasses or stripped branches employed as probes in feeding at insect nests; broad, rigid leaves used to shovel insects into the mouth; stones used as hammers for cracking hard shells of nuts are examples. What these cases clearly illustrate is that the critical features are in these circumstances the affordances of the materials relative to some task. Only grasses that are sufficiently long, sufficiently rigid, and graspable can be employed as a tool for eating. Sticks that are relatively straight and contain few branches are most useful for digging and probing the ground (Sugiyama, 1995). Leaves for eating need to be of an appropriate size and rigidity. Stones for hammering must be graspable, liftable, and resilient. In short, animals that use materials for a range of purposes, from building materials to sponging liquid, are typically exploiting the affordance properties of these materials (Reed, 1993). These affordances have functional significance in a particular niche, and found tools are one source of meaningful information in the environment for an animal.

What then is the difference between an affordance and a tool? Following the analysis offered by L. van Leeuwen, Smitsman, and C. Van Leeuwen (1994), a tool has a higher-order affordance structure. Whereas affordances refer to a relation between an agent and a feature of the environment, such that the relation is one of functional compatibility or fittedness, a tool refers to two functional compatibilities: a relation between an agent and the tool and a relation between the tool and the task. To illustrate this point, for a branch to function as a tool for a chimpanzee to probe a termite nest, the physical dimensions of the branch must be within a range whereby it can be grasped and wielded by the individual, and its physical dimensions must be such that it can be inserted into the nest to a sufficient depth. For a branch to serve as this sort of tool, it must have this dual or higher order affordance structure.

It can be seen that although the properties of tools, like those of affordances, exist in the environment apart from any users, they are relational features defined relative to certain tasks and users. (This apparent contradiction between objective and subjective properties has been addressed earlier, primarily in Part II.) As independent objects, tools reside potentially within an individual–environment relation. They are environmental features that can become appropriated into the goal-directed action of the individual; and in doing so, they extend or amplify actions, and they alter the body's phenomenal boundary during their use. When properly handled, and when the task to which they are applied goes smoothly, tools have a "functional transparency." At these moments, their presence goes unnoticed. As has often been pointed out, perhaps most notably by Polanyi (1962), a tool such as a pen when in use is experienced as an extension of one's hand, and the pen as such is not noticed. In Heideggerian terms (Dreyfus, 1991), the tool is "ready-to-hand." Of course, a detached, reflective stance can be adopted toward a tool, experiencing it as an object possessing independent properties in the environment ("present-to-hand"). Accordingly, there are two ways that we interact with tools: as extensions of our own functional capacities and as objects apart from us. Many phenomenological theorists have attempted to sensitize us to the experience of tools as being "ready-to-hand," but their analysis goes little beyond description. Conceptualizing tools as having a higher order affordance structure is a first step in giving this observation a much needed analytical foundation.

Artifacts—"an object shaped to some pre-existent conception of form"—are ubiquitous in human cultures. The examples of artifacts in the contemporary Western world are seemingly endless, from hammers and saws, pens and printers, spectacles and microscopes, to cars and airplanes (Petroski, 1994).

As with any categorical distinction, the boundary between tool and artifact is fuzzy. Consider a branch used as a tool for probing: An animal may modify the branch slightly by, for example, stripping off petioles for more effective use. Thus, the absence of modification of an object by users cannot serve as a definitive criterion for classifying a tool. Inversely, sometimes because of their specific affordance properties, some designed tools can be used for purposes for which they were not originally intended (i.e., they are treated as found objects). For example, the (ubiquitous) stapler on my desk is presently holding a book open to a specific page (and I admit even to have used it on occasion to hammer a nail into the wall). The stapler is a designed object; its present use, however, is found.

Where then is the boundary between tools and artifacts? Recognizing that the boundary is indistinct, it may be prudent to loosen the criteria and adopt the view that objects can be designated as tools as opposed to artifacts when there has been a minimal degree of modification from their found state. Or perhaps it is better to conceptualize tools and artifacts as being located on a continuum of "use objects," with "found" and "designed" being its end points.

More important for the present discussion, tools and artifacts differ in other ways than merely being found versus designed. First, artifacts have a far greater potential to embody cumulative knowledge in their design than does a tool. Because an artifact has been designed to solve some specific problem (i.e., its designer had some task in mind for which the artifact was fitted), it could be said that this problem solution is built into the object. For example, embodied in the design of a pen is some set of previous discoveries about how one can make a trace on a surface. This point becomes clearer if one were faced with the circumstance of trying to reinvent a writing implement that leaves a trace rather than creates a gouge. Among the task problems that must be faced would be to determine what sorts of substances could be used that would remain in liquid form while in a reservoir of some sort, but would dry rather quickly when spread thinly; and what sort of instrument could be used to deliver the liquid to the surface readily, while at the same time could be manipulated easily. There are different ways to solve these problems, and the various designs of pens reflect different ways to do so. What is important from a psychological perspective is that once the necessary knowledge about how the task can be carried out is built into the design of the pen, a user of the tool does not need to think much about it. Indeed, the user may remain ignorant as to how the instrument operates. The user only needs to know how to operate it. And, if it is properly designed, then how to operate the tool should be fairly apparent (Norman, 1988). Its affordance should be easily perceived.

Thus, through the availability of artifacts, an individual is the beneficiary of discoveries and the implementation of these discoveries made by countless other, typically unknown individuals. The results of our predecessors' efforts enable us to function in our contemporary world in ways that would otherwise be difficult, if not impossible. Hutchins (1995) stated this property of artifacts thusly: "In the Western tradition, physical artifacts became repositories of knowledge, and they were constructed in durable media so that a single artifact might come to represent more than any individual could know" (p. 96).

Artifacts differ from tools in a second way. Tools typically extend or amplify the body's action: A stick as a probe extends one's reach, and a rock as a hammer amplifies the force of one's blow. In each case, the action involved may need to be modified, but it is not structurally different from the form it takes in its unembellished version. One is still probing and hammering. Artifacts, however, usually require an additional, new set of skills in order to be utilized. There is the operation that the artifact performs, but also there is the operation the user employs in using the artifact; and typically these two operations are not structurally isomorphic. This difference in operational structure exists because the artifact is designed to perform an operation that is difficult for the individual to carry out in its absence. From the user's standpoint, one operation—manipulation of the artifact—substitutes for another or, commonly, a set of others. The artifact allows the individual to trade off a difficult task for what is presumably a comparatively easier one.

Consider, for example, a hand calculator. In a literal sense, an individual does not actually do mathematical operations on a calculator (although it is true that some mathematical reasoning is required); rather, what one actually does is operate this instrument. The individual pushes particular keys in a particular order, and the calculations are performed by the instrument. The operations required to use the calculator are less demanding than most of the mathematical operations it performs. So, in most cases, the artifact transforms the task, altering what the individual needs to know:

> The problem that confronts [the individual] is usually not one of figuring out how to process the information in order to get an answer; that has already been worked out. The problem, in most instances, is simply to use the existing [artifacts] and techniques to process the information gathered by the system. (Hutchins, 1995, p. 21)

The individual does not need to understand how to do the task that the artifact performs. Indeed, understanding the latter has increasingly become the province of only the highly specialized. The skills needed in order to function competently in everyday life have changed radically over a comparatively short time, as complex or taxing operations have been "off-loaded" to our artifacts. Needless to say, the psychological consequences of these changes are potentially enormous, and to date they have been little studied.[8]

These broader issues aside, two points should be emphasized: The environment into which an individual is born is already rich in "use meanings" constituted by its available affordances, tools, and artifacts.

---

[8]The ways in which artifacts alter what we need to know became very clear to me a few years ago when I learned to my surprise that many my brightest undergraduate students are incapable of performing relatively simple mathematical calculations "in their heads"—calculations that a generation ago were commonplace for individuals with far fewer years of formal education. Needless to say, implications of the loss of such skills vary from merely inconvenient (e.g., when a cashier cannot make change when the register is down) to worthy of concern (e.g., as when some fundamental skills are possessed by an increasingly smaller number of individuals over time).

And in the case of artifacts, these use meanings are explicitly created, and through their design, artifacts preserve in some relatively durable way previous gains in knowledge. Artifacts embody things that humans know about the world and about our actions in relation to the world (Pea, 1993).

Finally, a connection can be made between this discussion of tools and artifacts to the comments in the previous section concerning learning through the actions of others as intentional agents. A great deal of our knowledge about tools and artifacts is no doubt acquired through others, who either explicitly instruct or guide the learner, or who through their own activities demonstrate object uses without necessarily intending to do so. In these cases, individuals perceive how tools and artifacts are used by others in the context of intentional actions. That the affordances of tools and artifacts are typically learned in this manner demonstrates how deeply embedded they are in social processes. This way of thinking about how the uses of tools and artifacts are learned has a potentially significant implication for the issue of *perceived meaning*. In observing their use by an intentional agent, learners "do not learn just what they can do with an object, they learn what the object is for" (Tomasello, 1999c, p. 159). That is, in addition to learning about how to use an object, the individual learns the meaning of the object itself within the practices of the culture. To the extent that this possibility has merit, it is an important step in understanding how objects take on *conventional or culturally prescribed meanings* beyond their immediate use functions.

An example may help to clarify this distinction: Whereas a particular goblet may afford drinking from—this is its immediate use function— conventionally it may never be used for this purpose because of its sacred place in a religious practice. Both the immediate use function, that is, the immediate affordance, and the conventional affordance are perceived in the same manner, namely, in the context of action. Consequently, from the perspective of a relational account of perceiving, both kinds of affordance are directly perceived (Heft, 1989).[9] Perhaps this approach to understanding how the conventional meanings of objects are learned can be extended to the meanings of symbols and representations generally (Tomasello, 1999c).

---

[9]Tomasello (1999a) referred to the former type as a "natural affordances" and the latter as an "intentional affordances." These designations may encourage a misreading of this distinction along the lines of a natural/cultural dichotomy, so "immediate versus conventional affordances" may be preferable, which corresponds to James's percept/concept distinction.

Representations

Forms of preservation of knowledge gains by social groups extend well beyond the use of artifacts as implements. A wide range of knowledge about aspects of daily life, about techniques, about the group's history and rituals, and so on, are developed and sustained over time in a variety of ways. Such knowledge can be maintained through the actions of group members, including verbal communication, which reproduce this information with sufficient regularity to maintain a collective memory. In the absence of some minimal frequency of recurrence, however, such as a periodic demonstration and communication about how to make and use a particular tool, or how to plan and coordinate some group action, the 'know-how' would simply be lost, dropping out of the group's collective repertoire. In such cases, the longevity of a group's knowledge would be determined by the relative durability of individuals' pooled biological memory.

Gradually, over long stretches of time, methods were devised to overcome the limitations of fragile, relatively short-lived biological memories and less dependent on continual social transmission. This was achieved by developing ways to store knowledge in the inanimate environment itself. The possibility of creating representations[10] that convey information about such things as how to manufacture and to use certain implements, when and where to plant, where to find food, what to eat and what not to eat, how to build shelters, how large one's inventory of resources are at any given time, how to carry out group rituals, and so on, provided a new stability to collective living. Knowledge gains preserved in less fragile forms than biological traces, for example, in the form of tallies, pictograms, maps, or alphanumerics could, in principle, remain accessible over a lifetime and indeed over generations (Olson, 1994). These systems for preserving collective knowledge are quite flexible, not even requiring a graphic system. For example, the Luba of Zaire construct "memory boards," or *lukasa*, which are wooden, hand-sized boards decorated with beads and shells representing in their design the group's history and the landscape (M. N. Roberts & A. F. Roberts, 1996).

Quite possibly, the development of techniques to preserve knowledge gains in extra-somatic forms, and thereby overcoming the constraints and the corrigibility of biological memory, has been the wellspring for the surge of cultural changes that have been witnessed in the West in fits and starts since at least the 3rd century B.C. (Donald, 1991) and growing exponentially since at least the 15th century (A. W. Crosby, 1997).

---

[10]The term *representation* is used explicitly here (as Gibson did), to refer to concrete features of the environment. Obviously, this usage differs from how this term is typically employed in contemporary psychology where it refers to a mental content.

Being able to create representations of what is known, rather than relying solely on biological memory, has advantages beyond the obvious one of greater durability. Significantly, in the form of a representation, knowledge gains become *publicly* accessible to a degree never before possible. Information that is publicly available in other than a transient way (as is orally communicated information) can be more thoroughly scrutinized; and, importantly, it can more readily accumulate as representations are layered atop older ones. These possibilities enabled humans to capitalize more than ever before on the cultural gains of their predecessors and thereby more self-consciously attempt to shape their future.

Having the psychological means to store information in the environment in these ways is fundamental to processes of cultural evolution. As Cole (1996) put it, with the appearance of these capacities in *Homo sapiens* "a teleological, Lamarckian system is embedded in a blind, Darwinian one" (p. 167). This possibility for change through the intentional transmission of "acquired characteristics" sets us apart from all other life forms. And, in recent years, the pace of cultural evolution has reached what seems to most of us, bewildering speed.

In what sense is it reasonable to refer to mundane representations such as lists or tallies as "knowledge"? Knowledge is generally considered something more elevated that individuals have or possess in some *intrinsic* sense. This notion of what it means to possess knowledge is far too restrictive, however, and in many cases it is inaccurate. To take a simple example, although I can attempt to remember a street address by rehearsing it until I no longer need it, I would be more prudent to write the address down on a scrap of paper. When I am rehearsing the address, holding it in working memory, conventionally it would be said that I know or possess this information. But what about once I write the address down? Typically, claims that one possesses particular knowledge are reserved for information that we can reproduce without any environmental supports, that is, "out of our heads." Surely, this way of speaking about knowledge in our possession is too limited. After all, as the present example indicates, practically speaking I "have" the information more securely in certain respects by creating a extra-somatic representation of it that serves as a memory store than by entrusting it to biological memory systems. If possessing knowledge is taken to mean having ready access to certain information, then it is justifiable to refer to such representations as knowledge that I possess.

In addition, and most significantly, a system of representations can serve as a repository for the knowledge gains of others, both our contemporaries and predecessors. Our capacity as a species to create collective systems of knowledge representations is unique among living things.

The potential for building knowledge into features of the environment through, for example, the use of graphic systems or pictorial displays, confers numerous advantages to an individual, and by extension, to a group. Some of these advantages have been alluded to already; and these are summarized and expanded on here.

First, as mentioned, representation of knowledge such as by means of a written graphic system allows individuals to record information in a relatively durable form rather than needing to rely solely on maintaining this information in more fragile biological memory.

Second, not only does the act of graphically recording information afford possibilities for its more durable preservation, but also it increases the sheer amount of information that can be preserved. The recent improvements in information storage capacity with advances in computer technology powerfully illustrate this point.

Third, and significantly, information captured in a representation can more readily be improved on over successive revisions and modifications, becoming an increasingly richer collective repository of the products of individuals' activity. Obviously, oral traditions too are cumulative and collective enterprises (Rubin, 1995), but graphic and pictorial representations accelerate and broaden this property enormously. As Donald (1991) indicated:

> [Representations] are *crafted*; that is, they are symbolic inventions that have undergone a process of iterative examination, testing, and improvement. To a degree this may also be said of biological memory ... but the conceptual products of cognition themselves cannot undergo extensive refinement in a purely oral tradition. Only in elaborate exographic systems[11] ... can the products of thinking be frozen in time, held up to scrutiny at some future date, altered, and re-entered into storage, in a repetitive, iterative process of improvement. (pp. 315–316)

For example, the development of nautical maps drawn with an overlaid grid system in the 14th century was refinement of *portolani*, which were earlier drawings of coastlines with superimposed compass courses between ports (A. W. Crosby, 1997). As this illustrates, having information in concrete form facilitates thinking about how it can be represented in different and perhaps better ways. Similarly, having information in concrete form facilitates integration across different sources. To continue with the previous example, information from two or more different maps can be integrated into a single comprehensive repository of information. Indeed,

---

[11]Donald (1991) referred to these representations that exist in the world as "exograms"—a term he offered as a counterpart to Lashley's "engram" (i.e., the biological residua of prior experience). I am reluctant to use this term because it carries with it the internal/external distinction that has contributed to the problems of central concern to James and to Gibson.

the maps that many of us use everyday for travel are just this sort of collective repository produced by untold numbers of individuals over long stretches of time. In many cases, such as that of maps, it is iteration across many individuals, even individuals living at different times, that makes possible the elaboration of information. Further, it is the sharing of these representations that provides much coherence among different individuals sharing a common culture.

Fourth, information preserved as representations in the environment can be more widely disseminated than it can through oral communication. That is, knowledge embodied in graphic form can overcome the limited distances over which spoken language can be conveyed as well as overcome the transience of spoken language. Information in graphic form can be conveyed and reproduced across vast geographic distances and across centuries of time, as the far-reaching and lasting effects of "Gutenburg revolution" of the 15th century attests.

Fifth, and related to the previous point, representations are often portable, and in these cases, they can broaden opportunities for action. Consider, for example, the benefits of carrying around knowledge of the layout of the environment in the form of a map. In its absence, a traveler would be wise to stick to familiar ways of travel, not straying too far from previously traveled paths. Having a map in hand, and knowing how to read it, possibilities for exploration become greater and the risks are greatly reduced.[12] Might the differences in the territorial range of individual humans as compared to that of their closest genetic relatives be explainable to a great extent on these grounds?

The common link in all of these advantages conferred by the creation and refinement of representations is their *public accessibility*. From the fact of their concrete embodiment, representations overcome limitations of biological memory with regard to durability, storage capacity, ease of modifying and pooling of collective knowledge, dissemination possibilities, and portability.

But more than these changes, the existence of representations of knowledge alter *how* we think; and recognition of alterations in how we think as a result of the availability of representations clarifies a distinctive characteristic about *human cognition*.

The claim that human cultures have devised various ways to preserve knowledge by building it into the environment is not new, by any means, nor are considerations of the implications of this ubiquitous circumstance of our lives. Historians and social theorists have been writing about these

---

[12]Of course, maps have other functions as well. They can be used descriptively to indicate land elevations, the location of resources, and so on. The argument offered here can be readily applied to any of these other maplike representations.

changes for a very long time. Surprisingly, however, these phenomena have been explored only to a limited extent in psychology (Heft, 1998a). To be sure, psychologists have explored notions of information overload and the consequences of living in a demanding and shifting technological world. But recognition of the fact that information is built into facets of the environment has received only a little attention—and that just in recent years. As pointed out later in this chapter, recognition of this fact has wide-ranging implications for how cognition itself is conceptualized.

But before examining these issues, it is useful to consider some additional matters in order to head off anticipated points of confusion.

Direct and indirect knowing

Tools/artifacts and representations are mediators of action, and hence all are tools in the broadest sense of that term. But more than that, a representation, unlike a tool/artifact, stands for something else. Thus, tools/artifacts and representations differ in terms of whether they provide *primary* or *secondary experience*, that is, whether they offer, respectively, opportunities for direct or indirect experience (Reed, 1996b).

As discussed earlier, an individual perceives an artifact, such as a hammer, in terms of a higher order structure of affordances, which is specified by information in the ambient array. Perceiving this artifact is a matter of *direct perception*, inasmuch as it is based on immediate, information pickup. The individual can perceive what properties the tool has for the self in conjunction with some action. The individual engages the tool in primary, firsthand experience and can check the apparent properties of the tool within experience.

In contrast, a representation is a display of information; and in detecting it as a representation, there is a dual experience. To take the case of a drawing, it is perceived both as a drawing as such and as a drawing of something (J. J. Gibson, 1971). It is an object in the environment, and also it stands for another object. And in its function as a representation, the drawing provides secondhand information about another object. What one is perceiving directly, in this case, are the tracings on the paper, but not their referent. Knowledge of the reference is *indirect* or mediated. As a result, what one knows about the referent depends solely on the accuracy of the representation.

Some historically interesting examples of inaccurate representations are offered by Gombrich (1960). He reported cases where descriptions related by 19th-century European explorers resulted in drawings and engravings of rhinoceroses bearing armor-like plates as skin and of whales with appendages resembling forelimbs (see pp. 50–51). Whereas presumably these inaccuracies were committed innocently, inaccuracies can also be built into representations with the intention to mislead and deceive. It is primarily on these grounds that Reed (1996b) cautioned about the potential risks faced by a society, such as ours, whose citizens rely to such a great extent on second hand or indirect experience (also see Heft, 1998b)[13]

As the reader is probably aware, the preceding use of indirect experience, and indeed, of representation, differs considerably from its standard uses in psychology and cognitive science. More commonly, the idea of indirect experience is applied to all cases of perception. According to the received view, in no instance is perception considered to be direct because it is assumed that perception necessarily operates on mental representations of the environment. Of course, the epistemological thrust of Gibson's ecological theory was to show that this need not be the case, that perception does not by necessity operate on mental representations because information in the environment is sufficiently rich to make direct perception possible.

Gibson's theory does not dispense with representations, however. Instead, the term is employed in a literal manner. Representations are features of the world, as already discussed. The practice by philosophers and psychologists of using the idea of representation to describe an essential feature of mind reflects a long-standing tendency to import as concepts artifacts found in the world "into" the black box of the mind, and to use these concepts as inferred mental structures or processes. Conceptualizing vision along the lines of a *camera obscura* is an early instance of this tendency. More modern examples include viewing the mind/brain as a telephone switchboard, a sequential processing computer, or most recently, as a parallel processing system. Like these developments—although perhaps less obviously—mental representations, now so central to cognitive theories, are in the first instance *features of the world*:

---

[13]In the opening section of his novel *The Book of Laughter and Forgetting* (1980), Milan Kundera dramatically illustrated the distinction between primary and secondary experience. He described the following gathering of government leaders on a balcony overlooking the Old Town Square in Prague:

> Gottwald was flanked by his comrades, with Clementis standing next to him. There were snow flurries, it was cold, and Gottwald was bareheaded. The solicitous Clementis took off his own fur cap and set it on Gottwald's head.
>
> The Party propaganda section put out hundreds of thousands of copies of a photograph of that balcony with Gottwald, a fur gap on his head and his comrades at his side, speaking to the nation. On that balcony the history of Communist Czechoslavakia was born. Every child knew the photograph from posters, school-books and museums.
>
> Four years later Clementis was charged with treason and hanged. The propaganda section immediately airbrushed him out of history and obviously, out of all the photographs as well

(continued on next page)

Both "symbol" and "representation" have taken on the cognitive sciences interpretation of *mental* representation, deemphasizing the sociohistorical
fact that many of the kinds of notations that are considered to be among the
languages of "thought"—such as mathematical language, written language,
and scientific symbols—began their existence as external inscriptions
whose conventions of construction, interpretation, and use in activities had
to be acquired in cultural activities. (Pea, 1993, p. 61)

Suchman (1987) adopted a similar stance in a critical analysis of the notion of
plans as mental representations guiding actions. The organized nature of our
actions in collaboration with artifacts, as well as with other people, is often
taken to reflect an unobservable mental structure that guides our behavior.
But this view is mistaken: "What traditional behavioral sciences take to be
cognitive phenomena have an essential relationship to a publicly available,
collaboratively organized world of artifacts and actions" (p. 50). Bourdieu
(1977) offered this same critical stance on plans as mental representations.

What the emphasis on mental representations has succeeded in doing
is to deflect attention away from the role that *representations as features of
our environment* play in our daily transactions. In turn, this emphasis on
mental representation has misled us about the nature of cognition itself.

DISTRIBUTED COGNITION

Mainstream theorizing in psychology historically has limited its analysis of
cognition to psychological operations "in" the individual. This approach is
hardly surprising; indeed, it probably seems the natural course to follow because, after all, doesn't cognition refer to a set of *intra*-individual processes?
Often, however, what seems obvious and self-evident is so because of familiar, tradition-bound ways of thinking—and so it is here. Viewing cognitive processes as transpiring only "within" the person is part of the legacy psychology
has inherited from modern philosophy, and it may be too restrictive a view.

The first section of the present chapter has set the stage for broadening
the viewpoint about the nature of cognition. In many instances, cognition
appropriately can describe person–environment relations. When, for
example, an individual carries out actions in conjunction with tools,
artifacts, and representations, acts of cognition can be described with
justification as encompassing both person and environment as a functional
entity. Further, in many everyday circumstances, cognitive processes can be
described as being shared among a group of individuals, who are using
tools, artifacts, and representations and are participating in a common task.
Cases such as these two can be referred to as instances of *distributed*

---

[13] *(continued from previous page)*

Ever since, Gottwald has stood on that balcony alone. Where
Clementis once stood, there is only bare palace wall. All that remains of Clementis is the cap on Gottwald's head. (p. 3)

cognition. This term has been gaining currency in recent years in contrast to an exclusive intra-individual use of the term *cognition* in psychology.

Before exploring these ideas, it is useful to consider, if only briefly, why the notion of distributed cognition is likely to appear odd at first glance. The claim that cognition can extend beyond the body boundaries seems foreign because it is inconsistent with a central tenet of the Western intellectual tradition. When it comes to one's identity and place in the world, it seems natural and self-evident to evaluate ourselves as individuals bounded by the limits of our bodies and evaluated in terms of our own personal achievements. But this has not always been the case, nor is it in many quarters today. In Western European history, this view has been dominant among most of the population only for about the last five centuries. For at least the preceding millennium, understanding who one is and what one's tasks in life are was primarily a matter of identifying and then sustaining one's relation and place in a transcendent order. In *Sources of the Self*, C. Taylor (1989) traced the shift in this point of view through modern Western philosophy.

A critical moment in this history is the reemergence of the individual, in the more classical sense, during the period self-consciously referred to as the Renaissance (Toulmin, 1990). During this watershed in Western thought, the *humanistic* viewpoint, taking as it does the individual as its central focus, becomes the dominant metatheoretical perspective. Descartes' psychology, which has served as a historical point of origin for many of the ideas critically examined in this book, is certainly among the most influential, early humanistic positions. [Refer to C. Taylor (1989), Toulmin (1990), and to numerous other histories of modern philosophy and society to trace this vision through recent centuries.]

An emphasis on the individual considered apart from the environment readily took root in American soil where the ground was prepared by early European immigrants, who brought with them the individualist emphasis of Protestantism and the Enlightenment. By the time experimental psychology arrives on the American scene at the end of the 19th century, the "self-contained individual" is unquestionably the focus for the new science (Sampson, 1977). By mid-20th century in the society at large, the image of one person standing alone reaches mythic proportions verging on cliché.

The cultural legacy for the new science of psychology is an exclusive focus on the individual. Regardless of whether the sources of an individual's attributes were claimed to rest in biology or in environmental circumstances, all but a few early psychologists agreed that the individual is the appropriate unit of analysis for the study of psychology and that the locus of all psychological processes is within the boundaries of the body.

Proposals challenging this self-evident view have been steadily appearing over several decades. Gradually emerging has been a view that the appropriate starting point for psychological analyses is the environment and individual, taken as a relational, dynamic system (see chap. 3). Even so obvious a matter as where to fix the boundary between the individual and the environment is no longer clear, if it can be consistently established at all.

Situated Action

One of the early signs in mainstream experimental psychology of problems afoot with the individualistic focus were the devastating critiques of laboratory artifacts in social psychological research that began appearing in the 1960s (see the landmark book edited by Rosenthal & Rosnow, 1969). Laboratory settings were found to be far from psychologically neutral places. Participants in laboratory experiments invariably responded in ways that indicated their awareness of being in a scientific laboratory, as reflected in high levels of "evaluation apprehension" and "compliance" in their responses.

It is widely accepted that this work raised important methodological issues. But at its core lay a rarely acknowledged lesson about the nature of psychological processes. This is the fact that psychological processes are, by their very nature, situated. Psychological processes occur in places, and they need to be recognized as occurrences embedded in contexts. Apostates from mainstream social psychology, such as Altman (1976) and Proshansky (1976), asserted vigorously that "persons-in-context" is the fundamental and irreducible psychological entity of study. But apart from these few protesting voices, not many experimental psychologists fully embraced the deeper implications of the work of Rosenthal and others. It is remarkable that recognition of its import has been so slow in coming and so limited in its effects.

In order to overcome our intellectual habit of considering the individual apart from the immediate environmental context, it is necessary to recognize how problematic the notions of a person and environment as distinct entities are. In drawing this distinction, it is taken for granted that the person "ends" at the body boundary; and that all else is "outside" the person. An initial step in questioning the self-evident nature of that claim is to consider our relation to tools and artifacts.

Tools, Artifacts, and the Extension of the Body

As discussed earlier, tools and artifacts extend the body both in a functional and a phenomenal sense. Functionally, they augment what an individual can do. From a phenomenological point of view, when one is using a tool to carry out a task, that tool does not lay outside the field of action but *within it*. To employ on an often-cited example from Bateson (1972), for someone without sight a probe such as a cane extends the reach, enabling that person to tap surfaces while walking, and thereby guide and monitor action. In such a case, where is the boundary between the person and the environment? It depends on one's point of view. If we ask where does the body end and the environment begin in a *physical* sense, we arrive at one answer: where the hand meets the cane. But if we ask where does the body end and the environment begin psychologically, then the answer is different: *Psychologically,* the body boundary is at the tip of the cane because that is where the person experiences the environment. This assertion is consistent with James' notion of knowing or awareness as the selective engagement of environmental structure. If knowing is a relation between knower and object known established in a selective manner, then in the present example, the known is the environmental surfaces tapped and the cane is a part of the selective processes of the knower. This claim is warranted on experiential grounds because awareness is "located" at the tip of the cane, and what one is aware of is the surface being tapped.

This type of experience is common in everyone's daily life. The various implements and artifacts we use, engage, and even wear, shift the body boundary throughout the day and hence shift where we experience the world. We feel the grain of the paper we write on at the tip our pen, the relative firmness of the ground we are walking on under our shoes, the density of the food we are skewering at the end of our fork, the relative smoothness of the road we are riding across under the tires of our bicycle, and so on. Mundane observations of this nature have been a rich field for phenomenologists to mine. The following description by Merleau-Ponty (1942/1963) must certainly be among the most expressive (albeit a little dated):

> A woman may, without any calculation, keep a safe distance between the feather in her hat and the things which might break it off. She feels where the feather is just as we feel where our hand is. If I am in the habit of driving a car, I enter a narrow opening and see that I can "get through" without comparing the width of the opening with that of the wings, just as I go through a doorway without checking the width of the doorway against that of my body.[14] ... Habit expresses *our power of dilating our being in the world, or changing our existence by appropriating fresh instruments.* (p. 143, emphasis added)

From a psychological point of view, the location of our body boundaries is fluid. In Merleau-Ponty's words, with habitual use of tools and artifacts, we have the "power of dilating our being in the world," shifting our body boundaries in conjunction with the tools and artifacts that are part of the field of our actions. This lability of the environment–person boundary un-

---

[14]For experimental support for this phenomenological claim, see W. H. Warren and Whang (1987).

dercuts any effort to draw a fixed distinction between self and not-self. Psychologically, at least, the distinction is specious.

Tools, artifacts, and representations as mediators of action allow the individual to do things that are otherwise difficult or impossible to do. As such, they extend our range of possibilities. Collectively, they are not merely tools for action, in a limited sense of action, but more broadly, they are tools for thinking. To illustrate this point with an example offered by A. Clark (1997), when multiplying two numbers together, in all but the simplest cases the task becomes more manageable if the calculations are done on paper. In this case, we are thinking with pencil and paper. The reason why these implements are helpful is because, in contrast to attempting to perform the calculation on our own ("in our head"), we shift some of the weight of the task onto the paper. That is, the task becomes distributed across the person and the implements. Or, said differently, the implements become included within the field of action. This example usefully illustrates Salomon's (1993) claim that "once the idea of mediation through artifacts ... is seen as a distinctive characteristic of humans, the adoption of the distributed view of cognitions is inescapable" (p. xvi).

As for an example involving a representation rather than an artifact, consider again the difference between traveling in a somewhat unfamiliar city with or without the aid of a map. Without it, the individual would tend to keep to a route previously traveled. With map in hand, the individual has great flexibility in choosing alternate routes to familiar places and in determining new routes to yet-to-be visited places. This greater flexibility and adaptability is possible because navigating has become a collaborative process between the individual, the map, and the environment. Under such circumstances, the map is not a mere object in the environment, like that map across the room folded in my desk drawer; instead, it is a very real part of the cognitive function of navigating. As such, it extends what one knows and what one can do. In Donald's (1991) apt phrase, there is occurring a "cognitive symbiosis," or to use different terminology, the cognitive function of navigating "enfolds" both the individual and the artifact (Portugali, 1996).

Donald borrowed the term *network* from computer science to describe the phenomenon of distributed cognition, and it is indeed a useful analogy. In a computer network, the ongoing computational operations cannot be adequately understood by focusing solely on an individual facet of the network. For example, when I am retrieving information from some database at a geographically distant institution, where precisely are the computational operations taking place? Clearly, the operations are not occurring in any one place, but rather they are distributed across a network. Likewise, in any given instance of distributed cognition, what an individual needs to do to carry out some task is likely to be distributed among several components of a network, one of which is the individual him- or herself. As I am traveling through a new city with a map in hand, where is this cognitive operation taking place? The database, if you will, is the map in my hand, and I am employing the necessary psychological skills to extract the pertinent information. To limit cognition to considerations of intra-individual processes will not do. For one thing, how the information is presented on the map significantly influences its usefulness (e.g., Levine, 1982; D. H. Warren, Rossano, & Wear, 1990). The functional properties of the map and of the individual jointly collaborate to facilitate or impede navigation. Map-reading is a person–environment process, an act of distributed cognition.

Incorporating tools, artifacts, and representations into an account of cognitive functioning provides a way of addressing a paradox of cognitive development. This paradox is "the problem of explaining how individuals acquire a more powerful [cognitive] structure if they do not already possess that structure" (J. Miller, 1999, p. 88). This paradox is a variation of the classic problem in Plato's dialogue *The Meno*. The problem becomes more tractable when the role played by the environment is recognized, in the present case by tools, artifacts, and representations in learning. The "more powerful structure" that is needed for learning can reside sometimes in the relation between an individual and certain environmental features. Tools, artifacts, and representations make some operations possible that are otherwise beyond one's capabilities, and through their use the individual's cognitive skills can become expanded. Moreover, information that is embodied in some environmental features and some new skills required for utilizing these features can be appropriated by the individual through engaging them (Rogoff, 1990, 1993). To return to the map example, by traveling with the aid of a map, an individual can come to learn more about the structure of a place, and subsequently can navigate with greater skill without the map as a support. The individual has discovered more in the environment by using the map to mediate learning.

There is one last and related point that was already touched on earlier in the chapter. When cognition is distributed across an individual and a tool, artifact, or a representation, what operations the individual employs differs from those operations the individual uses when functioning in their absence. When acting in collaboration with an artifact or a representation, some of the burden of remembering how to perform the requisite task (in the case of artifacts) or remembering the needed information (in the case of representations) has shifted to a significant degree from the individual to the environmental feature in question. In doing so, typically there occurs more than a redistribution of what needs to be known; it is often necessary for the individual to develop particular skills specific to the these environmental resources. What the individual needs to know when acting alone as compared to when acting in conjunction with environmental features may be quite different.

Socially Distributed Cognition

The exploration of distributed cognition has been limited thus far to consideration of an individual's collaboration with inanimate features of the environment. Another vital part of many networks of distributed information is, of course, other individuals. As discussed earlier, others serve as the most important source of information about how to use tools, artifacts, and representations. Also, an individual can collaborate with others on a common activity or project, and in such instances, it is justifiable to say that information is distributed across a *social network*. These considerations eventually lead the discussion back to terrain initially examined with respect to Barker's analysis of behavior settings (chaps. 7–8).

Fields of Promoted Action. A critical feature of the environmental background against which our human lineage evolved is, as pointed out earlier, the actions of others. Briefly reconsider those issues here. Among other things, observed actions by intentional agents reveal information about the properties of objects and about the skills needed to utilize those properties. The young of our species is very adept at attending to how others manipulate and engage environmental features, and establishing acts of joint attention is critical for exploiting the available resources of the sociocultural environment. When all parties involved are aware of the coordination of attention among them, a *consensual frame* is established, and within the time-dependent boundaries of a consensual frame, object-focused actions unfold. Early in life these dialogical exchanges can be viewed as forms of proto-communication, perhaps providing the foundation for the development of language (Fogel, 1993; Tomasello, Kruger, & Ratner, 1993).

When participating in a consensual frame, an individual's field of action is expanded to include the other person and the object(s) of their shared attention. One outcome of this coordinated, triadic relation between child, caregiver, and object is to draw the child's attention to specific affordance properties of objects, as for example, when a caregiver points to a handle on a cup (Reed, 1993). Here with the caregiver's prompting, the child can discover some of the functional, tool-like properties of objects. Also, sometimes within the coordinated actions of a consensual frame, the caregiver will structure the task environment in such a way as to enable children to carry out tasks that otherwise are beyond their skill level. Such acts of *scaffolding* by caregivers enlarge the sphere of the child's actions through the mediation of others. Following Reed (1993), caregivers contribute in these ways to establish *fields of promoted action* for the child, and in so doing expand the *scope* of possibilities in the child's environment.

In addition to acts of scaffolding serving to extend the child's action possibilities on a specific task, through multiple experiences of others scaffolding their actions, children may begin to recognize that they themselves can promote the expansion of their own skill level by modifying how tasks are structured. These efforts, both small and large, are rightly seen as acts of environmental design, as children discover how affordance properties of features can be altered to promote new kinds of activities. These discoveries expand the child's repertoire and field of action. There is much need for longitudinal, naturalistic studies of children's play that illuminate the development of these aspects of environmental exploration and object play.

Some methods of scaffolding novices' actions appear to be more effective than others, and these differences reveal something about the learning processes involved. Offering verbal instructions and guidelines that by their very nature are separate from a perception-action activity in process is less effective than nonintrusive guidance opportunistically inserted into the flow of the novice's actions (Rogoff, Mosier, Mistry, & Göncü, 1993). Considering the latter from a dynamic systems view (see chap. 8), the guiding action by the "teacher" can be seen to function as one of several control parameters that collaborates in structuring the unfolding goal-directed action. That is, the teacher's actions are one constraining factor among many whose mutual convergence results in the observed pattern of action. A well-placed, well-timed, and nondisruptive action by a teacher, as a function of its position in the manifold of relationships constituting the action, can transform the learner's ongoing engagement of a particular environmental feature. In this way, some learning experiences of the child entail what Rogoff (1993) aptly called "the participatory transformation of action," whereby developmental change is a process occurring within the individual–environment transaction.

Thinking about learning as "the participatory transformation of action" differs sharply from the usual way of conceptualizing this process as involving the individual "internalizing" information or instruction. The latter view, in effect, makes the claim that information "out there" in the world is transported "inside" into the mind of the learner. A brief consideration of a recent example of this perspective in the domain of cognitive anthropology helps, by way of contrast, to illuminate the character of participatory transformation, and in turn clarifies the notion of distributed cognition.

A Representational Alternative.   Shore (1996) attempted to break new ground by linking ideas in cultural anthropology with recent developments in cognitive science. In doing so, however, his adoption of a representational theory of mind presents him with the problem of how information crosses the boundary between what is "outside" and what is "inside." Specifically, Shore drew a distinction between cultural forms of knowledge, that is, "instituted models," which are "conventional, patterned public forms [of action that are] ... part of the external social world" (p. 51), and mental models that are schematized cognitive analogues of these instituted models. The acquisition of culturally appropriate knowledge is seen by Shore as involving analogical transfer, that is, "translations between inner and outer experience models ... through a process I call 'analogical schematization,'" as individual mental models of cultural conventions are subjectively constructed (p. 345). As this implies, analogical schematization

> is not a passive mapping process. It is an intentional activity by a meaning-seeking agent. Analogies are constructed, not discovered. The manner in which conventional models are brought to mind is best thought of as a creative and contingent activity rather than as a determinate and passive replication process. (Shore, 1996, p. 371)

Culturally instituted models "act for members of a community as shared and ready-made source domains for analogical schematization" (p. 371). What Shore envisioned is a transfer of abstract relations from a cultural level of analysis to a psychological level of analysis. The "theoretical bridge" between the two is some version of a connectionist model of thinking. There is a mapping of cultural forms of action, via connectionist networks, to psychological forms of knowing. In view of the earlier examination of representational theories, Shore's conclusion is not at all surprising: "Culturally constituted meaning points ... *only to a probability of a significant overlap* within a community in how novel experiences will be reconstituted as memory" (p. 372, emphasis added).

Justifiably rejecting a passive copying of cultural forms onto the individual, Shore embraced an active theory of mind, but one raising the same difficulties with representational theories that were confronted earlier. His analysis did not offer at a psychological level of analysis an account of how external representations become translated into internal representations, nor can it do so. Like other representational theories, there is the problem of how something "external" to mind gets "into" mind. The approach adopted is that minds construct representations. But what is the nature of the 'point of contact' between world and mind? The best that can be done, as with other theories of this sort, is to skirt the question at a psychological level and appeal ultimately to neurophysiological models (e.g., neural networks). Further, by adopting a constructivist account, one is being forced to conclude that the degree of correspondence between an individual's knowledge of the world and the world itself—and importantly in this case, the degree of overlap of shared knowledge among individuals—bears a probabilistic relation. As argued earlier, this seems to be rather shaky ground on which to erect an account of collective, coordinated action. These two difficulties are, of course, related, and they may be most readily overcome by rejecting the dualism that lies at their foundation from the start.

The problem here is not the adoption of an active theory per se, but the kind of active theory adopted. Shore's is an active theory in the processing sense of action. Instead, Cole, Rogoff, Tomasello, and others adopted an approach along the lines proposed by Vygotsky, and took activity in a much more literal way: *Activity* occurs within a field of experience and is structured in relation to environmental features.

Transformation Through Participation.   Knowing is a process that occurs within experience, which from a radical empiricist perspective, refers to the dynamic and reciprocal relation between an active knower and environment of potential structure. Knowing is a relation of selectivity, an attunement of an active organism to structures of the environment. Viewed in this way, learning is a process of *"becoming,"* rather than a process of acquisition, as new features of the learning context are appropriated into action. To recall the earlier discussion of Aristotle's treatment of formal causality, what is being described here is a conveyance of structure (chap. 8). New knowledge does not pass across a boundary that separates the world and the mind. Rather, the person–environment field of experience is transformed, as heretofore unselected, and hence psychologically unrealized, latent features of the environment become appropriated into the ongoing, dynamic person–environment relation.

Rogoff (1993) distinguished different cases here: When the individual is acting alone, ways of engaging the environment are transformed through "participatory appropriation." In Jamesian terms, new features of the environment are selected by the knower (e.g., a new feature is differentiated from a constellation of perceived structure), and as a consequence the field constituting the knower-object known is transformed within this relational field. When others are co-actors with an individual on some task, action can be said to involve "guided participation." For example, a teacher adjusting a student's ongoing stream of action by changes in positioning of the body, eliminating some steps in the task, and introducing developmentally appropriate implements, are all actions that can be taken to transform the student's ongoing engagement with features of the environment. In such circumstances, the teacher is a part of the student's field of action, and thus changes occur as a transformation within, rather than an importation into, this relational field.[15]

What is being proposed, then, is that learning and development involve participatory adjustments of knowing-acting within the relational field of person and environment. When a solitary individual is utilizing a tool, artifact, or representation, knowing is a relation distributed across the person–implement relation. When another person(s) is present to guide an individual's engagement within the field of experience, it can be said that what is known—that is, what constitutes the task environment—is distributed among these co-actors sharing a common field.

Socially Distributed Networks

Guided participation is an interpersonal process that, if successful, eventuates in individuals functioning effectively on their own. Some interpersonal processes, however, remain shared activities throughout the duration of their expression because some goals are only attainable in the midst of group processes. Particularly when a task is complex, containing multiple steps and requiring multiple skills distributed over a number of locales, it may be necessary to divide the task up among a group of individuals. With such divisions of labor, individuals play specialized roles in conjunction with specific artifacts and representations. The task is a collaborative group effort, and an individual may only understand one portion of the overall task. In such instances, the requisite skills for carrying out the operations of the task as a whole do not rest with any one person, but rather they are distributed across a group of persons and the artifacts and representations they engage.

The most detailed analysis of such a system of socially distributed cognition to date is Hutchins's (1995) study of the navigational operations of a Navy ship. The task of navigating a large ship through open waters to some destination involves the coordination of a team of individuals assigned to various roles. The network of responsibilities among these individuals is not fixed, however, but can change with circumstances. For instance, entering or leaving a harbor is an event of greater potential hazard than piloting in open seas, and for this reason, the configuration of the navigation team becomes more differentiated and dispersed across a wider variety of instruments.[16] There is a redundancy of skills among the navigation team, both for

---

[15]In her more recent writings, Rogoff (1995) distinguished "guided participation" from "apprenticeship." Unlike guided participation, apprenticeship refers to processes occurring solely at the community level, and it refers to "active individuals participating with others in culturally, organized activity that has as part of its purpose the development of mature participation in the activity by the less experienced people" (p. 142).

[16]In the previous chapter, Lewin's field theory was described as a precursor to dynamic systems theory. In this discussion of socially distributed cognition, Lewin's prescience is again apparent. He proposed the psychological field (i.e., the life space) be conceptualized as changing with development and under certain situations by becoming more or less differentiated.

backup at any time and when actions become more differentiated, as on these occasions when greater vigilance is required. However, given the complexity of the ship's operations, no one person can be skilled at all tasks.

Hutchins argued that it is necessary to view the cognitive activity underlying these operations as distributed in two respects. First, any single individual is utilizing an instrument or representation that itself has information and computational operations built into it. That is, knowledge is distributed or extended across an individual and artifact and/or a representation. Second, functions are distributed across a network of individuals functioning within a common time frame. A difference between these two instances of distributed cognition is the unit of analysis. For example, in the first case, the unit of analysis is an individual engaged in some component of the overall task of navigating. In the second case, the unit of analysis is the ship as a whole, and cognitive functions involved here need to be examined across that entire entity. According to Hutchins (1995), "Any attempt to explain the cognitive properties of the integral parts [i.e., individuals] without reference to the properties of the larger system would be ... incomplete" (pp. 287–288). In a very real sense, the operations of a system of this degree of complexity is a cognitive operation that is socially distributed.

It is Hutchins's goal in this examination of a distributed cognitive system to "move the boundaries of the unit of cognitive analysis out beyond the skin of the individual" (p. 287). He did so by viewing the technical and social operations of the naval ship as "simultaneously cognitive systems in their own rights and contexts for the cognition of the people who participate in them" (p. 287). The primary functional characteristic of this distributed cognitive system is "the propagation of representational states across a series of representational media" (p. 117). The media are the various technical components of the complex system, including navigational and other instruments, and representations such as maps. Propagation of representational states occurs "by bringing the states of the media into *coordination* with one another" (p. 117), and thereby collectively controlling the operations of the ship. With this conceptualization of the functioning of a distributed cognitive system, Hutchins explained the role of individuals in such a system:

> One important aspect of the social distribution of this task is that the knowl-edge required to carry out the coordinating actions is not discretely con-tained inside the various individuals. Rather, much of the knowledge is intersubjectively shared among the members of the navigation team. This permits the human component of the system to act as a malleable and adaptable coordinating tissue, the job of which is to see to it that the proper coordinating activities are carried out. ... They provide the connecting tissue that moves representational states across the tools of the trade. In addition,

they dynamically reconfigure their activities in response to changes in the task demands. (p. 219)

A discussion of media for the transmission of information was included in Heider's framework for perceiving, but it is important not to confuse the two different ways the term is employed in each case. In Heider's treatment, "media" refers to that facet of the perceiving process that makes it possible for object structure to be made available to a perceiver. Media, in Heider's sense, collectively have the property of docility: Because of the relative independence of their constituent parts, media are able to convey structure without appreciably transforming it (see chap. 6). Hutchins used the term *media* in the more conventional sense to refer to artifacts and representations (i.e., human constructions) that have structure themselves, and this property distinguishes them from media in Heider's sense. The constituent elements of artifacts and representations are not independent, but have internal coherence. As a result, artifacts and representations convey information in certain forms but not in others because of the way they have been constructed. This means that the technical artifacts and representations in this distributed system alter information by representing it. At best, they selectively abstract information from another source, thereby preserving only some aspects of its structure.

The example of a map as a representational medium illustrates Hutchins's usage in contrast to Heider's. A map conveys a *representation*, which is a selection of some of the features of that which is being represented. In so doing, representational media provide opportunities for individuals to perceive aspects of the environment *indirectly*. Media in Heider's, and more specifically in Gibson's terms, carry *information* that specify features of the environment. Media, in this latter sense, do not selectively convey some information and not others, but rather carry an array of information that the individual, as an intentional agent, selectively engages. In this case, then, media allow individuals to perceive the environment *directly*

In Hutchins's analysis, individuals in the distributed cognitive system function as "connecting tissue" that coordinate a representational state across media (e.g., from charts to compass readings): "The individuals are a sort of flexible tissue that moves to ensure the propagation of task-relevant representational states" (Hutchins, 1995, p. 227). In this scheme, individuals approximate the function of media, in Heider's sense of the term[17]; their flexibility is revealed in their functioning as spurious units "compensat[ing] for local breakdowns by going beyond the normative procedures to make

---

[17]I offer a qualified statement here—that individuals approximate media—to indicate that whereas they have the capacity to propagate information without distorting it, in practice for individuals this may sometimes be difficult to achieve.

sure that representational states propagate when and where they should" (p. 228). Overall, the intended operation of the ship is "implemented in the coordination of representational states, and human participants coordinate their coordinating actions with one another" (p. 219).

Adaptive Agency

Can the functioning of the individual participants in this distributed system be more fully conceptualized? Hutchins is, in his own words, "agnostic" on this point. He described his conceptual strategy (like Gibson's) as beginning with the environment in which the individual is functioning. The structure of the environment is to be carefully detailed before any assumptions are made about the functional attributes of the individual. The reverse strategy of starting with the individual apart from the environment creates possibilities for positing unnecessary structures:

> Unfortunately, in order to get the cognitive game started in a mind that is profoundly disconnected from its environment, it is necessary to invent internal representations of a good deal of the environment that is outside the head. This requirement is simply not present in a mind that is in constant interaction with its environment. (Hutchins, 1995, p. 132)

Hutchins cited the advice of Latour, who proposed that in order to understand the nature of scientific knowledge the process should begin with a detailed analysis of task structure: "If, by some extraordinary chance, there is something still unaccounted for, then, and only then, look for special cognitive abilities" (Latour, 1987, cited in Hutchins, p. 132).

However, aspects of Hutchins's presentation belie his agnosticism. Whereas he claimed that this strategy of beginning with the task situation allows leaving the question of mental representation open until the analysis is sufficiently fleshed out, he also claimed that this strategy allows the investigator to remain "committed to the analysis of information processing and the transformation of representations 'inside the organism'" (p. 129). But how is it possible to remain committed to information processing and representations inside the organism and also to remain agnostic as to the status of mental representations? In fact, his terminology is inconsistent in its theoretical commitments. The propagation processes within a distributed system are described as "computations," albeit defined broadly. The terms *inside/outside* and *inner/outer* recur throughout his discussion, even while he roundly criticized the notion of a boundary between person and setting.

To raise these objections may seem to focus on trifles; but such distinctions are conceptually loaded, carrying with them a commitment to the received ontological distinction between environment and person that, importantly, Hutchins otherwise seemed to resist. The theoretical position he appeared to be moving toward is revealed in the following passage:

> With the focus on a person who is actively engaged in a culturally con-structed world, let us soften the boundary of the individual and take the indi-vidual to be a very plastic kind of adaptive system. Instead of conceiving the relation between person and environment in terms of moving coded infor-mation across a boundary, let us look for processes of entrainment, coordi-nation, and resonance among elements of a system that includes a person and the person's surroundings. (p. 288)

By describing the dynamic relations between person and environment as "processes of entrainment, coordination, and resonance," Hutchins was making efforts to distance himself from distinction of inside/outside and the like.

How should person processes best be characterized in this distributed and relational framework? To follow this analysis for a few additional steps, terms such as *entrainment, coordination*, and *resonance* are useful moves forward in helping to shed the dualistic trappings of inside/outside thinking. But at the same time, they may handicap thinking in a different way, by connoting a passive role for the individual in the relation. For example, a tuning fork resonates, and indeed, cannot help doing so *ceteris paribus*. But an individual selectively engages the environment; psychological processes do not passively mirror or correspond to the environment (recall James's criticism of Spencer's view of adaptation as the organism coming to terms with its environment, see chap. 1). Because knowing processes are marked by an individual selectively engaging the environment, a term with a more intentional connotation may better direct the thinking here. In this respect, *attunement* would seem to be more suitable.

The individual conceptualized as part of a person–environment system is an *adaptive agent*. Actions reflect an ongoing selective engagement of particular features of a setting, an attunement to some dynamic structures rather than others (Hecht, 2000; Heft, 1989, 1990). The individual is functionally flexible, adaptively shifting in the focus of intentional action and shifting with respect to contextual frames. In the case of a distributed cognitive system, the individual functions selectively and coordinately to maintain operations that encompass artifacts, representations, and other individuals.

One consequence of this admittedly sketchy perspective is the view that individuals develop an ensemble of actions in relation to the contexts they are faced with and the features and tasks they selectively engage. And to adopt this kind of conceptualization is to move away from the kind of "faculty" thinking that continues to influence psychology by assuming the presence of highly specialized mental functions. Instead, if psychological processes are an attunement to everyday environmental structures (i.e., if the situation and the task are constitutive factors in any psychological event occurrence), such specialized, environmentally independent characterizations are inadequate. As Lave wrote (1993), "There is no such thing as 'learning' *sui generis*, but only changing participation in the culturally designed settings of everyday life" (pp. 5–6). This perspective cuts deeply into how psychological processes are conceptualized:

> The difference may be at heart a very deep epistemological one, between a view of knowledge as a collection of real entities, located in heads, and of learning as a process of internalizing them, versus a view of knowing and learning as engagement in changing processes of human activity. ... [that individuals engage in] the production of knowledgeability as a flexible process of engagement with the world. (Lave, 1993, pp. 12–13)

Such a conceptualization seems well-suited for the kind of analysis of socially distributed cognition Hutchins has in mind.

Behavior Settings as Systems of Distributed Cognition

Hutchins's work is an important contribution to ecological psychology, taking the analysis of meaningful environmental structures to a level of complexity rarely considered. But as seen in the examination of Barker's analysis of behavior settings, Hutchins's attention to extra-individual environmental phenomena is not unique in psychology. The remainder of this chapter examines these two analyses in order to broaden the range of considerations prompted by either viewpoint alone.

Considering Hutchins's analysis with Barker's ecobehavioral program as a backdrop helps to override one potential misreading of Hutchins's claims. His study of the operations of a naval ship might suggest that processes of socially distributed cognition apply only to fairly technical or specialized domains. Barker's work, in contrast, is striking because of the rather mundane everyday settings he considered—in fact, the sophistication of his work has probably been underestimated at times because of his focus on children's activities in playgrounds, drugstores, school gymnasiums, and the like. Juxtaposing these two bodies of work leads to the consideration of the possibility that instances of socially distributed cognition are ubiquitous in everyday life.

Further, features that are especially apparent in Hutchins' analysis are rather subtle in Barker's, and vice versa. Consequently, the two viewpoints considered together illuminate their shared features. To be specific, a particularly striking feature of Hutchins's analysis is the assortment of technical equipment used to navigate the ship. It is not too difficult to make the case that built into these artifacts and representations is previously acquired knowledge. Nautical charts are the most obvious example. From this point, the claim that cognition is distributed across individuals and artifacts is straightforward. Turning to Barker's framework, it is more difficult to see that cognition is distributed across milieu features because the settings he described are so familiar and the milieu features are so nontechnical. The mundane character of behavior settings renders their milieu features functionally transparent. But the operations of a behavior setting are distributed across its standing pattern of behavior and its "milieu" (Fuhrer, 1993). And many of the milieu features (e.g., tools, artifacts, furnishings, and the layout of a setting) embody aspects of what an individual needs to know to be a participant in a particular setting.

Inversely, the most salient attribute of a behavior setting—indeed its defining property—is some requisite degree of interdependence among the individuals' actions. This quality is most readily evidenced in Barker and his colleagues' studies of the effects of departures from the optimum number of participants in a setting (e.g., R. Barker & Gump, 1964). The individuals comprising a distributed system such as one that Hutchins described may be so separated physically, working perhaps out of direct sight of one another, that their high degree of functional interdependence may not always be obvious. In fact, an issue that Hutchins did not address, and that Barker can provide assistance with, is locating the boundaries of the distributed cognitive system. Along these lines, does the naval ship he studied constitute one distributed cognitive system, or are there several distributed systems simultaneously in operation on board? For example, are crew members, whose responsibilities are primarily maintenance of the equipment, participants in the navigational system under examination, or do they constitute a somewhat separate system of distributed knowledge? Barker's efforts to determine the boundaries of behavior settings may be helpful here.

Behavior settings are more than a collection of individuals; they are relatively coherent, dynamic systems (see chap. 8); and coherence, reflected in interdependence of its constituents, is a criterion that can be employed to identify behavior settings. Interdependence among components of behavior settings is evidenced by settings functioning as quasi-stable equilibria. Barker operationalized interdependence by establishing empirically the degree to which actions in one part of a potential behavior setting affect operations in another part of the setting, using some minimal level of interdependence as a threshold (R. Barker, 1968, pp. 40–46).

Finally, Hutchins's analysis enriches the conceptualization of behavior settings in one other way. Many of the sources of system perturbation Hutchins considered originate beyond the immediate boundaries of the system, such as changes in weather conditions or in sea depth. The influence of conditions outside of the boundaries of behavior settings receives comparatively less attention in Barker's framework, and understandably so. Consideration of a ship's operations, in contrast to, for example, analysis of a high school basketball game a' la Barker, brings into relief the fact that it is not only factors within the behavior setting alone that can perturb the stability of the system. Clearly, the sorts of everyday behavior settings Barker considered can also be perturbed by occurrences whose sources lay outside setting boundaries. Barker was quite aware of this fact (see R. Barker, 1968, pp. 89–90); but these issues remain a relatively undeveloped part of his framework.

More generally, sensitivity to conditions that originate outside of behavior setting boundaries brings to the fore the fact that behavior settings themselves are sociocultural phenomena. As such, economic, political, and technical influences all bear on behavior setting possibilities and their operation. Bronfenbrenner's (1979) theoretical writings have done much to illuminate these "exosystem" influences. Along these lines, Cotterell (1998) recently examined behavior settings as constituents of "macroenvironments," by which he meant clusters of similar types of behavior settings whose operations are interdependent.

These considerations bring the present chapter full circle, returning to the viewpoint that human activity is always embedded in sociocultural structures. With this view of the conceptual foundation for psychological analyses, the central theme of this chapter that environments are meaningful may begin to receive more thorough-going attention than it has to date. This issue is discussed further in the concluding chapter.

SUMMARY AND CONCLUSION

This chapter explored why and in what ways it is reasonable to claim that environments are meaningful. An attempt was made to explain in what sense it is the case that individuals function in a shared environment that is already meaningful, rather than within multiple, idiosyncratic, cognitively encapsulated environments that each individual constructs "in the head." The meaningful features of the environment examined included affordances, tools, artifacts, representations, as well as behavior settings and other instances of distributed social knowing. The meaningful features of the environment comprise a tangible, publicly accessible repository of knowledge gains by those who have come before, and each individual subsequently sustains and contributes to this fund of ecological knowledge. In this way, meaningful environmental structures are maintained, and often transformed.

Over the course of our day, and indeed over our lifetimes, we each experience a wide range of affordances, tools, and representations in the social settings available to us and to which we contribute. In large measure, the course of our psychological development—the competencies we hone and the possibilities we envision - is rooted in a landscape of these various kinds of *ecological knowledge*. They amount to the *ecopsychological resources* of the environment. And as with any resource, they can be sustained over time or can fail to be renewed; they can be shared and made accessible to others or restricted to a few; and they can be enriched and hence be enriching, or can be allowed to stagnate and thereby become stultifying.

IV

Conclusion

The Scope of Ecological Psychology

The time has come to take stock of the ground that has been covered, and in so doing to locate ecological psychology in the broader context of the discipline of psychology. In part, this chapter is intended as an overview of what has preceded, tracing out its arc—although it is not a summary of all of the issues covered. Instead, the emphasis is on the beginning and end points of the presentation, attempting to take a longer view of the argument free of the distractions that may have been produced by the exposition of approaches, historical and philosophical discussions, and justifications for claims scattered throughout. In this way, the discussion intends to highlight some of the theoretical commitments of ecological psychology, both in order to identify some of the intentions of ecological psychology to date and to consider how it might contribute prospectively to the science of psychology.

THE RECIPROCAL AND NESTED FOCUS OF ECOLOGICAL PSYCHOLOGY

An initial step in exploring the implications of an ecological approach to psychology from the point of view of theory is to identify the focus of an ecological approach in the life sciences more generally. Beginning with the naturalistic assumption that phenomena in nature occur at multiple levels of organization, an ecological approach takes as its point of entry for analysis of the natural world the animal–environment relation. "Ecological" in the designation "ecological approach" refers then, in part, to a focus on natural phenomena occurring at the *scale* of an individual animal. This scale, or grain, of analysis can be identified with reference to what the individual animal selectively responds and selectively engages in its surround. The selective actions collectively exhibited by species members toward features of the environment bracket, as a first approximation, the range of phenomena that fall within the ecological level of analysis for that species.

Ecological also refers to the dynamic *reciprocity* that characterizes animal and environment relations. Animals adjust to prevailing environmental conditions and engage its features through perceiving–acting processes, while concurrently altering those conditions (to varying degrees across species) to better suit their functional aims. In short, reciprocal relations operate within the animal–environment level of organization.

An additional naturalistic assumption is that the various multiple levels of organization of natural phenomena exhibit nested interjacent and circumjacent reciprocal influences (i.e., between level relations). Single entities at a given level of organization participate in collectively giving rise to structures at a higher level of organization. Such between-level relations reflect the fact that the integrity of any higher-order structure is dependent on particular functional relations being maintained among those interjacent entities that constitute it. Reciprocally, a higher order structure, which is by definition circumjacent to its constituents, constrains the functional possibilities of its constituent entities.

In psychology, there are two sets of between-level relations directly operating: First, biological processes are nested within the higher order structure that is the whole organism. There are influences "from below," as the functional viability of the individual considered as a whole is dependent on the requisite functioning of the complex of constituent, biological processes. There are also influences "from above," as the functional integrity of the individual organism as a whole limits the degrees of freedom of its biological constituents in the sense of promoting the maintenance of particular functional relations. This set of between-level relations is primarily the province of neuroscience and related fields, and it falls outside of the scope of ecological psychology.

The second set of between-level relations operating in psychology concerns individual activities nested within extra-individual behavior-milieu entities (i.e., within *behavior settings*). Individuals acting in conjunction with environmental (milieu) features collectively generate quasi-stable, extra-individual systems. For certain settings to exist, particular functional relations among individuals must obtain. Reciprocally, behavior settings constrain the actions and, to some extent, the experiential possibilities of their constituent participants. These between-level relations are the province of ecobehavioral science, which falls within the broader designation of ecological psychology.

With this analysis as backdrop, the *scope* of an ecological approach in psychology can begin to be identified. An ecological approach in psychology adopts both a within-level of analysis and between-level of analysis of psychological phenomena. Importantly, it embraces a *dynamic, relational perspective* in both of these senses. As for the within-level analysis, the actions of the individual are considered in relation to their immediate environmental context taken with respect to that individual. Actions in relation to affordances are paradigmatic here. With respect to a between-level analysis, actions of individuals need to be considered in relation to the *behavior setting* in which they are presently participating. In short, individual functioning needs to be understood in relation to environmental features which the person is engaging (within-level relations) and in relation to the circumjacent setting in which those actions are occurring (between-level relations). Ecological psychology is a psychology of context in both of these respects.

The ecological approach overall has a *pluralistic* character as well. It is pluralistic in several senses, but for present purposes it means that because the natural world is organized in terms of multiple, nested levels of structure, no one level is in principle more fundamental than another. Because natural phenomena exist at multiple levels of organization, the conceptual tools associated with any particular level are not privileged as bases for description or explanation at all levels. An ecological viewpoint urges that the sciences resist reduction of natural phenomena to any single level of analysis. Depending on the natural phenomena under examination, sometimes relational accounts operating within a given level of analysis are required, sometimes accounts of the relation between adjacent levels of analysis are most appropriate, and sometimes both within- and between-level considerations are needed.

In addition to shared assumptions concerning hierarchically nested structure and the reciprocal relations among natural entities, more broadly an ecological approach to psychology is linked to an ecological perspective in science because of the common thread provided by evolutionary theory and its emphasis on adaptive organismic processes. The functional characteristics of humans reflect a phylogenetic history of adaptation and selection with respect to inanimate, animate, and (proto-) sociocultural features of the environment; and much of ontogenetic development can be viewed as an ongoing cumulative process of adaptation to and engagement of local environmental circumstances.

Ecological Psychology in Relation to Other Ecological Sciences

For the purposes of understanding the enterprise of psychology, as distinct from other life sciences, the matter cannot be left solely with evolutionary theory, with considerations of levels of organization in nature, and the like. This is because the problems identified as significant from a psychological standpoint do not initially come out of considerations of the life sciences. Instead, its problems come from a source that is unique to psychology in relation to the other life sciences.

Psychology is unique among the life sciences in that the phenomena selected for examination are significant because of their place in *human experience*. It is through attention to immediate experience that questions arise about ourselves; and philosophers and psychologists have been engaged by such issues for centuries. Questions such as how individuals acquire knowledge, in what ways the environment influences individual development, how it is possible to know other minds, what is the basis for ethical choices, and so on, are all, in the first instance, derived from and possess significance in relation to immediate experience (MacLeod, 1975). Recent students of the human condition, from James and Merleau-Ponty to Koffka and Gibson, have repeatedly demonstrated through their work that significant psychological issues are identified by close attention to everyday experience.

It is true, of course, that the phenomena studied in the other life sciences are also features of individuals' (viz. scientists') experience. However, the significance of these phenomena, unlike those in psychology, does not derive from their place in human experience, but rather from their significance among the systems under study.

There is an additional way in which psychology differs from other life sciences. Among the life sciences, only psychology has the potential to alter fundamentally aspects of its subject matter simply by their study. In other words, the way psychologists conceptualize and study human functioning—that is, the picture of humans offered through the authority of science—can transform how humans think about themselves, and hence how humans act. Other life sciences do not have this reflexive power.

Competing Psychological Approaches in Light of Evolutionary Theory

The approaches that psychology has adopted in the examination of long-standing problems about human functioning are built on philosophical traditions stretching far back into the past. These traditions are a valuable starting point. But something has changed since the mid-19th century. In the wake of the Darwinian revolution in thought, responses to long-standing philosophical questions must now fit agreeably with the tenets of evolutionary theory. Regrettably, many traditions that have most influenced the ideas of 20th century psychology do not.

I am referring here to the varieties of representational theory of mind that have been psychology's intellectual inheritance and are often hidden as tacit features of so much contemporary thinking. It is vital to remember that those conceptions of mind that have most directly shaped contemporary psychological thinking predate evolutionary theory. Although strenuous efforts have been made to modify these traditional analyses so as to render them compatible with evolutionary theory, at the heart of representational theories of mind is an assumption that impedes their ready transformation into a plausible functional account. This is the assumption that experience of the environment is always indirect. From the point of view of representational theories, the individual knower never experiences the world as such, but only a mental copy of it; and all human knowing, as well as that of other animals, is based on mental representations. Because of the assumed indirectness of environmental knowledge, there exists in all such theories an unbridgeable gap between the world as such and the knower's experience of it. The challenge then is to reconcile this view with the fundamental evolutionary tenet that psychological processes are adaptive with respect to environmental conditions possessing functional significance.

As just noted, psychologists have taken steps to adjust traditional representational views of experience to fit post-Darwinian expectations that knowledge and action have functional value for an individual in the environment. Most commonly, it has been proposed in various forms that mental representations have functional value to the extent that they bear a reasonably high probabilistic relation to the environment. For this reason, they can adequately mediate between the environment, on the one hand, and individual action and thought, on the other. Such an account no doubt works, conceptually speaking. It makes for a story that is consistent with some claims about how perceiving and knowing operate. But is it fundamentally plausible?

Naïve experience is at odds with such a view. And not just naïve experience. After stepping back and considering from an evolutionary perspective the adaptive demands on animals in the environment, doesn't it seem rather odd for animals to have evolved adaptive processes that admit at best indirect and probabilistic knowledge of even the most basic ecological resources and hazards?

But questioning the prima facie plausibility of a conceptualization is not by itself an adequate way of evaluating its merits. The history of science is rife with seemingly counterintuitive claims that have stood the test of time. And perhaps indirect knowledge of the environment is the best that could be achieved given the limitations imposed by the early paths taken in the evolution of sensory systems.

Plausibility does become a factor, however, when we are presented with an alternative(s) to the received view, and then the proffered approaches can be considered in terms of their relative congruence with other widely accepted ideas. In the case of a metatheoretical foundation for psychological theory in particular, plausibility can turn on how well the competing accounts of mind comport with the essential assumptions of the other life sciences, and with the backbone of the life sciences, evolutionary theory, in particular.

Until William James offered his philosophy of radical empiricism, there was no viable alternative conceptualization of mind that claimed compatibility with evolutionary theory other than those late 19th century representational theories adjusted to fit this view.[1] With radical empiricism, James attempted to provide philosophical grounds for the view that experience of the environment is direct. To the extent that radical empiricism succeeds in providing the groundwork for an account of direct knowing, it would seem to be more compatible than representational theories with the central feature of evolutionary theory—an organism's continuing adaptation to environmental conditions. From there, a radical empiricist approach to knowing would need to be able to offer an adequate account of processes of nonperceptual awareness, such as thinking and imagining.

It is not possible to argue conclusively for radical empiricism on these grounds. Indeed, it is unlikely that the choice of a representational account versus radical empiricism is resolvable on empirical grounds. As historical studies of clashes between scientific conceptual frameworks indicate, such disputes are rarely resolved empirically (Kuhn, 1970). The reasons why one conceptualization in science is embraced over another are not well understood; but one important factor appears to be how well the framework fits conceptually with the other ideas and "themata" prevailing in the science at the time (Holton, 1973). In the present case, a conceptualization of psychological functioning that allows for direct knowing of environmental conditions, while also offering an account of abstractions (concepts) derived from direct knowing, appears to be more congruent with the view that animal processes are fundamentally adaptive, than is a conceptualization that knowing is in all cases an indirect, mediated process.

RADICAL EMPIRICISM AND ECOLOGICAL PSYCHOLOGY

Radical empiricism offers a way of conceptualizing the environment–person relation that admits the possibility of individuals directly knowing the world, while also recognizing the critical place of reflective processes in human knowing. In order to provide grounds for direct experience, James ad-

---

[1]Thomas Reid proposed an account of direct perception in the 18th century without the benefit of evolutionary theory to provide a naturalistic explanation for why cognition is adaptive.

dressed the question, "What is the nature of existence such that the world can be known directly or immediately by a knower?" He proposed that such an analysis, and indeed, individual knowing, begin with the notion of "pure experience." Pure experience, as an idealization, is the fundamental and undifferentiated ground of experience. It is undifferentiated in that subsequent distinctions between knower and known, and among the constellations of features within each of these domains—all yet to be realized in experience from the outset—exist as possibilities in this ground.

What makes all subsequent differentiation possible are two factors: the latent structure of this experiential field and the essential functional characteristic of knowing, namely, *selectivity*. That is, the facet of the experiential field that is the knower has the potential to discover latent structure in the field. Importantly, this is a process of discovering structure within the field of experience. This process is perceiving. The potential relations discoverable in this ground of experience are, in principle, unlimited. Because relations are established within the field of experience that includes the knower, the knower is directly in contact with the object known. So nothing mediates between the knower and known, nothing plays an intermediary role of establishing a correspondence between a world "out there" and a mind "inside the head."

However, characteristics of the knower's immediate relation to the known through perceiving are constrained in their very immediacy. In order to overcome these limitations, humans (and to varying degrees other animals) developed the means for selectively engaging perceptual experience (percepts) and reflexively generating knowledge (concepts) derived from it. These reflexively derived forms of knowing create possibilities to extend understanding by allowing the knower to go beyond the limitations of immediate experience (recognizing that immediate experience is far richer than is usually assumed). But ultimately, the validity of concepts rests on their relation to ongoing, immediate experience of the environment. James's insistence that concepts continually be tested against immediate experience reveals an important way in which his approach to conception differs from others that may appear superficially similar. Whereas abstractions from perceiving conceptualized as indirect knowledge can never take the individual closer in touch with reality than the indirect knowledge itself—and even threatens to progressively distance us from reality—for James concepts that are tested against direct experience can put us closer in touch with reality while overcoming the limitations of perceiving.

What are the affinities between this view and an evolutionary perspective? As discussed, radical empiricism is a perspective developed with evolutionary theory as its template. In fact, all of James's psychology was informed by acceptance of an evolutionary point of view, as well as attention to human experience. Radical empiricism offers the view that the knower actively engages the environment, and in the process uncovers its structure. In this manner, the individual is an *adaptive agent* in relation to the prevailing environmental circumstances.

This view of the knower as being active in discovering properties of the environment may appear at first glance to be comparable to a number of other functional views of cognition (perhaps, most obviously Piaget's genetic epistemology). However, the perspective offered by radical empiricism is different from most others, as already noted. Whereas most functional views claim that adaptation of the individual to the environment involves establishing a correspondence between what is in the world and what is in mind, radical empiricism assumes that ultimately there is a direct relation between knower and known, and that knowing involves a participatory attunement of knower to environmental structure within the individual–environmental relation.

The Jamesian conceptualization of an organism progressively becoming attuned to environmental structure is in evidence when an evolutionary perspective is adopted and some functional characteristics of an individual animal in relation to its econiche are examined. For example, the visual sensitivities of humans reflect certain properties of the econiche, namely, the dominant range of wavelengths present under daylight levels of illumination. In this case, it can be said that what has been selected for over time are organismic processes that have the potential to take on (to resonate to) particular structural properties of the environment. Or, to take a quite different example, the selection of forelimbs and paws in arboreal mammals and subsequently in primates reflects a progressive attunement to graspable features of the econiche. Evolutionary theory, like radical empiricism, offers up a picture of environment–organism attunements, of adaptation as a process of structure shared between environment and organism, between knower and known.

Both evolutionary theory (as applied to a particular species) and radical empiricism also assume the presence of a background of relatively stable environmental structures, including regular, orderly change (i.e., events), against which natural selection and knowing processes, respectively, operate. The functional characteristics of a particular species can be understood in relation to the environmental structures that were in place when functions emerged. Similarly, from the point of view of radical empiricism, knowing processes operate against a background of structure already in place. Knowing is a process of adjusting to existing, latent structure, just as species adaptation is a process of selection in relation to existing environmental structure. It is important to add, however, that in both cases (but to varying degrees), individuals often contribute to the very background conditions against which they develop.

Finally, both evolutionary theory and radical empiricism view development, broadly construed, as an active, self-correcting, open-ended process. Species 'evolution is an ongoing process of adaptation and selection with respect to a changing environment (as long as the environment continues to be life-sustaining). Likewise, radical empiricism and its companion theory of truth, pragmatism, view knowing as an ongoing process of continuously evaluating what is known against what is currently experienced, of revising or updating the known as its inconsistencies relative to immediate experience are revealed; and so on without end. What is known is always a temporary and imperfect resolution to a question of fit between an adaptive agent and environmental structure. In Dewey's phrase, "the quest for certainty" is a chimera. However, and this point cannot be overemphasized, although changing and open-ended, what is known does not lack a foundation, as some would have it. Like the ground for species evolution, the foundation of knowing is the structure of the environment that can be directly experienced—but never in all of its multitude of facets. Possibilities for knowing, like potential econiches, are potentially inexhaustible; and like living organisms with respect to econiches, individuals seek out these structures.

The strong affinities between radical empiricism and evolutionary theory, as already noted, are no accident. Evolutionary theory was a formative influence on James's ideas. Unlike modern representational theories of mind that have been "retrofitted" to accommodate evolutionary theory, radical empiricism and pragmatism were from the outset intellectual products of Darwinian thinking.

Adience and "The Recession of the Stimulus"

Although James's philosophy of radical empiricism is deeply psychological in many respects, most of its psychological implications remain to be developed. In what ways can radical empiricism be extended to the concerns of psychology, especially those receiving greatest attention in the 20th and 21st centuries? During roughly the first decade of the 20th century, experimental psychology made a decisive turn, taking as its overarching goal a functional analysis of psychological processes. Emulating the search in the natural sciences for lawful relations among variables, psychology sought to uncover lawful relations between stimulus conditions and behavior. In what ways can radical empiricism inform this sort of functional analysis? James's student E. B. Holt took some important, initial steps in this direction.

Holt sought ways of conceptualizing aspects of James's philosophical views in behavioral terms. As for the selectivity of knowing that is so central to James's position, Holt developed the behavioral notion of adience. He proposed that a primitive characteristic of responses is their adience: When an organism is stimulated, it responds by directing action toward the source of stimulation in order to maintain and prolong exposure to it. Over time adient responses become fine-tuned, and concurrently, the environmental stimulation toward which they are directed becomes differentiated. Apart from one difference to be noted shortly, the concept of adience is more or less a straightforward translation of Jamesian selectivity into the conceptual language of behavior and physiology circa 1930.

Perhaps more significant than adience is Holt's proposal of the "recession of the stimulus." The lawful relations sought between environment and behavior were idealized by most behaviorists as a relation between proximal physical stimuli and peripheral sensory and motoric responses. Holt opposed this peripheralistic tendency in behaviorism. He argued instead that in psychology's attempts to identify lawful relations between stimulus conditions and behavioral variables, the *grain* of this functional analysis should not be considered fixed and maintained, as it typically is, at a molecular level. As the behavior or action in question becomes considered in increasingly molar terms (e.g., when considering actions of the whole organism rather than fragments of behavior), the effective stimulus (or environmental correlate) of behavior "recedes" into distal layers of the environment.

This claim has at least two significant consequences for the development of psychological theory. First, whereas the dominant view among most behaviorists was that psychology would ultimately benefit from defining its variables in the reductionistic language of physics and physiology, Holt's was the strongest voice within the early behaviorist camp promoting a nonreductive analysis of behavior. He was soon surpassed as the foremost representative of this position by his student Edward Tolman. Second, by proposing that the effective stimulus recedes as increasingly complex behaviors are considered, and thereby pointing to the limitations of molecular, proximal stimuli in accounting for behavior qua the individual, Holt invited a reconceptualization of the environment from a psychological point of view. The connection between radical empiricism and the recession of the stimulus here is subtle, but important. By looking for functional relations between environment and behavior in increasingly distal features of the environment, Holt was following James in seeking an account of action and knowing, resulting in the selection of structure *within the field of an individual's experience*. In doing so, Holt prepared the way for Gibson's exploration of higher order variables in the stimulus array.

Coupling the claim of the recession of the stimulus with the notion of adience offered a conceptualization that was unique in psychology, although its roots can be found in James as well as in Dewey. The individual is viewed as actively engaging its environment, as responding adiently to stimulation with distal sources for the purpose of achieving a goal *intrinsic* to this relation. The individual is not seeking stimulation solely to meet some extrinsic need, for instance to reduce some biologically based drive. Instead, the individual is seeking out stimulation in order to uncover more about it. And such epistemic goals are dispositions or intentions of individuals considered as whole entities.

A difficulty with this viewpoint, however, is that the term *stimulation* connotes something that is imposed on an organism (J. J. Gibson, 1960), and indeed Holt posited that adient responses are initially triggered by stimulation. But this aspect of the conceptualization is not completely consonant with the Jamesian view of selectivity, which has a thorough-going intentional character. The language of stimulation will not do at a molar level of analysis of behavior. Once it is recognized that this language distorts the intentional character of action, what alternative conceptualization other than stimulation can be offered to describe the properties of the environment that perceivers selectively engage?

James Gibson, Holt's student, provided an answer: Animals do not respond to stimulation, instead they seek out stimulus *information*. One important difference between information and stimulation is that, by and large, animals must act to detect information; by contrast, stimulation is something that is imposed. In this way, Gibson's concept of stimulus information is far more compatible with James's view of knowing as selection than is stimulation. Moreover, because the critical underpinning of Gibson's notion of information is *structure*, it provides an opening for developing a conceptualization of the environment that is psychologically meaningful. This too is thoroughly Jamesian in spirit.

Environmental Information, Meaning, and Sociocultural Processes

Gibson proposed in the case of vision that information available to be perceived in the ambient array of reflected light specifies functionally significant properties of the environment taken with reference to an individual. These functionally significant properties of environmental features taken at this grain of analysis (i.e., with reference to the actions of an individual), are *affordances*. The actions of an individual in a setting can be lawfully related to the affordances available to be engaged in that setting. For instance, an assessment of the affordances available for an individual in a setting can be used as a basis for predicting what actions are possible.[2] The concept of affordance implements Holt's notion of "the recession of the stimulus." Ac-

---

[2]In view of the fact that action is intentional, what an individual actually will do is not something that can be predicted, except in those exceedingly rare conditions where the possibilities for meaningful actions (i.e., actions which lead to some outcome) are extremely narrow (as in the case of an operant chamber) or specific motivations are artificially elevated, (e.g., through deprivation). Normally, only a macrodeterminancy is possible (Weiss, 1969).

tions of an individual qua individual are systematically related to properties of the environment taken at a commensurate level of analysis, rather than to proximal, molecular stimuli.

Likewise, Barker's concept of a *behavior setting* can be viewed incidentally as an implementation of Holt's notion of the "recession of the stimulus." When the grain of analysis is the actions of an individual as a participant in a group, as opposed to individual action qua individual, the environmental property that is lawfully related to action of a group is a behavior-milieu synomorph with specifiable geographical and temporal boundaries—that is, a behavior setting. As the level of analysis of activity increases in scale, the effective environmental feature "recedes" commensurately to a more molar level.

Especially significant about affordances and behavior settings is that from the point of view of the actions of the individual they are perceptually meaningful features of the environment. Affordances are environmental features that are enfolded in goal-directed actions, that is, they are constitutive aspects of action. The object's meaning derives from a particular set of intrinsic properties that it possesses in relation to the perceiver and are perceived in the context of a goal-directed action. In principle, affordances are specified by stimulus information. Included among the categories of affordances to be found in most human cultures are tools, artifacts, representations, and places.

Behavior settings are perceivable dynamic environmental structures of collective, interdependent actions and milieu. An individual typically chooses to participate in a particular behavior setting for the sake of some end that is largely intrinsic to the character of that setting. The meaning of a behavior setting is assumed to be a perceivable functional property of behavior and milieu.

It was proposed earlier that psychology is unique among the life sciences because its fundamental problems are significant in the context of human experience. Recognizing the importance of firsthand experience as the well-spring for the discipline's most central questions brings with it the recognition that addressing meaning in experience is a question that is inescapable for a science of human phenomena. The problem is how to approach such a formidable problem within the standards of natural science? Affordances and behavior settings can serve as prototypes for conceptualizing some meaningful aspects of experience, namely, the experience of meaningful environmental features. In this respect, they stand in marked contrast to physicalistic concepts that are traditionally employed to describe the effective stimuli for behavior but are absent of any meaning. But like physicalistic terms, affordances and behavior settings are objective in principle—that is, they are perceivable properties of the environment that can be specified independently of any single individual's experience.

Finally, how can the claim that there are meaningful structures in experience be brought into line with evolutionary considerations? As properties of the environment, meaningful features such as affordances and the social processes that generate behavior settings can be viewed as part of the context against which actions of modern humans have evolved. For instance, tools and the functional capacity to use them co-evolved; and early hominids that could most effectively exploit such functionally meaningful resources would have a selective advantage. Likewise, meaningful social information supporting communication provides the ground against which the requisite skills for learning in social contexts can develop and interdependent group structures can emerge. Both archaeological evidence and contemporary field observations of higher primates are consistent with the claim that functionally meaningful features of the environment and meaningful social processes constitute parts of the econiche with respect to which humans evolved. Just as biosensory systems can be viewed as adaptations to certain extant environmental properties, so too certain actions of the animal as a whole can be viewed as adaptations to extant environmental properties—namely, the presence of information specifying meaningful features of the environment. Indeed, it is possible to view human beings as a species that is distinctive for its exploitation of potential meanings in the environment. And much of ongoing human activity can be viewed as efforts toward discovering meaning and structure in the surround.

Fundamental to human cultural evolution is the elaboration of meaningful environmental features and their preservation in durable forms. New tools affording particular actions were discovered, and artifacts facilitating the ease and increasing the yield of actions were developed. Representational systems of meanings, such as symbol systems, were created. Extra-individual social structures, such as behavior settings and social institutions, were generated through patterns of action that sustain meaning.[3] One particularly important feature of artifacts, symbolic representations, and social structures is that knowledge acquired by individuals and collectively by social groups can be "off-loaded" onto them. In so doing, the amount of knowledge that can be retained over time increases enormously, and the accumulation and refinement of knowledge through iterations across generations becomes possible. These innovations, in effect, create possibilities for knowledge to become distributed across the environment–person(s) relation, considered at varying levels of complexity. In short, humans co-evolved with meaningful environmental features, and the subsequent elaboration

---

[3]This is not intended to be an exhaustive list of the ways knowledge is preserved and conveyed through sociocultural processes. Omitted are phenomena such as mimetic systems (e.g., ritual and art, just to name some others; see Donald, 1991).

of them has been the springboard for many of the recent products of sociocultural history.

ECOLOGICAL PSYCHOLOGY AS AN ESSENTIAL PART OF A HUMAN SCIENCE

It is time to reflect on the place of ecological psychology in the field of psychology as a whole, and in so doing, to bring this study to a close. Some of the ways that ecological psychology can contribute to psychology should be apparent at this point. Because their rationale has been covered at length in the preceding chapters, they are stated here in the briefest of terms. There is also a little more new ground to break as well.

Some Implications of an Account of Direct Perception

Ecological psychology offers the discipline a much needed focus on the environment considered from a psychological and relational point of view. In doing so, it is not proposing a mere shift in emphasis, from a decontextualized organism to an organism-free environment. Looking at psychological phenomena from an ecological vantage point produces significant consequences for psychological theory and method. As for theory, which has been the sole focus of this book, consideration of the environment from a psychological, relational perspective has direct bearing on how the nature of knowing (cognitive) processes is conceptualized.

The standard approach of conceptualizing the environment in physical terms typically leaves it relatively unstructured; and accordingly, what is required of the organism in order to maintain an adaptive relation with environmental conditions places an enormous epistemic burden on cognitive processes. Moreover, in the process of imposing some order on what is otherwise a relatively disordered experience of the environment, each individual organism would construct a subjective, private, mental realm. As a result, even granting that cognitive models can be proposed that meet these considerable epistemic demands, such a task would be accomplished at the expense of forever cutting off each organism from direct contact with the environment, including with other organisms.

If instead, by adopting a psychological level of analysis of the environment, a case can be made that the environment available to be perceived is structured (and empirical support is accumulating for this claim), thus what is required of cognitive processes is radically different. Instead of needing each individual to construct a private, subjective environment, the individual would need to possess the means for detecting structure already present in the environment. Such an analysis would provide grounds for the possibility that features of the environment are directly perceived by an individual, even while these properties exist independently of that individual. If directly perceivable environmental features exist independently of an individual, they can be viewed as features of a common environment that are accessible in principle to anyone. In short, the gap between the individual knower and the known can be bridged (side-stepped actually), and the common grounds for shared, mutual understanding, although still leaving vast freedom for differences between knowers, becomes a possibility.

A Natural Science Approach to a Human Science

Beyond the foregoing, there is a further contribution yet to be considered that ecological psychology can make to the discipline of psychology as a whole. It is entirely reasonable to expect that the analysis of the human condition that the discipline of psychology has to offer addresses some of our most basic questions and concerns and also is recognizable to us as a description of ourselves. It must be a "human science", that is, a psychology at a minimum, adequate to the task of capturing the distinctive qualities of what it is to be human. Ecological psychology contributes to the promotion of a human science in several ways, but perhaps most essentially because of its fundamental claim that individuals engage a meaningful environment and because it provides some footholds for rigorously explicating this claim. Even in those circumstances where there is an apparent absence of environmental meaning, it is assumed that individuals take measures to discover extant meaning or, when necessary, to create meaning in the environment. Ecological psychology is not alone in its emphasis on the centrality of meaning in human experience. This point of view has been the centerpiece of several approaches for quite some time. What is unique to ecological psychology is its approach to meaning in human experience from a natural science perspective.

One of the many fault lines running through the diverse discipline of psychology has created two distinct intellectual territories: one that takes a natural science perspective as its standard, and another (and a far smaller region) that resides fully in what is often broadly called an existential/humanistic perspective. The principal reason for this schism is the apparent lack of a place for meaning in a naturalistic perspective. But must a naturalistic approach preclude treatment of meaning in human experience?

The strategy of employing concepts of the physical sciences to describe the properties of the environment was very justifiable for psychology at the outset, and it remains so in many areas of psychology because the discipline needs a precise language to describe its variables. Terms grounded in physical concepts meet this criterion. In addition, the use of physicalistic language gives psychology a clear place among other natural sciences. Sometimes physical concepts were not readily available, so the desire for physicalistic precision was instantiated into a procedure for defining variables in terms of how they are measured or how they are produced. This is, of course, the ubiquitous *operational definition*, which students of psychology have cut their teeth on for decades.

Striving to maximize precision in its conceptual language is essential for any science. There is no argument about that. But as Koch (1975/1999a) argued, by formalizing how concepts are to be admitted into the discipline, historically the scope of psychology became increasingly restricted:

> Beliefs concerning the magical potency of a device called "operational definition" have been the most stable of the inheritances from that paradigm of science which began to regulate psychological inquiry in the early thirties. ... This deeply ingrained lore exerts no trivial impact on inquiry. For any set of rules which stipulate how concepts *must* be *introduced* into a field of inquiry—which stipulate, in fact, how concepts and thus systematic relations built upon them must be linked to the world—must delimit the admissible subject matter of that field. (p. 148)[4]

At best, the consequences of this procedure can produce a field that addresses with precision and care a small, select set of phenomena, while neglecting other phenomena. But often, in addition to narrowing the range of topics acceptable for disciplinary study, attempts at maximizing the precision of its language have sometimes come at the expense of verisimilitude. That is to say, the resulting lexicon has had less and less bearing on the human condition and may even unintentionally offer up a distorted picture of "human nature." Possessing as it does the imprimatur of science, this would be an authoritative enterprise with the power to transform how we think about ourselves and others, and in turn what we become (Koch, 1964; Sampson, 1977; Schwartz, 1986; Shotter, 1975). The alternative need not be to abandon methodological rigor, but rather to explore ways of describing human phenomena both rigorously and meaningfully.

Koch argued that psychology's quest to purify its conceptual tools has produced two problematical styles of thought. First, it has engaged in "ameaningful thinking." This pattern of thought is characterized by a slavish commitment to a fixed procedure, rather than procedures that are modified in relation to problem contexts. Second, it has led to "a-ontologism", which he described in the following way:

---

[4]A clarification about the two dates here and in the subsequent citations from Koch's writings. The 1999 date refers to an invaluable collection of Koch's most significant essays recently edited by Finkelman and Kessel. This volume contains excerpts from Koch's essays. The first and earlier date indicates when the paper from which the excerpt was extracted appeared.

The terms and relations of the object of inquiry or the problem are seen, as it were, through an inverted telescope: detail, structure, quiddity, are obliterated; relative to the state of affairs in meaningful thinking, objects of knowledge become faceless. Being caricatures, being faceless—*they lose reality*; they are not inhabited by mind, not caressingly explored in that they have little interest or color. They are dealt with, conjured with, arranged into relatively *gross means-end or antecedent–consequent relationships*. The world becoming relatively flaccid, the object of knowledge becoming relatively indistinct, the world or any given part of it is not felt fully or passionately, is perceived *devoid of objective value*. (Koch, 1965/1999b, p. 241, emphases added)

The world of immediate human experience becomes unrecognizable from this vantage point. It takes on the colorless and value-neutral character of our conceptualization of the physical domain. Is this the necessary price to be paid for scientific precision and rigor?

Meaning and Value as an Environmental Property

Through his often iconoclastic writings, Koch offered incisive, harsh, sometimes witty, sometimes cynical analyses. But he was more than a nay-sayer. He also made efforts to put forward the beginnings of a positive program that, with attention to rigor, would help place meaning and value as qualities of human experience at the forefront of psychology's concerns. His overarching goal was to effect a rapprochement between psychological science and the humanities.[5]

Koch did not identify himself as an ecological psychologist; his theoretical and philosophical interests were broader than that. But his approach helps to illuminate one role that ecological psychology can play in the development of psychology as a human science. Koch (1969/1999c) argued that "major psychological problems cannot be addressed except at levels of experiential sensitivity commonly cultivated in the past in the humanities" (p. 196). But the physicalistic and operational approach that the discipline has employed over much of the 20th century omits those very qualities of experience. Further contributing to the resulting paucity of understanding about the dimensions of human experience has been an issue that has only received incidental attention up to this point in the preceding chapters, and that is psychology's approach to the basis for

---

[5]Koch (1965/1999) identified the problem that occupied his concerns as follows:

From the beginning, some pooled schematic image of the *form* of science was dominant: respectability held more glamour than insight, caution than curiosity, feasibility than fidelity or fruitfulness. A telling consequence ... was the ever-widening estrangement between the scientific makers of human science and the humanistic explorers of the content of man. (p. 244)

action—(i.e., the problem of the motivation). Although it has been emphasized throughout (following James, Dewey, and others) that action is intentional, the bases for action have not been explicitly considered.

In truth, psychology's understanding of human motivation is really quite meager. The standard approach to motivation has historically attempted to understand actions, both animal and human, as means–ends relations in which the ends produced (i.e., the gains or benefits) are external to the action. The actions are engaged in for some other purpose beyond the action itself. Consequently, individuals are understood to act in order to satisfy a biological need, an ego need, a curiosity need, a need for play, and so forth. An action is rarely considered in terms of its intrinsic qualities. Although it is no doubt true that in some limited ways an individual's actions can be viewed as means to some such extrinsic ends as these, this focus excludes a vast array of distinctively human actions. Moreover, even in the case where extrinsic needs are being served, such accounts "convey nothing whatsoever with respect to the *intrinsic character*" of the action (Koch, 1969/1999c, p. 200).

The intrinsic character of an action is a critical dimension for understanding why one specific action in relation to particular environmental features rather others was engaged in. Putting the matter in terms of "needs" does little to explain what it is about some particular environment–action relation that makes it something an individual chooses to participate in; and it leaves untouched those many daily actions for which it is difficult to identify any extrinsic benefit. An emphasis on extrinsic goals has blinded psychologists to the "quiddities" of human experience.

The intrinsic characteristics of any particular action have to do with its experiential qualities as a *situated action*—that is, in terms of qualities residing within a particular environment–person relation. Looking at motivation from this vantage point puts the account "outside of the *idiom of needs*" (Koch, 1969/1999c, p. 202):

> I have been drawn to these activities, and not others, because (among other reasons) they "contain," "afford," "generate" specific properties or relations in my experience toward which I am adient. *I like these particular activities because they are the particular kinds of activities they are*—not because they reduce my "play drive," or are conducive to my well-being (often they are not), or my status (some of them make me look quite ludicrous), or my virility pride. (Koch, 1969/1999c, p. 202)

Why then is an individual drawn to engaging particular environmental features rather than others? How are psychologists to think about the motivational grounds for engaging these features of experience in other than external terms? Koch explained it in the following way:

I like them by virtue of something far more *definite*, "real," if you will, than anything that could be phrased in the extrinsic mode. Each one I like because of *specific* properties or relations immanent, intrinsic, within the given action. Or better, the properties and relations *are* the "liking." (p. 202)

Koch called these properties of experience "value properties."

A concrete example drawn from Koch may help at this point. Whereas eating has, no doubt, an "in-order-to," extrinsic character—people eat in-order-to reduce hunger—leaving this activity at that barely scratches its surface, omitting its most interesting human qualities. Eating is a discriminating perceptual experience. It offers inexhaustible possibilities of a gustatory, olfactory, tactile, auditory, and visual nature. The source of these possibilities rests in a multitude of factors in the food and other ingredients, in the manner of their preparation and presentation, and so on. Cooking in many cultures has been elevated arguably to an art form, and the perceptual sensitivities accompanying eating can be developed to a very high degree. From the vantage point of considering its intrinsic qualities, the value of the act takes on a high degree of specificity rooted in particular features of the environment. Moreover, if this example is any indication of possibilities in other domains of experience, then these qualitative features can be described with considerable precision:

It is already possible for most of us to comment on a meal in a more particulate way than some such exclamation as "Delicious!" Great chefs ... members of gourmet communities, professional wine and tea tasters, have in fact achieved a gastronomic-experience language of expressive differentiation and specificity. (Koch, 1969/1999c, p. 206)

The high level of connoisseurship found in many domains of human experience provides ample evidence that structure in the field of experience can be described with a high level of precision. Having identified, even in a preliminary way, the intrinsic qualities of experience, the psychological, the sociocultural, and the biological processes involved can be further explored with greater rigor and specificity while the analysis remains rooted in the domain of human experience.

This example is but one of many that could be offered to illustrate the following: First, there is seemingly an exhaustible richness within perceptual experience. Second, this field of potential experience is not neutral; it has value properties. It is comprised of "a plurality of particulate 'goods' and 'bads'" (Koch, 1969/1999c, p. 209). Third, a description of value properties captures many of the distinctive qualities of human experience while acknowledging the vast experiential differences that exist. Fourth, this field of experience can be described with some degree of precision.[6] Fifth, within the context of individual–environment relations, value properties can be viewed as being objective, in the sense that they reside in properties of environment that, in principle, are accessible to any perceiver. Finally, by attending to the subtleties of experience, some possibilities for a renewed convergence and collaboration between psychology and the humanities around common concerns begin to appear (see Koch, 1969/1999c, pp. 201–217).

This discussion of value properties is very much in the spirit of James's radical empiricism and the approach to psychological experience he developed. James argued that knowing, which *always has both cognitive and affective qualities,* is a relation between a knower and an object known, and the qualities of experience are intrinsic to this relationship. Koch's analysis of value properties, and especially his efforts to effect a reconciliation between the natural sciences and the humanities, is quite Jamesian in character.[7]

Koch identified a vast area of exploration for psychology that is fundamental to any understanding of what it is to be human. His proposals should not be dismissed as merely relevant to aesthetics, at least in any narrow sense of that term. He was pointing to the need for better understanding the full spectrum of situated human experience, because "the search for the structure of experience *is* the lived experience" (McDermott, quoted in Hickman, 1992, p. 29).

How does one proceed with this sort of research enterprise? Koch (1969/1999c) proposed that "the chief research 'instrument' for disembedding value properties can only be human discrimination" (p. 216). When he looked to contemporary experimental psychology (circa 1970) for approaches of this nature, one of the few programs he could find that was consonant with his viewpoint was Gibson's perceptual psychology. Koch described Gibson's position as a rare example of an "ontology-revealing framework."[8] By this he meant a theoretical frame-

---

[6]The historically oriented reader may object that this kind of approach has been attempted before in various ways, and without success. A case in point is the efforts of introspectionists to describe the sensations comprising conscious experience. Such a catalogue of sensations is not at all what is being suggested here. For one thing, value properties, although relational, can be said to reside in the object in the same vein that affordances reside in the object (chap. 5). The introspectionists' "stimulus error"—describing mental experience in terms of the object of experience—is close to what the investigator of value properties seeks. In this regard, sensations are the product of a reductionistic attitude, the attempt to find elementary units; whereas the value properties Koch is identifying are complex, higher-order phenomena.

[7]For biographical consideration of James's deep and early interests in the arts, see Bjork (1983) and Feinstein (1984).

[8]Koch (1969/1999a) cited Tolman's purposive behaviorism, with its phenomenological qualities, as an "ontology-respecting framework," and Skinner's program, with its highly restricted language base, as an example of "ontology-distorting framework" (pp. 187–188).

work that tells us more about human experience than otherwise we would know. The development of the program of ecological optics "has pointed to the possibility that there may be many dimensions of physical stimulation specification—the 'higher-order variables' of stimulation—which have not been touched by classical sensory psychology" (Koch, 1975/1999a, p. 189).[9] He continued, "To the extent that a program of this sort is successful, it supplements and refines the previously achieved discriminations of the human race bearing upon the domain not only of psychology but of physics" (p. 189).

This is a lofty endorsement for Gibson's (literally) down-to-earth program. But it is warranted because Gibson drew attention to significant aspects of perceptual experience that otherwise received little notice, especially in experimental psychology. In the domain of vision alone, these phenomena include optic flow fields and ego motion, occluding edges and the perceiving of hidden surfaces, texture gradients and depth-at-an-edge, invariant information specifying object size and object shape, invariants of surface structure under changing illumination, varieties of rigid and nonrigid motion, the ways that objects go out of sight and ways they go out of existence, the dual nature of picture perception, and affordances. All of these phenomena have refined our appreciation of perceptual experience. Additional fruits of the research inspired by Gibson over the past 20 years, including many significant investigations of perceptual and cognitive development, could be added to this list. Clearly, our appreciation for properties of perceptual experience has been greatly enhanced by Gibson's investigations and of those working from his perspective. And as outlined in earlier chapters, the advances in perceptual theory based on these explorations have been notable.

In addition, by applying Holt's notion of "the recession of the stimulus" further than Gibson did, the treatment of value properties can be expanded to a wider range of phenomena than suggested earlier. The concepts of affordances and behavior settings, which are tangible results of following this Holtian line of thought, are suggestive of a rich array of yet-to-be articulated environmental structures operating at various levels of complexity that are perceptually meaningful and have explanatory merit from a psychological perspective.

---

[9]Koch did not employ Gibson's term *ecological optics*, and he did not discuss Gibson's theory as an ecological approach. The latest of Gibson's writings referred to is the 1966 book, but even so it is clear that Koch's familiarity with Gibson is primarily based on J. J. Gibson's (1959) contribution to *Psychology: A Study of A Science*, which Koch edited. As a result, the language Koch used, although accurate circa the 1960s, does not fully reflect Gibson's later ecological views.

ECOLOGICAL PSYCHOLOGY AND ITS PROSPECTS

The field of experimental psychology encompasses a bewildering range of topics operating at distinguishable levels of analysis, from the molecular level (e.g., neurobiological structures, sensory processes) to higher order organizational and sociocultural structures. Whether the field can continue to cohere under the strain of such divergent issues and grains of analysis continues to be in doubt. Is there a center to this excess of diversity? What, if anything, holds psychology as a field of study together?

Reflecting on the first century of psychology, George Miller (1985) pointed out:

> With all of the centrifugal forces presently at work, the real question is not whether psychology is a unified discipline, but why so many psychologists believe it should be. ... What is the binding force? ... I believe the common denominator is a faith that somehow, someday, someone will create *a science of immediate experience*. (p. 42, emphasis added)

Miller took the study of immediate experience to be "the constitutive problem of psychology."

A science that self-consciously embraces immediate experience as its core problem would at all times keep in view those phenomena that bear a fundamental relation to human experience. Such an enterprise would be more than descriptive. It would also uncover processes operating at various levels of analysis, both circumjacent and interjacent to the person, that comprise the present context as it has developed historically and that play an essential role in making us what we are.

An ecological psychology rooted in William James's radical empiricism and brought to an initial stage of fruition by James Gibson, offers the best hope for such an enterprise. This approach provides the foundation for a rigorous science of psychology whose "constitutive problem" is immediate experience.

To summarize three of its main features:

Ecological psychology's entry point for the examination of psychological issues is the dynamic, ongoing, environment–person relation. Identification of this relationship as the principal unit of analysis highlights the primacy of relational, temporally dependent phenomena of a psychological nature. These phenomena clearly reveal the fact that psychological processes are situated processes, never fully isolable from their contexts.

Ecological psychology adopts the view held by other facets of the life sciences that natural processes are structured in a nested hierarchy of relations. Consequently, in addition to reciprocal influences within the psychological level of analysis, also operative are between-level relations. Of these, the between-level relations of greatest interest to ecological psychology are influences from "above" that is, from circumjacent, extra-individual structures, that create opportunities for individuals even as they constrain action.

Ecological psychology assumes that what is most distinctive about human activities, to a greater degree than other complex forms of life, is their efforts toward meaning. The environment is viewed as being rich in features with functional significance, and a focal point of human evolution was the exploitation and subsequent elaboration of meaningful functional resources in the environment. Environmental features, both inanimate and animate, and operating at multiple levels of complexity, have perceivably meaningful properties for action. Individuals function to discover and sometimes to create these meanings, and they act in concert with these features. Psychologically meaningful and perceptible structures are immanent in tools, are created and embedded in artifacts, are displayed in all manner of symbolic representations, and are generated by collective social processes. Beyond supporting individual actions, these resources permit individuals to participate in functionally meaningful activities that are socially distributed across social networks. The basis for much of this distinctively human activity, these efforts toward meaning, is to be found in the value properties of the environment.

The ecological approach, with radical empiricism at its foundation, provides in J. J. Gibson's (1967b) apt phrase "reasons for realism." Apart from any other attribute, its commitment to realism is the ecological approach's most unique and most important feature. Psychology and the social sciences have long needed a framework that can provide a common ground for human experience.

Most fundamentally, the source of much of the tension among the inhabitants of this planet is the necessarily selective nature of perceiving, exacerbated by diverging belief systems constructed on the differences resulting from this initial selectivity. But it is important to remember that differences arise out of a common ground of immediate experience. Because human beings share this common ground, the possibilities for much needed mutual understanding can grow prosperously in its soil.

Although it may be the case that the vantage point from which I view something may differ from yours, the information I discriminate at this moment may differ from what you are able to discriminate, and the information having been made available to each of us historically may differ, the fact remains—if the viewpoint offered by ecological psychology is roughly correct—that the perceptual information in question is publicly accessible. This means there is a possibility for us eventually to experience the same world, even as we live variously within it. That claim of ecological psychology is reason for hope.

CHAPTER 10

References

Allen, T. F. H., & Starr, T. B. (1982). *Hierarchy: Perspectives for ecological complexity*. Chicago: University of Chicago Press.

Allport, F. H. (1955). *Theories of perception and the concept of structure*. New York: Wiley.

Altman, I. (1976). Environmental psychology and social psychology. *Personality and Social Psychology Bulletin, 4,* 109–126.

American Psychological Association (1965). Award for distinguished scientific contribution: Fritz Heider, *20,* 153.

Ashby, W. R. (1956). *An introduction to cybernetics.* New York: Wiley.

Banks, R. (1985). *Continental drift.* New York: Ballantine.

Barker, J. (1999). *Street-level democracy: Political settings at the margins of global power.* West Hartford, CT: Kumarian Press.

Barker, R. G. (Ed.). (1963). *The stream of behavior.* New York: Appleton-Century-Crofts.

Barker, R. G. (1968). *Ecological psychology: Concepts and methods for studying the environment of human behavior.* Stanford, CA: Stanford University Press.

Barker, R. G. (1978). *Habitats, environments, and human behavior: Studies in ecological psychology and eco-behavioral science.* San Francisco: Jossey-Bass.

Barker, R. G. (1987). Prospecting in environmental psychology: Oskaloosa revisited. In I. Altman & D. Stokols (Eds.), *Handbook of environmental psychology* (Vol. 2, pp. 1413–1432). New York: Wiley.

Barker, R. G. (1989). Roger G. Barker. In G. Lindzey (Ed.), *A history of psychology in autobiography* (Vol. 8, pp. 3–35). Stanford, CA: Stanford University Press.

Barker, R. G. (1990). Settings of a professional lifetime. In I. Altman & K. Christensen (Eds.), *Environment and behavior studies: Emergence of intellectual traditions. Human Behavior and Environment,* Vol. 11, (pp. 49–78). New York: Plenum.

Barker, R. G., Dembo, T., & Lewin, K. (1941). Frustration and regression: A study of young children. *University of Iowa Studies in Child Welfare, 18.*

Barker, R. G., & Gump, P. (1964). *Big school, small school: High school size and student behavior.* Stanford, CA: Stanford University press.

397

Barker, R. G., & Schoggen, P. (1973). *Qualities of community life: Methods of measuring environment and behavior applied to an American and an English town*. San Francisco: Jossey-Bass.

Barker, R. G., & Wright, H. F. (1951). *One boy's day*. New York: Harper & Row.

Barker, R. G., & Wright, H. F. (1955). *Midwest and its children*. New York: Harper & Row.

Barkow, J. H., Cosmides, L., & Tooby, J. (Eds.). (1992). *The adapted mind: Evolutionary psychology and the generation of culture*. New York: Oxford University Press.

Barnes, J. (1982). *Aristotle*. Oxford, England: Oxford University Press.

Barzun, J. (1983). *A stroll with William James*. New York: Harper & Row.

Bateson, G. (1972). *Steps towards an ecology of mind*. New York: Ballantine.

Bechtel, R. B. (Ed.). (1990). *The Midwest psychological field station: A celebration of its founding, Environment & Behavior, 22*, 435–552.

Beck, J. (1972). *Surface color perception*. Ithaca, NY: Cornell University Press.

Beek, P. J., Verschoor, F., & Kelso, S. (1997). Requirements for the emergence of a dynamical social psychology. *Psychological Inquiry, 8*, 100–104.

Benesh-Weiner, M. (1988). *The notebooks/Fritz Heider: Vol. 2. Perception*. New York: Springer-Verlag.

Ben-Zeev, A. (1984). The Kantian revolution in perception. *Journal for the Theory of Social Behavior, 14*, 69–84.

Bergson, H. (1960). *Time and free will: An essay on the immediate data of consciousness*. New York: Harper & Row (original work published 1888).

Bergson, H. (1988). *Matter and memory*. New York: Zone Books (original work published 1910).

Berlin, I. (1980). The counter-enlightenment. In H. Hardy (Ed.), *Against the current: Essays in the history of ideas* (pp. 1–24). New York: Viking.

Bjork, D. W. (1983). *The compromised scientist: William James in the development of American psychology*. New York: Columbia University Press.

Boesch, C. (1991). Teaching among wild chimpanzees. *Animal Behavior, 41*, 530–532.

Boorstin, D. (1983). *The discoverers: A history of man's search to know himself and his world*. New York: Random House.

Bourdieu, P. (1977). *Outline of a theory of practice*. Cambridge, England: Cambridge University Press.

Brewer, W. (1999). Schemata. In R. A. Wilson & F. C. Keil (Eds.). *The MIT Encyclopedia of the cognitive sciences* (pp. 729–730). Cambridge, MA: MIT Press.

Brown, H. C. (1931). This material world. Supplementary essay in E. B. Holt, *Animal drive and the learning process: An essay toward radical empiricism,* (Vol. 1, pp. 265–287). New York: Henry Holt.

Brown, R. (1989). Roger Brown. In G. Lindzey (Ed.), *The history of psychology in autobiography,* (Vol. VIII, pp. 37–62). Stanford, CA: Stanford University Press.

Bronfenbrenner, U. (1968). *The ecology of human development: Experiments by nature and design*. Cambridge, MA: Harvard University Press.

Brooks, R. (1995). Intelligence without reason. In L. Steels & R. A. Brooks (Eds.), *The artificial life route to artificial intelligence: Building embodied situated agents* (pp. 25–81). Hillsdale, NJ: Lawrence Erlbaum Associates.

Bruner, J. S. (1983). *In search of mind: Essays in autobiography*. New York: Harper & Row.

Brunswik, E. (1956). *Perception and the representative design of psychological experiments*. Berkeley and Los Angeles: University of California Press.

Brunswik, E. (1966). Samples of Egon Brunswik's early conceptualizations, (L. W. Brandt, trans.). In K. R. Hammond (Ed.), *The psychology of Egon Brunswik* (pp. 514–534). New York: Holt, Rinehart & Winston.

Buber, M. (1970). *I and thou*. New York: Scribner's.

Burtt, E. A. (1954). *The metaphysical foundations of modern science*. Garden City, NY: Doubleday Anchor.

Buss, D. (1995). Evolutionary psychology: A new paradigm for psychological science. *Psychological Inquiry, 6*, 1–49.

Butterworth, G. (1995). Origins of mind in perception and action. In C. Moore & P. J. Dunham (Eds.), *Joint attention: Its origins and role in development* (pp. 29–40). Hillsdale, NJ: Lawrence Erlbaum Associates.

Calpaldi, E. J., & Proctor, R. W. (1999). *Contextualism in psychological research?: A critical review*. Thousand Oaks, CA: Sage.

Carello, C., Grosofsky, A., Reichel, F. D., Solomon, H. Y., & Turvey, M. T. (1989). Visually perceiving what is reachable. *Ecological Psychology, 1*, 27–54.

Carmichael, L. (1946). Edwin Bissell Holt: 1873–1946. *American Journal of Psychology, 59*, 478–480.

Carpenter, M., Tomasello, M., & Savage-Rumbaugh, S. (1995). Joint attention in children, chimpanzees, and enculturated chimpanzees. *Social Development, 43*, 217–237.

Carr, D. (1986). *Time, narrative and history*. Bloomington, IN: Indiana University Press.

Chatwin, B. (1987). *The songlines*. New York: Penguin Books.

Chisolm. R. M. (Ed.). (1960). *Realism and the background of phenomenology*. Atascadero, CA: Ridgeview Publishing.

Chow, S. L. (1989). An intentional analysis of "affordances" revisited. *Journal for the Theory of Social Behavior, 19*, 357–365.

Clark, A. (1997). *Being there. Putting brain, body, and world together again*. Cambridge, MA: MIT Press.

Clark, R. W. (1971). *Einstein: The life and times*. New York: World Publishing.

Cohen, S. M. (1992). Hylomorphism and functionalism. In M. C. Nussbaum & A. O. Rorty (Eds.), *Essays on Aristotle's De Anima* (pp. 57–73). Oxford, England: Oxford University Press.

Cole, M. (1996). *Cultural psychology: A once and future discipline*. Cambridge, MA: Belknap Press.

Conant, J. (1997). The James/Royce dispute and the development of James' "solution." In R. A. Putnam (Ed.), *The Cambridge Companion to William James* (pp. 186–213). Cambridge, MA: Harvard University Press.

Corkum, V., & Moore, C. (1995). Development of joint attention in infants. In C. Moore & P. J. Dunham (Eds.) *Joint attention: Its origins and role in development* (pp. 61–84). Hillsdale, NJ: Lawrence Erlbaum Associates.

Cornus, S., Montagne, G., & Laurent, M. (1999). Perception of a stepping-across affordance. *Ecological Psychology, 11*, 249–267.

Costall, A. (1986). The "psychologist's fallacy" in ecological realism. *Teorie & Modelli, 3*, 37–46.

Costall, A. (1989). A closer look at "direct perception." In A. Gellatly, D. Rogers, & J. A. Sloboda (Eds.), *Cognition and social worlds* (pp. 10–21). Oxford, England: Clarendon.

Costall, A. (1993). Beyond linear perspective: A cubist manifesto for visual science. *Image and Visual Computing, 11*, 334–341.

Costall, A. (1995). Socializing affordances. *Theory and Psychology, 5*, 467–481.

Costall, A. (1999). An iconoclast's triptych: Edward Reed's ecological philosophy. *Theory & Psychology, 9*, 411–416.

Costall, A., & Still, A. (1989). Gibson's theory of direct perception and the problem of cultural relativism. *Journal for the Theory of Social Behavior, 19*, 431–444.

Cotterell, J. L. (1998). Behavior settings in macroenvironments: Implications for the design and analysis of places. In D. Görlitz, H. J. Harloff, M. Günter, & J. Valsiner (Eds.), *Children, cities, and psychological theories: Developing relationships* (pp. 383–404). Berlin: deGruyter.

Crosby, A. W. (1997). *The measure of reality: Quantification and western society 1250–1600*. Cambridge, England: Cambridge University Press.

Crosby, D. A., & Viney, W. (1992). Toward a psychology that is radically empirical: Recapturing the vision of William James. In M. E. Donnelly (Ed.), *Reinterpreting the legacy of William James* (pp. 101–118). Washington, DC: American Psychological Association.

Cutting, J. E. (1986). *Perception with an eye for motion*. Cambridge, MA: MIT Press.

Danziger, K. (1990). *Constructing the subject: Historical origins of psychological research*. New York: Cambridge University Press.

Dawkins, R. (1982). *The extended phenotype: The gene as a unit of selection*. San Francisco: Freeman.

Dent-Read, C., & Zukow-Goldring, P. (Eds.). (1997). *Evolving explanations of development: Ecological approaches to organism–environment systems*. Washington, DC: American Psychological Association.

Dewey, J. (1896). The reflex arc concept in psychology. *Psychological Review, 3*, 357–370.

Dewey, J. (1922). *Human nature and conduct*. New York: Henry Holt.

Diamond, J. (1992). *The third chimpanzee*. New York: Harper Collins.

Diggins, J. P. (1994). *The promise of pragmatism: Modernism and the crisis of knowledge and authority*. Chicago: University of Chicago Press.

Donald, M. (1991). *Origins of the modern mind: Three stages in the evolution of culture and cognition*. Cambridge, MA: Harvard University Press.

Downs, R. (1981). Maps and mapping as metaphors for spatial representation. In L. Liben, A. H. Patterson, & N. Newcombe (Eds.), *Spatial representation and behavior across the life span: Theory and application* (pp. 143–166). New York: Academic Press.

Dreyfus, H. L. (1991). *Being-in-the world: A commentary on Heidegger's Being and time, Division I*. Cambridge, MA: MIT Press.

Edelman, G. M. (1998). Building a picture of the brain. *The Brain, Daedalus, 127*, 37–69.

Edie, J. M. (1964). Introduction. In J. M. Edie (Ed.), *Maurice Merleau Ponty: The primacy of perception and other essays on phenomenological psychology, the philosophy of art, history, and politics* (pp. xiii–xix). Chicago: Northwestern University Press.

Edie, J. M. (1987). *Williams James and phenomenology*. Bloomington, IN: Indiana University Press.

Eiseley, L. (1958). *Darwin's century: Evolution and the men who discovered it*. Garden City, NY: Doubleday.

Elman, J. L., Bates, E. A., Johnson, M. H., Karmiloff-Smith, A., Parisi, D., & Plunkett, K. (1999). *Rethinking innateness. A connectionist perspective on development*. Cambridge, MA: MIT Press.

Epstein, W, & Hatfield, G. (1994). Gestalt psychology and the philosophy of mind. *Philosophical Psychology, 7*, 163–181.

Feinstein, H. (1984). *Becoming William James*. Ithaca, NY: Cornell University Press.

Feldman, A., & Acredolo, L. (1979). The effect of active versus passive exploration on memory for spatial location in children. *Child Development, 50,* 698–704.

Flanagan, O. (1997). Consciousness as a pragmatist views it. In R. A. Putnam (Ed.), *The Cambridge Companion to William James* (pp. 25–48). New York: Cambridge University Press.

Fodor, J., & Pylyshyn, Z. (1981). How direct is perception? Some reflections on Gibson's "ecological approach." *Cognition, 9,* 139–196.

Fogel, A. (1993). *Developing through relationships: Origins of communication, self and culture*. Chicago: University of Chicago Press.

Forgas, J. P. (1979). *Social episodes: The study of interaction routines*. New York: Academic Press.

Fuhrer, U. (1990). Bridging the ecological-psychological gap: Behavior settings as interfaces. *Environment & Behavior, 22,* 518–537.

Fuhrer, U. (1993). Behavior setting analysis of situated learning: The case of newcomers. In S. Chaiklin & J. Lave (Eds.), *Understanding practice: Perspectives on activity and context* (pp. 179–211). Cambridge, England: Cambridge University Press.

Gale, R. M. (1997). John Dewey's naturalization of William James. In R. A. Putnam (Ed.), *The Cambridge companion to William James* (pp. 49–68). New York: Cambridge University Press.

Geertz, C. (1973). *The interpretation of cultures: Selected essays*. New York: Basic Books.

Gibson, E. J. (1969). *Principles of perceptual learning and development*. New York: Appleton-Century-Crofts.

Gibson, E. J. (1982). The concept of affordances in development: A renascence of functionalism. In W. A. Collins (Ed.), *The concept of development: The Minnesota Symposium on Child Development*, Vol. 15 (pp. 55–81). Hillsdale, NJ: Lawrence Erlbaum Associates.

Gibson, E. J. (1991). *An odyssey in learning and perception*. Cambridge, MA: MIT Press.

Gibson, E. J. (1994). Has psychology a future? *Psychological Science, 5,* 69–76.

Gibson, E. J., & Pick, A. D. (2000). *An ecological approach to perceptual learning and development*. New York: Oxford University Press.

Gibson, J. J. (1939). The Aryan myth. *Journal of Educational Sociology, 13,* 164–171.

Gibson, J. J. (1941). A critical review of the concept of set in contemporary psychology. *Psychological Bulletin, 38,* 781–817.

Gibson, J. J. (1950a). *The perception of the visual world*. Boston: Houghton-Mifflin.

Gibson, J. J. (1950b). The implications of learning theory for social psychology. In J. G. Miller (Ed.), *Experiments in social process: A symposium on social psychology* (pp. 120–133). New York: McGraw-Hill.

Gibson, J. J. (1953). Social psychology and the psychology of perceptual learning. In M. Sherif & M. O. Wilson (Eds.), *Group relations at the crossroads*. New York: Harper & Brothers.

Gibson, J. J. (1957). Survival in a world of probable objects. Review of E. Brunswik, *Perception and the representative design of psychological experiments. Contemporary Psychology, 2,* 33–35.

Gibson, J. J. (1958). Visually controlled locomotion and visual orientation in animals. *British Journal of Psychology, 49,* 182–194.

Gibson, J. J. (1959). Perception as function of stimulation. In S. Koch (Ed.), *Psychology: A study of a science* (Vol. 1), (pp. 456–501). New York: McGraw-Hill.

Gibson, J. J. (1960). The concept of the stimulus in psychology. *American Psychologist, 16*, 694–703.

Gibson, J. J. (1962). Observations on active touch. *Psychological Review, 69*, 477–491.

Gibson, J. J. (1966). *The senses considered as perceptual systems.* Boston: Houghton-Mifflin.

Gibson, J. J. (1967a). James Gibson. In E. G. Boring & G. Lindzey (Eds.), *A history of psychology in autobiography* (Vol. 5, pp. 125–144). New York: Appleton-Century-Crofts.

Gibson, J. J. (1967b). New reasons for realism, *Synthese, 17*, 162–172.

Gibson, J. J. (1970). On the relation between hallucination and perception. *Leonardo, 3*, 425–427.

Gibson, J. J. (1971). The information available in pictures. *Leonardo, 4*, 27–35.

Gibson, J. J. (1976). *What is it to perceive?* Unpublished manuscript. (available at http://www.trincoll.edu/depts/psyc/perils/folder6. html)

Gibson, J. J. (1979). *The ecological approach to visual perception.* Boston: Houghton-Mifflin.

Gibson, J. J., & Crooks, L. E. (1938). A theoretical field analysis of automobile-driving. *American Journal of Psychology, 51*, 453–471.

Gibson, J. J., & Gibson, E. J. (1955). Perceptual learning: Differentiation or enrichment? *Psychological Review, 62*, 32–41.

Gibson, J. J., Kaplan, G., Reynolds, H., & Wheeler, K. (1969). The change from visible to invisible: A study of optical transitions. *Perception & Psychophysics, 5*, 113–116.

Giddens, A. (1984). *The constitution of society: Outline of the theory of structuration.* Berkeley: University of California Press.

Ginsburg, G. P. (1990). The ecological perception debate: An affordance for the Journal for the Theory of Social Behavior. *Journal for the Theory of Social Behavior, 20*, 347–364.

Glotzbach, P., & Heft, H. (1982). Ecological and phenomenological contributions to the psychology of perception. *Nous, 16*, 108–121.

Goldfield, E. C. (1995). *Emergent forms: Origins and early development of human action and perception.* New York: Oxford University Press.

Goldstein, K. (1995). *The organism.* New York: Zone Books. (Original work published 1934)

Gombrich, E. H. (1960). *Art and illusion: A study in the art of pictorial perception.* Princeton, NJ: Princeton University Press.

Grene, M. (1963). *A portrait of Aristotle.* Chicago: University of Chicago Press.

Hamlyn, D. W. (1961). *Sensation and perception.* London: Routledge & Kegan Paul.

Hamlyn, D. W. (1990). *In and out of the black box: On the philosophy of cognition.* Oxford, England: Blackwell.

Hammond, K. R. (1966). Probalistic functionalism: Egon Brunswik's integration of the history, theory, and method of psychology. In K. R. Hammond (Ed.), *The psychology of Egon Brunswik* (pp. 15–80). New York: Holt, Rinehart & Winston.

Harlow, V. E. (1931). *A bibliography and genetic study of American realism.* Oklahoma City, OK: Harlow Publishing.

Hatfield, G. (1990). *The natural and the normative: Theories of spatial perception from Kant to Helmholtz.* Cambridge, MA: MIT Press.

Hayek, F. A. (1952). *The sensory order.* Chicago: University of Chicago Press.

Hayek, F. A. (1967). Rules, perception, intelligibility. In F. A. Hayek, *Studies in philosophy, politics, and economics* (pp. 43–61). London: Routledge & Kegan Paul.

Hayek, F. A. (1969). The primacy of the abstract. In A. Koestler & J. R. Smythies (Eds.), *Beyond reductionism: New perspectives in the life sciences, The Alpbach Symposium 1968* (pp. 309–333). Boston: Beacon Press.

Hazen, N. L., Lockman, J. J., & Pick, H. L., Jr. (1978). The development of children's representations of large-scale environments. *Child Development, 49,* 623–636.

Hecht, H. (2000). The failings of three event perception theories. *Ecological Psychology, 30,* 1–25.

Heft, H. (1980). What Heil is missing in Gibson: A reply. *Journal for the Theory of Social Behavior, 10,* 187–193.

Heft, H. (1981). An examination of constructivist and Gibsonian approaches to environmental psychology. *Population and Environment: Behavioral and Social Issues, 4,* 227–245.

Heft, H. (1988a). Affordances of children's environments: A functional approach to environmental description. *Children's Environments Quarterly, 5,* 29–37.

Heft, H. (1988b). The development of Gibson's ecological approach to perception: A review essay. *Journal of Environmental Psychology, 8,* 325–334.

Heft, H. (1989). Affordances and the body: An intentional analysis of Gibson's ecological approach to visual perception. *Journal for the Theory of Social Behavior, 19,* 1–30.

Heft, H. (1990). Perceiving affordances in context: A reply to Chow. *Journal for the Theory of Social Behavior, 20,* 277–284.

Heft, H. (1993). A methodological note on overestimates of reaching distance: Distinguishing between perceptual and analytical judgments. *Ecological Psychology, 5,* 255–271.

Heft, H. (1996). The ecological approach to navigation: A Gibsonian perspective. In J. Portugali (Ed.), *The construction of cognitive maps* (pp. 105–132). Dodrecht: Kluwer Academic Publishers.

Heft, H. (1997). The relevance of Gibson's ecological approach to perception for environment-behavior studies. In G. T. Moore & R. W. Marans (Eds.), *Advances in environment, behavior, and design* (Vol. 4, pp. 71–108). New York: Plenum.

Heft, H. (1998a). Essay review: The elusive environment in environmental psychology. *British Journal of Psychology, 89,* 519–523.

Heft, H. (1998b). Why primary experience is necessary. *Contemporary Psychology, 43,* 450–451.

Heft, H., & McFarland, D. (1999). *Children's and Adult's Assessments of a Step Affordance for Self and Others.* Poster presented at the meetings of the Society for Research in Child Development, Albuquerque, N.M.

Heft, H., & Nasar, J. (2000). Evaluating environmental scenes using dynamic versus static displays. *Environment and Behavior, 32,* 301–322.

Heft, H., & Wohlwill, J. F. (1987). Environmental cognition in children. In I. Altman & D. Stokols (Eds.), *Handbook of environmental psychology.* (Vol. 1, pp. 175–204). New York: Wiley.

Heidbreder, E. (1933). *Seven psychologies.* New York: Century.

Heidbreder, E. (1973). Functionalism. In M. Henle, J. Jaynes, & J. J. Sullivan (Eds.), *Historical conceptions of psychology* (pp. 276–285). New York: Springer.

Heider, F. (1958). *The psychology of interpersonal relations.* New York: Wiley.

Heider, F. (1959a).Thing and medium. *On perception and event structure, and the psychological environment, Psychological issues, 1*, Monograph 3, 1–34. (Original work published 1926)

Heider, F. (1959b). The function of the perception system. In *On perception and event structure, and the psychological environment Psychological issues, 1*, Monograph 3, 35–52. (Original work published 1930)

Heider, F. (1959c). On Lewin's methods and theory. *On perception and event structure, and the psychological environment Psychological issues, 1*, Monograph 3, 108–119.

Heider, F. (1983). *The life of a psychologist: An autobiography*. Lawrence, KS: University Press of Kansas.

Heider, F. (1989). Fritz Heider. In G. Lindzey (Ed.), *A history of psychology in autobiography*, Vol. 8 (pp. 127–156). Stanford, CA: Stanford University Press.

Heil, J. (1979). What Gibson's missing. *Journal for the Theory of Social Behavior, 9*, 265–269.

Heil, J. (1981). Gibsonian sins of omission. *Journal for the Theory of Social Behavior, 11*, 307–311.

Held, R. (1965). Plasticity in sensory-motor systems. *Scientific American, 213*, 84–94.

Heller, M. A. (1984). Active and passive touch: The influence of exploration time on form recognition. *Journal of General Psychology, 110*, 243–249.

Henle, M. (1974). On naïve realism. In R. B. MacLeod & H. L. Pick, Jr. (Eds.), *Perception: Essays in honor of James J. Gibson* (pp. 40–71). Ithaca, NY: Cornell University Press.

Hergenhahn, B. R. (1992). *An introduction to the history of psychology* (2nd ed.). Pacific Grove, CA: Brooks/Cole.

Herrmann, H. (1998). *From biology to sociopolitics: Conceptual continuity in complex systems*. New Haven, CT: Yale University Press.

Hickman, L. A. (1992). *John Dewey's pragmatic technology*. Bloomington, IN: Indiana University Press.

Hilgard, E. R. (1987). *Psychology in America: A historical survey*. San Diego, CA: Harcourt Brace Jovanovich.

Hochberg, J. (1968). In the mind's eye. In R. N. Haber (Ed.), *Contemporary theory and research in visual perception* (pp. 309–331). New York: Holt, Rhinehart, & Winston.

Hochberg, J. (1974). Higher-order stimuli and inter-response coupling in the perception of the visual world. In R. B. MacLeod & H. L. Pick, Jr., (Eds.), *Perception: Essays in honor of James J. Gibson* (pp. 17–39). Ithaca, NY: Cornell University Press.

Holt, E. B. (1903). Eye-movement and central anaesthesia. *The Psychological Review Monograph Supplement, 4*, 3–45.

Holt, E. B. (1912). The place of illusory experience in a realistic world. In E. B. Holt et al. (Eds.), *The new realism: Cooperative studies in philosophy* (pp. 303–377). New York: MacMillan.

Holt, E. B. (1915a). *The Freudian wish and its place in ethics*. New York: Henry Holt.

Holt, E. B. (1915b). Response and cognition I: The specific-response relation. *The Journal of Philosophy, Psychology, and Scientific Methods, 7*, 365–373.

Holt, E. B. (1915c). Response and cognition II: Cognition as response. *The Journal of Philosophy, Psychology, and Scientific Methods, 7*, 393–409.

Holt, E. B. (1920). Professor Henderson's "fitness" and the locus of concepts. *Journal of Philosophy, Psychology, and Scientific Methods, 17*, 365–381.

Holt, E. B. (1931). *Animal drive and the learning process: An essay toward radical empiricism* (Vol. 1). New York: Henry Holt.

Holt, E. B. (1934). The argument for sensationalism as drawn from Dr. Berkeley. *Psychological Review, 41*, 509–533.

Holt, E. B. (1935). The whimsical condition of social psychology, and of mankind. In H. Kallen & S. Hook (Eds.), *American philosophy today and tomorrow* (pp. 171–202). New York: Lee Furman.

Holt, E. B. (1937). Materialism and the criterion of the psychic. *The Psychological Review, 44*, 33–53.

Holt, E. B. (1973). *The concept of consciousness*. New York: Arno Press. (Original work published 1914)

Holt, E. B., Marvin, M. T., Montague, W. P., Perry, R. B., Pitkin, W. B., & Spaulding, E. G. (1910). The program and first platform of six realists. *Journal of Philosophy, Psychology, and Scientific Methods, 7*, 393–401. [reprinted in Holt, E. B. et al. (Eds.), *The new realism: Cooperative studies in philosophy* (pp. 471–480). New York: MacMillan.

Holt, E. B., Marvin, M. T., Montague, W. P., Perry, R. B., Pitkin, W. B., & Spaulding, E. G. (1912). *The new realism: Cooperative studies in philosophy*. New York: MacMillan.

Holton, G. (1973). *Thematic origins of scientific thought: Kepler to Einstein*. Cambridge, MA: Harvard University Press.

Hothersall, D. (1995). *History of psychology*. New York: McGraw-Hill.

Hutchins, E. (1995). *Cognition in the wild*. Cambridge, MA: MIT Press.

Ingold, T. (1993). Tool-use, sociality, and intelligence. In K. R. Gibson & T. Ingold (Eds.) *Tools, language and cognition in human evolution* (pp. 429–445). Cambridge, England: Cambridge University Press.

Irwin, D. E. (1996). Integrating information across saccadic eye movements. *Current Directions in Psychological Science, 5*, 94–100.

James, W. (1911). The Ph.D. octopus. In *Memories and studies* (pp. 328–347). New York: Longmans, Green. (Original work published 1903)

James, W. (1920a). Remark's on Spencer's definition of mind as correspondence. In *Collected essays and reviews* (pp. 43–68). New York: Longmans, Green. (Original work published 1878)

James, W. (1920b). The knowing of things together. In *Collected essays and reviews* (pp. 371–400). New York: Longmans, Green. (Original work published in1895).

James, W. (1958). *Talks to teachers on psychology: And to students on some of life's ideals*. New York: Norton. (Original work published 1899)

James, W. (1976). *Essays in radical empiricism*. Cambridge, MA: Harvard University Press. (Original work published 1912)

James, W. (1978). *Pragmatism*. Cambridge, MA: Harvard University Press. (Original work published in 1907)

James, W. (1978). *The meaning of truth*. Cambridge, MA: Harvard University Press. (Original work published in 1909)

James, W. (1981). *The principles of psychology*. Cambridge, MA: Harvard University Press. (Original work published 1890)

James, W. (1985). *Psychology: The briefer course*. Notre Dame, IN: University of Notre Dame Press. (Original work published 1892)

James, W. (1996). *A pluralistic universe: Hibbert Lectures at Manchester College on the present situation in philosophy.* Lincoln, NE: University of Nebraska Press. (Original work published 1909)

James, W. (1996). *Some problems of philosophy: A beginning of an introduction to philosophy.* Lincoln, NE: University of Nebraska Press. (Original work published 1911)

Jaynes, J. (1973a). Introduction. In J. Jaynes, M. Henle, & J. J. Sullivan (Eds.), *Historical conceptions of psychology* (pp. ix–xii). New York: Springer.

Jaynes, J. (1973b). The problem of animate motion in the seventeenth century. In M. Henle, J. Jaynes, & J. J. Sullivan (Eds.), *Historical conceptions of psychology* (pp. 166–179). New York: Springer.

Johansson, G., von Hofsten, C., Jansson, G. (1980). Event perception. *Annual review of psychology, 31,* 27–63.

Johnson, M. G., & Henley, T. B. (1990). *Reflections on The Principles of Psychology: William James after a century.* Hillsdale, NJ: Lawrence Erlbaum Associates.

Jones, M. R., & Boltz, M. (1989). Dynamic attending and responses to time. *Psychological review, 96,* 459–491.

Kadar, E., & Effken, J. (1994). Heideggerian meditations on an alternative ontology for ecological psychology: A response to Turvey's (1992) proposal. *Ecological Psychology, 6,* 297–341.

Kallen, H. (1916). Philosophic formalism and scientific imagination. *Journal of Philosophy, Psychology, and Scientific Methods, 16,* 597–607.

Kallen, H. (1937). Remarks on R. B. Perry's portrait of William James. *The Philosophical Review, 46,* 68–78.

Kaplan, G. (1969). Kinetic disruption of optical texture: The perception of depth at an edge. *Perception and Psychophysics, 6,* 193–198.

Katz, D. (1935). *The world of color.* (R. B. MacLeod & C. W. Fox, trans.). London: Kegan Paul, Trench, Trubner. (Original work published 1911)

Katz, D. (1989). *The world of touch* (L. E. Kruger, trans.). Hillsdale, NJ: Lawrence Erlbaum Associates. (Original work published 1925)

Katz, S. (1987). Is Gibson a relativist? In A. Costall & A. Still (Eds.), *Cognitive in question* (pp. 115–127). Brighton: Harvester.

Koch, S. (1964). Psychology and emerging conceptions of knowledge as unitary. In T. W. Wann (Ed.), *Behaviorism and phenomenology: Contrasting bases for modern psychology* (pp. 1–41). Chicago: University of Chicago Press.

Koch, S. (1999a). A theory of definition: Implications for psychology, science, and the humanities. In D. Finkelman & F. Kessel (Eds.), *Psychology in human context: Essays in dissidence and reconstruction* (pp. 147–191). Chicago: University of Chicago Press. (Original work published in 1975)

Koch, S. (1999b). The allures of a meaning in modern psychology. In D. Finkelman & F. Kessel (Eds.), *Psychology in human context: Essays in dissidence and reconstruction* (pp. 233–266). Chicago: University of Chicago Press. (Original work published in 1965).

Koch, S. (1999c). The concept of "value properties" in relation to motivation, perception, and the axiological disciplines. In D. Finkelman & F. Kessel (Eds.), *Psychology in human context: Essays in dissidence and reconstruction* (pp. 192–230). Chicago: University of Chicago Press. (Original work published in 1969).

Koch, S. (1999d). *Psychology in a human context: Essays in dissidence and reconstruction* (D. Finkelman & F. Kessel, Eds.). Chicago: University of Chicago Press.

Koffka, K. (1935). *Principles of Gestalt psychology*. New York: Harcourt, Brace & World.

Köhler, W. (1938). *The place of value in a world of facts*. New York: Liveright.

Köhler, W. (1947). *Gestalt psychology: An introduction to new concepts in modern psychology*. New York: Liveright.

Kossyln, S. M. (1994). *Image and brain: The resolution of the imagery debate*. Cambridge, MA: MIT Press.

Klatzky, R. L., & Lederman, S. J. (1987). The intelligent hand. In G. H. Bower (Ed.), *The psychology of learning and motivation* (Vol. 21, pp. 121–151). San Diego: Academic Press.

Kuhn, T. S. (1970). *The structure of scientific revolutions*. Chicago: University of Chicago Press.

Kuklick, B. (1977). *The rise of American philosophy: Cambridge, Massachusetts 1860–1930*. New Haven, CT: Yale University Press.

Kundera, M. (1980). *The book of laughter and forgetting*. New York: Knopf.

Lakoff, G. (1987). *Women, fire, and dangerous things*. Chicago: University of Chicago Press.

Landes, D. S. (1983). *Revolution in time: Clocks and the making of the modern world*. Cambridge, MA: Harvard University Press.

Langfeld, H. S. (1946). Edwin Bissell 1873–1946. *The Psychological Review, 53*, 251–258.

Large, E. W., & Jones, M. R. (1999). The dynamics of attending: How people track time-varying events. *Psychological Review, 106*, 119–159.

Lamberth, D. C. (1999). *William James and the metaphysics of experience*. New York: Cambridge University Press.

Lashley, K. (1950). In search of the engram. In *Symposium of the Society of Experimental Biology: Vol. 4. Physiological mechanisms in animal behavior* (pp. 454–482). New York: Cambridge University Press.

Lashley, K. S. (1951). The problem of serial order in behavior. In L. A. Jeffress (Ed.), *Cerebral mechanisms in behavior: The Hixon symposium* (pp. 112–135). New York: Wiley.

Latour, B. (1987). *Science in action*. Cambridge, MA: Harvard University Press.

Lave, J. (1993). The practice of learning. In S. Chaiklin & J. Lave (Eds.), *Understanding practice: Perspectives on activity and context* (pp. 3–32). Cambridge, England: Cambridge University Press.

Leahey, T. H. (1994). *A history of psychology: Main currents in psychological thought* (3rd ed.). Englewood Cliffs, NJ: Prentice-Hall.

Lee, D. N. (1974). Visual information during locomotion. In R. B. MacLeod & H. L. Pick, Jr. (Eds.), *Perception: Essays in honor of James J. Gibson* (pp. 250–267). Ithaca, NY: Cornell University Press.

Lee, D. N., & Lishman, R. (1977). Visual control of locomotion. *Scandanavian Journal of Psychology, 18*, 224–230.

Leeper, R. W. (1963). Learning and the fields of perception, motivation, and personality. In S. Koch (Ed.), *Psychology: A study of a science* (Vol. 5, pp. 365–487). New York: McGraw-Hill.

Leudar, I., & Costall, A. (1996). Situating action IV: Planning as situated action. In A. Costall & I. Leudar (Eds.), *Special issue: Situating action. Ecological Psychology, 8*, 153–170.

Levine, M. (1982). You are here maps: Psychological considerations. *Environment & Behavior, 14*, 221–237.

Levinson, H. S. (1996). Introduction. *A pluralistic universe* by William James. Lincoln: University of Nebraska Press.

Lewin, K. (1951a). Defining the "field at a given time." In D. Cartwright (Ed.), *Field theory in social science: Selected theoretical papers* (pp. 43–59). New York: Harper Torchbooks. (Original work published in 1943)

Lewin, K. (1951b). Psychological ecology. In D. Cartwright (Ed.), *Field theory in social science: Selected theoretical papers* (pp. 170–187). New York: Harper Torchbooks. (Original work published 1943)

Lewin, K. (1951c). Behavior and development as a function of the total situation. In D. Cartwright (Ed.), *Field theory in social science: Selected theoretical papers* (pp. 238–303). New York: Harper Torchbooks. (Original work published in 1946)

Lewis, R. W. B. (1991). *The Jameses: A family narrative*. New York: Farrar, Straus, & Giroux.

Lindberg, D. C. (1976). *Theories of vision from Al-Kindi to Kepler*. Chicago: University of Chicago Press.

Lombardo, T. J. (1987). *The reciprocity of perceiver and environment: The evolution of James J. Gibson's ecological psychology*. Hillsdale, NJ: Lawrence Erlbaum Associates.

Lovejoy, A. (1930). *The revolt against dualism*. LaSalle, IL: Open Court.

Lynch, K. (1976). *What time is this place?* Cambridge, MA: MIT Press.

MacLeod, R. B. (1964). Phenomenology: A challenge to experimental psychology. In T. W. Wann (Ed.), *Behaviorism and phenomenology: Contrasting bases for modern psychology* (pp. 47–73). Chicago: University of Chicago Press.

MacLeod, R. B. (1969). Introduction: James as phenomenologist. In R. B. MacLeod (Ed.), *William James: Unfinished business* (pp. v–ix). Washington, DC: American Psychological Association.

MacLeod, R. B. (1974). A tribute to J. J. Gibson. In R. B. MacLeod & H. L. Pick, Jr. (Eds.), *Perception: Essays in honor of James J. Gibson* (pp. 11–13). Ithaca, NY: Cornell University Press.

MacLeod, R. B. (1975). *The persistent problems of psychology*. Pittsburgh, PA: Duquesne University Press.

Malle, B. F., & Ickes, W. (2000). Fritz Heider: Philosopher and psychologist. In G. A. Kimble & M. Wertheimer (Eds.), *Portraits of pioneers in psychology* (Vol. 4, pp. 194–213). Washington, DC: American Psychological Association.

Mark, L. S. (1987). Eyeheight-scaled information about affordances: A study of sitting and stair climbing. *Journal of Experimental Psychology: Human Perception and Performance, 13*, 361–370.

Mark, L. S., Balliett, J. A., Craver, K. D., Douglas, S. D., & Fox, T. (1990). What an actor must do in order to perceive the affordance for sitting. *Ecological Psychology, 2*, 325–366.

Marrow, A. (1969). *The practical theorist: The life and work of Kurt Lewin*. New York: Basic Books.

McDermott, J. J. (1977). *The writings of William James: A comprehensive edition*. Chicago: University of Chicago Press.

McGinn, C. (1999). *The mysterious flame: Conscious minds in a material work*. New York: Basic Books.

McGrew, W. (1992). *Chimpanzee material culture*. Cambridge: Cambridge University Press.

McGrew, W. (1998). Culture in nonhuman primates? In W. H. Durham, E. V. Daniel, & B. B. Schieffelin (Eds.), *Annual review of anthropology, 27*, 301–374.

McLellan, D. (1975). *Marx*. Glasgow: Fontana.

Megarry, T. (1995). *Society in prehistory: The origins of human culture*. New York: New York University Press.

Merleau-Ponty, M. (1962). *The phenomenology of perception*. (C. Smith, trans.). London: Routledge & Kegan Paul.

Merleau-Ponty, M. (1963). *The structure of behavior*. (A. L. Fisher, trans.). Boston: Beacon Press. (Original work published 1942)

Meserve, B. E. (1955). *Fundamental concepts of geometry*. Cambridge, MA: Addison-Wesley.

Michaels, C. F., & Carello, C. (1981). *Direct perception*. Englewood Cliffs, NJ: Prentice-Hall.

Milgram, S., & Jodelet, D. (1976). Psychological maps of Paris. In H. M. Proshansky, W. H. Ittelson, & L. Rivlkin (Eds.), *Environmental psychology* (2nd ed, pp. 104–124). New York: Holt, Rhinehart & Winston.

Miller, G.A. (1985). The constitutive problem in psychology. In S. Koch & D. E. Leary (Eds.), *A century of psychology as science* (pp. 40–45). New York: McGraw-Hill.

Miller, G. A., Galanter, E., & Pribram, K. H. (1960). *Plans and the structure of behavior*. New York: Holt, Rhinehart, & Winston.

Miller, J. (1999). Cultural psychology: Implications for basic psychological theory. *Psychological Science, 10*, 85–91.

Moller, M. S. (1997). *William James's quandary: Radical empiricism, consciousness and the Miller-Bode objections*. Unpublished doctoral dissertation, Washington University.

Montague, W. P. (1960). The story of American realism. In W. G. Muelder, L. Sears, & A. V. Schlabach (Eds.), *The development of American philosophy: A book of readings 2nd Ed.* (pp. 479–489). Boston: Houghton-Mifflin. (Original work published 1937)

Moore, C., & Dunham, P. J. (Eds.). (1995). *Joint attention: Its origins and role in development*. Hillsdale, NJ: Lawrence Erlbaum Associates.

Morphy, H. (1996). Proximity and distance: Representations of the Aboriginal society in the writings of Bill Harney and Bruce Chatwin. In J. MacClancy & C. McDonaugh (Eds.), *Popularizing anthropology* (pp. 157–179). London: Routledge.

Myers, G. E. (1986). *William James: His life and thought*. New Haven, CT: Yale University Press.

Nagel, T. (1974). What is it like to be a bat? In *Mortal questions* (pp. 165–180). New York: Cambridge University Press.

Neisser, U. (1978). Gibson's ecological optics: Consequences of a different stimulus description. *Journal for the Theory of Social Behavior, 7*, 17–28.

Neisser, U. (1988). Five kinds of self-knowledge. *Philosophical Psychology, 1*, 35–59.

Noble, W. (1981). Gibsonian theory and the pragmatist perspective. *Journal for the Theory of Social Behavior, 11*, 65–85.

Norman, D. (1988). *The psychology of everyday things*. New York: Basic Books.

Nussbaum, M. C., & Putnam, H. (1992). Changing Aristotle's mind. In M. C. Nussbaum & A. O. Rorty (Eds.), *Essays on Aristotle's De Anima* (pp. 27–56). Oxford, England: Oxford University Press.

Olson, D. R. (1994). *The world on paper: The conceptual and cognitive implications of writing and reading*. Cambridge, England: Cambridge University Press.

Oyama, S. (1985). *The ontogeny of information: Developmental systems and evolution*. New York: Cambridge University Press.

Pattee, H. H. (1973). The physical basis and origin of hierarchical control. In H. H. Pattee (Ed.), *Hierarchy theory: The challenge of complex systems*. (pp. 71–108). New York: Braziller.

Pea, R. D. (1993). Practices of distributed intelligence and designs for education. In G. Salomon (Ed.), *Distributed cognitions: Psychological and educational considerations* (pp. 47–87). New York: Cambridge University Press.

Perry, R. B. (1935). *The thought and character of William James*. Boston: Little, Brown.

Petroski, H. (1994). *The evolution of useful things*. New York: Vintage.

Pick, A. D. (1997). Perceptual learning, categorizing, and cognitive development. In C. Dent-Read & P. Zukow-Goldring (Eds.), *Evolving explanations of development: Ecological approaches to organism-environment systems* (pp. 335–370). Washington, DC: American Psychological Association.

Pick, H. L., Jr. (1993). Organization of spatial knowledge in children. In N. Eilan, R. McCarthy, & B. Brewer (Eds.), *Spatial representation: Problems in psychology and philosophy* (pp. 31–42). Oxford: Basil Blackwell, Ltd.

Pick, H. L., Jr., Rieser, J. J., Wagner, D., & Garing, A. E. (1999). The recalibration of rotational locomotion. *Journal of Experimental Psychology: Human Perception and Performance, 25*, 1179–1188.

Pinker, S. (1994). *The language instinct*. New York: Morrow.

Pizlo, Z. (1994). A theory of shape constancy based on perspective invariants. *Vision Research, 34*, 1637–1658.

Pizlo, Z., & Stevenson, A. K. (1999). Shape constancy from novel views. *Perception & Psychophysics, 61*, 1299–1307.

Polanyi, M. (1962). *Personal knowledge 2nd ed.* Chicago: University of Chicago Press.

Port, R. F., & van Gelder, T. (Eds.). (1995). *Mind in motion: Explorations in the dynamics of cognition*. Cambridge, MA: MIT Press.

Portugali, J. (1996). Inter-representation networks and cognitive mapping. In J. Portugali (Ed.), *The construction of cognitive maps* (pp. 11–44). Dordrecht, The Netherlands: Kluwer Academic.

Povinelli, D., Bierschwale, D. T., & Cech, C. G. (1999). Comprehension of seeing as a referential act in young children, but not juvenile chimpanzees. *British Journal of Developmental Psychology, 17*, 37–60.

Proshansky, H. M. (1976). Environmental psychology and the real world. *American psychologist, 4*, 303–310.

Putnam, H. (1990). *Realism with a human face*. Cambridge, MA: Harvard University Press.

Putnam, H. (1995). *Pragmatism*. Oxford, England: Blackwell.

Putnam, R. A. (1997). *The Cambridge companion to William James*. New York: Cambridge University Press.

Reaux, J. E., Theall, L. A. Povinelli, D. J. (1999). A longitudinal investigation of chimpanzees' understanding of visual perception. *Child Development, 70*, 275–290.

Reed, E. S. (1988). *James J. Gibson and the psychology of perception*. New Haven, CT: Yale University Press.

Reed, E. S. (1990). Space perception and the psychologist's fallacy in James's *Principles*. In M. G. Johnson & T. B. Henley (Eds.), *Reflections on the Principles of Psychology: William James after a century* (pp. 231–248). Hillsdale, NJ: Lawrence Erlbaum Associates.

Reed, E. S. (1991). James Gibson's ecological approach to cognition. In A. Still & A. Costall (Eds.), *Against cognitivism: Alternative foundations for cognitive psychology* (pp. 171–198). New York: Harvester Wheatsheaf.

Reed, E. S. (1993). The intention to use a specific affordance: A conceptual framework for psychology. In R. H. Wozniak & K. W. Fischer (Eds.), *Development in context: Acting and thinking in specific environments* (pp. 45–76). Hillsdale, NJ: Lawrence Erlbaum Associates.

Reed, E. S. (1996a). *Encountering the world: Toward an ecological psychology.* New York: Oxford University Press.

Reed, E. S. (1996b). *The necessity of experience.* New Haven, CT: Yale University Press.

Reed, E. S. (1997). *From soul to mind: The emergence of psychology from Erasmus Darwin to William James.* New Haven, CT: Yale University Press.

Rieser, J. J., Guth, D. A., & Hill, E. W. (1986). Sensitivity to perceptive structure while walking without vision. *Perception, 15,* 173–188.

Rieser, J. J., Pick, H. L., Jr., Ashmead, D., & Garing, A. E. (1995). Calibration of human locomotion and models of perceptual-motor organization. *Journal of Experimental Psychology: Human Perception and Performance, 21,* 480–497.

Roberts, M. N. & Roberts, A. F. (Eds.). (1996). *Memory: Luba art and the making of history..* New York: Museum of African Art.

Robinson, D. (1981). *An intellectual history of psychology.* New York: MacMillan.

Robinson, D. N. (1989). *Aristotle's psychology.* New York: Columbia University Press.

Rochat, P. (1995). Perceived reachability for self and for others by 3- to 5-year old children and adults. *Journal of Experimental Child Psychology, 59,* 317–333.

Rock, I. (1990). A look back at William James's theory of perception. In M. G. Johnson & T. B. Henley (Eds.), *Reflections on the Principles of Psychology: William James after a century* (pp. 197–229). Hillsdale, NJ: Lawrence Erlbaum Associates.

Rogoff, B. (1990). *Apprenticeship in thinking: Cognitive development in sociocultural activity.* New York: Oxford University Press.

Rogoff, B. (1993). Children's guided participation and participatory appropriation in sociocultural activity. In R. H. Wozniak & K. W. Fischer (Eds.), *Development in context: Acting and thinking in specific environments* (pp. 121–154). Hillsdale, NJ: Lawrence Erlbaum Associates.

Rogoff, B. (1995). Observing sociocultural activity on three planes: Participatory appropriation, guided participation, and apprenticeship. In J. V. Wertsch, P. Rio, & A. Alvarez (Eds.), *Sociocultural studies of mind* (pp. 139–164). New York: Cambridge University Press.

Rogoff, B., Mosier, C., Mistry, J., & Göncü, A. (1993). Toddlers' guided participation with their caregivers in cultural activity. In A. A. Forman, N. Minick, & C. A. Stone (Eds.), *Contexts for learning: Sociocultural dynamics in children's development* (pp. 213–229). New York: Oxford University Press.

Rorty, R. (1999). *Philosophy and social hope.* New York: Penguin.

Rosenthal, R., & Rosnow, R. L. (Eds.). (1969). *Artifact in behavioral research.* New York: Academic Press.

Rubin, D. C. (1995). *Memory in oral traditions: The cognitive psychology of epic, ballads, and counting-out rhymes.* New York: Oxford University Press.

Salomon, G. (1993). Editor's introduction. In G. Salomon (Ed.), *Distributed cognitions: Psychological and educational considerations* (pp. xi–xxi). New York: Cambridge University Press.

Sampson, E. E. (1977). Psychology and the American ideal. *Journal of Personality and Social Psychology, 35,* 767–782.

Sampson, E. E. (1993). *Celebrating the other: A dialogic account of human nature.* Boulder, CO: Westview Press.

Sanders, J. T. (1997). An ontology of affordances. *Ecological Psychology, 9,* 97–112.

Sanders, J. T. (1999). Affordances: An ecological approach to a first philosophy. In G. Weiss & H. F. Haber (Eds.), *Perspectives on embodiment: The intersections of nature and culture* (pp. 121–141). New York: Routledge.

Scheffler, I. (1974). *Four pragmatists: A critical introduction to Pierce, James, Mead, and Dewey.* London: Routledge & Kegan Paul.

Schoggen, P. (1963). Environmental forces in the everyday lives of children. In R. G. Barker (Ed.), *The stream of behavior* (pp. 42–69). Appleton-Century-Crofts.

Schoggen, P. (1978). Environmental forces on physically disabled children. In R. G. Barker & Associates, *Habitats, environments, and human behavior* (pp. 125–145). San Francisco: Jossey-Bass.

Schoggen, P. (1989). *Behavior settings: A revision and extension of Roger G. Barker's Ecological Psychology.* Stanford, CA: Stanford University Press.

Schwartz, B. (1986). *The battle for human nature: Science, morality, and modern life.* New York: Norton.

Seigfried, C. H. (1978). *Chaos and context: A study in William James.* Athens, OH: Ohio University Press.

Seigfried, C. H. (1990). *William James's radical reconstruction of philosophy.* Albany, NY: State University of New York Press.

Sellars, R. W. (1960). Knowledge and its categories. In W. G. Muelder, L. Sears, & A. V. Schlabach (Eds.), *The development of American philosophy: A book of readings 2nd Ed.* (pp. 490–498). Boston: Houghton-Mifflin. (Original work published in 1920).

Shank, R. P., & Abelson, R. C. (1977). *Scripts, plans, goals, and understanding.* Hillsdale, NJ: Lawrence Erlbaum Associates, Inc.

Sherrington, C. S. (1906). *The integrative action of the nervous system.* New Haven, CT: Yale University Press.

Shore, B. (1996). *Culture in mind: Cognition, culture, and the problem of meaning.* New York: Oxford University Press.

Shotter, J. (1975). *Images of man in psychological research.* London: Metheun.

Shotter, J. (1983). "Duality of structure" and "intentionality" in ecological psychology. *Journal for the Theory of Social Behavior, 13,* 19–43.

Simon, H. (1973). The organization of complex systems. In H. H. Pattee (Ed.), *Hierarchy theory: The challenge of complex systems.* (pp. 1–28) New York: Braziller.

Simon, H. (1969). *The sciences of the artificial.* Cambridge, MA: MIT Press.

Simon, L. (Ed.). (1996). *William James remembered.* Lincoln, NE: University of Nebraska Press.

Simon, L. (1998). *Genuine reality: A life of William James.* New York: Harcourt Brace.

Slife, B. D., & Williams, R. N. (1995). *What's behind the research?: Discovering hidden assumptions in the behavioral sciences.* Thousand Oaks, CA: Sage.

Sommer, R. (1994). Two ecological couples: The Gibsons and the Barkers. *The International Society for Ecological Psychology Newsletter Supplement,* 1–8.

Sprigge, T. L. S. (1993). *James and Bradley: American truth and British reality.* Chicago: Open Court Publishing.

Steadman, P. (1995). In the studio of Vermeer. In R. Gregory, J. Harris, P. Heard, & D. Rose (Eds.), *The artful eye* (pp. 353–372). Oxford, England: Oxford University Press.

Stebbing, L. S. (1960). "Furniture of the earth. " In A. Danto & S. Morganbesser (Eds.), *Philosophy of science* (pp. 69–81). Cleveland, OH: The World Publishing. (Original work published 1937)

Steel, R. (1980). *Walter Lippman and the American century*. Boston: Little, Brown.

Stoffregen, T. A. (1985). Flow structure versus retinal location in the optical control of stance. *Journal of Experimental Psychology: Human Perception and Performance, 11*, 554–565.

Stoffregen, T. A., & Bardy, B. G. (in press). On specification and the senses. *Behavioral and Brain Sciences*.

Stoffregen, T. A., Gorday, K. M., Sheng, Y., & Flynn, S. B. (1999). Perceiving affordances for another person's actions. *Journal of Experimental Psychology: Human Perception and Performance, 25*, 120–136.

Suchman, L. A. (1987). *Plans and situated actions: The problem of human machine interaction*. Cambridge, England: Cambridge University Press.

Suckiel, E. K. (1982). *The pragmatic philosophy of William James*. Notre Dame, IN: University of Notre Dame Press.

Sugiyama, S. (1995). Tool-use for catching ants by chimpanzees at Boussou and Monts Nimba, West Africa. *Primates, 36*, 193–205.

Taylor, C. (1989). *The sources of the self: The making of modern identity*. Cambridge, MA: Harvard University Press.

Taylor, E. I. (1992). The case for a uniquely American Jamesian tradition in psychology. In M. E. Donnelly (Ed.), *Reinterpreting the legacy of William James* (pp. 3–28). Washington, DC: American Psychological Association.

Taylor, E. I., & Wozniak, R. H. (1996). *Pure experience: The response to William James*. Bristol, England Thoemmes.

Thelen, E. (1995). Time-scale dynamics and the development of an embodied cognition. In R. F. Port & T. van Gelder (Eds.), *Mind in motion: Explorations in the dynamics of cognition* (pp. 69–100). Cambridge, MA: The MIT Press.

Thelen, E., Kelso, J. A. S., & Fogel, A. (1987) Self-organizing systems and infant motor development. *Developmental Review, 7*, 39–65.

Thelen, E., & Smith, L. B. (Eds.). (1993). *A dynamic systems approach to development: Applications*. Cambridge, MA: MIT Press.

Thelen, E., & Smith, L. B. (1994). *A dynamic systems approach to the development of cognition and action*. Cambridge, MA: MIT Press.

Thines, G., Costall, A., & Butterworth, G. (Eds.) (1991). *Michotte's experimental phenomenology of perception*. Hillsdale, NJ: Lawrence Erlbaum Associates.

Tolman, E. C. (1932). *Purposive behavior in animals and men*. New York: Appleton-Century.

Tolman, E. C. (1956). Egon Brunswik (1903–1955). *American Journal of Psychology, 69*, 315–342.

Tolman, E. C., & Brunswik, E. (1966). The organism and the causal texture of the environment. In K.R. Hammond (Ed.), *The psychology of Egon Brunswik (pp. 457–486)*. New York: Holt, Rhinehart & Winston (Original work published in 1935).

Tomasello, M. (1995). Language is not an instinct. *Cognitive Development, 10*, 131–156.

Tomasello, M. (1999a). The cultural ecology of young children's interactions with objects and artifacts. In E. Winograd, R. Fivush, & W. Hirst (Eds.), *Ecological ap-*

proaches to cognition: Essays in honor of Ulric Neisser (pp. 153–170). Mahwah, NJ: Lawrence Erlbaum Associates.

Tomasello, M. (1999b). *The cultural origins of human cognition*. Cambridge, MA: Harvard University Press.

Tomasello, M. (1999c). The human adaptation for culture. In W. H. Dunham (Ed.), *Annual review of anthropology, 28*, 509–552.

Tomasello, M., Kruger, A. C., & Ratner, H. H. (1993). Cultural learning. *Behavioral and Brain Sciences, 16*, 495–552.

Tomasello, M., Savage-Rumbaugh, S., Kruger, A. C. (1993). Imitative learning of actions on objects by children, chimpanzees, and enculturated chimpanzees. *Child Development, 64*, 1688–1705.

Tooby, J., & Cosmides, L. (1992). The psychological foundations of culture. In J. H. Barkow, L. Cosmides, & J. Tooby (Eds.), *The adapted mind: Evolutionary psychology and the generation of culture* (pp. 19–136). New York: Oxford University Press.

Toulmin, S. E. (1990). *Cosmopolis: The hidden agenda of modernity*. Chicago: University of Chicago Press.

Turvey, M. T. (1990). Coordination. *American Psychologist, 45*, 938–953.

Turvey, M. T. (1992). Affordances and prospective control: An outline of an ontology. *Ecological Psychology, 4*, 173–187.

Valsiner, J. (1987). *Culture and the development of children's actions*. New York: Wiley.

Valsiner, J. (1993). Making of the future: Temporality and the constructive nature of human development. In G. Turkewitz & D. A. Devenny (Eds.), *Developmental time and timing* (pp. 13–40). Hillsdale, NJ: Lawrence Erlbaum Associates.

Van Leeuwen, C. (1998). Perception. In W. Bechtel & G. Graham (Eds.), *A companion to cognitive science* (pp. 265–281). Oxford, England: Blackwell.

Van Leeuwen, L., Smitsman, A., & Van Leeuwen, C. (1994). Affordances, perceptual complexity, and the development of tool use. *Journal of Experimental Psychology: Human Perception and Performance, 20*, 174–191.

Von Hofsten, C. (1982). Eye-hand coordination in newborns. *Developmental Psychology, 18*, 450–467.

Vygotsky, L. (1978). *Mind in society: The development of higher psychological processes* (M. Cole, V. John-Steiner, S. Scribner, & E. Souberman, (Eds.). Cambridge, MA: Harvard University Press.

Waddington, C. H. (1971). The theory of evolution today. In A. Koestler & J. R. Smythies (Eds.), *Beyond reductionism: New perspective in the life science, The Alpbach Symposium 1968* (pp. 357–374). Boston: Beacon Press.

Warren, D. H., Rossano, M. J., & Wear, T. (1990). Perception of map-environment correspondence: The roles of features and alignment. *Ecological Psychology, 2*, 131–150.

Warren, R. (1976). The perception of egomotion. *Journal of Experimental Psychology: Human Perception and Performance, 2*, 448–456.

Warren, W. H. (1984). Perceiving affordances: Visual guidance of stair climbing. *Journal of Experimental Psychology: Human Perception and Performance, 10*, 683–703.

Warren, W. H. (1998). Visually controlled locomotion: 40 years later. *Ecological Psychology, 3 & 4*, 177–220.

Warren, W. H., & Whang, S. (1987). Visual guidance of walking through apertures: Body-scaled information for affordances. *Journal of Experimental Psychology: Human Perception and Performance, 13*, 371–383.

Watson, J. (1913). Psychology as the behaviorist views it. *Psychological Review*, *20*, 158–177.

Watson, J. (1970). *Behaviorism*. New York: Norton. (Original work published in 1930)

Watson, R. I. (1971). *Selected writings in the history of psychology*. New York: Oxford University Press.

Watson, R. I. (1978). *The great psychologists* (4th Ed.) Philadelphia: Lippencott.

Weimer, W. B. (1982). Hayek's approach to the problems of complex phenomena: An introduction to the theoretical psychology of *The sensory order*. In W. B. Weimer & D. S. Palermo (Eds.), *Cognition and the symbolic processes* (Vol. 2, pp. 241–286). Hillsdale, NJ: Lawrence Erlbaum Associates.

Weiss, P. (1969). The living system: Determinism stratified. In A. Koestler & J. R. Smythies (Eds.), *Beyond reductionism: New perspectives in the life sciences* (pp. 3–42). Boston: Beacon Press.

Wertsch, J. V. (1985). *Vygotsky and the social formation of mind*. Cambridge, MA: Harvard University Press.

White, M. (1947). *Social thought in America: The revolt against formalism*. Boston: Beacon Press.

Whitehead, A. N. (1925). *Science and the modern world*. New York: MacMillan.

Whyte, W. H. (1983). *The social life of small urban spaces*. Washington, DC: Conservation Foundation.

Wicker, A. W. (1987). Behavior settings reconsidered: Temporal stages, resources, internal dynamics, context. In I. Altman & D. Stokols (Eds.), *Handbook of environmental psychology* (Vol. 1, pp. 613–654). New York: Wiley.

Wicker, A. W. (1992). Making sense of environments. In W. B. Walsh, K. H. Craik, & R. H. Price (Eds.), *Person-environment psychology: Models and perspectives* (pp. 157–192). Hillsdale, NJ: Lawrence Erlbaum Associates.

Wild, J. (1969). *The radical empiricism of William James*. New York: Doubleday.

Wilshire, B. (1968). *William James and phenomenology: A study of "The Principles of Psychology."* Bloomington, IN: Indiana University Press.

Wimsatt, W. C. (1976). Reductionism, levels of organization, and the mind-body problem. In G. G. Globus, G. Maxwell, & I. Savodnik (Eds.), *Consciousness and the brain: A scientific and philosophical inquiry* (pp. 205–268). New York: Plenum.

Wimsatt, W. (1984). Reductionistic research strategies and their biases in the units of selection controversy. In E. Sober (Ed.), *Conceptual issues in evolutionary biology: An anthology* (pp. 142–183). Cambridge, MA: MIT Press.

Wittgenstein, L. (1953). *Philosophical investigations*. New York: MacMillan.

Wright, H. F. (1967). *Recording and analyzing child behavior*. New York: Harper & Row.

Wohlwill, J. F. (1973). The environment is not in the head! In W. F. E. Preiser (Ed.), *Environmental design research* (Vol. 1, pp. 166–181). Stroudsburg, PA: Dowden, Hutchinson, & Ross.

Wohlwill, J. F. (1976). In search of the environment in environmental cognition research. In G. T. Moore & R. G. Golledge (Eds.), *Environmental knowing* (pp. 385–392). Stroudsburg, PA: Dowden, Hutchinson, & Ross.

Author Index

Smith, L., 54, 322, 323
Smitsman, A., 341
Solomon, H., 123, 131
Sommer, R., 324
Spaulding, E., 66, 73, 74, 75, 81
Sprigge, T., 26, 27, 28, 34, 35, 116, 164,
    167, 194, 210
Starr, T., 237, 238
Steadman, P., 175
Stebbing, L., 47, 48
Steel, R., 62
Stevenson, A., 151
Still, A., 123
Stoffregen, T., 120, 121, 177
Suchman, L., 311, 313
Suckiel, E., xxxii, 26, 42
Sugiyama, S., 341

T

Taylor, C., 353
Taylor, E., xxxii, 17, 20
Theall, L., 337
Thelen, E., 54, 316, 322, 323
Thines, G., 117
Tolman, E., 8, 9, 10, 83, 128, 229
Tomasello, M., 199, 291, 336, 337, 338,
    339, 340, 345, 358
Tooby, J., 6, 335
Toulmin, S., xxviii, 3, 351
Turvey, M., xxiv, 123, 131, 196, 316

V

Valsiner, J., 198, 317
van Gelder, T., 54, 323
van Leeuwen, C., 50, 341
van Leeuwen, L., 341

Verschoor, F., 316
Viney, W., 17, 20
von Hofsten, C., 150, 186
Vygotsky, L., 198

W

Waddington, C., 316
Warren, D., 357
Warren, R., 120
Warren, W., 120, 123, 130, 287, 355
Wagner, D., 192
Watson, J., 21, 24, 83
Watson, R., xviii, 121
Wear, T., 357
Weimer, W., 261, 318
Weiss, P., 237, 240, 244, 274, 383
Wertsch, J., 198
Whang, S., 123, 355
Wheeler, K., 122
White, M., 106
Whitehead, A., 16, 132
Whyte, W., 293
Wicker, A., 264, 265, 267, 269, 291
Wild, J., 114, 137
Williams, R., 286
Wilshire, B., 114
Wimsatt, W., 238, 239, 241, 243, 244
Wittgenstein, L., 130
Wright, H., 250, 251, 263, 264, 288,
    291, 292, 293
Wohlwill, J., 156, 191, 285
Wozniak, R., xxxii

Z

Zukow-Goldring, P., 323

Subject Index

A

Adaptive agency, xxiii, 365–367, *see also* Intentionality
Adience, *see* Edwin B. Holt, adience
Aesthetics, *see* Value properties of the environment
Affordances,
    and behavior settings, 280–282, 286–301, 308, 383–384
    and the body as a frame of reference, 131, 136
    as compared to concepts, 130–132
    as components of places, 296–297
    their dual nature, 125, 132–135
    early treatment by Gibson, 221–222
    environmental sources, 292–294
    errors in judging, 131 fn. 7
    and formal cause, 286–287
    and functionalism, 126, 146
    influence of Gestalt psychology, 220–221
        differences with, 216–218
    multiple properties, 131, 222
    parallels in Tolman, 128
    phenomenological roots, 123–124, 219–222
    of places, 297–298
    potential, 132, 197
    and radical empiricism, 126–132, 135
        as percepts, 129–131
        and affectional experience, 128
    and recession of the stimulus, 383
    their relational nature, 124–125
    and the selective nature of perceiving, 133
    and sociocultural processes, 134, 293, 383–386
    sources, 292–294
    and tools, 341–342
    see also External relations and realism; Reciprocity, animal and environment; Value properties of the environment
Alexander, Samuel, 65
Allport, Floyd, 140 fn. 9
Anamorphic art, 168 fn. 11
Animate beings, *see* Sciences of the inanimate and animate
Appearance versus reality, 115
Apprenticeship, *see* Guided participation
Appropriation, versus internalization, 361–362
Apriori knowledge, *see* Idealism
Aristotle, *see* Causality
Artifacts, *see also* Tools
    definition, 342–343
    functional properties of, 343–345
    and transmission of knowledge, 343
Artifacts in laboratory research, *see* Experimental methods

423

Reciprocity, animal-environment, 7, 109–111, 373–374
in Dewey, 14
and sociocultural processes, 134, see also, Structuration
see also, James J. Gibson, affordances; Interactionism
Reductionism, 70–71, 203–204
and the reflex arc, 14
Reid, Thomas, 161, 378 fn. 1
Relational view of knowing, xxxii, see also William James, radical empiricism, reciprocity
Relations, in pure experience and the ambient array, 143–152
see also James Gibson; William James
Remembering, see Cognition, from an ecological perspective; Edwin B. remembering
Renaissance, 3
Representations, artifacts, 346–350
and cultural evolution, 346–347, 385–386
direct versus indirect knowing, xxxiv, 350–352
properties of, 348–349
see also maps
Representations, mental, see also Cognitive maps; Plans and scripts
cause maps, 264–268
indirect realism, 115, 163, 283–284
minimal, 314 fn. 11
and sociocultural processes, 358–359
Representational theory of perception, 78, 165
see also Edwin B. Holt, critique of mental representations; William James, objection to mental representation
Resonance, 366
see also Attunement
Retinal stimulation, 148, 151, 175
implications for perception, 31, 278–279
and the present, 178 fn. 5
see also Proximal-distal stimulus distinction
Royce, Josiah, 33, 61, 66, 166
and Idealism, 68–69,

S

Sartre, Jean-Paul, 116
Scaffolding, see Guided participation; Zone of proximal development
Schema, see Plans and scripts
Schlick, Moritz, 116
Schoggen, Phil, xxvi fn. 4, 269–271
Sciences of the inanimate and animate, xxii–xxiv
Scripts, see Plans
Selectivity in knowing, see Awareness; Edwin B. Holt, selectivity; Intentionality; William James, selectivity of knowing; Exploration
Self, 120–122
ecological, 121
empirical, 120–121
and radical empiricism, 136–137
Sherrington, Charles, 91
Skinner's operant psychology, 383 fn. 2, 392 fn. 8
Situated action, 313, 354, 390
see also Affordances; Behavior settings; Distributed cognition;
Ecological knowledge
Skepticism, 33
see also David Hume
Sociocultural processes,
and biological evolution, 332–338
and ecological structures, 339–369
and the individual, 330–332
and ontogenetic development, 291–292, 338–339
and radical empiricism, 332
theoretical approaches, 330–339, 360–361
see also Guided participation, Joint attention, Meaning
Social constructionism, 267
Socially distributed cognition, see Distributed cognition
Spatial updating with locomotion, 192
Specious present, see William James, specious present
Spencer, Herbert, 15, 17
see also William James, criticism of Spencer

RITTER LIBRARY
BALDWIN-WALLACE COLLEGE

DATE DUE

JUN 1 3 2005			
JUN 0 7 2006			
OhioLINK			

WITHDRAWN

DEMCO 38-297